FUNDAMENTALS OF VIŚIṢṬĀDVAITA VEDĀNTA

FUNDAMENTALS OF *Viśiṣṭādvaita Vedānta*

A STUDY BASED ON VEDĀNTA DEŚIKA'S TATTVA-MUKTĀ-KALĀPA

S. M. SRINIVASA CHARI

MOTILAL BANARSIDASS PUBLISHERS
PRIVATE LIMITED • DELHI

First Published: 1988
Reprint: Delhi, 1998

ISBN: 81-208-2066-7

MOTILAL BANARSIDASS

41 U.A. Bungalow Road, Jawahar Nagar, Delhi 110 007
8 Mahalaxmi Chamber, Warden Road, Mumbai 400 026
120 Royapettah High Road, Mylapore, Chennai 600 004
Sanas Plaza, Subhash Nagar, Pune 411 002
16 St. Mark's Road, Bangalore 560 001
8 Camac Street, Calcutta 700 017
Ashok Rajpath, Patna 800 004
Chowk, Varanasi 221 001

PRINTED IN INDIA

BY JAINENDRA PRAKASH JAIN AT SHRI JAINENDRA PRESS,
A-45 NARAINA INDUSTRIAL AREA, PHASE I, NEW DELHI 110 028
AND PUBLISHED BY NARENDRA PRAKASH JAIN FOR
MOTILAL BANARSIDASS PUBLISHERS PRIVATE LIMITED,
BUNGALOW ROAD, DELHI 110 007

To the Revered Memory of

H. H. ABHINAVA RANGANATHA

PARAKALASWAMI

With Profound Respects and Gratitude

Foreword

VIŚIṢṬĀDVAITA is one of the great religio-philosophical systems of the world. There are very few modern critical expositions of it based on the bhāṣya, supplemented by later erudite works.

Dr. Srinivasa Chari has acquired quite a profound knowledge of Viśiṣṭādvaita from great pandits with whom he studied for years the texts in original. His modern education has endowed him with the capacity to present classical ideas in a lucid and connected way.

Depending on the original texts, in particular on Vedānta Deśika's *Tattva-muktā-kalāpa*, Dr. Chari has written an excellent monograph which authoritatively expounds Viśiṣṭādvaita. Moreover, it attempts to establish that this is a system of philosophy in conformity with logic and experience.

I hope this learned work will be read widely.

K. SATCHIDANANDA MURTY

Vice Chairman
University Grants Commission
New Delhi-110002

Preface

THIS BOOK attempts to present in a systematic way the fundamental doctrines of Viśiṣṭādvaita Vedānta associated with Śrī Rāmānuja based on the study of *Tattva-muktā-kalāpa,* the *magnum opus* of Śrī Vedānta Deśika, who was one of the most distinguished successors of Rāmānuja. Although in recent years quite a few books have been written in English on the philosophy and religion of Rāmānuja, Viśiṣṭādvaita as a sound system of philosophy has not received the treatment it deserves. The emphasis placed by Rāmānuja on the acceptance of *saviśeṣa* Brahman or the personal Supreme Being endowed with attributes as the ultimate Reality of philosophy on the strength of the scriptural evidence has led some scholars to feel that Rāmānuja's system is essentially theological. Theology, understood in the correct sense as an enquiry into the nature of God, is no doubt an important part of Viśiṣṭādvaita, even as it is in the case of many other Indian philosophical systems. But the Viśiṣṭādvaita system has both a philosophical as well as theological aspect, and the former is of greater importance for the reason that it gives meaning and value to the latter. The metaphysical doctrines, developed by the Viśiṣṭādvaitin on the basis of which the system is founded, cannot be understood easily unless one has made a deep study of ancient treatises in the original. Next to the *Śrī-bhāṣya* of Rāmānuja, there are two outstanding philosophical classics, *Tattva-muktā-kalāpa* and *Śatadūṣaṇī,* written by Vedānta Deśika. A study of these texts is an essential prerequisite for getting a deeper insight into Viśiṣṭādvaita tenets. But these are highly technical works written in terse Sanskrit and presented in the classical style replete with subtleties of dialectical arguments. The two texts have therefore remained beyond the approach of ordinary scholars and modern students of philosophy. It is significant that, barring passing references to the works, an authentic translation of them has not been attempted in any European language. Even among the existing scholars, brought up strictly in the traditional disciplines of scholarship, there are very few who can claim to have studied them fully. Realising the importance of these two treatises for a fuller understanding of Viśiṣṭādvaita, I published in 1961 a book, *Advaita and Viśiṣṭādvaita*, covering a study of *Śatadūṣaṇī*, which is an important polemical work. I have now attempted to cover *Tattva-muktā-kalāpa*, the other important classic, in the present book.

The main objective of this task is to remove a prevalent impression that Viśiṣṭādvaita is primarily theology and establish that it is essentially a system of philosophy. It is a system which has been developed, apart from an appeal to scriptural authority, on the basis of well-formulated epistemological, ontological, cosmological and religious doctrines. If there is a single authentic work in which this fact has been demonstrated, it is in *Tattva-muktā-kalāpa* of Vedānta Deśika.

The scope of this book is not confined to an exposition of *Tattva-muktā-kalāpa*. Nor is it aimed merely at presenting a narrative account of Viśiṣṭādvaita philosophy and religion. On the basis of the rich material contained in the original Sanskrit text, I have endeavoured to present a critical and comparative account of the basic doctrines of Viśiṣṭādvaita in their logical sequence. In discussing these doctrines, I have paid greater attention to the underlying issues in order to bring out their philosophic significance. I have therefore avoided, to the extent possible, appeal to scriptural authority. I have also tried to present the doctrines in their original orthodox style, so characteristic of the ancient Ācāryas, and therefore refrained from temptations to use the familiar concepts of western philosophy by way of comparison, because this can often prove misleading.

So far as I am aware, it is for the first time that an attempt is being made to present in English the Viśiṣṭādvaita doctrines comprehensively on the basis of this authoritative text. Anyone interested in an in-depth study of Viśiṣṭādvaita Vedānta will find this book invaluable. The doctrines discussed in the book are related to the fundamental epistemological and philosophical issues, which are common to all schools of philosophic thought whether in the East or the West. The book will therefore be useful to all those who are interested in understanding the basic problems of philosophy.

In a work of this type it is difficult to avoid the use of technical terms in Sanskrit. I have however tried to minimise their use. Wherever I have adopted the Sanskrit words in the body of the text for want of an appropriate English equivalent, I have given the nearest English equivalent. Wherever I have used English terms, I have also given in bracket the Sanskrit words to avoid possible misunderstanding. Sanskrit quotations used in the body of the book have also been explained in English. Except the commonly used words, all Sanskrit words have been diacritically marked. I have also given a glossary of the Sanskrit terms. I have taken special pains to express the highly technical subject matter in as simple and lucid manner as possible, so that even lay readers should have little difficulty in understanding the book.

In the preparation of this book I have confined my study mainly to the original Sanskrit works on Viśiṣṭādvaita, drawing material primarily from Vedānta Deśika's *Tattva-muktā-kalāpa* and the commentaries thereon, *Śatadūṣaṇi*, *Nyāya-siddhāñjana* and *Nyāya-pariśuddhi* as well as Rāmānuja's *Śrī-bhāṣya* along with *Śruta-prakāśikā*. The other books consulted are indicated in footnotes. I have also consulted the leading scholars in South India on Vedānta in an attempt to make this book as authoritative a version of the Viśiṣṭādvaita doctrines as possible. I hope the book will be a useful contribution to the study of philosophy in general and Vedānta in particular.

It is with great pleasure that I record my obligations. I must first pay my respects to my revered guru, the late Sri Gostipuram Sowmyanarayanacharyaswami (1878-1943), under whose feet I had the rare privilege and fortune of studying Vedānta in the traditional manner. But for his initiation into the essentials of the Viśiṣṭādvaita philosophy and his blessings it would have been impossible for me to accomplish the study of *Śatadūṣaṇi* and *Tattva-muktā-kalāpa*. I also owe my success in the present undertaking to another guru, the late Sri Madhurantakam Veeraraghavacharyaswami (1900-83) under whom I studied the original text. I am deeply indebted to both these Ācāryas.

I should also pay my respects to His Holiness Abhinava Ranganatha Brahmatantra Parakalaswami (1884-1966) whose blessings received in my early age have enabled me to understand Viśiṣṭādvaita philosophy. Though I could not study directly under him, I have had the opportunity of receiving considerable knowledge and benefit in the preparation of the present book from three of his learned disciples—Sri Saragur Varadachar, Sri K. S. Varadachar and Sri E. S. Varadachar. As a token of my gratitude to them and also in recognition of the unique contribution made to Viśiṣṭādvaita Vedānta by H.H. Parakalaswami by his scholarly commentaries on *Śrī-bhāṣya* and *Tattva-muktā-kalāpa*, I respectfully dedicate the book to him.

I owe a debt of gratitude to Prof. S. Srinivasaraghavan who was kind enough to go through the entire manuscript and offer valued criticism and helpful suggestions. I am also grateful to my esteemed friends, Prof. L. V. Rajagopal and Sri S. Srinivasachar, who have read through the entire typescript and made useful suggestions for improvement. I should also thank Prof. S. S. Raghavachar, Dr. N. S. Anantharangachar, Sri K. S. Krishna Tatachar and Sri A. Srinivasaraghavan who looked through a portion of the typescript and offered useful comments. Prof. T. R. V. Murti, who recently passed away, went through the typescript and came out with a number of valuable suggestions. I express my indebtedness to the departed soul. My thanks are due to all those who have helped me in one way or other and, in particular, to my wife without whose loving co-operation I would not have been able to complete this book. I should also express my grateful thanks to the esteemed Professor K. Satchidananda Murty for evincing keen interest in my work and for graciously writing the Foreword.

Bangalore S. M. Srinivasa Chari
2nd October, 1987

Contents

Scheme of Transliteration

Vowels	a ā i ī u ū ṛ ṝ ḷ e ai o au
anusvāra	ṁ
visarga	ḥ
Consonants	
gutturals	k kh g gh ṅ
palatals	c ch j jh ñ
cerebrals	ṭ ṭh ḍ ḍh ṇ
dentals	t th d dh n
labials	p ph b bh m
semi-vowels	y r l v
sibilants	s as in *sun*
	ś palatal sibilant pronounced like the soft *s* of Russian
	ṣ cerebral sibilant as in *shun*
aspirate	h

List of Abbreviations

AI	*Aaitareya Upaniṣad*
AV	*Advaita and Viśiṣṭādvaita*
BG	*Bhagavad-gītā*
Br	*Bṛhadāraṇyaka Upaniṣad*
Ch	*Chāndogya Upaniṣad*
HIP	*History of Indian Philosophy*
IP	*Indian Philosophy*
Ka	*Kaṭha Upaniṣad*
Mund	*Muṇḍaka Upaniṣad*
NP	*Nyāya-pariśuddhi*
NS	*Nyāya-siddhāñjana*
OIP	*Outlines of Indian Philosophy*
RB	*Rāmānuja Bhāṣya on Vedānta-sūtras*
SB	*Śaṁkara Bhāṣya on Vedānta-sūtras*
SD	*Śatadūṣaṇī*
SS	*Sarvārtha-siddhi*
Sub	*Subālopaniṣad*
Svet	*Śvetāśvatara Upaniṣad*
Tait	*Taittirīya Upaniṣad*
TMK	*Tattva-muktā-kalāpa*
Up	*Upaniṣads*
VP	*Viṣṇu-purāṇa*
VS	*Vedānta-sūtra*

Introduction

I. MEANING OF THE TERM VIŚIṢṬĀDVAITA

THE system of philosophy as expounded by Śrī Rāmānuja is called Viśiṣṭādvaita. The term *advaita* means non-dualism (*na dvaitam*) emphasising the oneness of the ultimate Reality. Though all schools of thought upholding monism agree that the ultimate Reality is one only, they differ widely from one another when it comes to determining the sense in which Reality is one. The fundamental problem of monism is to account for the world of plurality as well as the infinite number of souls. The issue with which a monist is confronted is : how does the 'one' become 'many' and how is the one Reality related to the manifold universe of matter and spirit? There are two ways of resolving this important metaphysical problem. According to one view, which upholds absolute monism as propounded by Śaṁkara, the universe is not ultimately real but a phenomenal appearance of Reality. The ultimate Reality is absolutely one in the sense that it does not admit of any kind of differentiation, either internal or external. Such an absolute identity would imply denial of ultimate reality to individual souls and the universe. This type of monism advocated by Śaṁkara is known as Advaita Vedānta.

According to the second view held by Rāmānuja, the ultimate Reality, though one, is not the Absolute without any differentiation since such a transcendental undifferentiated Being is inconceivable and also logically untenable. We have to admit the reality of the universe with which we are surrounded and also of the individual souls which experience the external world. Accordingly, Rāmānuja acknowledges three fundamental real entities—matter (*acit*), soul (*cit*) and God (*Īśvara*)—and on the basis of the principle of organic relation, upholds that ultimate Reality is one as a unity. *Īśvara* as the creator of the universe is the immanent ground of existence and also the inner Self of all things in the universe and as such He sustains and controls *cit* and *acit*. *Cit* and *acit* depend on *Īśvara* for their very existence and are organically related to *Īśvara* in the same way as the physical body is related to the soul within. The oneness of Reality is to be understood not in the sense of absolute identity but as an organic unity (*viśiṣṭaikya*). As Vedānta Deśika says, Brahman alone, as organically related to the entire *cit* and *acit*, is the one ultimate Reality (*aśeṣa-cidacit-prakāraṁ brahmaikameva tattvam*).[1] Though there is absolute difference between *Īśvara* and the two other reals and also among the individual souls and matter, the ultimate Reality is considered as one because as an organic unity it is one.[2] In this sense, the system of Vedānta expounded by Rāmānuja is described as Viśiṣṭādvaita which means oneness of the organic unity (*viśiṣṭasya advaitam*).[3] The soundness of this view as against the absolute non-dualism of Śaṁkara is discussed in the concluding chapter.

II. DEVELOPMENT OF VIŚIṢṬĀDVAITA AS A SYSTEM OF PHILOSOPHY

Viśiṣṭādvaita as a well-formulated philosophical system or *darśana* with properly developed epistemology and ontology on logical ground as well as on the basis of correct interpretation of the supporting scriptural statements, was expounded by Rāmānuja in his monumental commentary on *Vedānta-sūtras* known as *Śri-bhāṣya*. In view of this, Rāmānuja may be regarded as the founder of the Viśiṣṭādvaita system. But Rāmānuja himself does not claim this distinction. In the opening para of *Śri-bhāṣya* he says that he is writing a commentary on the *sūtras*

[1]NS, p. 1.

[2]*Ibid.*, *tatra prakāra-prakāriṇoḥ prakārāṇām-ca mitho atyanta-bhede api viśiṣṭaikyādi-vivakṣayā ekatva-vyapadeśaḥ.*

[3]It may be noted that the term Viśiṣṭādvaita is not used by Rāmānuja in any of his works. It was adopted at a later period by his followers on the basis of the definition offered by Vedānta Deśika in *Nyāya-siddhāñjana*. It is generally rendered into English as qualified monism or pan-organismal monism. Both do not bring out the fuller implications of the term. A better expression which approximates to the concept is *pan-en-theism*. Pan-en-theism. as understood in the Western philosophy, refers to the view that 'deity as eternal is distinguishable from and independent of any and all relative items and yet as an actual whole, it includes all relative items'.

in accordance with the views contained in an elaborate and extensive *vṛtti* or glossary written by Bodhāyana which has been abridged by earlier teachers.[4] Though the Bodhāyana *vṛtti* as well as the works of these ancient teachers are not extant, there is ample internal evidence to show from the quotations cited by Rāmānuja that there were eminent exponents of Viśiṣṭādvaita Vedānta such as Bodhāyana, Ṭaṅka, Dramiḍa, Guhadeva, Kapardi and Bhāruci.[5] Rāmānuja quotes a few statements of Bodhāyana who is also known as *Vṛttikāra* and from *Dramiḍa-bhāṣya*.

According to Vedānta Deśika, Nāthamuni, who lived in the tenth century, was the first exponent of Viśiṣṭādvaita as a system of philosophy (*Nāthopajñaṁ pravṛttaṁ*).[6] He wrote two important works : *Nyāya-tattva* and *Yoga-rahasya*, but unfortunately these are also not extant. However, it is evident from the numerous quotations cited by Vedānta Deśika in his *Nyāya-siddhāñjana* that *Nyāya-tattva* is an important philosophical treatise which had considerable influence on both Rāmānuja and Vedānta Deśika.[7]

After Nāthamuni, Ālavandar, also known as Yāmuna, who lived sometime between A.D. 916-1036 developed the system by contributing a few independent philosophic works.[8] The most important of these is *Siddhitraya* consisting of three parts—Ātmasiddhi, Īśvarasiddhi and Saṁvitsiddhi—each being devoted to one of the three fundamental doctrines of Viśiṣṭādvaita. The

[4]RB I-1-1. *Bhagavad-bodhāyana-kṛtāṁ vistīrṇāṁ brahma-sūtra-vṛttiṁ pūrvācāryaḥ saṅcikṣipuḥ; tanmatānusāreṇa sūtrākṣarāṇi vyākhyāsyante.*

[5]*Vedārtha-saṁgraha,* p. 102. *Bhagavad-bodhāyana-ṭaṅka-dramiḍa-guhadeva-kapardi-bhāruci-prabhṛtya-vigīta-śiṣṭa-parigrahīta-purātana-veda-vedānta-vyākhyāna.* This statement of Rāmānuja establishes the antiquity of Viśiṣṭādvaita philosophy.

[6]TMK V-136. *Nāthopajñaṁ pravṛttam* is interpreted by Vedānta Deśika as *Nāthamuni ārabhya pravṛttam.* This indicates that Nāthamuni is the first to present it as a system.

[7]The theory of *yathārtha-khyāti* and the theory of subject-object relation as one of *saṁyoga* advocated by Rāmānuja are based on the views expressed by Nāthamuni in *Nyāya-tattva.* See TMK IV-10. *Nāthaiḥ uktā yathārthā vimala-mati-rapi nyāya-tattve tadetat bhāṣye anūktaṁ.* Also TMK V-59. *Saṁyogaṁ bhāṣyakārāḥ prathamamukathayat nyāyatattvānusārāt.*

[8]TMK V-136. *bahubhiḥ yāmuneya-prabandhaiḥ upacitam.* Yāmuna is the author of eight works : *Āgama-prāmāṇyam Mahā-puruṣa-nirṇaya. Ātmasiddhi, Īśvarasiddhi, Saṁvitsiddhi, Gītārtha-saṁgraha, Stotraratnam* and *Catuḥ-ślokī.*

teachings of Yāmuna have greatly influenced both Rāmānuja and Vedānta Deśika as they have used the logical arguments advanced by him in the refutation of Advaita doctrines.

Rāmānuja who came after Yāmuna (born in A.D. 1017) further developed and strengthened the Viśiṣṭādvaita system of philosophy.[9] Besides his commentary on *Vedānta-sūtras* known as *Śrī-bhāṣya*, he wrote eight other works: *Vedārtha-saṁgraha*, an independent treatise containing the exposition of the philosophy of the Upaniṣads; *Vedānta-sāra* and *Vedānta-dīpa* containing brief commentaries on *Vedānta-sūtras*; *Gītā-bhāṣya* commenting on the *Bhagavad-gītā*; *Nitya-grantha* dealing with forms of worship; and three *Gadyas* or prose works which expound the greatness of *prapatti* or the doctrine of self-surrender to God as means to *mokṣa*. Through these scholarly treatises Rāmānuja systematised the teachings of Viśiṣṭādvaita in its metaphysical, moral and theological aspects.

For nearly two centuries after the advent of Rāmānuja, there was no significant contribution to the Viśiṣṭādvaita system by way of major philosophic works. The Ācāryas who succeeded Rāmānuja, though some of them were eminent Vedāntins such as Parāśara Bhaṭṭa, Viṣṇucitta, Vātsya Varada, Sudarśana Sūri and Ātreya Rāmānuja, confined their attention primarily to the dissemination of the philosophy of Rāmānuja by teaching *Śrī-bhāṣya* or writing further glossaries on it. Some of the Ācāryas such as Pillān, Nanjīyar, Periavaccān Pillai, etc. who were attracted by the devotional hymns of the Ālwars in Tamil were preoccupied with writing elaborate commentaries on them. During this period the theological aspect of Viśiṣṭādvaita received much greater emphasis and importance than its philosophy. The only important works that were written during this period are : *Tattvaratnākara* by Parāśara Bhaṭṭa, *Prameyasaṁgraha* by Viṣṇucitta, *Prajñāparitrāṇa* by Varada Nārāyaṇa Bhaṭṭāraka, *Śrī-bhāṣya-vivaraṇa* by Rāmamiśra, *Prameya-mālā* and *Tattva-sāra* by Vātsya Varada, *Śruta-prakāśikā* by Sudarśana Sūri, *Nyāyakuliśa* by Ātreya Rāmānuja and *Nyāyadyumaṇi* by Meghanādāri.[10] With the exception of *Śruta-prakāśikā* which is more

[9]TMK V-136. *trātam samyag yatīndraiḥ.*

[10]Except *Śruta-prakāśikā*, *Nyāyakuliśa*, *Tattvasāra* and *Nyāyadyumaṇi*, none of these works is available. However, Vedānta Deśika has referred to these works in his *Nyāya-siddhāñjana* with relevant quotations from them.

a commentary than an independent philosophic work, none of these can be considered as a philosophical classic. They are no match to what was written later by Vedānta Deśika. It appears that during this period the Viśiṣṭādvaita system was exposed to criticism by several rival schools of thought and in particular from the Advaitins. Rāmānuja had vigorously attacked Māyāvāda of Śaṁkara in his *Śrī-bhāṣya*. The *mahāpūrvapakṣa* containing an excellent summary of the Advaita position and the *mahāsiddhānta* covering a detailed and systematic refutation of Advaita doctrines constitute a classic example of dialectical criticism rendered in a dispassionate, impersonal and academic way. Naturally, the Advaita scholars of post-Rāmānuja period had attempted to defend their doctrines against the criticism of Rāmānuja. Even among the followers of Rāmānuja, differences of opinion on some of the basic concepts of Viśiṣṭādvaita had cropped up though such conflicts of opinion were more pronounced on the doctrinal side. This is evident from the fact that Vedānta Deśika refers to such views as of the *sayūthyas*, meaning the followers of the same school of thought. Thus, there was need for the advent of an able philosopher who could consolidate further the basic teachings of Rāmānuja and establish the Viśiṣṭādvaita system of philosophy on a stable foundation making it unassailable from all conceivable criticism not only by the rival schools but also from among the followers of Rāmānuja.

III. VEDĀNTA DEŚIKA AND VIŚIṢṬĀDVAITA

This important mission came to be fulfilled by Veṅkaṭanātha, popularly known as Vedānta Deśika, who was born in the year 1268.[11] It is said that Veṅkaṭanātha's future role as the re-establisher of Rāmānuja's philosophy was prophesied even when he was a child of five by Vātsya Varadācārya, a spiritual descendent of Rāmānuja. The story goes that when the child accompanied by his maternal uncle met the Ācārya for the first time, the latter was so attracted by the extraordinary intelligence of

[11]For a biographical sketch of Vedānta Deśika and his works, see author's *Advaita and Viśiṣṭādvaita*, pp. 1-4.

the boy that he blessed him in the following words : 'May you establish the Vedānta on a firm basis, vanquishing the theories of rival schools of thought; may you become the respected of the orthodox Vedāntins and the abode of abundant auspiciousness.'[12] Vedānta Deśika acknowledges with gratitude the blessings received from his spiritual guru in the opening verses of *Tattva-muktā-kalāpa* and *Adhikaraṇa-sārāvali*.[13]

It is important to note in this connection that Vedānta Deśika had to accomplish two major tasks in order to establish Viśiṣṭādvaita as a sound and acceptable system of philosophy. The first one was the refutation of the *māyāvāda* of Śaṁkara which undermined the fundamental tenets of Viśiṣṭādvaita. This task was fulfilled by writing an independent polemical work entitled *Śatadūṣaṇi*. As the title suggests, one hundred philosophical issues were chosen for systematic criticism by adopting the dialectical method. Vedānta Deśika claims with some justification in his *Tattvaṭikā* that the refutation of Śaṁkara's Advaita was completed in his *Śatadūṣaṇi*.[14] The second and a greater task was to present a constructive exposition of the fundamental doctrines of Viśiṣṭādvaita with a view to proving their soundness by a critical evaluation of the theories opposed to Viśiṣṭādvaita. Until the advent of Vedānta Deśika, apart from Rāmānuja's *Śrī-bhāṣya* and the commentaries thereon, there was no single work presenting comprehensively and critically all the doctrines of Viśiṣṭādvaita along with the corresponding doctrines of other systems of philosophy. As we observed earlier, the literature that appeared in the post-Rāmānuja period laid greater emphasis on the theological aspect of Viśiṣṭādvaita than on the philosophical aspect. The *Śrī-bhāṣya* of Rāmānuja and the *Śruta-prakāśikā* of Sudarśana Sūri no doubt contain most of the doctrines of Viśiṣṭādvaita including criticisms of theories opposed to Viśiṣṭādvaita. But these texts, intended primarily as an exposition of the *Vedānta-sūtras* were devoted mainly to the interpretation of the *sūtras* and the connected scriptural texts. Thus, there was need for an independent treatise presenting in

[12] *Pratiṣṭhāpita-vedāntaḥ pratikṣipta-bahirmataḥ / bhūyāḥ traividya-mānyastvam bhūrikalyāṇa-bhājanam//*

[13] TMK 1-2. *Varadagurukṛpālambhitoddāmabhūmā. Adhikaraṇasārāvalī*, verse 2) *Varadācārya-Rāmānujābhyām samyagdṛṣṭena sarvam.*

[14] *Tattvaṭikā*, (Stanza 5). *śātitaḥ śatadūṣaṇyām śaṁkarādi-mudhāgrahaḥ.*

a consolidated and logical way the epistemological, ontological, cosmological and eschatological doctrines of Viśiṣṭādvaita more on the basis of logic than on scriptural evidence. This need came to be fulfilled with Vedānta Deśika's independent and comprehensive philosophic treatise titled *Tattva-muktā-kalāpa* followed by a scholarly commentary thereon known as *Sarvārtha-siddhi*.

IV. TATTVA-MUKTĀ-KALĀPA AS A PHILOSOPHICAL TREATISE

Vedānta Deśika was a prolific writer and he wrote more than hundred works not only in the realm of philosophy and religion but also in the field of poetry and drama. His chief philosophic works are : *Tattva-muktā-kalāpa* along with *Sarvārtha-siddhi*, *Nyāya-pariśuddhi*, *Nyāya-siddhāñjana*, *Seśvaramīmāṁsā*, *Mīmāṁsā-pādukā*, *Śatadūṣaṇi* and *Adhikaraṇa-sārāvali*. His other philosophical works which are in the form of commentaries are: *Tattva-ṭikā* (a commentary on *Śri-bhāṣya*), *Tātparya-candrikā* (a gloss on Rāmānuja's *Gitā-bhāṣya*), *Īśāvāsyopaniṣadbhāṣya* (a commentary on *Īśāvāsyopaniṣad*), *Rahasya-rakṣā* (a commentary on Yāmuna's *Stotra-ratna* and *Catuḥśloki* and Rāmānuja's *Gadyatraya*) and *Gitārtha-saṁgraha-rakṣā* (a commentary on Yāmuna's *Gitārtha-saṁgraha*). Among the philosophic works, *Tattva-muktā-kalāpa*, *Nyāya-pariśuddhi*, *Nyāya-siddhāñjana* and *Śatadūṣaṇi* occupy important place because in these works Vedānta Deśika attempts to establish Viśiṣṭādvaita as a sound system of philosophy.

Of the philosophical treatises of Vedānta Deśika *Tattva-muktā-kalāpa* stands out as the most important work. *Nyāya-pariśuddhi* is an epistemological work devoted primarily to a discussion of the nature of *pramāṇas* and other epistemological theories of Viśiṣṭādvaita. In the closing chapter of this book a brief reference is made to the *prameyas* or the ontological doctrines of Viśiṣṭādvaita. A detailed exposition of the *prameyas* referred to in *Nyāya-pariśuddhi* is taken up in *Nyāya-siddhāñjana*. The objective of this work, as stated in the opening verse, is to expound in a clear way the metaphysical doctrines.[15] The text which is in prose deals with the various Viśiṣṭādvaita

[15]NS, p. 1. *samyak-tattva-nirikṣaṇāya tanute sat-tarkasiddhāñjanam.*

doctrines in the same order in which they are found in *Tattva-muktā-kalāpa*. It comprises six sections covering the six major topics in the following order: *jaḍa-dravya*, *jīva*, *Īśvara*, *nitya-vibhūti*, *buddhi* and *adravya*. *Tattva-muktā-kalāpa* which is written in verse comprises only five sections since *nitya-vibhūti* instead of forming a separate section, is included in the section dealing with *Īśvara*. Apart from this minor change the text of *Nyāya-siddhāñjana*, in the form in which it is extant, is incomplete. Another important difference between the two works lies in the fact that the section dealing with *buddhi* or theory of knowledge in *Nyāya-siddhāñjana* is very brief and does not discuss the *pramāṇas* and the theories of truth and error. *Tattva-muktā-kalāpa*, on the contrary, seeks to deal with the theory of knowledge in a very comprehensive way.

Śatadūṣaṇī to which we have referred is an important polemical work devoted mainly to the refutation of the doctrines of Śaṁkara's Advaita Vedānta by adopting dialectical arguments. It is designated as a *Vāda-grantha*, the aim of which is to refute the doctrines of the Advaita Vedānta with a view to establishing the Viśiṣṭādvaita Vedānta on a logical basis. In view of this, it is compared to a sword (*śastra*) used to destroy the opponents in contrast to the purely constructive work *Sarvārtha-siddhi*, which is compared to a shield (*kheṭa*) that is used to defend oneself.[16]

While *Śatadūṣaṇī* is confined to the criticism of only one school of thought, namely, Advaita, *Tattva-muktā-kalāpa* makes critical appraisal of several rival schools of thought including Advaita Vedānta.

Unlike *Śatadūṣaṇī*, *Tattva-muktā-kalāpa* is a *prakaraṇa-grantha*, a treatise intended primarily to present Viśiṣṭādvaita doctrines with a critical evaluation of corresponding theories of rival schools of thought. Unlike *Nyāya-siddhāñjana* and *Nyāya-pariśuddhi*, it is a comprehensive philosophical classic of Viśiṣṭādvaita Vedānta covering all topics in the realms of Metaphysics, Ontology, Epistemology, Cosmology, Eschatology and Theology. It is the *magnum opus* of Vedānta Deśika.

[16]*Saptatiratna-mālikā* (Verse 48). *sarvārthasiddhiḥ śatadūṣaṇī ca dve kheṭa-śastre kathak āgragāṇām*

V. NATURE AND SCOPE OF TATTVA-MUKTĀ-KALĀPA

This work contains five hundred verses composed in the *sragdharā* metre. It is neither easy nor usual to express dialectical arguments in verse form but Vedânta Deśika, with his versatility both as a poet and a philosopher, has achieved this task with remarkable effect. The book is divided into five parts devoted to five major topics : *dravya* (substance), *jiva* (individual self), *Īśvara* (God), *buddhi* (knowledge) and *adravya* (non-substance). Each part is named *sara*, meaning a strand. Each verse or a group of verses in a *sara* which deals with a philosophical topic is compared to a pearl, signifying its precious value. Each part comprising specific number of verses is therefore regarded as a *sara* meaning a strand of pearls. The five *saras* combined together constitute an ornament (*kalāpa*) in the form of a pearl necklace of five strands. Thus the text bears the title *Tattva-muktā-kalāpa*. *Kalāpa* means an ornament, *muktā* means pearl and *tattva* stands for a metaphysical doctrine. *Tattva-muktā-kalāpa* is a philosophical classic devoted to an exposition of *tattvas*.[17]

The main objective of *Tattva-muktā-kalāpa*, as stated in one of the opening verses, is to establish the doctrines of Viśiṣṭâdvaita Vedânta on a sound basis through a critical evaluation of the corresponding doctrines advocated by rival schools of thought.[18] It covers all the important philosophical, epistemological, cosmological and religious doctrines of the Viśiṣṭâdvaita system. As Vedânta Deśika claims, there is no topic in philosophy which is not discussed in this work. What is not considered here cannot be found elsewhere (*yannāsmin kvāpi naitat*).[19] In the conclud-

[17]According to tradition, this book was dedicated by Vedânta Deśika to Lord Raṅganâtha in the same way as an ornament is offered to God in devotion. The book is therefore described as a special ornament (*bhūṣaṇa*) comprising pearls in the form of *tattvas* or metaphysical doctrines of the Viśiṣṭâdvaita Vedânta.

In *Viṣṇupurāṇa*, the different *tattvas* such as the individual soul, *prakṛti*, *mahat*, *buddhi*, *mind*, *indriyas*, etc. are described as different ornaments of *Īśvara*. It is therefore justified to treat the book which deals with *tattvas* as an ornament of God. See Introduction to TMK by Uttamur Viraraghavacharya.

[18]TMK I-4. *nirdhūta-sarva-pratimata-vimatim sādhaye sarvamartham.*

[19]TMK V-134. This reflects the statement made by Vyâsa in the *Mahābhārata*: *yad ihāsti tad anyatra*; *yan nehāsti na tat kvacit.*

ing portion of the book he says: 'I have examined in this book very carefully almost all topics relating to both *pramāṇas* and *prameyas* at some place or the other; if I have overlooked any philosophic issue or expressed the same in a manner that may appear ambiguous, no one else would be capable to decide it other than myself.'[20] Though this looks like an exaggerated claim, it is in fact not so, because until this day the only source of authority for deciding any controversial philosophical and epistemological issue in Viśiṣṭādvaita is the views of Vedānta Deśika as expressed in *Tattva-muktā-kalāpa* and *Sarvārtha-siddhi*. Truly *Tattva-mukā-kalāpa* is an important compendium of all topics of Viśiṣṭādvaita.

The schools of thought which come up for critical evaluation in *Tattva-muktā-kalāpa* are: Nyāya and Vaiśeṣika, Sāṅkhya and Yoga, Pūrva-Mīmāṁsā of both Prabhākara and Kumārila, Vedānta as presented by Bhāskara, Yādava and Śaṁkara, Buddhism covering the four schools of Vaibhāṣika, Sautrāntika, Yogācāra and Mādhyamika, Jainism and Cārvāka. Only such of the theories of these schools as stand opposed to those upheld by the Viśisṭādvaitin are taken up for critical examination. The main objective of the criticism is to expound the doctrines of Viśiṣṭādvaita and reaffirm their soundness by exposing the defective nature of the corresponding theories held by the rival schools of thought. Unlike the method followed in the *Śatadūṣaṇi*, dialectic is not adopted here except in a few places, to overthrow the rival theories. On the contrary, the theories are subjected to critical analysis in a systematic manner and their soundness is evaluated with reference to three accepted *pramāṇas* —perception, inference and revealed scripture. What is evident to perceptual experience is not rejected as invalid. In matters which are outside the purview of perceptual experience, scriptural evidence is accorded greater importance than perception as well as logic while determining the validity of a theory. As for inference, it is acknowledged that it has a limited role since logic cannot establish conclusively the supersensuous realities. However, logic is adopted to support the theories established by scripture. It is also used extensively to disprove the views advanced by the opponents and defend one's own theory,

[20]TMK V. 135.

insofar as it does not conflict with scriptural texts. Nowhere in this work does Vedānta Deśika adopt dialectical arguments to condemn a theory of the rival school in a dogmatic way, but rather he uses them to elucidate and establish the soundness of his own theory by pointing out the defects in the views of the opponents.

The original Sanskrit text has a few valuable commentaries on it written in Sanskrit language. The most outstanding commentary is the one contributed by Vedānta Deśika himself under the title *Sarvārtha-siddhi*. In the words of its author, it is a glossary (*vṛttiḥ*), neither too lengthy nor too brief intended to provide elucidation of points mentioned in the verses.[21] As the title signifies, it contains all that is to be known by a student of philosophy. It is a very scholarly and comprehensive commentary, exhibiting the author's encyclopaedic knowledge of the other systems of Indian philosophy. This is evident from the way he has stated succinctly the views of the other schools of thought by quoting the relevant statements from their original works.[22] According to tradition, Vedānta Deśika was conferred the title of *Sarvajña*—as one possessing comprehensive philosophic knowledge *par excellence*—on the basis of his masterly work, *Tattva-muktā-kalāpa* and *Sarvārtha-siddhi* (*sarvajñatvam tattva-muktā-kalāpe*).

There are a few other commentaries on *Sarvārtha-siddhi*. The important one among these is known as *Ānanda-dāyini*, also called *Nṛsiṁharājiyam* written by Nṛsiṁharāja, a Viśiṣṭādvaita scholar of the 16th century. It is a brief one written in the form of a glossary and part of it is published by the Oriental Research Institute, Mysore.

Gūḍhārtha-vivṛtiḥ by Vādhūla Śrīnivāsācārya[23] is a brief glossary on *Sarvārtha-siddhi*. This is available in full and is published by Uttamur Viraraghavacharya along with his glossary on *Sarvārtha-siddhi*.

[21]See the opening verse of *Sarvārtha-siddhi*: *nātivyāsa-vyatikaravatī nātisaṅkoca-khedā vṛttisseyam viśada-rucirā kalpyate asmābhireva*.

[22]See Sri Parakalaswami's Preface to TMK Vol. I published by Oriental Research Institute, Mysore.

[23]It is difficult to determine the exact period of this author as there are more than one Vādhūla Śrīnivāsa among the Vaiṣṇava Ācāryas. If he is the pupil of *samara-puṅgava*, as the opening verse indicates, and the teacher of Mahācārya, we may take the period of this work as 15th century.

Gūḍhartha-prakāśaḥ contributed by Saumya Varada Rāmânuja[24] is an incomplete glossary and available up to the end of first *sara*. This is also published along with the *Gūḍhārtha-vivṛtiḥ* by Uttamur Viraraghavacharya.

Among the recent commentaries, *Bhava-Prakāśaḥ* written by H.H. Abhinava Ranganatha Brahmatantra Parakala Swamin (1884-1966) of Parakal Mutt, Mysore, provides an extensive and scholarly commentary on *Sarvārtha-siddhi*. But unfortunately, it covers only the first part, *jaḍa-dravya-sara*, and the first 30 verses of the second part, *jiva-sara*. It is published in three volumes by the Oriental Research Institute, Mysore. In recent years another eminent Sanskrit scholar, the late Sri Uttamur Viraraghavacharya of Madras, has published *Tattva-muktā-kalāpa* with *Sarvārtha-siddhi* along with his own glossary entitled *Alabhya-lābhaḥ*.

VI. SUBSTANCE OF TATTVA-MUKTĀ-KALĀPA

The *tattvas*, according to Vedānta Deśika, fall under two broad divisions: *dravya* (substance) and *adravya* (non-substance). *Dravya is* that which serves as the substratum for modifications (*avasthāvat*). What is other than *dravya* is *adravya*. It is defined as that which cannot be the substratum of anything else (*anupādāna*) but is necessarily dependent upon *dravya*. On the basis of this definition, Vedānta Deśika enumerates six *dravyas*: *prakṛti* (cosmic matter), *kāla* (time), *Īśvara* (God), *jiva* (individual self), *jñāna* (knowledge) and *nitya-vibhūti* (transcendental spiritual matter). The *dravyas* are of two kinds: *jaḍa* (material) and *ajaḍa* (non-material). *Prakṛti* and *kāla* are the material substances. The remaining four are regarded as non-material or spiritual substances. A further distinction is made among the non-material substances as *pratyak* (self-revealed) and *parāk* (revelation for another). *Īśvara* and *jiva* are of the former type, whereas *jñāna* and *nitya-vibhūti* belong to the latter.

[24]According to the opening verse of this commentary the author is a disciple of Śrīnivāsa guru and Tātārya who belonged to the 15th century. We may therefore fix the period of this author as 16th century.

The *adravyas* are reckoned as ten. These are: the three cosmic attributes or the characteristics of the cosmic matter, viz. *sattva, rajas* and *tamas*; the qualities of the five gross elements (*bhūtas*), viz. *śabda* (sound), *sparśa* (touch), *rūpa* (colour), *rasa* (taste) and *gandha* (odour); *śakti* (potency) and the last *adravya* is *saṁyoga* (conjunction).

The sixteen *tattvas*—the six *dravyas* and the ten *adravyas*—constitute the fundamental metaphysical categories of Viśiṣṭādvaita system. The *Tattva-muktā-kalāpa* is a detailed and critical exposition of these categories.

The sixteen categories are dealt with in five parts, each part being known as *sara*: (1) *Jaḍa-dravya-sara,* (2) *Jiva-sara,* (3) *Nāyaka-sara,* (4) *Buddhi-sara* and (5) *Adravya-sara.*

The *Jaḍa-dravya-sara* deals with the nature of cosmic matter (*prakṛti*) and its evolutes, the order and manner in which evolution takes place, the theory of causality, and the concept of substance and theories of time and space. While considering these important topics, the Buddhist doctrine of momentariness which undermines the very concept of substance and attribute comes up for critical examination. Similarly, the views of the Cārvāka which deny the concept of cause and effect, the theory of Nyāya-Vaiśeṣika upholding *paramāṇus* as the cause of the universe and the Sāṅkhya theory of evolution are taken up for critical examination. The conclusion reached is that *prakṛti* which is an eternal and non-sentient substance is the *vibhūti* (property) of *Īśvara* and that it evolves itself into various modifications as *mahat, ahaṁkāra,* eleven sensory and motor organs including *manas,* five subtle elements (*tanmātras*) and five gross elements (*bhūtas*). Though *prakṛti* undergoes evolution, Brahman, being the ground (*ādhāra*) and inner controller (*niyantā*) of *prakṛti* is the material cause of the universe.

The *Jiva-sara,* the second part, is devoted to a detailed discussion of the nature of the individual self. The theories of *jiva* as advocated by some of the other schools such as Cārvāka, Jaina, Buddhist, Nyāya-Vaiśeṣika and Advaita Vedānta are examined and refuted. It is established that *jivas* are eternal, manifold and distinct from Brahman though they are inseparably related to Brahman; they are not all-pervasive, as the Naiyāyika believes but monadic (*aṇu*); they are of the nature of knowledge (*jñānasvarūpa*) and also constitute the locus for *jñāna* (*jñānāśraya*)

The *jīva* is also both the agent of action (*kartā*) and the enjoyer (*bhoktā*) of pleasure and pain. The eligibility of *jīva* for *mokṣa*,, the ways and means of achieving it and the nature of *mokṣa* are also dealt with in this part.

The *Nāyaka-sara*, which is the third part, is primarily concerned with the discussion on the nature of God. At the very outset, it is established with supporting arguments based on śruti and smṛti texts, that the Absolute or Brahman of the Upaniṣads is the same as the personal God of Religion. It is also pointed out that the existence of God cannot be proved by means of logical arguments but it is to be accepted on the basis of scriptural authority. Another important theory which is discussed in detail in this section is the material causality (*upādāna-kāraṇatva*) of Brahman. While upholding the *pariṇāma-vāda* of the Viśiṣṭādvaita system, the *vivarta-vāda* as advocated by the Advaita Vedānta is subjected to a critical examination. In this connection the Advaitin's doctrine of *avidyā* comes up for detailed criticism. The theory of incarnation of God, his essential attributes and the concept of *nitya-vibhūti*, which is one of the *dravyas* in this system, also figure in this section.

The *Buddhi-sara*, the fourth part which is the most important and the biggest, discusses in great detail the Viśiṣṭādvaita theory of knowledge and the nature of *pramāṇas* and their validity. In presenting the Viśiṣṭādvaita view of knowledge as an essential and eternal attribute of the self and having a reference to an object, the theories of knowledge as advanced by the Buddhists, Nyāya-Vaiśeṣika, Mīmāṁsā and Advaita Vedānta come up for criticism. While upholding the self-validity of knowledge, the various other theories of truth and error are critically examined. The *yathārtha-khyāti* advocated by Rāmānuja combined with the *akhyāti* of Mīmāṁsaka is accepted as the sound theory of truth and error.

In examining the nature of various *pramāṇas*, Vedānta Deśika discusses the nature and content of perception and establishes that perception even in the initial stage reveals an object only as qualified by some characteristic. He also examines the theories of perception advanced by the rival schools of thought. Regarding *anumāna*, he takes up a critical evaluation of the views held by the Naiyāyikas on the components of syllogism, the method of formulation of logical concomitance, the logical fallacies and the rules regulating philosophic debate. With regard to *śabda* or verbal testimony, he discusses the different theories regarding the function of words and sentences and their logical import. While establishing revealed scripture as the most authoritative source of knowledge in matters which are supersensuous Vedânta Deśika maintains that smṛtis as well as the Pâñcarâtra Âgama, which have their source in Vedas are also authoritative as opposed to the non-Vedic âgamas.

The fifth and final part is presented under the title *Adravya-sara*. It is mainly devoted to a critical examination of the various attributes or *guṇas* as admitted by the Nyâya-Vaiśeṣika system. It is pointed out that the fundamental attributes known as *adravya* in the Viśiṣṭâdvaita system are ten in number; *sattva, rajas, tamas, śabda, sparśa, rūpa, rasa, gandha, śakti* and *saṁyoga*. The twenty-four *guṇas* admitted by Nyāya-Vaiśeṣika are critically examined with a view to pointing out that there is no logical justification for postulating these attributes as independent categories. The doctrine of substance-attribute and the theory of relation which constitute the pivot of Viśiṣṭâdvaita are also discussed in this section. In this connection, the Jaina *saptabhaṅgi-vāda*, Bhāskara's *bhedābheda-vāda* and Advaitin's theory of *bheda* as illusory come up for critical examination. It is established that substance and attribute are distinct but inherently related.

VII. CENTRAL THEME OF TATTVA-MUKTĀ-KALĀPA

Though *Tattva-muktā-kalāpa* is a treatise devoted to an exposition of the fundamental metaphysical categories, it is directed to the discussion of the metaphysics of substance-attribute on the basis of which Viśiṣṭâdvaita is founded. The three realities—Brahman, *cit* (*jīva*) and *acit* (cosmic matter) accepted in this system—constitute in a sense the substance-attribute relation. According to the Viśiṣṭâdvaitin, substance and attribute are distinct but inseparable. A pure substance devoid of attribute is inconceivable; in the same way an attribute which inheres in the substance does not have an independent existence. Every real entity in the universe is a complex whole, having two aspects—a substantive aspect and an attributive aspect. A substance is always a characterised entity (*viśiṣṭa-vastu*). This principle applies to *Īśvara* and the universe consisting of the *jivas* and cosmic matter. *Īśvara* is the primary substance and in relation to Him, *jivas* and cosmic matter are His attributes or modes (*prakāra*) insofar as the latter depend for their existence on *Īśvara* and are controlled by Him. The relationship between *Īśvara* and the universe of *cit* and *acit* is conceived in the same way as the body is related to the soul. The body is regarded as *śarira* in the technical sense that it depends wholly and necessarily on the soul for its existence; it is controlled by the soul and it exists for the use of the soul. The soul is *śariri* or *ātman* in the sense that it serves as the basis for the existence of body (*ādhāra*), it controls the body (*niyantā*) and it uses it for its purpose (*śeṣin*). The same explanation holds good in respect of Brahman and the universe, and the two are organically related in the form of body to the soul.

This organic relationship of Brahman to the universe consisting of *cit* and *acit* constitutes the central doctrine of Viśiṣṭādvaita Vedānta. Vedānta Deśika describes it as *pradhāna-pratitantra. Pratitantra* means a doctrine which is unique to one's own system but not accepted by any other school of thought. The classification of the realities into *dravya* and *adravya* and the detailed discussion of these fundamental metaphysical categories in *Tattva-muktā-kalāpa* is intended to bring out the philosophic significance of Viśiṣṭādvaita.

VIII. SCOPE OF THE PRESENT BOOK

It is believed by some Western as well as Indian scholars that the Vedānta expounded by Rāmānuja is a system of theology rather than a system of philosophy. It is thus designated as 'Theology of Rāmānuja' or 'Theism of Rāmānuja' or to use a better expression 'Philosophy of Religion'. Presumably the reason for holding such a view is that Rāmānuja, unlike Śaṁkara, adopts the theistic interpretation of Vedānta and emphasises the identity of the Absolute of philosophy with the personal God of Religion. One other possible reason is that

Râmânuja has developed his system more on the basis of scripture than logic.

This view of Viśiṣṭâdvaita is not correct. Theology, understood in the correct sense as systematic enquiry into the nature of God, no doubt forms an important part of the Viśiṣṭâdvaita Vedânta. But a philosophical system or *darśana*,[25] concerned with an enquiry into the nature of ultimate Reality, cannot be totally divorced from religion.[26] In fact no system of Indian philosophy including the orthodox Advaita and atheistic Buddhism excludes religion. Philosophy and religion are generally treated together in all schools of Indian thought. The former represents the theoretical side of the system dealing primarily with an enquiry into the nature of ultimate Reality, while the latter covers the practical side of the system concerned with the ways and means of realisation of Reality. *Tattva-jijñâsâ* should culminate in *tattva-sâkṣâtkâra*, as emphasised in the Upaniṣad: 'He who knows Brahman attains the highest.'[27] The *Vedânta-sûtras* on which the different systems of Vedânta are developed emphasise both these aspects as they deal with *tattva* (Reality), *hita* (means) and *puruṣârtha* (goal). The first two *adhyâyas* of the *Vedânta-sûtras* deal with the Reality, the third with the ways and means of realising it and the last with the supreme goal. The acceptance of personal God as the ultimate Reality of philosophy will not therefore render the system theological in character. As will be shown later the concept of ultimate Reality conceived only as a personal Supreme Being can be sustained philosophically.

Though religion forms an important part of the Viśiṣṭâdvaita system, we should take note of the distinction between the religion of Viśiṣṭâdvaita and the philosophy of Viśiṣṭâdvaita. The former is known as *Śrî-vaiṣṇavism*. It is a well-established and distinctive cult developed on the belief that Viṣṇu is the

[25]The word *darśana*, according to its root meaning, means vision or philosophic knowledge. But it is also understood as a system of philosophy, as adopted by the Naiyâyikas and the author of *Sarvadarśana-saṅgraha*. It is in the latter sense I am using the term. See Dasgupta's HIP, vol. I, p. 68.

[26]The word religion is taken in the sense, as explained by Prof. M. Hiriyanna, of a way of life that helps one to reach an ideal or the highest goal in life. See OIP, p. 18.

[27]Tait *brahmavid âpnoti param*.

Supreme Deity, the creator of the universe and redeemer of suffering humanity. It emphasises the exclusive worship of Viṣṇu as the only means of final liberation from bondage. More than its ideologies it has laid down a pattern of life which covers a variety of rigorous, religious practices including certain sacraments. There is extensive literature dealing with this religious aspect. In fact, the vast literature that has appeared in the post-Deśika period gives more prominence to religion than philosophy. As a result of the overemphasis given to the theological aspect, the metaphysical doctrines on which Viśiṣṭādvaita is developed have been overshadowed. The Vaiṣṇava religion is much older than the Viśiṣṭādvaita system as developed by Rāmānuja and it can be traced back to *Ṛg-veda*, Viśiṣṭādvaita as a system of philosophy or as a *darśana* which, as we have observed earlier, had its beginning in the tenth century with Nāthamuni and is developed primarily on the basis of the Upaniṣadic teachings, the *Vedānta-sūtras* and the *Bhagavad-gītā*. Like any other full-fledged system of philosophy or *darśana*, it is also developed on the basis of well-formulated epistemology, ontology, cosmology and eschatology as is evident from the *Tattva-muktā-kalāpa*. It is therefore important that we should not lose sight of this distinction between what constitutes religion and what constitutes philosophy of Viśiṣṭādvaita. The confusion between these two aspects has often led to the conclusion that Viśiṣṭādvaita is only theology or theism.

It is true that Rāmānuja has developed his system primarily on the strength of the scriptural texts. In this respect he is no different from Śaṁkara or other Vedānta schools for the obvious reason that in matters which are supersensuous scripture is taken as the sole authority. This does not mean that logic or reasoning is excluded. Logic does find an important place in all the philosophical discussion. Some of the philosophical truths established in the Upaniṣads are also based on logical analysis and arguments as is evident from the dialogues between a teacher and his pupil. The Upaniṣad, while teaching the ways and means of self-realisation, lays equal emphasis on *manana* or arguing within oneself with reasoning for a conviction of what is heard from the sacred texts (*śravaṇa*). The *Vedānta-sūtra* which are regarded as *naya-sūtra*[28], are intended to provide the logical arguments in support of the theories advanced in Vedânta. Râmânuja acknowledges the need of reasoning for determining the meaning of the scriptural texts.[29] While logic is given due importance, it is not to be depended on as the sole means or *pramāṇa* for establishing supersensuous realities. Whenever a conflict arises between reason and revelation, the latter is accorded greater authority than the former. This is due to the fact that reason has its own limitation and cannot as such conclusively establish a truth which is beyond the scope of normal experience. There cannot be any finality about the nature of ultimate Reality, if it is to be determined only by reasoning.[30] Secondly, revelation is accorded greater validity on the ground that knowledge derived from it is self-valid. This point is discussed in a later chapter. The fact that the Vedânta of Râmânuja is based on scriptural evidence does not make it theological in character.

As we have observed earlier, the Viśiṣṭādvaita system is developed not solely on the basis of scripture but also on the metaphysics of substance-attribute. It is in a broad sense a substance-attribute philosophy corresponding to the substance-quality philosophy of some of the well-known Western philosophers. Viśiṣṭādvaita is founded on three important metaphysical concepts : (*a*) the concept of substance and attribute; (*b*) the concept of relation and (*c*) the concept of cause and effect. This truth has been well brought out by Vedânta Deśika in the *Tattva-muktā-kalāpa*. He has discussed in this work the underlying philosophical issues and established the doctrines of Viśiṣṭādvaita more on logical basis than on scriptural evidence. An objective study of this treatise will reveal without any shadow of doubt that Viśiṣṭādvaita is truly a sound system of philosophy and not a mere theology.

[28]The *sūtras* are of two types : *naya-sūtra* and *upadeśa-sūtra*. The former is the one which contains the essence of teaching in brief but expressed in the form of logical argument. The latter is the one intended to convey certain ideas or facts, *Pāṇini-sūtras*, *Yoga-sūtras*, etc. are of this type.

[29]RB II-1-4. *tarkānugṛhīta-śāstrārtha-pratiṣṭhāpanam.* See also *Manusmṛti* XII-106. *yastarkeṇānusandhatte sa dharmaṁ veda netaraḥ.*

[30]See VS II-1-11. *tarkāpratiṣṭhānādapi.*

In order to remove the wrong impression about the Viśiṣṭādvaita system and restore it the place that it is entitled to among the great philosophical systems, I have attempted to present the fundamental doctrines of Viśiṣṭādvaita based on a critical study of *Tattva-muktā-kalāpa.*

This book is not a rendering into English of the original text, nor is it aimed merely to present a narrative account of Viśiṣṭādvaita philosophy and religion. On the basis of the rich and thought-provoking material contained in the original Sanskrit text, I have endeavoured to present a comparative and critical account of the basic doctrines of Viśiṣṭādvaita in their logical sequence. In discussing these topics I have focused my attention on the main issues in order to bring out the underlying philosophic significance of the doctrines. With the same purpose, I have avoided, as far as possible, any discussion of the scriptural texts, because the soundness of a theory should have its roots firmly fixed in logic and experience even more than in scripture.

With a view to presenting a coherent account of the doctrines of Viśiṣṭādvaita, I have modified the order in which the topics have been discussed in the original text. I have taken first the fundamental metaphysical categories and concepts which constitute the logical foundation for Viśiṣṭādvaita. These are discussed in the original text partly in the first and the last *sara*. Next comes the Theory of Knowledge in all its aspects including the *pramāṇas* or the means of knowledge which is the subject matter of *Buddhi-sara*. This is covered in Chapters II-V of this book. Next in order comes the discussion of the ontological theories : (*i*) the doctrine of individual self which is dealt with in the first half of *Jiva-sara*; (*ii*) the doctrine of *Iśvara*; (*iii*) Brahman and universe which form the subject of *Nāyaka-sara*. These are presented in chapters VI, VII and VIII respectively. Next comes the discussion of Eschatology of Viśiṣṭādvaita which is contained in the later half of *Jiva-sara*. This is taken up in Chapter IX under the title of *Sādhana* and *Mukti*. Then follows chapter X on *Prakṛti* and its evolutes, which is actually the subject matter of the first *sara* (*Jaḍa-dravya-sara*)) in *Tattva-muktā-kalāpa*. The last but one Chapter (XI) deals with the fundamental attributes and other logical categories covered in the final section of the original text. The final Chapter (XII)—General Estimate and Conclusion—makes a critical evaluation of Viśiṣṭâdvaita as a sound system of philosophy.

In my presentation of Viśiṣṭâdvaita philosophy, I have drawn upon material mainly from the original Sanskrit works and in particular the text of *Tattva-muktā-kalāpa*. For detailed explanation of the arguments contained in the verses, I have consulted available commentaries and in particular *Sarvārtha-siddhi*. I have also drawn material from Râmânuja's *Śri-bhāṣya* and Vedānta Deśika's *Nyāya-pariśuddhi*, *Nyāya-siddhāñjana* and *Śatadūṣaṇi*. Though I have made use of *Sarvārtha-siddhi*, I have not included in my exposition all the points found therein in the interest of brevity. There are far too many details, some dialectical in character and as such more useful for a debate than for understanding the essentials of Viśiṣṭâdvaita. I have therefore omitted some of these details which have no direct bearing on the main doctrines. However, in my interpretation of the text, I have remained faithful to it and endeavoured to bring out the spirit and the underlying significance of the verses as clearly as possible. I hope the book will help in understanding Viśiṣṭâdvaita Vedānta in all its facets and serve as an important text for an in-depth study of this philosophical system.

CHAPTER ONE

Fundamental Metaphysical Categories

BEFORE we enter into a discussion of the doctrines of Viśiṣṭādvaita Vedānta, we need to understand clearly the fundamental metaphysical categories and concepts on the basis of which Viśiṣṭādvaita as a system of philosophy is developed. A proper comprehension of the true nature of the *tattvas* or categories is considered very essential for getting a deeper insight into Vedānta and thereby for the attainment of spiritual realization.[1] Vedānta Deśika has therefore attempted to present in *Tattva-muktā-kalāpa* a comprehensive and critical account of the nature of these categories. In fact, it is for the first time in the history of Viśiṣṭādvaita that such a detailed study of this important subject is undertaken.

I. DEFINITION AND CLASSIFICATION OF CATEGORIES

What are the *tattvas*? The term *tattva* means a real entity, that is, an entity which exists and which is not negated by any of the *pramāṇas* (*abādhita vastu*). In a technical sense, *tattva* also refers to *padārtha*[2] or category, logical as well as metaphysical. Taken in this sense, *tattvas* cover not only the ontological entities such as *Īśvara*, *jiva* and *prakṛti* but also the fundamental attributes of cosmic matter such as *sattva*, *rajas*, *tamas*, etc.

Vedānta Deśika classifies the *tattvas* under two broad headings: *dravya* (substance) and *adravya* (non-substance).[3] *Dravya* is defined as that which has states or modifications (*avasthāvat*). In other words, whatever serves as the substratum for modification is *dravya*.[4] An *avasthā* or modification is defined as an

[1]TMK I-4.

[2]SS I-6. *atra tattvamiti padārtha-mātroktiḥ.*

[3]*Ibid. dravyādravya-prabhedān mitam ubhayavidhaṁ tadvidas tattvam āhuḥ.*

[4]SS I-7, p. 6. *dravyam daśāvat; vikāradharmavat ityarthaḥ.* See also NS, p. 187.

adventitious quality which should be inseparably related to the substance.[5] The implication of this is that any transitory modification to which a substance may be subjected cannot be regarded as an *avasthā* unless it is inherently related to the substance. Thus, for instance, when a jar is placed on the ground, the latter assumes a changed condition insofar as it is associated with the former; but it is not an *avasthā* even though transitory because the jar is separable from the ground. Further a permanent *dharma* or an attribute of a substance cannot be an *avasthā* even though it is inseparably related to the substance. Cowness (*gotva*), for instance, is inseparable from cow but insofar as it is not an adventitious quality, it is not considered as an *avasthā* of cow. Only such an adventitious quality as is inseparably related to the substance so long as the two last is regarded as an *avasthā*. Such passing states or modifications should necessarily belong to an entity. That entity which serves as a substratum for the *avasthās* is considered as a *dravya*. The clay is a substance but the various modes it assumes in the form of a lump—two halves, a pot, vase, etc.—are its *avasthās* or modifications. It is a *dravya* because it is the substratum of the various modifications it assumes. Thus the term *dravya* bears a special connotation in this system. In this sense, it is applicable not merely to a physical object as is commonly understood but even to the ontological entities. The fuller significance of the concept of *dravya* as formulated by Vedānta Deśika becomes clearer in the course of the discussion of the ontological entities in later chapters.

Answering to the definition given above, Vedānta Deśika enumerates six *dravyas*. They are *Īśvara* (God), *jiva* (individual self), *jñāna* (knowledge), *nitya-vibhūti* (transcendental matter), *prakṛti* (cosmic matter) and *kāla* (time). All these are classified as *dravyas* because they serve as substrate for modifications.[6] The six *dravyas* are divided into two classes—*jaḍa* (material substance) and *ajaḍa* (non-material or spiritual substance). *Prakṛti* and *kāla* come under the former class and the remaining four under the latter class. A further distinction is also made among the *ajaḍa dravyas* as *pratyak* (self-revelation) and *parāk* (revelation for

[5]SS V-2, p. 262. *āgantuḥ apṛthaksiddha-dharmaḥ avasthā.*

[6]For explanation as to how *Īśvara* assumes *avasthās*, see the Section 'Viśiṣṭādvaita Theory of Brahma as Material Cause of Universe' in Chapter VII.

others). *Jīva* and *Īśvara* are of the former type, whereas *nitya-vibhūti* and *jñāna* belong to the latter group.

The term *adravya* also bears a special connotation in this system. What is other than *dravya* is *adravya*. It is defined as that which cannot be the substratum of anything else (*anupādāna*) but is necessarily dependent upon *dravya*.[7] A mere quality (*dharma*) of an entity cannot be regarded as *adravya*. It should be such a quality or property of a substance as it does not become a substrate for another quality and should also be integrally related to the substance. *Jñāna* or knowledge, for example, is a *dharma* of the *jīva* for the Viśiṣṭādvaitin, but the former, though inseparably related to the latter, is not *adravya* because it serves as a substrate for its modifications. *Rūpa* or colour as a quality is *adravya* since it is not the substrate for any other qualities and at the same time it is inseparable from the substance in which it inheres. In view of this, *adravya* is also defined as that which cannot admit conjunction with another quality.[8]

In the light of the above explanation, Vedānta Deśika enumerates ten fundamental *adravyas*. These are: *sattva*, *rajas* and *tamas*—the three attributes of *prakṛti*; *śabda* (sound), *sparśa* (touch), *rūpa* (colour), *rasa* (taste) and *gandha* (odour) —the five attributes of gross elements (*pañcabhūtas*); *saṁyoga* (conjunction) and *śakti* (potency). The enumeration of ten attributes does not mean that there are no other qualities found in the substances. There are numerous other qualities belonging to the substances which have to be accepted in conformity with the *pramāṇas*.[9] The mention of ten *adravyas* is intended to emphasise the fact that these are the basic or fundamental metaphysical attributes.

From the foregoing account it may be observed that the two terms *dravya* and *adravya* are comprehensive in character and also mutually exclusive. What is a *dravya* can never be an *adravya* and what is an *adravya* can never become a *dravya*. In view of this, the terms such as *dharma-dharmi*, *viśeṣaṇa-viśeṣya*, *guṇa-guṇi*,

[7]SS V-2, p. 262. *adravyasya anupādānatvam lakṣaṇam nijagaduḥ; avasthāvat dravyam; tad-vyatiriktam adravyam.*

[8]NS, p. 246. *saṁyogarahitam adravyam.*

[9]TMK V-15.

ādheya-ādhāra, etc. which may mean in a loose sense attribute-substance, do not necessarily stand for *adravya* and *dravya* respectively for the obvious reason that these being relative concepts are not mutually exclusive. Thus, for example, *jñāna* is an attribute (*dharma*) of the self but the same is regarded as substance (*dharmi*) with reference to its modification. In the expression 'blue jar', jar is a substance and blueness a quality; but in the expression 'the ground with the jar' (*bhūtalam ghaṭavat*), jar becomes a quality of the ground.

The logical soundness of the classification of the categories (*padārthas*) offered by Vedānta Deśika becomes apparent if we compare it with that provided by the Nyāya-Vaiśeṣika. Besides *dravya* and *guṇas*, they have admitted five other *padārthas* —*karma* (action), *sāmānya* (generality), *viśeṣa* (individuality), *samavāya* (inherence) and *abhāva* (non-existence). *Dravyas* are nine in number and these are the five elements—*pṛthivī* (earth), *ap* (water), *tejas* (fire), *vāyu* (air) and *ākāśa* (ether)—*kāla* (time), *dik* (space), *manas* (mind) and *ātman* (soul). The *guṇas* are twenty-four in number and these include, besides the attributes of the five elements and *saṁyoga* (conjunction) admitted by the Viśiṣṭādvaitin under *adravyas*, a long list of various other *guṇas*[10] in a somewhat arbitrary way. The *sattva*, *rajas* and *tamas* which are the fundamental cosmic attributes and *śakti* or potency which is an important property of causal substance do not figure in the list of *guṇas* enumerated by the Nyāya-Vaiśeṣika. *Buddhi* or knowledge which is accepted as a substance by the Viśiṣṭādvaitin is included among the *guṇas*. As will be shown later, Vedānta Deśika considers the classification and analysis of *padārthas* as expounded by Naiyāyikas defective. He has therefore presented a different classification which in his opinion is far more satisfactory and logically tenable, apart from the fact that it is in conformity with experience and scriptural teachings.

We shall discuss in detail in the succeeding chapters the nature of each of the six dravyas — *jñāna*, *jiva*, *Iśvara*, *prakṛti* *kāla*, *nitya-vibhūti*, and the *adravyas*. Underlying these doctrines there are three fundamental metaphysical concepts which constitute the pivot of the Viśiṣṭādvaita system. These are: (*i*) the

[10]See Section 'Nyaya-Vaiśeṣika Theory of Attributes' in Chapter XI.

concept of substance and attribute; (*ii*) the concept of relation; and (*iii*) the concept of cause and effect.

The central theme of Viśiṣṭādvaita Vedānta is that *cit* (the individual souls) and *acit* (the cosmic matter) are organically related to *Īśvara*, in the same way as an essential attribute is related to a substance. The term Viśiṣṭādvaita thus presupposes that substance and attribute are distinct but the two are integrally related and, as an integral and complex whole, it is one (*viśiṣṭasya advaitam*). It also presupposes that cause and effect are the different states of the same substance (*viśiṣṭayoḥ advaitam*). Thus the soundness of Viśiṣṭādvaita system depends on the soundness of the above metaphysical concepts. We shall therefore discuss these concepts in the present chapter.

II. THE CONCEPT OF SUBSTANCE AND ATTRIBUTE

Viśiṣṭādvaita View

This is the most important doctrine in the Viśiṣṭādvaita system as it constitutes the very basis for *saviśeṣādvaita*. Just as the attribute is inseparable from the substance (*apṛthak-siddha*) the universe is also inseparable from the Absolute.[11] Based on valid *pramāṇas* and in particular our common experience, the Viśiṣṭādvaitin accepts the concept of substance and attribute. The two, according to him, are distinct but integrally related.[12] Whenever we perceive an object we comprehend it as qualified by an attribute. Thus, for instance, when we perceive a blue lotus, we see the flower along with its colour. That which is substrate or basis for the colour is regarded as substance; the colour that cannot exist by itself but only in relation to the substance is the attribute. Since both the substance and the attribute are capable of being cognised at the same time, they are known to exist together. What is well established by experience is undeniable.

The very distinction made between substance and attribute is questioned by the critics. The existence of substance other than the attributes is not accepted by some Buddhists. Similarly, the real existence of attributes other than the substance is denied by

[11]TMK V-1. See also SS, p.262. *tadvadeva viśvamapi parasya apṛthak-siddham.*
[12]*Ibid. idam ca adravyam dravyāt atyantabhinnam.*

the Advaitins. But some who accept the reality of both regard that substance and attribute are different as well as non-different. All these points need clarification to prove the validity of the substance-attribute concept.

The first point of criticism is that the distinction between substance and attribute is logically untenable. If the two are absolutely distinct (*atyanta-bhinna*) as the Viśiṣṭādvaitin believes, how are they related to each other? If the two are related by a relation, then there will be three entities—substance, attribute and relation. How is the relation related to the substance and attribute? If another relation is assumed to bring about its relationship to substance and attribute, it would lead to an infinite regress (*anavasthā*). If a relation is not accepted, then the relationship itself is not established.

This objection which is based on dialectic is met easily. Since substance and attribute by their very nature are inseparably related, there is no need to postulate a third element to account for their relationship. Thus there is no room for the fallacy of infinite regress. The Naiyāyikas admit the relation of inherence (*samavāya*) to account for the relationship between two inseparable entities. Such a relation does not require another relation to account for its relationship to the relata. Without accepting *samavāya* as a separate relation, the Viśiṣṭādvaitin adopts the concept of *apṛthak-siddhi* or inseparability to explain the relation of attribute to substance. What the nature of *apṛthak-siddhi* is and whether it satisfactorily explains the relation existing between substance and attribute will be discussed later when we deal with the concept of relation. For the present, it may be noted that whenever we perceive an object we comprehend the attribute as related to the substance. The attribute which is different from substance has the inherent character of revealing itself as related to the substance.[13] It is not appropriate to question what is well established by experience.

The second criticism is also directed against the untenability of the distinction between substance and attribute on the assumption that the two cannot be known together at the same

[13] TMK V-2. See also SS, p. 263. *idam ca anupadhikam samavāyādi-sambandhābhāvena svabhāvād eva dravyam viśimṣyāt.*

time. The term *adravya* is taken to mean in a negative sense as that which is other than *dravya* (*na dravyam*). If this be so, unless *dravya* is known, *adravya* cannot be known; unless *adravya* is known, *dravya* cannot be understood because the nature of an object can be comprehended only through its quality, which is an *adravya*. Thus the two are inter-dependent (*anyonya-sāpekṣa*), and either of them not being proved both stand unproved.

This objection is controverted on the ground that both substance and its attribute are comprehended together at the same moment, since both are the content of a single perception.[14] Thus the question of a vicious circle does not arise. The term *adravya* is not, strictly speaking, a negative concept. It refers to positive qualities inhering in a substance. The two terms *dravya* and *adravya* have clear-cut connotations and do not give rise to any confusion. Whatever is the substratum for the attribute is *dravya* and what cannot exist except in relation to a substance is *adravya* or attribute. The former is called *ādhāra* or substratum and the latter *ādheya* or that which inheres in it.[15]

Criticism of Buddhist View Denying Substance

A major criticism against the theory comes from the Vaibhāṣika Buddhists who question the very existence of substance as a separate entity. According to the Vaibhāṣikas, there are only four ultimate entities—colour, taste, smell and touch—which are themselves qualities and which do not inhere in any other thing. These are grasped by the respective sense organ.[16] Apart from these qualities, there is no separate entity called substance.

Vedānta Deśika refutes the above theory. We have a perceptual experience of an object by means of two different sense organs in the form: 'I touch what I have seen.' This is not a case of doubt because there are no two conflicting ideas involved in it. Nor is it a case of illusion because it is not contradicted by any other later experience as in the case of the illusion of

[14]TMK V-3.

[15]*Ibid. ādhāre dravya-śabdaḥ; anāśraye tadadhikaraṇake tu anyat.*

[16]See SS I-8 p. 6. *evam āhuḥ vaibhāṣikāḥ: nirādhārā nirdharmakāśca rūpādayaḥcatvāraḥ padārthāḥ, te cakṣurādy-ekaika-indriya-grāhyā iti.* The later Vaibhāṣikas have added *śabda* or sound to the four entities.

snake in rope. Such an experience is therefore valid and unquestionable (*dṛḍhatarā*). It is an experience in the form of *pratyabhijñā* or recognition of an object which was not only seen but is also being touched.[17] This recognition does not refer merely to the visual experience of the colour (*rūpa-mātra*), because the colour sensation does not involve the tactile; otherwise even a blind person who has the tactile experience should be able to perceive the colour. Nor does it refer merely to the tactile experience, because it does not involve the vision of the colour; otherwise one should get the feeling of touch through visual perception, even when the object is not being touched. We cannot say that the recognition refers to the experience of both touch and colour because each one of these sense-data is grasped separately by two different sense organs. *Rūpa* and *sparśa* are two different qualities insofar as the two are experienced by two different sense organs. It is therefore, obvious that the experience in question in the form of *pratyabhijñā* refers to an object to which both the qualities of colour and touch belong. If this be not admitted, it would not be possible to say that one touches what one has already seen.[18]

It may be argued that though colour and touch are experienced by different sense organs, they can be cognised at the same time when these qualities exist together (*saṅghāta*). What is meant by their being together? If it means coexistence, as two individuals seen together, a common ground is needed. If, on the other hand, it means becoming one like water and milk when mixed together, such a possibility does not hold good for two different qualities. Coexistence of two qualities presupposes a basis or substratum other than the qualities. The fact that the two different qualities cannot be combined together leads to the conclusion that the object to which they belong is different from them.[19]

Further, when we see an object located at a distance, we do not notice clearly the object but we get a vague awareness of it without knowing its specific characteristics (*aviśada-grahaṇam*). When we go near the object and observe it, we see its colour, its

[17]TMK I-8. *ekārtha-pratyabhijñā bhavati, dṛḍhatarā darśana-sparśanābhyām.*

[18]SS, p. 6. *ataḥ iyam pratyabhijña rūpādy-atiriktam tadāśrayabhūtam vastu prakāśayati, idam rūpa-sparśavaditi.*

[19]TMK I-8. *saṅghātāderayogād avagamayati sā vastu-rūpādito'nyat.*

true shape, etc. and realise that in the earlier perception of the object we had not grasped its colour and other features (*viśada-grahaṇam*). If the sense data and its basis, viz. the substance were not different, such an experience would not have taken place.[20]

Why can we not say that colour, taste, etc. are one single entity but appear to be as different sense-data, because the sense organs that cognise them are different? This is untenable, because it leads to the fallacy of vicious circle. How do we prove that the sense organs are different? If this is proved on the basis of the difference in respect of sense-data, then we are begging the question. The sense-data are different because the sense organs apprehending them are different. The sense organs are different because the sense-data are different. It is therefore logically sound to accept substance as distinct from attributes.[21]

The theory of substance and non-substance as two distinct entities presupposes the existence of either substrate (*dharmi*) as distinct from quality (*dharma*) or that which constitutes the basis (*ādhāra*) as different from what inheres in it (*ādheya*). In fact, what is accepted as *dravya* constitutes the *dharmi* for the *dharma* and *ādhāra* for the *ādheya*. Some Buddhists do not accept any of these concepts and on that ground they reject the theory of substance and attribute.

The dialectical argument advanced against *dharma* and *dharmi* is as follows. When we speak of the attribute of an object, the question is asked whether the attribute has further quality (*sadharmaka*) or whether it is without a quality (*nirdharmaka*). If it be the latter, it cannot be known. An object becomes known only through its special characteristic. If the attribute is devoid of any further qualities (*nirdharmaka*), it cannot be grasped. To overcome this difficulty, if it be admitted that attribute has further qualities, the question arises whether these qualities have any further qualities in them, and in this way it goes on *ad infinitum*.[22]

Vedānta Deśika refutes this dialectical argument. What is considered to be a *dharma* or attribute need not possess further qualities for it to be known. On the contrary, a *dharma* reveals

[20]TMK I-8. [21]*Ibid.* [22]SS I-9, p. 9.

itself and also the object to which it belongs. This is technically called *svaparanirvāhaka*. Light, for instance, reveals objects but it does not require another light to reveal itself. It reveals itself as well as the objects. The same explanation holds good for *dharma* also.

Further, the classification of *dharma* and *dharmi* is not a rigid one. For what is *dharma* in one context could be *dharmi* in another and vice versa. To illustrate this point, let us take two examples, 'blue jar' (*nīlo ghaṭaḥ*) and 'the ground having the jar' (*bhūtalam ghaṭavat*). In the former case, the jar is the *dharmi* or substance as qualified by blueness and in the latter case the jar is the qualification of the ground. Thus, what in one case is a *dharma* could as well become a *dharmi* in another.

The main point to be taken into consideration is that, according to the Viśiṣṭādvaitin, the *dharma* or an essential characteristic of an entity serves as a basis for differentiating that object from another belonging to a different class. Thus, for instance, the special characteristic of cow known as *gotva* distinguishes the cow from another animal, say, buffalo or horse. It is therefore regarded as *bheda* or difference insofar as it serves as the basis for the judgment we make later that cow is different from horse. The unique characteristic which is possessed by cow-class only is not found in another class of animals. Therefore, it is only on that basis that a cow is distinguished from a buffalo. In view of this explanation it is maintained that in some instances the *dharma* could also become a *dharmi*.[23] If the *dharma* itself could become *dharmi*, would not *dharmi* presuppose a *dharma* as its quality? Vedānta Deśika answers this question by pointing out that in such special cases, the very substance (*viśeṣya*) of that *dharma* becomes its *viśeṣaṇa*. Taking the example of the cow, the *gotva* when it is regarded as a *dharmi* has for its qualification the cow itself. That is, in such cases when the term has specific connotation and denotation (*niṣkarṣa-prayoga*), it refers to the *vyakti* or object itself as its dharma.[24]

With regard to the concept of *ādhāra* and *ādheya*, the Buddhists put forward a similar dialectical argument to disprove it. It is generally believed that a quality inheres in a substance, as for

[23]TMK I-9. *kaścit dharmo'pi dharmī.*

[24]*Ibid. tanniṣkarṣa-prayogeṣvapi tasya dharmī punaḥ viśeṣaḥ bhavati.*

example, that *gotva* (cowness) belongs to '*go*' or cow. The question is asked: whether the quality belongs to that which has no quality or to that which has it? Taking the present example, does *gotva* as the quality inhere in the object devoid of *gotva* or in the object possessing the quality of *gotva*? The former alternative would imply the existence of an entity in its negation which is impossible; for then everything would exist everywhere. If the latter alternative is accepted, it would amount to saying that a quality exists in a quality. That is, if *gotva-viśiṣṭa* is *ādhāra* for *gotva*, *gotva* being already included in the former, it would follow that *gotva* is *ādhāra* for itself. This is absurd. Either way the concept of *ādhāra* and *ādheya* is unintelligible.

The above argument is rejected by Vedānta Deśika. The quality actually belongs to the object. *Gotva* as a *dharma* subsists only in '*go*' which is its *ādhara*. *Gotva* neither exists in *gotva-śūnya* entity or in the *gotva-viśiṣṭa* entity but only in '*go*'.[25] If this explanation is not accepted it would involve self-contradiction. When we say 'pot exists on the ground', it is absurd to ask whether it exists on the ground devoid of pot or on the ground qualified by pot. The correct answer, as warranted by experience, is just that the 'pot exists on the ground'. If such an obvious experience is questioned, then all empirical knowledge would end up in confusion. Dialectic has its limitation and should not be used to deny valid experience.

Criticism of Advaitin's Theory of Difference as Illusory

Another important criticism against the concept of substance-attribute comes from the Advaitin who denies the ultimate reality for the attributes. According to him, only substance or Being is real, whereas the attributes are illusory in character. The basis for holding such a view is that the concept of difference is logically unintelligible and as such the distinction between substance and attribute is ultimately untenable. A dialectical argument is adopted to prove the illusory character of difference. Is difference the nature of the object or its attribute? If it were the former, the illusion would not arise. Illusion arises only when the true nature of the object is not cognised. Shell is mistaken for silver because the difference between the two is

[25] TMK I-10.

not cognised. If, according to the present position, the cognition of shell itself makes known the difference of it from silver, how can there be the apprehension of silver in the shell? If difference is the attribute of the object, then is this attribute different from its substrate or not? If it were not different, then the attribute and the substrate would become identical, and, in the absence of any attribute whatsoever, there cannot be a difference of attributes. If the attribute be different from the substrate, then is that difference between substrate and attribute the very nature of the substrate or an attribute of it? If it be the latter, we are launched on an infinite regress. Thus, the concept of difference is logically unintelligible, and difference therefore is not real.[26]

Vedānta Deśika refutes this theory. The concept of difference can never be denied as its denial would amount to a contradiction of one's own words. The very questions raised by the Advaitin whether *bheda* is *dharma* or *svarūpa* of an object presuppose the admission of difference. If the two alternatives are raised after accepting the difference in general, then it is meaningless to refute it. If the notion of difference is totally rejected, there would be no room for the alternatives.

It may be argued that difference is accepted as *presented* but denied as *real*. In other words, the alternatives are in respect of the difference that is spoken of in the empirical world, while the criticism of it refers to the difference that is contended to be ultimately real. This will not do, says Vedānta Deśika, because the difference in question (*vimarśa-bheda*) is not admitted by the Advaitin to be ultimately real and there is no need to refute it. If it were admitted, it would result in the contradiction of one's own position.

Coming to the question whether difference is the nature of the object or its attribute, Vedānta Deśika replies that, in some cases, it is the nature of the thing, and, in some other cases, it is an attribute of an object depending upon the circumstances.[27] Wherever the cognition of the difference helps to remove the illusion, there difference is *dharma*. In all other cases, it is the

[26]SS V-13, p. 268. See also SD, vāda, 13. These dialectical arguments are drawn from *Brahma-siddhi*, pp. 47-48.

[27]TMK V-13. *dharmaḥ kvāpi svarūpam kvaciditi ca yathā-dṛṣṭi.*

very *svarūpa* of the object.[28] Difference is defined as that which gives rise to the empirical usage, viz. 'that it is different' (*vyāvṛtta-vyavahāra-hetuḥ*).[29] Such a usage is caused sometimes by the very nature of an object and sometimes by the attribute of an object. When we distinguish between two objects, we do so on the basis of the characteristic which one possesses and the other does not. Insofar as the essential characteristic or attribute gives rise to the judgment that one object is different from the other, it is treated as difference.

The question might arise whether or not the attribute that stands for the difference is different from the substrate. It should be admitted as different, for, otherwise there would be no meaning in saying that attribute constitutes difference. If that be the case, what is this difference again? Is it a quality of the attribute or the very nature of it? Vedānta Deśika answers that it is not a quality; if it were a quality, it would lead to an infinite regress. It is, on the contrary, the very nature of the attribute. The attribute which stands for the difference of two objects stands also for the difference of itself from its substrate. There is no need to postulate another quality to account for the difference of the attribute from its substrate. There is no contradiction in admitting that one and the same thing accounts for others as well as for itself. Knowledge, for instance, reveals objects as well as itself. Similarly, colour reveals itself as well as the thing that has the colour. Likewise, an attribute that stands for the difference of its substrate from other objects can also account for its own difference from its substrate.[30] Thus, the concept of difference being intelligible, the difference between substance and attribute is valid.

Vedānta Deśika further points out that difference is also cognised by perception. The Advaitin's contention that perception does not cognise difference is based on the supposition that difference presupposes the knowledge of its counter-correlate and also its substrate and perception being momentary apprehends only Being, while difference is imposed on it later by thought. This argument is controverted by the Viśiṣṭādvaitin by upholding the fact that perception can cognise even in one moment both the object and its characteristic, since both are capable of being

[28]TMK V-13. [29]SD, vāda 13. [30]*Ibid.*

grasped by the same sense organ.[31] The special characteristic of an object as already explained constitutes the difference, and in this sense perception cognises difference. The judgment that one object is different from another arises later only after the substrate and its counter-correlate are known. Insofar as the basis for this judgment is the essential attribute of the object which is grasped by the single perception it is perfectly logical to assert that perception apprehends difference.

Some Buddhists also hold the view that all attributes which are changing modes (*vikāra*) are illusory. Some others who accept the qualities as real regard them as part of the substance, as for instance, that *pṛthivi* is of the nature of *rūpa*, *rasa*, *gandha* and *sparśa*. All these views are unsound. If, according to the Buddhists, the objects are devoid of qualities (*nirdharmaka*) and also momentary, how could such entities which are without qualities be regarded as attributes too? If a distinction between *dravya* and *guṇa* is not accepted, how can they say that air is of the quality of touch, fire is of the qualities of colour and touch only, water is of the nature of colour, touch and taste and earth is of the nature of all four qualities. All these statements imply the distinction between *dravya* and *guṇa*. As pointed out earlier, *pratyabhijñā* in the form 'I touch what I have seen' implying the distinction of the object and its qualities becomes inexplicable.

The Buddhists accept the modifications in the physical objects in the form of origin, decay and destruction. Similar modifications in respect of internal organ (*citta*) are admitted. These are known as *caitya*. These modifications cannot be the very nature of objects. In that case all the three forms of change should take place at the same time. If they are different from the objects, it would amount to the admission of these as qualities of the objects. Thus, in some form or the other, the acceptance of the distinction between substance and attribute is inevitable.

Criticism of Bhāskara's Theory of Bhedābheda

That substance is distinct from attribute may be questioned by those who regard the relationship between the two as one of difference-cum-non-difference. According to Bhāskara, who is

[31]TMK V-14. *yogya-dharmaiḥ yugapat grahaḥ*. See also RB I-1-1.

the upholder of *bhedābheda-vāda*, substance and attribute are different and non-different. The main justification for holding such a view is that in the perception of an object, in the first instance, we do not see it as distinct from its attribute.[32] Thus, for instance, when we first see a cow, we do not at the same time apprehend the distinction between cow and its characteristic, viz. *gotva*. Only when two cows are perceived, do we recognise the fact that both belong to the same cow-class (*gotva-jāti*). Even the judgment we make in the form 'This is cow' indicates that the object (*vyakti*) and its generic character (*jāti*) are one but not distinct. All these facts point out that there is only a relation of difference and non-difference between *jāti* and *vyakti*. If *bheda* alone were true, then we would not have had the experience of the object as one entity. If *abheda* alone were true, we would not be able to speak of difference between them at a later stage. The correct view, according to Bhāskara, is that substance and attribute are different and non-different.

The Viśiṣṭādvaitin who rejects the above theory asserts that the perception of an object as one entity means that the object (*vyakti*) as characterised by its essential attribute (*jāti*) is one (*tad-viśiṣṭaikya-buddheḥ*). Even in the initial perception of an object, the cognition arises in the form 'It is such and such'. As Rāmānuja says all our cognitions reveal the objects only as characterised. In the experience of an object that this is such and such, the 'this' element is the substance (*dharmī*) and the 'such and such' aspect refers to the character of the object (*dharma*).[33] There is no experience of an object devoid of any quality.

An objection may be raised against this position. If *dharma* and *dharmi* are different, we should be able to perceive them separately, just as we see separately two objects which are different. We do not see them as separate but, on the contrary, as one qualified entity. The two cannot therefore be absolutely different. This objection is met by pointing out that *dharma* and *dharmi* are inherently related (*apṛthaksiddha*), and as such they are always apprehended together as one characterised

[32]SS, p. 266. *prathama-piṇḍa-grahaṇeṣu bhedenāpratyayāt.*

[33]SS V-8, p. 266. See also RB I-1-1.

entity. They are not two separable entities like two physical objects but, on the contrary, they are inseparable being inherently related by their very nature. Because of the inseparable character of *dharma* and *dharmi*, the object is cognised as a qualified entity.[34] Though they are inseparable, they are distinct because they are perceived as such. There is no evidence to prove that *dharma* and *dharmi* are non-different.

An inferential argument is adopted to prove that *jāti* and *vyakti* are non-different. The argument is expressed in the form of a syllogism: '*jāti* is not different from *vyakti* because it is always cognised along with *vyakti*; whatever is different from another entity, that is perceived even without the other; as for example, cloth which is different from pot is perceived even in the absence of pot.' The main point of the argument is that the two are always cognised together (*sahopalambha*) and not separately without the other, and therefore they must be regarded as non-different.

The above inference is rejected as fallacious because it is contradicted by the perceptual experience. When it is evident to perception that *jāti* and *vyakti* are different, an inference cannot prove something which is against perceptual evidence. Besides, the principle of invariable association (*sahopalambha*), which is borrowed from the Buddhists is not favourable to the Bhedābhedavādin. The concept of *sahopalambha* implies *bheda*. That is, if only a distinction between two entities is accepted, it is possible to speak of their being associated invariably. It is thus opposed to the idea of non-difference.[35]

One other argument is put forward by the Bhedābhedavādin in support of his theory. Generally if an entity is found qualified, the term denoting it is expressed with the suffix '*mat*' meaning that it is characterised by the particular quality. Thus, in the expression 'ground associated with pot' (*bhutalam ghaṭavat*), the term *ghaṭa* (pot) has the affix '*mat*' and it then

[34]TMK V-8. *tad-vaiśiṣṭya-pratītiḥ nirupadhiḥ apṛthak-siddhi-mātreṇa sidhyet.* The word *nirupadhi* is explained as *svābhāvika* or natural. That is, the *dharma* and *dharmī* by virtue of their intrinsic character are inherently connected and there is no need for a separate relation like *samavāya* to account for their relation. See SS p. 266. See also the Section 'Viśiṣṭādvaita Theory of Apṛthak-siddhi' for a fuller discussion of the concept.

[35]SS V-9, p. 266. *sāhityam bheda eva niyatam, abheda-gandhamapi na sahata iti.*

becomes obvious that the entity as characterised is one, implying the distinction between *vyakti* and *jāti*. But in the case of the terms such as '*go*' (cow), there is no such affix and it cannot therefore be assumed that '*go*' and '*gotva*' are distinct. On the contrary, they are non-different, as distinction is not implied by the term unlike the other example cited.

This argument is not tenable. It is not necessary, contends Vedānta Deśika, that terms should have the affix of '*mat*' to denote that the object as qualified is one. Wherever the entity is the basis for both *dharmi* and *dharma*, the term denoting it need not have the *mat-pratyaya*. Thus, for example, the term *gau* implies both the *go-vyakti* and its *jāti* (*gotva*). Because the term denoting it does not have the *mat-pratyaya*, *gotva* and '*go*' do not become identical.

Criticism of the Jaina Theory of Anekāntā

According to the Jainas who advocate the doctrine of *anekānta*, the nature of the objects in the universe is not of one uniform character but manifold. In other words, nothing can be affirmed absolutely as all affirmations are true only under certain conditions and limitation. When we look at a thing from different viewpoints, we arrive at different conclusions. Thus, a jug is a *dravya* in the sense that it is of the nature of collection of atoms but it is not a *dravya* like another substance such as *ākāśa*. It is a *dravya* in one sense and not a *dravya* in another sense. In the same way, an object looked at from different standpoints could be described as of different character. By adopting such a theory it is quite possible to conceive that objects may be both different as well as non-different.

The above theory is not sound because it conflicts with our experience (*dhi-viruddha*). *Bheda* and *abheda* are mutually opposed and cannot exist together. It may be possible to overcome this objection by admitting difference and non-difference from two different standpoints. In fact, this is the view of the Jainas. For instance, all cows are the same (non-different) in the sense that they all possess certain general common character (*sāmānyākārā*) but they are also different in the sense that each cow as an individual entity is different from the other. Thus, from the standpoint of a common factor they are non-different but from the standpoint of special feature they are different.

Vedānta Deśika controverts this argument. If an entity is regarded as different as well as non-different in character from the two standpoints of *vyakti* and *jāti*, (that is, as *vyakti* different and on the basis of *jāti* non-different), the question is raised whether or not there is any difference between the concept of *vyakti* and concept of *jāti*. If it be admitted that the two are different, then the *anekāntavāda* falls to the ground. The implication of the criticism is that, according to the *anekānta* theory, an entity should admit difference as well as non-difference; but, on the basis of accepting *jāti* as different from *vyakti*, only difference becomes established and not non-difference. To escape this difficulty, the other alternative, viz. that *jāti* and *vyakti* as non-different is accepted, then, according to Jaina logic we need a common character or feature to prove that all *jāti* and *vyakti* are non-different. Two entities are regarded as non-different on the basis of certain common character or feature between them. What is the common feature between *jāti* and *vyakti*? If something as a common feature is admitted, then the question is asked whether this common feature is different or non-different from *jāti-vyakti*. If it be non-different, it needs another common feature and so on *ad infinitum*. Thus, it would lead to the fallacy of infinite regress.[36]

If the doctrine of *anekānta* is applicable to all things in the universe as Jainas believe, there would be utter confusion in our thinking, in making judgments about the nature of things and in determining the correct nature of logical and philosophical truths. How could one determine the difference between *pūrvapakṣa* and *siddhānta* and between what is logically tenable and what is not tenable? If there be no difference between one's own view and that of the opponent, there is no point in criticising the latter. If there be difference, *anekānta* theory cannot be justified. Hence this doctrine will end up in utter chaos.[37]

If the nature of the thing is unchanging and well established, the Jainas ask why two different views should be held on a theory by the exponents belonging to the same school of thought? Thus, for instance, some Naiyāyikas believe that memory (*smṛti*) is not a valid knowledge, while some other Naiyāyikas hold

[36]TMK V-10. [37]TMK V-10.

the view that it is valid knowledge. Even among the Viśiṣṭādvaitins, *nitya-vibhūti* (transcendental matter) is *jaḍa* (material) for some, while for others it is *ajaḍa* (non-material). If the theory of *anekānta* is accepted, such different views about the same matter would be explicable.

Vedānta Deśika's reply to this objection is that the different views about the same matter are due to the difference of opinion among the two thinkers (*bhinnāśaya*). This does not mean that the nature of the object itself is manifold (*anekānta*). In some cases, two different statements about the same theory may be an expression of doubt (*saṁśayokti*) or even a case of exaggerated description (*vaibhavokti*). There is absolutely no justification to resort to the doctrine of *anekānta*.

The Jainas justify the theory of *anekānta* or the possibility of different conclusions regarding the nature of an entity from different viewpoints on the basis of another important doctrine known as *syādvāda*, advocated by them. The word *syād* means 'maybe'. The reality, in their opinion, is extremely indeterminate in its nature and it is not possible to make any affirmation which is universally and absolutely valid. They conceive of seven possible alternatives in respect of describing the nature of reality, and each of them is partially true in some sense or the other. The Jainas think that reality is so complex in its structure, while everyone of these views is true as far as it goes but none is completely so. Accordingly, they enunciate its nature in seven steps described as *saptabhaṅgi* or the seven-fold formula. The seven-fold description of reality is expressed as follows :[38]

(1) Maybe, is (*syād asti*).
(2) Maybe, is not (*syān nāsti*).
(3) Maybe, is and is not (*syād asti nāsti*)
(4) Maybe, is inexpressible (*syād avyaktavyaḥ*).
(5) Maybe, is and is inexpressible (*syād asti ca avyaktavyaḥ*).
(6) Maybe, is not and is inexpressible (*syān nāsti ca avyaktavyaḥ*).
(7) Maybe, is, is not and is inexpressible (*syād asti ca nāsti ca avyaktavyaḥ*).

Sattva means existence or being and *asattva* is non-existence

[38]OIP, p. 164.

or non-being. Generally, it is believed that these two are mutually opposed and cannot be affirmed of the same object. But, according to the Jainas, it is possible that the same object may be a being as well as non-being, depending upon the viewpoint from which we look at it. Thus, a jug is or exists as a jug but it is not or does not exist as a pot. A jug exists in a particular place but does not exist elsewhere. A jug exists at this time but not at a later time. Thus, every object in the universe may have contrary characteristics with reference to the material, time, space and condition.

We need not go into the details of the Jaina doctrine. What is relevant for our purpose is, as Vedānta Deśika observes, that the Jainas unfortunately apply the seven-fold formula even to the concept of substance and attribute.[39] The qualities are called *paryāyas*, modes or changes as distinguished from enduring substance. These are modifications taking place in the substance and are accidental in character. Both the features—substance and the modes—are admitted in respect of the same identical object and, at the same time, on the basis of *syādvāda* doctrine. This means that permanence and change or unity and difference could coexist in the same object and at the same time. Judged as an enduring entity substance is permanent (*nitya*) and non-different (*abhinna*), and the same with reference to the various modifications it constantly undergoes is non-permanent (*anitya*) and different (*bhinna*).

The above theory is summarily rejected by Vedānta Deśika on the ground that two mutually opposed characteristics cannot be affirmed in respect of one and the same entity. If a clear-cut distinction is not admitted between two entities, as evidenced by our experience, the question of establishing one's own theory and the criticism of the theory of the opponent does not arise. The idea of defeat and success in a debate is meaningless since the two are not different for the Jainas.[40]

[39]TMK V-12. *saiṣā saptabhaṅgī jinasamayajaḍaiḥ dravya-paryāya-varge uktā.*

[40]TMK V-12. The defect of this theory as voiced by other critics is that the sevenfold description of reality falls short of determining precisely the nature of reality. Thus it does not offer a satisfactory solution to the metaphysical problem. See OIP, p. 173.

III. THE CONCEPT OF RELATION

The doctrine of substance and attribute is linked with the concept of relation. If substance and attribute are distinct, we have to provide a satisfactory explanation for their relationship. The theory of relation assumes greater significance as it has a bearing on the ontological issue concerning the relationship between Brahman and the cosmic universe of *cit* and *acit*.. The major problem of Vedānta is how does the 'one' become 'many', and how are the two related. The Advaitin attempts to resolve the issue by dismissing the ultimate reality of the many. The Absolute alone is real and the manifold universe is a phenomenal appearance of Reality. The Viśiṣṭādvaitin, on the other hand, who admits the reality of the manifold universe including the individual souls, explains the relationship between the Absolute and the universe on the basis of the relation that holds good between the substance and attribute.

Nyāya-Vaiśeṣika Theory of Samavāya

We have already referred to the criticism against the concept of relation. If substance and attribute are different, how are they related? If the two are related by a relation, then the question is asked how that relation is related to the relata. If another relation is assumed to bring about its relationship to the relata, it would lead to an infinite regress. If, on the contrary, a relation is not accepted, then the relationship between substance and attribute is not established.[41] Thus, the concept of relation is logically untenable.

Nyāya-Vaiśeṣika meets this objection by admitting the relation of inherence known as *samavāya* between substance and attribute. It is a relation which holds good between two entities which are inseparable (*ayutasiddha*), unlike the relation of *saṁyoga* or conjunction that obtains between two separable things (*yuta-siddha*). The latter is an external relation, whereas the former is a kind of internal relation. *Samavāya* is an inherent relation because the separation of the relata connected by it necessarily implies the destruction of one at least of them.

[41]The same kind of argument is adopted by F.H. Bradley. See Bradley's *Appearance and Reality*, p. 28 (2nd edn.).

Such relata are described as *ayuta-siddha* which means that of the two entities one is invariably connected with the other. According to Nyāya-Vaiśeṣika, there are five types of *ayuta-siddha* entities which alone admit of *samavāya* relation. These are: (*a*) *dravya* and *guṇa*, (*b*) *dravya* and *karma*, (*c*) *vyakti* and *jāti*, (*d*) ultimate things and *viśeṣa*; and (*e*) whole and parts. As regards the objection pointed out above, the Naiyāyikas maintain that *samavāya* relation does not require another third element to relate it to the relata. If another relation is assumed, it would no doubt lead to the fallacy of infinite regress. By adopting the principle of *svaparanirvāhaka*,[42] Naiyāyikas explain that *samavāya* as a relation could relate itself with the two relata without the need of a third relation.

Viśiṣṭādvaita Theory of Apṛthak-siddhi

Vedānta Deśika does not accept *samavāya* as a separate relation between substance and attribute. In fact, both Rāmānuja and Śaṁkara have rejected the concept of *samavāya* relation on the basis of *vedānta-sūtra*.[43] According to the Viśiṣṭādvaitin, substance and attribute are inseparable by their very nature. As explained earlier, an attribute cannot be separated from its substance; similarly, a substance cannot be conceived without its attribute. Taking the example of blue lotus, the blueness which is a quality cannot be separated from the lotus. Nor can the lotus be thought of without its blueness. According to the epistemological position of Viśiṣṭādvaita, when an object is perceived it is seen as inherently connected with the quality. In view of this, it is maintained that substance and attribute are inseparable. The technical term used to describe the inseparable character of substance and attribute is *apṛthak-siddhi*. *Pṛthak* means separate and *apṛthak* means not separate. *Siddhi* implies two things: *sthiti* or existence and *pratiti* or cognition.[44] *Apṛthak-sthiti* means that attribute and substance cannot exist as two separate entities unlike two physical objects. *Apṛthak-pratiti* signifies that substance and attribute cannot be comprehended separately. Thus, attribute is dependent

[42]See Section 'Criticism of Buddhist View Denying Substance' in Chapter I.

[43]VS II-2-12 (acg. to R.B) II-2-13 (acg. to S. B.).

[44]See *Śrutaprakāśikā* I-1-13.

on substance for its existence (*sattā*). Being inherent in substance it forms an integral part of it. Substance, which is the basis for attribute does not however depend on the latter for its existence, but nevertheless it needs attribute because the *svarūpa* of an entity is determinable only through its essential attributes. According to the Viśiṣṭādvaitin, a *svarūpa* devoid of attributes is a non-entity.[45] When substance and attribute are already related by virtue of their intrinsic character, it is superfluous to postulate a separate relation such as *samavāya*, In view of this, Vedānta Deśika asserts that we do not see any separate relation other than the very *svarūpa* of substance and attribute.[46] If an additional relation other than the inseparable character of the relata is admitted, the fallacy of infinite regress is inescapable. Any relation which falls outside the terms to be related requires a relation to relate it to the terms and so on *ad infinitum*. If it is argued that there is no need for another relation and that the very *samavāya* relation itself can account for itself and its relationship to the relata on the basis of the principle of *svaparanirvāhaka*, then it is more appropriate to accept that the very relata—substance and attribute—by virtue of their nature can account for the relationship between substance and attribute.[47]

It may be noted that *apṛthak-siddhi* is not strictly a separate relation (*sambandha*) like *samavāya*. It is a name given to the inseparable character of the relata. As already mentioned, there are two types of entities in the universe: (*i*) those that are separable (*yuta-siddha*) such as a pot and cloth and (*ii*) those which are inseparable such as the rose and its colour (*ayuta-siddha*). In the case of the former, when the two entities are brought together their relation is described as *saṁyoga* or conjunction. This is purely an external relation and ceases to exist the moment the objects are separated. In the case of the latter, we have to conceive an inherent relation or internal relation. The Naiyâyikas describe such a relation as *samavāya*. Instead of *samavāya*, the Viśiṣṭādvaitin uses the expression

[45]See Section 'God and His Attributes' in Chapter VII.

[46]TMK V-126. *bandham na adhyakṣayāmaḥ samadhikaṁ apṛthak- siddhayoḥ tatsvarūpāt*. See also SS, p. 317. *apṛthak-siddhayoḥ samavâyākhyam svarūpād adhikaṁ kalpyamānaṁ sambandham na pratyakṣayāmaḥ*

[47]SS V-2, p. 263.

apṛthak-siddhi. However, there is an important difference between the two schools. For Naiyâyika *samavāya* is a separate relation; it is regarded as one of the six independent *padārthas* or categories and it is *nitya* in the sense that it is not produced. For the Viśiṣṭâdvaitin *apṛthak-siddhi* is not a separate relation or even a separate category. It is just a name used to describe the nature of the relation that already exists between the substance and the attribute. It is the very nature of the relata. In this sense it may be regarded as a unique relation (*svarūpa-sambandha*) that exists between the two inseparable entities. Further, *apṛthak-siddhi* conceived as a relation is not *nitya* or eternal in all cases. If the relata are non-permanent, such as the rose and its redness, its relationship is also non-permanent. That is, it lasts or exists as long as the relata exist. It is permanent or *nitya* in the case of eternal entities such as *jiva* and its attributive knowledge. As will be shown presently, the Viśiṣṭâdvaitin admits *apṛthak-siddhi* between two ontological substances such as *Īśvara* and *jiva*. The concept of *apṛthak-siddhi* is not strictly speaking the same as *samavāya* conceived by the Naiyâyikas and as such the criticisms levelled against the latter do not hold good in respect of the former.

Is it appropriate to regard the very *svarūpa* of the relata as a *sambandha*? Vedânta Deśika answers in the affirmative. In the case of knowledge and external object, even the Naiyâyikas do not postulate a separate relation other than the fact that knowledge (*viṣayi*) stands related to the object (*viṣaya*). Such a relation is known as *viṣaya-viṣayibhāva* or subject-object relation.[48] In the same way the very *svarūpa* of the substance and attribute which are inseparable accounts for their relationship. Such an explanation is logically justified if we understand the proper meaning of the term 'relation'. A relation, according to Vedānta Deśika, is that which causes the empirical usage, viz. that two entities in question are related (*vastunor-viśiṣṭavyavahāra-janana-svabhāvatvam*).[49] If the relation that obtains in respect of the two relata could give rise to such a judgment, it is rather superfluous to postulate another relation in order to account for

[48]The theory of subject-object relation is discussed in the chapter on 'Knowledge and External World'.

[49]SD, vâda 17.

the relation in question. A relation, like knowledge, is capable of accounting for itself as well as another relation. Wherever the relata themselves are found to be capable of giving rise to the judgment that the objects are related (as in the case of the substance and attribute), there the very relata constitute the relation inasmuch as they bring about the judgment of relation. Wherever a relation is evident as in the case of *saṁyoga* and *viṣaya-viṣayi-bhāva*, there is no need to postulate any additional relation other than what is apparent to experience.

One possible objection may be raised against the concept of *apṛthak-siddhi*. If the substance and attribute are inseparable, would it be justified in regarding them as distinct? Some critics have taken the view that the concept of *apṛthak-siddhi* is postulated to separate what is supposed to be one.[50] This objection is not valid. The concept of *ayuta-siddhi* or *apṛthak-siddhi* is meaningful only if there are two distinct relata. We have already discussed in the earlier section that substance and attribute are distinct. The two are not identical. Even, according to the Naiyāyikas, *ayuta-siddha* does not imply identity since the two things which are inseparable are not one in reality. The form of fire and the ball of iron are distinct from each other.[51] The term *apṛthak-siddhi* is synonymous with the word *ayuta-siddha*. If two relata are inseparable they cannot be treated as identical. The nature of quality is different from that of substance. A quality as such cannot subsist by itself but it must necessarily inhere in a substrate. Similarly, a pure substrate devoid of a quality is inconceivable. As long as the nature of the two concepts is different the distinction between substance and attribute is undeniable. Perceptual experience also proves that the two are distinct. According to the epistemological position of Viśiṣṭādvaita, when an object is perceived, we comprehend at the same time the quality as well as the substance to which it belongs. As Rāmānuja has stated, we do not see in visual perception merely an indeterminate entity but, on the contrary, we perceive the *rūpa* (quality) and the *rūpi* (substance) and also the two as inherently connected together.[52] The implication of it is that *dharma* (quality) and *dharmi* (its substrate)

[50]See OIP, p. 409. [51]See IP, vol II. p. 217. [52]See RB I-1-1, p. 54.

as well as the *sambandha* between the two are all apprehended together insofar as all the three are capable of being cognised by the same sense organs.[53] Vedânta Deśika therefore comes to the conclusion that substance and attribute, though inherently related, are distinct.

The Concept of Body-Soul Relation

The relation of *apṛthak-siddhi* obtains not only between substance and attribute but also between two substances (*dravyas*). Thus, according to the Viśiṣṭâdvaita Vedânta, the physical body (*śarira*) and the soul within (*ātman*), though both are *dravyas*, are inseparable. Similarly, the universe comprising *cit* (souls) and *acit* (matter) is inseparable from *Iśvara*. Such an organic relation obtaining between the body and soul is described as *śarirātma-sambandha*. This constitutes the most important doctrine in Viśiṣṭâdvaita (*pradhâna-pratitantra*)[54]. The soundness of Viśiṣṭâdvaita depends on the logical tenability of this doctrine and it therefore calls for fuller discussion to avoid any possible misunderstanding.

We shall first take up the relation of the physical body to the soul. How do we prove that the two are inseparable? We may concede an inseparable relation between the substance and attribute which is evident to experience. But we cannot say that in the same way we apprehend the inseparability of the soul and body. In order to admit that soul and body are inseparable, we have to prove that one cannot exist without the other (*apṛthak-sthiti*) and that we also comprehend them as inseparable (*apṛthak-pratiti*).

The Viśiṣṭâdvaitin explains that the body is dependent upon the soul for its very existence. When the soul leaves the body, the latter ceases to be a living body. As long as the living body lasts, it is not separable from the soul. As will be explained shortly, the very concept of *śarira* or physical body necessarily presupposes its relation to a soul. A body as a living organism cannot exist by itself without a soul to sustain it.

We do also have the awareness (*pratiti*) of the body being intimately related to the soul. Thus, in the judgment 'I am a

[53]See NP, p. 96. *dharmavad-dharmivacca tat-sambandhasyāpy-aindriyikatva-aviśeṣeṇa grahaṇasambhavât.*

[54]See the Section on 'Central Theme of Tattva-muktā-kalāpa' in 'Introduction'.

human being' (*manuṣyo'ham*) we cognise that the characteristic of being human (*manuṣyatva*) which is an essential property of the physical body is intimately connected with the notion of 'I', which is the soul. The assumption here is, based on Viśiṣṭādvaita epistemology, that what is regarded as an essential attribute, like cowness (*gotva*) in the case of a cow, is inseparable from the substance. That is why one gets an experience in the form of the judgment 'I am human being' where the terms standing for substance and attribute respectively are found in apposition.[55]

It is no doubt true that in the present experience, viz. 'I am a human being' the soul is not cognised along with the body in the same way as a material substance is perceived along with its attribute. This is due to the fact that soul is a supersenuous entity, and it is not an object of perception.[56] However, its existence is known by means of revealed scripture which is the authoritative *pramāṇa* in spiritual matters. The direct vision of the soul is also possible for an individual endowed with *yogic* perception developed through the practice of *yoga*.

How do we prove that Brahman and universe of *cit* and *acit* are inseparable ? As Brahman is beyond the scope of perceptual experience, the Viśiṣṭādvaitin seeks to establish the truth on the strength of scriptural testimony. The Antaryāmi Brāhmaṇa of *Bṛhadāraṇyaka Upaniṣad*[57] states explicitly that the non-sentient matter and the sentient souls constitute the *śarira* or body of Brahman. It mentions in an exhaustive way the various kinds of being that form the *śarira* of Brahman starting from the five elements which constitute the physical world of space and time and concluding with *jiva* or *vijñāna*. Similarly, the *Subāla Upaniṣad* declares that matter and soul in all their states constitute the body of the Supreme Self and concludes by saying that Brahman is the inner Self of all beings (*eṣa sarvabhūtāntarātmā*).[58] The smṛti texts reiterate the same truth by describing the universe as *tanu* (body) of Brahman.[59]

[55]See RB I-1-1, pp. 150-51, See also RB on BG XIII-1.

[56]*Ibid. ātmanastu acākṣuṣatvāt cakṣuṣā śarira-grahaṇa-velāyām ātmā na gṛhyate.*

[57]Br Up V-7 (III-7 accg. to SB).

[58]Sub Up VII.

[59]*Viṣṇupurāṇa* 1-12-38. *tat sarvam vai hareḥ tanuh.* Also see BG XV-7. *mamaivāṁśo jivaloke jīvabhūtas sanātanaḥ.* According to some Viśiṣṭā-

The term *śarira* as defined by Rāmānuja bears a special connotation and it implies that which is regarded as *śarira* should be inseparable from the soul or *ātman*. What is the exact and correct definition of the term *śarira*? In ordinary usage, *śarira* means the physical structure of a living being. Thus, it is applicable to the bodies of all living beings such as worms, insects, moths, snakes, quadrupeds and human beings. The physical structure of these various kinds of living beings is not uniformly the same and as such the term *śarira* cannot bear the same connotation in respect of the various kinds of bodies. The Vedas also use the expression *śarira* in respect of the bodies of *Īśvara*, other divine beings and the elements such as *pṛthivi* which are all of different nature. We should, therefore, adopt a definition for the word which should be applicable to all kinds of bodies described both in the Vedas and those that are referred to in our ordinary usage. The Naiyāyikas have defined the body as that which is the seat or abode of activity, sense organs and experience in the form of pleasure and pain.[60] This definition is considered defective as it is too wide or too narrow. If body is the seat of activity, even a pot becomes a *śarira* insofar as it is the locus of *ceṣṭā* or some activity. Again a body in the state of swoon does not have any activity but it still continues to be the body. The definition of body as the abode of sense organs is too narrow as it excludes such material entities which are regarded as bodies but do not have the sense organs. That body is the basis for the experience of pleasure and pain is faulty, because such experience belongs to the soul or the

---

dvaitins, the *Bṛhadāraṇyaka Upaniṣadic* text *'Neha nānāsti kiñcana'* directly speaks of the inseparable relation between Brahman and universe. The word *nānā*, according to *Pāṇini-sūtra*, stands for *vinā* meaning separate (*pṛthak*). *Na nānā* in this text therefore means that the universe is not separate from Brahman. The same truth is stated more explicitly in the *Gitā* (*na tadasti vinā yat syāt mayā bhūtam carācaram* BG.X-39). The meaning of this verse, according to Rāmānuja, is that there is nothing in the universe which exists without having Brahman as the inner controller. Because Brahman is the inner Self of the Universe, the two are inseparable (*ātmatayā avasthitena avinābhāvam*). See the commentary of Uttamur Viraraghavacharya on Br Up VI-4-19, p. 358

[60] *Nyāya-sūtra* I-1-11 *ceṣṭendriyārthāśrayaḥ Śarīram*.

empirical ego but not the physical body. Further, the definition offered by the Naiyāyikas does not apply to the physical elements such as *pṛthivī* which are described by the Upaniṣad as *śarīra* of *Īśvara*.

After critically examining the various other definitions of the term *śarīra*, Rāmānuja offers the following definition : *yasya cetanasya yaddravyam sarvātmanā svārthe niyantuṁ dhārayituṁ ca śakyaṁ taccheṣataika-svarūpaṁ ca tat tasya śarīram.*[61] It means: 'Any substance which a sentient self can completely control and support for its own purposes and which stands to the self in an entirely dependent relation is called its *śarīra*.' This definition which is very significant has certain implications. The concept of *śarīra* is applicable only to a substance in relation to a knowing subject or conscious self. That is, the body-soul relation is conceivable only between a sentient self and a substance and not between any two substances. Secondly, the concept does not apply to *dharma-bhūta-jñāna*, even though it is a substance because *jñāna* is an integral part of the self. It is also not applicable to *guṇa* (quality) and *karma* (action), even though the latter are inseparable from the substance. A mere dependence of one entity on the other or one being under the control of the other cannot also be the determinant of *śārīratva*. Thus, for instance, an attendant is dependent on his master to some extent and is also controlled by him, but the latter cannot be regarded as the *śarīra* of the former because of the fact that the attendant is not wholly and always (*sarvātmanā*) controlled by the master nor wholly dependent on him. This implies that unless the substance is necessarily, and as long as it endures, dependent on the self, it will not qualify to become a *śarīra*.

The above definition is very comprehensive and it applies to both the physical body of the living being in relation to its soul and also to the physical universe in relation to the Brahman. The physical body is necessarily dependent upon the soul for its existence; it ceases to be a body the moment the soul departs from it. It is wholly controlled by the soul. It exists wholly for the use of the self. Because there is an intimate or inseparable relation between the self and the body, it is possible that the latter can be supported, controlled and used for its purpose by the former.

[61]RB II-1-9, p. 457.

In view of this, Vedānta Deśika gives the following definition of *śarira* to bring out the *apṛthak-siddhi* relation between soul and body: 'That substance which is inseparable from the self, similar to its *dharmabhūta-jñāna*, is called its *śarira*.'[62] For each individual self there are two entities which are inseparable from it. One is its *dharmabhūta-jñāna* and the second is its physical body. *Jñāna* is not a *śarira* for the reason already explained but it is inseparable from the soul. The only other substance which is inseparable from the soul is the physical body. From this it follows that what is considered as a body or *śarira* should necessarily be inseparable from its soul.

On the basis of the above theory of body-soul relation, the Viśiṣṭādvaita Vedānta maintains that the entire universe of *cit* and *acit* stands in relation of a body to the soul. All sentient and non-sentient beings constitute the *śarira* or body of *Īśvara* in the technical sense that the former are wholly dependent on the latter for their existence; they are completely controlled by *Īśvara* and they subserve the purpose of the Supreme Being. *Īśvara* is called the *ātman* or *śaririn* because He is the ground (*ādhāra*) for the universe, He is the controller (*niyantā*) and He uses it for His own purpose. The three concepts used to explain comprehensively the organic relationship that exists between Brahman and universe of *cit* and *acit* are: *ādhāra-ādheya* (the sustainer and sustained), *niyantā-niyāmya* (the controller and controlled) and *śeṣi-śeṣa* (the self-subsistent and dependent). The fuller ontological significance of this threefold relationship is discussed in the chapter on Brahman and universe. For the present we may take note of the fact that on the analogy of the inseparable relation that obtains between body and soul and also on the strength of the Upaniṣadic statements, the Viśiṣṭādvaitin affirms that the universe of *cit* and *acit* is organically related to Brahman.

The concept of *apṛthak-siddhi*, on the basis of which the body-soul relation is formulated, has an important logical and philosophical significance. It accounts for both unity as well as difference. That is, wherever we find that two entities are inseparable by their nature, such as substance and attribute, soul and body and *Īśvara* and universe, we can

[62] TMK IV-83. *yad-dhī-tulyāśrayam, apṛthak-siddhimat dravyam yat, idam asya vapuḥ.*

uphold both difference and unity. There is difference between these two entities because by virtue of their intrinsic nature they are distinct. Nevertheless, they constitute one entity as an integral and complex whole. As a substance characterised by the attribute, it is one, but as substance and attribute they are two. This principle holds good in respect of Brahman and universe. The two by virtue of their character are distinct but Brahman as the inner self of the universe and as a *viśiṣṭa entity* is one. Where two entities are absolutely different (*bhinna*) and are separable, like a pot and cloth and where there is no inherent relation, unity cannot be affirmed except in a secondary sense as an aggregate of parts. We have to acknowledge two kinds of *bheda* or difference. One kind of *bheda*,, which is absolute may be found in separable entities such as two physical objects. The other kind of *bheda* obtains between two inseparable entities. The latter type of *bheda* is such as it allows for difference and also admits non-difference or unity in the sense of an integral and complex whole or as a qualified substance. The *apṛthak-siddha* entities are always cognised as one and as expressed in the judgments 'I am a human being'. In all such statements, which are regarded as *samānādhikaraṇa vākya* or judgments in which the two terms are in apposition, the implication is not absolute identity devoid of any differentiation but unity in the sense of a *viśiṣṭa entity* or substance qualified by its attribute.[63] This is the significance of the concept of *apṛthak-siddhi* in Viśiṣṭādvaita.

IV. THE CONCEPT OF CAUSE AND EFFECT

Ontological Implications of Causality

The concept of cause and effect is the most fundamental metaphysical category. It assumes greater importance than the other concepts we considered earlier as it provides the key to the understanding of the knotty problem of how the 'one' becomes 'many'. The Sadvidyā of *Chāndogya Upaniṣad*[64] raises the issue

[63]See Section 'The Import of Samānādhikaraṇa Vakya' in Chapter III for further discussion.

[64]Ch Up. VI-1-3.

in a striking manner: 'What is that by knowing which everything else is known? 'If we take into consideration the illustration of clay and its products cited by the Upaniṣad, it would imply that by knowing the material cause the effects too become known. Such a thing is possible if cause is immanent in the effect and non-distinct from it (*ananya*). The underlying issue involved in the theory of causality with reference to the universe as an effect and Brahman as material cause is whether cause and effect are different (*anya*) or not different (*ananya*). The Ārambhaṇādhikaraṇa of *Vedānta-sūtras* is mainly devoted to the discussion of this fundamental problem.[65] We shall deal with the ontological aspect of this subject at the appropriate place and consider here the general issues relating to the concept of cause and effect.

According to one school of thought, cause and effect are not the same. The effect is a product of the cause but the former is not already existent in the cause. This is known as *asat-kāryavāda*, attributed to the Nyāya-Vaiśeṣika system. According to another school of thought, the effect exists in the cause in a potential form and it is only a manifestation of what already exists. This is the *sat-kāryavāda* held by the Sāṅkhya system. There is another view which does not accept either of the above theories. The effect does not exist in the cause nor is it distinct from the cause. The two are different states of one and the same substance (entity). This is the theory of Viśiṣṭādvaita Vedānta which is regarded as a modified *sat-kāryavāda*.

As against these accepted views, we have other theories of causality which question the very basic concept of cause and effect. Thus, according to the Cārvāka school, there is no such thing as cause and effect. The Buddhists for whom everything is momentary also deny the very existence of cause and effect as real enduring entities. The Advaitins, though they accept the concept of cause and effect, deny ultimate reality to it because causal relation is logically unintelligible. Vedānta Deśika examines all these theories critically with a view to bringing out the soundness of the Viśiṣṭādvaita concept of causality on the basis of which the metaphysical problem of one and many is explained in the system.

[65]VS II-1-15.

Criticism of Cārvāka View of Causality

We shall first take up the Cārvāka view which denies the basic concept of cause and effect. A dialectic is adopted to criticise the notion of causality. Does the effect already exist prior to causai operation? If so, it should exist all the time like space and it cannot be brought about as an effect. If it does not already exist, it can never be produced as an effect as in the case of the sky-flower. What is non-existent cannot be produced as otherwise even sky-flower should have been produced.

Does the cause bring about the effect as related to the effect or as unrelated to it? If it be the former alternative, the cause will have no relation to what is going to be produced at a later period. If it be the latter alternative, then any cause can produce any effect Insofar as there is no relation between cause and effect.

When we say pot is produced, the question is asked whether production (*janma*) is produced or not. If we admit that production of pot is produced, then, the production being a different entity from pot, the question will arise whether that production is further produced, and by stretching the argument further, it would lead to an infinite regress. If we say that the production of pot is not produced, then it amounts to saying that pot is not produced at all.[66]

All these dialectical arguments are untenable, contends Vedānta Deśika, because they stand opposed to our experience and contradict the human endeavour as well as philosophical discussion. Human effort is directed to achieve some specific objective, and if there be no causal relation between effort and goal, an endeavour to achieve something is futile. Even the opponent's statement that there is no cause-effect relation, which is obviously aimed to disprove a theory, becomes meaningless.[67]

[66]TMK I-32.

[67]This is a general reply to Cārvāka's criticism. Vedānta Deśika has also offered a detailed reply to each of the dialectical arguments in the *Sarvārtha-siddhi*.. As the counter-arguments are more of a dialectical character, these are not stated here. Besides, somewhat similar dialectical arguments are advanced by the Advaitin and the replies given to them cover the objections raised by the Cārvāka.

Criticism of Advaitin's Theory of Causality

Similar dialectical arguments in greater detail are advanced by the Advaitin to prove the logical untenability of the causal relation. While the Cārvāka adopts the dialectic to question the very concept of cause and effect, the Advaitin uses the dialectic to prove the illusory character of the effect on the ground that the relation between cause and effect is logically unintelligible. The assumption here is that two entities as real with different nature cannot be identical. If one is real and the other illusory, then it is possible to regard them as non-distinct. On the basis of this logic, which arises from the ontological position of Advaita Vedānta, the Advaitin asserts that only cause is real, whereas the effect is illusory. By adopting this principle, the causal relationship between Brahman and the universe is explained. Brahman as the material cause of the universe is real, whereas the universe as an effect is illusory. The latter is the phenomenal appearance of the former and in this sense the two are non-distinct (*ananya*) as against the Naiyāyika position which holds that cause and effect are different.

How do we prove that all effects are illusory? This is proved by showing the logical untenability of the causal relation. The following are in brief the arguments put forward by the Advaitin.[68]

Is the effect produced out of the cause as related to it or unrelated? If the former, the cause and the effect being but two relata connected together by relation, there is no reason why the effect should be produced by the cause and not the cause by the effect. If the cause produced the effect without being related to it, then anything might produce anything.

Is the effect totally different from the cause or not? If totally different, then difference being common to all, objects which are different from one another would produce one another. If the effect be non-different from the cause, then there would be nothing to distinguish the effect from the cause.

Again, is the effect derived from a material cause which has undergone any transformation or from one that has not had any

[68]The details of the dialectical arguments are given in the *Śatadūṣaṇī* (vāda 55) and only the important ones are mentioned here.

transformation? If it be the former, then it can be asked whether or not this transformation is produced by some other transformation. If this question is pursued further, we are condemned to an infinite regress. If it be the latter, then the effect would abide all the time the material cause continues.

Further, does the effect exist already in the cause or not? If it does not exist in the cause, how can it be produced from it? If the effect exists already, then it cannot be considered to have been produced.

Again, is the effect produced from a positive entity or from a negative entity? It cannot be either; for an effect, say, a pot, cannot be produced from its cause, the lump of earth, without effecting some change in it. If a change is effected in it, it would no more be called a positive entity. On the other hand, if the effect is brought forth from a being which is not positive (which does not exist), then the effect would itself be unproduced. Thus, any attempt to understand the causal relation logically would involve a self-contradiction. Effects are therefore illusory and the universe too, insofar as it is regarded as an effect, is illusory.

Vedānta Deśika refutes these dialectical arguments on the basis of proper explanation of the concept of cause and effect. With regard to the question whether the effect is produced as related to the cause or unrelated, he replies that the effect is unrelated to the cause. From this it does not follow that all that is unrelated to the cause should be the effect, because mere unrelatedness itself does not cause the effect. The special powers associated with the causal entities are responsible for the production of particular effects. This fact is established by logical concomitance. That is, in the presence of special factors in the causal entities the effect is produced, while in their absence no effect is produced.

In reply to the question whether the effect is different or non-different from the cause, he says that the effect is in a sense different from the cause. The pot, for instance, is produced as different from the stick and the potter's wheel. If it be admitted that the effect is non-different from the cause, then it would amount to the rejection of what is an essential condition of causal relation. The relation of the cause to the effect is only based on their difference. If therefore it is held that the two are non-different, then it would result in the acceptance of what is not an essential condition to the causal relation or rejection of what is an essential condition.

The Advaitin asks whether the effect is produced from the cause that undergoes modification or from that which does not. If by modification (*vikāra*) is meant an association of an entity with any accidental characteristic (*āgantuka-dharma*), then it is admitted that the effect is produced from a modified cause, for any change in the cause, even the proximity of an accessory condition, would be a modification. If the term modification is understood in the sense in which the effect is regarded as a modification it is said that the effect is produced by an unmodified cause. It cannot be said that if an effect be produced from an unmodified cause, any and every effect might be produced from any and every unmodified cause, for an effect is produced from an unmodified cause subject to the time factor and in relation to the requisite accessory factors.

To the question whether the effect does exist or not in the cause, Vedânta Deśika replies that in the sense of a substance (*dravya*) the effect exists in the cause. On this ground it cannot be said that the effect is not something produced (*sādhya*). For, an effect or *kārya* is called so because of the new state assumed by the cause (*avasthāntarāpatti*). An effect in the sense of an effect-state (*kāryāvasthā*) does not exist in the cause. The objections that if the effect-state did not exist in the cause it could not be produced and that similarly anything could be produced from anything are untenable, for the effects are produced by specific powers which manifest themselves as effects subject to spatial and temporal conditions.

To the question whether the effects are produced from a positive or a negative entity, Vedânta Deśika replies that if by positive entity is meant a substance that exists, then the substance persists in the effects produced from that particular substance. Only the states and conditions change when the effect is produced. For, in the production of an effect there is change only in the causal state and not in the causal substance. There is thus an agreement between the cause and the effect only so far as substance is concerned but not with reference to their actual states, for it is by the negation of the causal state that the effect state arises. Thus, the relation between cause and effect is logically intelligible and on that account the effect cannot be regarded as illusory.

Vedānta Deśika offers an acceptable explanation of cause and effect. Effect is something which is brought into existence at a particular time (*kādācitkasya*). The immediate antecedent factors existing prior to the effect which are responsible for the production of the effect at a particular time constitute the cause.[69] Take, for instance, a pot which is a product or effect. It is produced only at a specified time when the requisite antecedent factors for its production are present. If it could be produced without a cause, why should it not have come into existence at any time other than the specified one or even at some later time? Only at a time the requisite causal factors are present, the effect too is brought into existence. If we take the example of the flame of the lamp (*dipa*), it is produced only when all the causal factors such as lamp, wick, oil, matchstick, etc. are brought together. These antecedent factors, present prior to the flame of the lamp, constitute the cause of the latter.

It cannot be said that the prior non-existence of an effect (*prāgabhāva*) could serve as the antecedent causal factor. The mere prior non-existence cannot cause the effect. It is beginningless and the question would arise as to why the effect was not produced even earlier. Certain positive factors other than mere *prāgabhāva* are needed to bring about the effect. It is necessary to admit a cause for the effect. If an effect could come into existence without a cause, then it would be either a permanent entity like *ākāśa* (space) or a non-existent entity like the sky-flower. Both these do not have a cause. It may be said that it is in the very nature of the physical objects to come into existence at some time or the other, just as blueness is the natural concomitant of the sky and the fact of non-existence that of sky-flower, and it is not therefore necessary to postulate a cause for them. This will not do since our experience shows that effects are produced at specified time and by specified causal factors. If this is not accepted, then the combination of water and earth should produce cloth and the combination of thread and weaving should produce a pot. This is not so.

[69]TMK, 1-33. *kādācitkasya ; kālāvadhiniyatikaram pūrvasatkāraṇam syāt.*

There is a regulated causal relationship between the cause and effect and when the requisite causal factors come together, the specified effects are produced at specified points of time.[70] The concept of cause and effect should therefore be accepted.

Criticism of Nyāya-Vaiśeṣika Theory of Cause and Effect

As opposed to the Viśiṣṭādvaita theory that cause and effect are two different states of the same substance, the Nyāya-Vaiśeṣika maintains that effect as a product is different from cause. The implication of this is that effect does not exist in its cause but is newly produced. Taking the common example of the threads and cloth as cause and effect, the latter was not already existent in the former but is brought into existence anew by the collection of various causal factors. Cause and effect are regarded as two distinct entities on the following grounds. What is accepted as a cause is known by a name different from that which is an effect. Thus, for instance, the cause of cloth is named thread, whereas its effect is known as cloth. By number (*saṅkhyā*) the two are different. The threads are numerous, whereas cloth is a single entity. By function (*vyavahāra*), they are not the same. Cloth covers the body, whereas the threads do not serve such a purpose. The knowledge of the thread is not the same as our knowledge of the cloth (*buddhi-bheda*). Cause and effect differ also in respect of shape (*ākāra*). The shape of thread is different from that of cloth. There is also temporal differenee between the two. Threads are first made and cloth appears later. Because of these several factors, effect is distinct from cause (*anya*).[71]

Vedānta Deśika does not agree with this view. Thread may be different from cloth but nevertheless the two can be regarded as different states of the same entity, as in the example of the scroll of palm leaf and an earring made out of it by just rolling it into the shape of an earring. When it is flat, it is called a scroll; but when it is rolled up, it is known as earring. In this case the two entities as cause and effect are different by virtue of the name, function, shape, etc. but still the two are the modifications or states of the same substance.[72] If this position is not accepted, there would be difficulty in respect of two

[70]TMK I-33. [71]TMK I-20. See also RB II-1-15, p. 466. [72]TMK I-20.

tangible objects (*sparśavattva*) coming together. According to the Nyāya doctrine, the whole known as *avayavi*, which is the effect, is formed out of parts known as *avayavas*, which is the material cause. Two tangible objects as, for example, the palm leaf and earring made of it cannot exist together in the same space and at the same time. If the two are entirely different, they have to occupy either a large space or a small space. In the same way, if the thread—the *avayava* or cause—and the cloth—*avayavi* or effect—are absolutely different, they cannot exist together in the same place. Further, if cloth and thread are different, the weight of the cloth which is the product of the thread should be double, according to the Naiyāyika position. None of these problems will arise, if the effect or the whole (*avayavi*) is regarded as only a modified state of the parts (*avayava*) or the material cause.

An objection can be raised against the above explanation. If cloth is not regarded as different from thread, one can as well say that thread too is not different from cotton. Such an argument may be stretched further to include the *paramāṇus* or the atoms which are the primal cause of the objects of the universe and assert that cloth is not different from *paramāṇus*. This is absurd because the cloth is a gross physical object, whereas *paramāṇus* are invisible subtle entities and the two cannot be the same.

This is not a valid objection. Though the *paramāṇus* are the smallest ones, they can assume a dimension when they are combined together to fill up a measurable space. From this angle, it is possible to conceive that a physical object is larger in size than the *paramāṇus*. The whole (*avayavi*) which is a combination of the parts (*avayava*) is different from the parts. Thus, for instance, an assembly of persons is different from an individual person; a jungle of trees is different from a single tree; and a heap of grains is different from a single grain. In the same way, the cloth is different from threads.

Our experience in the form of recognition (*pratyabhijñā*) points out that material cause and effect are two states of the same substance, even though it undergoes modifications. A person has seen in the morning only the threads, but later in the day when he sees the woven cloth he recognises that it is the same threads which appear as a piece of cloth. The basic substance, even if it undergoes modification into another state, does not become different. This is illustrated by a heap of grains. By adding some more quantity to it or even by taking off some from it the heap remains as such, and the reduction or addition of grains does not change its character. On the same basis, an *avayavi* or whole which is produced by the combination of parts does not become different from the parts. If it is held that the increase or decrease of the *avayavas* or *paramāṇus* causes a change or produces a new *avayavi*, then the entire universe (which is the product of the *paramāṇus* according to the Nyāya system) is subjected to constant change as a result of storms, tornadoes, uprise of ocean waves, forest fires, etc. and as such the universe should have been different from what it is believed to be.[73] Vedānta Deśika therefore comes to the conclusion that the theory of cause and effect as maintained by Nyāya-Vaiśeṣika is unsound.

Criticism of the Sāṅkhya Theory of Cause and Effect

As against the theory of Nyāya-Vaiśeṣika, the Sāṅkhya system maintains the view that the effect is already existent in the cause in a latent form. What is potentially existent is made manifest as effect by the causal operation. Two arguments are advanced in support of this theory. What does not exist (*asat*) cannot be produced. If that were possible, then oil should have been produced from sand. Because oil is pre-existent in the oil seeds, it is made manifest by the causal operation. Secondly, no one has seen that what is not related to the cause is ever produced. That is, the causal factors unrelated to the effect cannot produce the effect. If that were so, the potter's wheel, the staff, etc. needed for the production of the pot, should have caused the cloth and similarly the cloth, loom, etc. should have produced the pot. Therefore, there should be a causal relation between the specific cause and specific effect. This means that the effect is pre-existent in the cause. The presence of the effect in a latent form in the cause is known as *śakti* or power. The oil seeds in which oil is present are capable of producing the oil but not the sands in which this power does not exist. On the basis of these arguments the Sāṅkhyas conclude that the

[73]TMK I-22.

effect is already pre-existent in the cause. Hence this theory is called *satkāryavāda*.[74]

The Viśiṣṭādvaitin who also upholds *satkāryavāda* (in a modified form) does not agree with the Sāṅkhya explanation. It is not necessary that the effect should be pre-existent in the cause in order to be produced. The appropriate causal factors bring into existence the particular effect, even without the latter being present in a latent form in the former. There are two types of causes: (*a*) material cause (*upādāna kāraṇa*) and (*b*) the instrumental cause (*nimitta kāraṇa*). The lump of clay is the material cause and the potter's wheel is the instrumental cause for the pot. The pot does not exist in any form in the potter's wheel but, nevertheless, it is regarded as its cause, though it is not the primary cause. In the same way it is not wrong to consider the lump of clay as the cause of the pot, even if the pot is not pre-existent in it. There are certain factors whose presence is necessary for the production of the effect, and in their absence the effect does not come into existence. Only such factors constitute the cause and not so much the pre-existence of the effect in a latent form.[75]

There are difficulties in accounting for the *satkāryavāda* as conceived by the Sāṅkhyas. It is held by them that the causal operation manifests only what is latent. The question is raised whether this manifestation (*abhivyakti*) is also pre-existent in the cause or is it produced newly. If it were there already, the effect too should become manifest in the cause. If not, it would only amount to the acceptance of *asatkāryavāda*. If, on the other hand, it is said that *abhivyakti* too exists in the cause in a latent form and that it becomes manifest later, then it would need some other manifesting agent to make it manifest and in that way it would lead to an infinite regress. If, on the contrary, it is said that *abhivyakti* does not exist in the cause but that it is only produced newly, then it would be more appropriate to accept that the pot is produced newly and not from what was already existent in a latent form.[76]

For the Viśiṣṭādvaitin pot is not something which is made

[74]See *Sāṅkhya-kārikā*, verse 9. *asad-akaraṇād upādāna-grahaṇāt sarva-sambhavābhāvāt| śaktasya śakya-kāraṇāt, kāraṇa-bhāvāc-ca satkāryam.*

[75]TMK I-24. [76]*Ibid.*

manifest from what was latent but, on the contrary, what is actually produced. The two concepts, manifestation (*abhivyakti*) and production (*utpatti*), are different. It may be possible to raise the same dialectical arguments against the idea of production (*utpatti*). Is *utpatti* produced anew or was it pre-existent? If it already existed, then the difficulties pointed out in respect of *abhivyakti* would also arise. If it be produced, then the *utpatti* would need another *utpatti* and in this way it would lead to an infinite regress.

Vedānta Deśika argues that these problems do not arise in respect of Viśiṣṭādvaitin's theory. The *utpatti* which produces the effect is itself the cause of *utpatti*. It does not require another *utpatti* for this purpose. If this logic is applied to the Sāṅkhya view which speaks of *abhivyakti*, the effect would stand manifested all the time. The Sāṅkhya view is not therefore tenable. For the Viśiṣṭādvaitin, effect is a passing state of the substance (*āgantuka-dharma*). The basic substance (the clay) continues to be the same, even if it assumes the form of the pot. Prior to the state of the pot, the clay exists in the form of two halves; the pot when broken assumes the form of potsherd. Thus, the effect is a modified state of the cause. The cause and effect are two different states of the same substance. In this sense, the effect and cause are *ananya* or non-different. The same logic is adopted to account for the causal relationship between Brahman and universe. This is discussed in the relevant chapter.

Criticism of the Buddhist Doctrine of Momentariness

The Buddhist doctrine of momentariness undermines the very existence of cause and effect as real and enduring entities. Vedānta Deśika therefore takes up the doctrine for a detailed critical study.

The Buddhists contend that whatever is an existent (*sat*) is momentary (*kṣaṇikam*), like the series of water particles; whatever is not momentary is a non-existent (*asat*), like the sky-flower. If all the logical concepts such as cause and effect are not momentary, they would be reduced to the status of the non-existents.[77]

[77]See SS I-25, p. 31. *yat sat tatkṣaṇikam, yathā jaladhārāḥ santaśca bhāvā iti; yad akṣaṇikam tad avastu yathā kha-sūnam.*

The implication of this argument is that change constitutes the very reality. Unlike the commonly accepted view, there is no such a thing as a permanent reality or Being as related to Becoming. The Buddhist altogether denies it and the only reality is Becoming. Change is not something that endures through it, but it is total and also perpetual. That is, it is the very nature of the thing that it undergoes change every moment. The seed stored in the barn is not the same as the one which sprouts. If it were the same, the one in the barn should also be the cause of the sprouting. They are therefore different.

The doctrine of momentariness is refuted mainly on the ground that *pratyabhijñā* or experience in the form of recognition reaffirms the permanent character of an object. When an object seen earlier is perceived again at a later period, we do realise that it is the same object. In such an experience in the form of recognition, the object seen earlier does not present itself with different qualities. If the object seen earlier and the one seen at a later period were different, as Buddhist claims, then we should not have had the experience that it is the same object. *Pratyabhijñā* or recognition, therefore, proves beyond doubt the permanent character of the objects (*vastu-sthairya*).[78]

It may be asked why the seeds stored in the barn did not sprout, whereas those sown in the ground sprout. This is not due to the fact that the seeds in the ground are different from those in the barn. The reason for this is that certain accessory causal factors such as water, good soil, etc. which are required for the seeds to sprout were not present in the barn, whereas the same are found in the ground. Since the capacity to sprout and the absence of it are two opposed qualities, how can both belong to the same seeds? Vedānta Deśika replies that it is possible that one and the same object can possess two different qualities at two different times (*kālabhedāt*). The seed which is planted in the wet soil has the capacity to sprout, whereas the seed in the barn does not have it. The seeds belonging to two different times can possess two different qualities depending upon the presence or absence of the accessory causal factors. Thus, the association of an object with two different qualities is justifiable on the basis of temporal difference. Even the

[78]TMK I-25. *vastu-sthairyam viruddhānupahita-viṣayā sādhayet pratyabhijñā.*

Buddhists have to accept such a possibility on the basis of spatial difference (*deśa-bheda*). They too have to admit that a particular seed planted in one place at a particular moment cannot sprout in another place at the same moment. This amounts to the acceptance of two opposed qualities, viz. the presence and absence of the power to sprout in respect of the same at two different places. If, on the basis of spatial difference, the association of two different qualities with the same object can be justified, it would certainly be appropriate to admit such a possibility on the temporal basis.[79] Thus *pratyabhijñā* does not support the doctrine of momentariness.

The Buddhists question the very validity of *pratyabhijñā*. The judgment, based on recognition, is expressed in the form 'That is this' (*soyam*), that is, what was seen earlier is same as seen now. This has two aspects—'that' aspect referring to the object as belonging to a past time (*atitakāla-sambandha*) and 'this' aspect referring to the object as belonging to the present time (*vartamāna-kāla-sambandha*). The former is called *tattva* and the latter *idaṁtva*, and both of them are attributed to the same object. The question is asked whether the two factors—*tattva* and *idaṁtva*—are attributed to the same object at the same time or at different times. It cannot be attributed at the same time to the same object for the obvious reason that the two units belonging to two different times are opposed to each other. The past and the present cannot coexist together. To avoid this difficulty, if it is said that the two units belong to different times, then how are they brought together? The judgment 'That is this' implies the presence of both the time factors together in the object. If, in order to bring them together, we seek another two time units, then there would be no end to it and it would lead to an infinite regress.[80] Thus, all recognition involves a reference to past time which perception is not competent to apprehend as well as to present time which memory cannot refer to. To regard it as a single unit of knowledge, overlooking its hybrid character, is erroneous. *Pratyabhijñā* does not therefore establish the permanent character of the object.

Vedānta Deśika refutes this argument. It is possible to attribute two different time factors to the same object. Time, accord-

[79]TMK I-25. [80]TMK I-26.

ing to the Viśiṣṭādvaitin, is infinite (*akhaṇḍa*), and, on the basis of limiting adjunct such as the movement of the sun, we speak of its division as minute, hour, day, etc. The life of an object is also measured in terms of units of time. The jar which lasts for a year is characterised as one-year old jar. This is known as *ghaṭa-kāla*. In the same way an object can be characterised as belonging to the past time or to the present time. That is, when we speak of the jar existing at the present time, we describe it as 'this' jar; when we refer to a jar of the past, we refer to it as 'that' jar. Thus, there is absolutely no contradiction in one and the same object being characterised by two different time units. The *ghaṭa* and *kāla* are not opposed to each other. The two can coexist. If we speak of the existence of jar at the time when it does not exist, then it involves self-contradiction. The past time of the jar is its very characteristic (*ghaṭasya kāla*) and similarly, the present time of the jar is also its characteristic. The two *dharmas* of the jar are not opposed and as such it is possible to have *pratyabhijñā* or recognition of an object of the past as the same as it is at present. From the standpoint of the jar, the two time factors, the past and present, are experienced together. Further, time or *kāla* does not require another *kāla* to account for it. Therefore, the fallacy of infinite regress does not arise. That is, if the coexistence of two time units is accounted for on the basis of another two time units or as belonging to a different time units, then the fallacy of infinite regress is inevitable. This is not so. Here *kāla* is conceived as a characteristic of the object and it does not require another *kāla* to account for its association with the object. Thus, there is no room either for the fallacy of infinite regress or for self-contradiction if two time factors are present in the same object.[81]

The Buddhists attempt to prove the momentariness of the objects by means of perception. They argue that perception reveals the object of the present time. When it reveals the object of the present, it also manifests that it is different from that of the past and future. That is, the perception of an object as existing at present negates its existence in the past and the future. This is similar to the perception of blue colour which distinguishes it from other colours. Negation of the existence of

[81] *Ibid.*

the object in the past and future amounts to its existence in the present instant only. This, in other words, means that objects are momentary, as proved by perception.[82]

The above argument is unsound, contends Vedânta Deśika. Perception no doubt reveals that an object exists at the present time but it does not prove that it exists only at present and will not exist at any other time. The perception of an object at the present time only negates its non-existence at that time.[83] When the existence of an object at other times is well established by means of other *pramāṇas*, how can the perception of the object as existing at present deny its existence at other times? When we see a blue object, the perception of blueness negates its being red or as some other colour different from it but not all other qualities, such as its shape, number etc. In the case of the perception of an object of the present time, it negates its non-existence in the present time which is opposed to it but not the future and past time which are not opposed to its present existence. Thus, on the basis of perception, it is not possible to prove the momentariness of objects.

One other stronger argument is advanced by the Buddhists to prove that things are momentary. It is contended that all that originates is also subject to destruction. No extraneous causes are necessary for destroying a thing. The germs of destruction are inherent in every object.[84] Destruction is of two types. When we hit a pot with a stick, it is supposed to be destroyed. This is what is generally understood by destruction. The second type of destruction is that at every moment the object undergoes change leading to destruction. The very first moment the object originates, it undergoes destruction at the next moment; again at the subsequent moment it originates and is followed with destruction and in this way the series goes on. The first type of destruction which takes place when the pot is broken with a stick is a gross form of destruction and is visible, whereas the second type is a subtle one which occurs

[82]TMK I-27. According to the Buddhists what is *kṣaṇika* or momentary is the instantaneous present devoid of an existence either earlier or at a later instant. See *Sarva-darśana-saṁgraha*, p. 25. *pūrvāpara-bhāga-vikala-kāla-kalāvasthitir-lakṣaṇa-kṣaṇikatā*.

[83]*Ibid.*. *sataḥ vartamānatva-bodhaḥ tatkālāsattvameva hyapanayati.*

[84]SS I-28, p. 34.

without any cause (*ahetuka*). The latter type of destruction is inferred on the basis of the fact that all objects are momentary. The following syllogistic argument is advanced in support of this theory: 'Destruction does not need a cause because it is necessary (inevitable)' (*dhvaṁsaḥ hetu-nirapekṣaḥ dhruvabhāvitvāt*).[85]

Vedānta Deśika subjects this syllogistic argument to a critical analysis and rejects it as untenable on the ground that it suffers from various logical fallacies. The probans *dhruvabhāvitva* is faulty. What does it mean? It may be resolved into six alternatives: (*i*) that which necessarily happens (*avaśyatvamātra*), (*ii*) devoid of any production, i.e. that which exists always (*janana-vidhuratā*), (*iii*) coming into existence immediately after the advent of its counter-correlate (*tat-kṣaṇānukṣaṇatva*), (*iv*) coming into existence in the next moment after the advent of its counter-correlate (*anukṣaṇatva*), (*v*) to become the very *svarūpa* of the counter-correlate (*tattvam*), and finally (*vi*) what is brought into existence by its counter-correlate (*tajjanyatā*).

None of these alternatives is free from logical defects. Taking the first alternative, pot does not undergo destruction on its own. It needs a cause (*hetu-sāpekṣa*). The probandum (*nirhetukatva*) does not apply to it but the *hetu* is present in it. This is the fallacy of *vyabhicāra*.

Regarding the second alternative, the syllogism suffers from the fallacy of *asiddhi*. The probans adopted by the *vādi* should also be acceptable to the opponent. According to the Viśiṣṭādvaitin, destruction is not uncaused. The proposition that *dhvaṃsa* is without *utpatti* stands unproved (*asiddhi*).

The third alternative is also fallacious. Pot is the counter-correlate of its destruction. The moment pot is produced, destruction also should take place simultaneously. This is not so. The *hetu* therefore becomes unproved.

As regards the fourth alternative, *anukṣaṇa* means that which follows in the next moment. In the case of two events one succeeding the other, the former which precedes the latter becomes the cause of it. If *dhvaṁsa*, according to this position, is with a cause, it is a contradiction to assert that it is without a cause (*ahetuka*).

The fifth alternative is also untenable. The counter-correlate

[85]TMK, I-28.

(*pratiyogi*) (in this case *ghaṭa*) and its destruction (*dhvaṁsa*) are mutually opposed. Therefore, *dhvaṁsa* can never become the *svarūpa* of counter-correlate. The probans becomes unproved.

The sixth alternative suffers from the fallacy of *virodha* (contradiction). If we say that destruction is without cause because it is produced by the counter-correlate, the assertion that it is without cause involves a contradiction. If *dhvaṁsa* is produced by *pratiyogi*, then it would be dependent on it. It cannot then be said that it is *hetu-nirapekṣa*. Thus, in whatever manner we interpret the term *dhruvabhāvitva* (which is the *hetu* in the present syllogism), the syllogism suffers from logical fallacy. It is not therefore possible to prove momentariness on the basis of the inferential argument in question.

The destruction or *dhvaṁsa* for the Buddhist is not only without a cause (*hetu-nirapekṣa*), but it is also total (*niranvaya*). That is, when a thing is destroyed, it does not persist in a different form. It is described as *niranvaya-vināśa* (total destruction) as opposed to the *sānvaya-vināśa* (partial destruction). The example given to illustrate the former type is the cessation of the last flame of a lamp (*antya-dīpa*). When the last flame dies it disappears totally, and there is no continuance of it in any other form. The lamp flame however changes every moment as the wick and oil go on diminishing. As the new flame appears, the earlier flame disappears. This is the second type of destruction. On the basis of this theory, the Buddhists maintain that similar total destruction also takes place in respect of the physical objects which undergo constant change every moment.[86]

The Vedāntins do not accept this view. For them the objects even after destruction continue in some other form. When the pot is destroyed with a stick, it persists as potsherd or broken pieces. Destruction is therefore *sānvaya-vināśa*. Even in the case of the disappearance of the lamp-flame, the subtle elements of light dwindle and spread themselves all over and become invisible. Even if we assume that the lamp-flame has undergone total destruction, it is not possible to assert on the basis of this one example that all physical objects undergo similar destruc-

[86]SS 1-31, p. 37.

tion as it is not warranted by our experience. As total destruction is not possible in the case of physical objects, we should admit that in respect of the lamp-flame also there is no total destruction. Just as salt disappears from sight when it is put in water, the subtle elements of flame spread out themselves in the air and become invisible.[87]

The doctrine of momentariness is also criticised on a different ground. In Buddhism, all things in the universe are destroyed every moment and then produced in the next moment. The previous moment is the cause of the production in the next moment. Since Buddhists do not admit the reality of time or space, the very instant (*kṣaṇa*) stands for reality. In view of this, pot is called a *kṣaṇa*. The origin as well as destruction taking place every moment is invisible. The pot we saw earlier is not the same as the one seen later. Nevertheless, the series of moments are continuous. The one series gives raise to the other series. When the seed transforms itself into a shoot, the seed series is replaced by shoot series. Each series is different from the other. On the same basis every *vijñāna*, which is the only reality admitted in the system, is a continuous series of ideas. Because it is a continuous series the mental impression is transferred from the previous *vijñāna* to the next one on the basis of which memory is explained.

The above explanation offered by the Buddhist is not tenable, if proper cause-effect relation is not accepted. Cause is that which precedes the effect invariably (*avyavahita-pūrva-kālāvasthā*). According to the metaphysical position of Buddhist, time and space are not realities, and as such the previous moment could be the cause of not only the next moment but all the subsequent moments in the series as there is no difference between the one instant and the other. In the case of the *vijñāna* series, with the destruction of one *vijñāna* the *saṁskāra* also becomes destroyed and its transference to the next one is inexplicable. In the absence of such a transference memory cannot take place. To defend their position, the Buddhists cite the example of the cotton seed, which when soaked in a red solution, is supposed to produce the red cotton. Even though the seed series cease to exist after they pass on to the sprout series, the red colour

[87]TMK 1-31..*durdarśāvasthā syuḥ payasi lavaṇavat līna-dīpādi-bhāgāḥ.*

in the seed is transferred to the cotton. In the same way, if one *vijñāna* ceases to exist after next one arises, the *saṁskāra* could be transferred to it. But such an explanation does not hold good, contends Vedānta Deśika. When seeds are transformed into plants, the subtle particles of the seeds along with the colour get transferred to the plants and thereby to the cotton. Colour which is a quality cannot be separated from its substance. If a permanent soul is not admitted, it is not possible to account for the transference of the *saṁskāra* from one *vijñāna* to the other.[88]

The most crucial argument in defence of the Buddhist doctrine of momentariness is based on one important assumption: 'Whatever is considered to be real should be momentary.' The argument is expressed in the form of a syllogism. 'Things in the universe are momentary, because they exist, as for example the absolute instant.'[89] From the type of illustration given the Buddhist believes that an absolute instant (*kṣaṇa*) is an actual existent.

Vedānta Deśika refutes this argument. What is sought to be proved by the Buddhist stands negated by perceptual experience. The absolute instant, which is cited as an illustration, is not an existent. It is not accepted as strictly momentary by the Viśiṣṭādvaitin. What is considered as absolutely momentary is non-momentary. The word *kṣaṇa* means for the Viśiṣṭādvaitin the conglomeration of various causal factors which have not been operative in producing the effect (*kārya-śūnyā sāmagrī kṣaṇaḥ*).[90] Thus the word *kṣaṇa* is applicable even to what is permanent. The causal factors are not momentary. The moment they become operative, the effect is produced. *Kṣaṇa* understood in this sense is not strictly momentary, as Buddhists believe. It is not therefore possible to uphold the doctrine of momentariness on the basis of this argument.

[88]TMK I-29. See also SS, p. 35.

[89]TMK I-30. *idam vigītam jagat kṣaṇikam, meyatvāt (sattvāt), kṣaṇopādhivat*.

[90]SS, p. 36. The term *kṣaṇika* can mean either that which exists for a moment or that which is associated with a minimal time. Since the Buddhists do not accept time as a reality, it is not possible to understand *kṣaṇikatva* in either sense. Besides Pratyabhijñā disproves it.

Conclusion

The critical evaluation of the theory of substance-attribute and the doctrine of momentariness leads to the conclusion that it is impossible to establish, either on the basis of perceptual experience or the inferential arguments, that everything in the universe is momentary. The objects of the external world have a permanent character, even though they may be subjected to change. Every real entity in the universe which exists (*abādhita vastu*) is differentiated in character. That is, it is constituted of two aspects—a substantive aspect and an attributive aspect. These two are distinct, but substance as a qualified entity or a complex whole is one. The distinction between substance and attribute is undeniable. The relation between the two is not logically untenable. Nor the causal relation between substance as the material cause and its product as the effect is logically unintelligible. The principles involved in the three fundamental metaphysical concepts equally apply to the ultimate reals, viz. *Īśvara*, soul and matter accepted in the system. A proper understanding of the metaphysical categories will help to get a correct knowledge of the nature of the ultimate realities and their organic unity.

CHAPTER TWO

Pramāṇas and Their Validity

A STUDY of the *pramāṇas* or the means of valid knowledge is an indispensable prolegomena to all metaphysical investigation.[1] Every school of thought has to show that the doctrine advanced by it has the solid support of valid pramāṇas. In the absence of such a proof it is open to criticism and gets rejected by opponents. We shall therefore discuss at the very outset the nature of the *pramāṇas* accepted by the Viśiṣṭādvaitin on the basis of which the metaphysical doctrines of his system are established.

Pramāṇa is defined as that which is the means of *pramā* or valid knowledge.[2] According to Viśiṣṭādvaita, a knowledge to be valid should fulfil two conditions. It should reveal things as they are and should also serve the practical interests of life.[3] *Pramāṇa* therefore signifies the essential means of arriving at valid knowledge.

The Viśiṣṭādvaitin admits three *pramāṇas*. These are perception (*pratyakṣa*), inference (*anumāna*) and verbal testimony (*śabda*). Some schools of thought admit more than three *pramāṇas*. Thus the Mīmāṁsakas as well as some Advaitins regard *upamāna* (comparison), *arthāpatti* (presumption) and *anupalabdhi* (non-apprehension) as additional *pramāṇas*. As against this the Cārvākas regard perception as the only valid *pramāṇa*. The Buddhists, on the other hand, regard perception and inference as the only *pramāṇas* and deny authority to verbal testimony. Vedānta Deśika therefore discusses this matter in detail to determine the nature and validity of each *pramāṇa*.

Pratyakṣa is the valid knowledge which is generated by direct

[1]*mānādhīnā meya-siddhiḥ.*

[2]*Nyāya-pariśuddhi*, p. 86. *pramā-karaṇaṁ pramāṇam.* The word *pramāṇa* is also applicable to the very valid knowledge (*pramaiva pramāṇam*).

[3]*Ibid.*, p. 90. *yathāvasthita-vyavahārānuguṇam jñānam pramā.*

contact of the sense organs with the objects.[4] *Anumiti* is the knowledge of the probandum (*sādhya*) based on the probans (*hetu*) established by logical concomitance.[5] *Śābda* or the verbal knowledge is that which arises from the spoken words or verbal statement through the comprehension of the connected meaning.[6]

Of the three *pramāṇas*, *pratyakṣa* is the most important and basic source of knowledge as the other two are dependent on it.[7] Inference is based on the invariable concomitance established by means of perception. *Śabda* or verbal testimony takes place on the basis of hearing of the sound of a word and comprehension of its meaning. It thus depends on both perception and inference. Verbal testimony is of two types—empirical (*laukika*) and non-empirical (*alaukika*). The latter covers the revealed scripture (*āgama*) which includes the Vedas, the Upaniṣads as well as the Smṛtis which are based on the Vedas.

I. PERCEPTION

Nature and Content of Pratyakṣa

Knowledge, in this system, is defined as that which reveals an object (*artha-prakāśaḥ*). Its function is to manifest an object to a knowing subject or the conscious self. It is thus related to a subject as well as an object outside it. The objects exist independent of knowledge and they are therefore regarded as real. That which exists is alone cognised and knowledge devoid of an object is inconceivable.[8] Accordingly, perceptual knowledge reveals the external object as it exists. In the act of perception, knowledge flows out from *jīva* through the mind and the sense organs,[9] comes into contact with the objects and reveals it. The process of perception as accepted in Viśiṣṭādvaita is similar to what other realist schools of thought have admitted.

[4]TMK IV-31. *sākṣāt prātipat.* See also NP, p. 95. *sākṣātkāri-pramā pratyakṣam.*

[5]*Ibid. vyāpyataḥ vyāpake dhīḥ anumitiḥ.*

[6]*Ibid. vācā arthabuddhiḥ.* See also SS. *vākyena viśiṣṭārthadhīḥ.*

[7]TMK IV-133. *akṣajanyā manīṣā iha sarvopajīvyā.*

[8]See RB II-2-29. *na kevalasya arthaśūnyasya jñānasya bhāvaḥ sambhavati.*

[9]The nature of the sense organs and how they function are discussed in the chapter on 'Prakṛti and its Evolutes'.

The important point to be considered in connection with perception is with regard to the nature of the content of perception. The issue involved here is whether or not perception at the initial stage reveals an object as one devoid of characteristics. This is an important epistemological problem which has a bearing on the ontological question relating to the nature of ultimate Reality. According to the Viśiṣṭādvaitin, knowledge in general including perceptual cognition reveals an object only as qualified by characteristics.[10]

Advaitin's Theory of Nirvikalpaka Pratyakṣa

The Advaitin maintains that perception, caused by the first contact of the sense organs with the object, has for its content an object devoid of *all* characteristics. Following the Nyāya classification, he recognises two types of perception: indeterminate perception (*nirvikalpaka pratyakṣa*) and determinate perception (*savikalpaka pratyakṣa*). The former, it is held, reveals the mere being or bare existence (*sat*) devoid of all characteristics, while the latter reveals the object with its characteristics.[11]

According to the Viśiṣṭādvaitin, the perception of an object devoid of all characteristics is a psychological myth. When an object is perceived it is comprehended along with some qualities. As Rāmānuja points out, the apprehension of a mere 'being' without any characteristic whatsoever does not in the first place take place, and secondly, such an experience is impossible. It is never found to take place because all cognitions are in terms of 'this is such and such'.[12] Nothing can be apprehended apart from some particular feature or structure of the object, as for instance, the triangularly shaped dewlap of a cow. Even the indeterminate perception, Vedānta Deśika urges, has for its object

[10]TMK IV-32. *ādyākṣayogaiḥ janitā buddhiḥ viśiṣṭam prathayati.*

[11]This is the view which is criticised by Rāmānuja. According to the later Advaitins (see Dharmarāja's *Vedānta-paribhāṣā*) *nirvikalpaka* perception is a non-relational knowledge of the perceived object and *savikalpaka* is relational knowledge. As an example of the former, the judgment *so'yam Devadattaḥ* (he is the same Devadatta) is cited, which, according to the Advaitin, implies bare identity without any difference. This view is also rejected by Vedānta Deśika. *Pratyabhijñā* is also determinate in character and does not refer to bare identity. See SS IV-32, p. 205.

[12]RB I-1-1, p. 51. *kenacid viśeṣeṇa idam-itthamiti hisarvā pratītir upajāyate.*

only what is marked by characteristics because it is on the basis of indeterminate perception that an object is recognised as qualified with generic character, etc. in the determinate perception.

If indeterminate perception is the apprehension of an object devoid of some qualification, what then is the distinction between indeterminate and determinate perception? Rāmānuja explains the difference between the two by an illustration. When an object, say, a cow, is perceived for the first time, such a perceptual experiencc is regarded as indeterminate. When another object belonging to the same class is again seen, this second or subsequent apprehension constitutes determintate perception.[13] In the apprehension of the first individual cow, one sees it along with the special shape which constitutes the generic character of the class 'cows'; he is not aware at this stage that this generic character extends to other cows also. This fact becomes known when the second and third cow is perceived. In the indeterminate perception there is only the apprehension of the generic character, and there is no awareness that this character is common to the other individual cows as there is no perception of the other individuals. But, in the perception of the second individual and so on, the generic character is recognised as common to the whole class. Thus, what was indeterminate in the perception of the first individual is made determinate in the perception of the second and subsequent individuals. That is, the initial cognition of cow, which can be expressed in the form of a judgment 'this is a cow', is indefinite but not absolutely indeterminate in character; the later cognition of the cow, which is expressed in the form of a judgment 'this is also a cow' based on the revival of similarity of structure noticed earlier, determines the nature of the object in relation

[13]Rāmānuja uses the expressions *prathama-piṇḍa-grahaṇam* or apprehension of first individual and *dvitīyādi-piṇḍa grahaṇam* or apprehension of second, third individual, etc. of the objects of the same class to distinguish betwcen the two types of perception. It may be noted that the *dvitiya-piṇḍa-grahaṇa* does not necessarily imply *savikalpaka* perception unless the person seeing it does have the revival of the impression of the cow seen earlier. These are given as illustrations and do not stand for a definition of *saviklpaka* and *nirvikalpaka* The perception of the second individual cow can be indeterminate if one does not have the revival of the impression of the first cow. See SS, IV-32. p. 205.

to other similar objects. It is on this basis that the distinction between the indeterminate and determinate perception is to be made. In view of this, Vedānta Deśika gives the following definitions :

> *Savikalpaka* perception is the apprehension involving recognition because of its being produced by the sense organs influenced by *Saṁskāra*; *nirvikalpaka* perception, on the other hand, is the apprehension which is produced by mere sense organs without the influence of the *Saṁskāra*.[14] Thus, perception, whether it be determinate or indeterminate, reveals an object as qualified with some characteristics. In the words of Rāmānuja, perception can never have for its content an object that is totally devoid of characteristics.[15]

The Naiyāyikas also admit the distinction between the *savikalpaka* and *nirvikalpaka* perception. The latter, according to them, is the perception of an object without its qualities, while the former comprehends the relation between the qualified and the qualifications.[16] The determinate perception is regarded as complex in character involving substance-attribute relation (*viśiṣṭa-jñāna*) and it should therefore be preceded by the perception of the isolated elements such as *jāti* (genus), *guṇa* (quality) and relation.

Vedānta Deśika does not accept this theory. As already pointed out, perception of an object as totally uncharacterised cannot take place even at the initial stage. This is against all experience. Naiyāyikas cite the example of the perception of the infants, dumb persons and the animals in support of indeterminate perception. Even such perceptions, Vedānta Deśika contends, are determinate in character as it is evident from their reaction in the form of spontaneous likes or dislikes

[14]TMK IV-32. See also SD, vāda 11. *saṁskāra-sahakṛta-indriya-janyatayā sapratyavāmarśaṁ jñānaṁ savikalpakam; saṁskāra-nirapekṣa- kevala-indriyajanyaṁ jñānaṁ nirvikalpakam.*

[15]RB I-1-1. p. 51. *ataḥ ; pratyakṣasya : kadācidapi na nirviśeṣa-viṣayatvam.*

[16]According to some Naiyāyikas, in indeterminate perception we perceive an object alone with its genus (*jāti*), quality (*guṇa*) and also its relation but we do not however know at this stage that they are related to each other in the form of subject-predicate relation (*viśeṣaṇa-viśeṣya-bhāva*). But this fact becomes known in the determinate perception.

towards the objects seen. If the objects seen by them were totally devoid of all characteristics, it would not be possible to account for attractive or repulsive behaviour of the infants and animals.[17]

Further, it is not necessary that all determinate perception or knowledge (*viśiṣṭa-jñāna*) should be preceded by the cognition of the qualities separately. This may be true in certain cases where the substance and quality are to be grasped by different sense organs, as for example, the flower with its fragrance. In this case, prior knowledge of the quality is required before the object is known as a qualified entity (*viśiṣṭa*). But where it is possible to cognise both the quality and the substance in a single perception insofar as they are capable of being grasped by the same sense organ, as, for instance, the flower and its colour, the prior knowledge of quality is not required. It is not therefore correct to postulate a stage of perception in which the object is seen as devoid of all characteristics.[18]

Is it not a self-contradiction to assert that *nirvikalpaka pratyakṣa* apprehends an object qualified by characteristics? This is a question raised by the critic on the assumption that the term *nirvikalpaka* should mean a perceptual knowledge devoid of characteristics (*niṣprakāraka-jñānam*) as defined by the Naiyāyikas. Vedānta Deśika replies to this question in the negative. As there cannot by any apprehension of a mere 'being', without any characteristic whatsoever, it becomes necessary to restrict the import of the term *nirvikalpaka* to mean as devoid of some characteristics. The word *daridra* (poverty-stricken), for instance, does not mean that one is totally devoid of money but is having very little money (*alpa-dhana*).[19] In view of this, Vedānta Deśika has offered a different definition of the two terms to justify the maintenance of a distinction between the two stages or kinds of perception.

Criticism of Buddhist Theory of Savikalpaka Pratyakṣa

The Buddhists question the validity of determinate perception. According to them, in the first stage of perception we get a mere sensation of the object. What is then perceived is the

[17]SS VI-32, p. 204. See also NP, p. 96. [18]*Ibid.*
[19]SS, p. 205. *alpadhane daridra vyavahāravat.*

unique momentary particular, a 'Thing-in-Itself', which is technically termed *sva-lakṣaṇa.* This stage of perception is described as indeterminate and that alone is valid. At the next stage of perception, the conceptual elements or *sāmānya-lakṣaṇas,* as they are termed, are superimposed by the mind upon the object. This type of perception is known as *savikalpaka* or determinate which is the perception as it is familiarly known. The Buddhists regard that all *savikalpaka* knowledge is not wholly true, because it is greatly influenced by the *saṁskāra* or the innate mental disposition. What is true is only the *sva-lakṣaṇa,* the bare unrelated particular presented in the first stage of perception. The following argument is advanced in support of this view: 'All *vikalpa-jñāna* is erroneous, because it is determinate in character (*vikalpatvāt*), just as the determinate cognition of shell-silver.'[20]

This inference is rejected by Vedānta Deśika as fallacious. It is not possible to prove that all knowledge is erroneous on the ground that perceptual knowledge is determinate in character. At this rate even the very syllogistic argument becomes erroneous, because it is determinate in character; as such it cannot establish that all knowledge is erroneous.

The main point of criticism is that the mere fact that sense organs through which the objects are known in the first instance, are influenced by the innate mental disposition (*saṁskāra*) does not render the cognition of the object erroneous. *Saṁskāra* is only an aid to the sense organs; it does not actually generate the knowledge as in the case of memory. Perceptual knowledge does not depend either on *vyāpti-jñāna* as in the case of inference or on verbal testimony in which case it would become mediate. On the contrary, it arises through direct contact of the sense organs with the object. Such an immediate knowledge cannot be regarded as erroneous, simply because it is determinate in character. No doubt, when we see the cow for a second time we say that it is the same cow as was seen earlier. But nevertheless, despite the fact that the impression created by the perception of the cow earlier continues when the second cow is seen, the

[20]SS IV-33, p. 206. *vikalpaḥ sarvo'pi apramā, vikalpatvāt, śukti-rūpya vikalpavat. Vikalpa,* according to the Buddhists, means conceptual construction, the subjective activity of thought interpreting the object. It is a subjective form lacking reality.

determinate perception does not cease to be perception. It is as valid as the first stage of indeterminate perception.

Criticism of Bhartṛhari's Theory of Śabdādhyāsa

It is normally believed that perception takes place through the contact of sense organs with the external objects which exist independently of knowledge. As against such a commonly accepted theory, some idealists who do not admit the reality of external objects maintain extreme views of perception. According to one school of thought ascribed to Bhartṛhari,[21] the perception of the so-called object takes place through the hearing of the sound of the word (*śabda*) and not independent of it. For Bhartṛhari, *śabda* itself projects or manifests as object; this is known as *śabdādhyāsa*. There is no difference between *śabda* of a word and the object denoted by the word. The two are one and the same. Because of such an identity the cognition of the object takes place the moment the *śabda* is known.

The other views which are somewhat similar to this are advanced by Yogācāra Buddhist and the Advaitin. According to Yogācāra, *vijñāna* or consciousness which alone is real, projects itself in the form of external objects. In other words, the so-called objects are the creation of the mind or the *vijñāna*. This is known as *vijñāna-vivarta-vāda*. The Advaitin does admit the empirical reality of objects, but from the transcendental standpoint the objects are considered illusory. They appear to exist as such because of the influence of *avidyā*. This is known as *vivartavāda*. As already pointed out, perception, according to some Advaitins, cognises only the undifferentiated Being, and the cognition of differentiated objects is due to the influence of *ajñāna* or ignorance. Both these theories will be discussed later. We shall take up here for examination the *śabdādhyāsa-vāda*.

Vedānta Deśika criticises this theory on the ground that *śabda* and object are distinct and can never be identical. The object exists even prior to the origin of *śabda* and it continues to exist even after the cessation of *śabda*.[22] Further, the sound

[21]Bhartṛhari is the famous grammarian who is the author of *Vākyapadīya*. He was a predecessor of Śaṁkara and is believed to have died about A.D. 650. See IP Vol. II, p. 465.

[22]TMK IV-34. *śabdāt prāk, paramapi artha-siddheḥ.*

of the word (*śabda*) and the object (*artha*) denoted by it are to be grasped by two different sense organs. *Śabda* is known through the ear, whereas the object is perceived through the visual organ. The two do not become manifest at the same time. A word may have different meanings but at the time of hearing a word, we grasp only one particular meaning. If sound and object are identical, then all the meanings of the word should have occurred to our mind, when the word is first heard. This is not so. There are different words which are synonymous but they all refer to the same object. When we get the knowledge of the object, then all the synonymous words should have come to our attention. But this does not happen. Therefore the two—*śabda* and *ártha*—cannot be identical.

Nor is it possible to explain the identity between *śabda* and *artha* on the basis of *adhyāsa* or illusory superimposition. When the shell is mistaken for silver, silver is superimposed on the shell because of similarity in respect of whiteness and glitter between the two. To take another example, a white crystal appears as red when the former is brought into close proximity with a red flower. In both cases illusion is caused either due to similarity or juxtaposition. Either of these factors is not found in respect of *śabda* and *artha*. *Śabda* may originate at a distant place and *artha* may be close to us and vice versa. In the absence of proximity between the two, the possibility of *śabdādhyāsa* is ruled out.[23]

Similar to the theory of *śabdādhyāsa*, there is another theory which maintains that all empirical experience depends on *śabda*. There is a close relationship between *śabda* and *artha*; whenever the sense organs are in contact with the objects, the objects are perceived along with the words denoting them. In other words. *śabda* is closely associated with the awareness of the objects. This theory is called *śabdānuvedha*.

This view is also rejected by Vedānta Deśika as unsound. Only after the objects are perceived do the words denoting them become known. Just as the idea of the elephant boy comes to the mind only after the elephant is seen, it is only after the object is seen that its name comes to our mind. Further, it is not correct to say that both *śabda* (sound) and *artha* (object) manifest simultaneously. Thus, for instance, infants as

[23]TMK IV-34.

well as deaf and dumb persons who see the objects do not have any knowledge of the words denoting the objects seen by them. It cannot be said that such persons have the knowledge of some kind of supernormal or subtle sound as there is no proof in support of the existence of a subtle sound. The mention of subtle forms of sound in religious literature[24] is intended for purposes of meditation and it has no bearing on the sound as we commonly understand it.

The Theory of Supernormal Perception

In considering the nature and content of perception, the question arises whether perception could apprehend supernormal objects. According to some,[25] even supernormal objects can be seen by perception. The argument in support of this view is that whatever exists should be known by means of perception and as supernormal things also exist, they should be perceived.[26]

The above argument is fallacious. Merely because a thing exists, it does not follow that it should be the object of perception. There is no concomitance between that which exists (*sattva*) and perceptibility (*pratyakṣatva*). If something is not the object of perception, we cannot say that it does not exist. If by perception we mean empirical perception, we cannot take it that everything becomes known. If it be non-empirical perception, such a perception could even be hallucination. It cannot be said that by perception we mean *Īśvara-pratyakṣa* because the *pratyakṣa* of *Īśvara* which is not dependent on the sense organs is not strictly perception.

It may be argued that as there is variation in the capacity of sense organs from person to person, there may be an indi-

[24]*Mantra-śāstra* speaks of four types of *śabda*: (*a*) *Sūkṣma* or *para*, which is the root of the universe; (*b*) *Paśyantī*—the original sound made manifest inside the organism near the navel; (*c*) *Madhyamā*—subtle air in its course towards the heart manifesting subtle form of letters or speech which is the form of letters flashing in our mind while repeating mantras during meditation; (*d*) *Vaikharī*—the audible sound which is externally and universally perceptible. This is used as means of communication.

[25]This theory is ascribed to some Buddhists. See NP, p. 95.

[26]SS IV-36. *dharmādayaḥ kasyacit-pratyakṣāḥ sattvāt.*

vidual who possesses the power to see everything. This argument cannot be accepted, because it is not possible to prove the existence of a person with such a supernormal power. Each sense organ has its specific and restricted function. Eyes grasp colour but they cannot hear. It is not therefore possible to assume that sense organs can comprehend everything.[27]

It may be contended that there are variations with regard to the capacity of the sense organs in individuals. Thus, for example, the owl has the capacity to see in darkness, while human beings do not possess this ability. In the same way, some individuals may be gifted with the capacity of perceiving supernormal things.

It is no doubt true that the nocturnal vision of the owl is more powerful than that of a human being, but the function of all visual organs is restricted to seeing. That is, the eyes can only see but cannot hear. There may be instances of two different functions being performed by one organ as in the case of snakes which are believed to hear the sound through their eyes. Even in such cases, Vedānta Deśika observes, the two different organs are located in the same area where the eyes are found and it is therefore possible for the snakes to hear through eyes. The eyes of snakes as such do not hear but, on the contrary, the auditory organ which is located in the eyes (or close to the eyes) apprehends the sound. He therefore concludes that perception caused by the direct contact of sense organs with object is restricted in scope and it cannot grasp supernormal objects.

This conclusion should not be taken to mean that Vedānta Deśika rejects *yogi-pratyakṣa* or perception of supernormal things by yogis. The Viśiṣṭādvaitin accepts *yogi-pratyakṣa*. But it is different from the normal perception. The latter is dependent on sense organs, whereas the former is caused by special potency (*adṛṣṭa*) acquired by yogic practice.[28] It may also be acquired by an individual through the grace of God as in the case of the intuitive knowledge of the sages. It is then regarded as divine perception (*divyam*).[29]

[27]TMK IV-36. *iha nirupadhiḥ akṣaprakarṣaḥ te durvacaḥ.*

[28]NP, p. 95. *yogi-pratyakṣam prakṛṣṭādṛṣṭa-viśeṣajam . . . sa ca adṛṣṭa-viśeṣaḥ yogābhyāsa-tapaścaryādibhiḥ jāyate.*

[29]*Ibid. bhagavat-prasāda-labdha-yogipratyakṣam divyam.*

II. INFERENCE

Anumāna as a Valid and Independent Pramāṇa

The very first question that needs to be discussed is whether or not *anumāna* or inference is a separate *pramāṇa* and, if separate, whether it is a valid one. According to the Cārvāka school, *pratyakṣa* is the only *pramāṇa* and *anumāna* which is regarded as part of perception does not enjoy a separate status as a *pramāṇa*.

It is generally accepted that the presence of fire is inferred from the observation of smoke and the knowledge of the fire is inferential in character or *anumiti*. The critic questions this assumption. Just as the cognition of smoke is considered perceptual in character, why should not the knowledge of fire also be regarded as perceptual? No doubt, there is direct contact of the sense organs only with the smoke, but because of the fact that smoke is invariably connected with fire, it should be possible to consider the knowledge of fire, too, as perceptual.

The above argument may hold good in respect of one who is actually seeing the smoke on the hill. But there are instances when a person not having any direct contact of the visual organ with the smoke gets the inferential knowledge of fire either on the basis of the recollection of the smoke seen earlier elsewhere or on the basis of the verbal statement made by someone else. It cannot therefore be said that in all cases the inferential knowledge of fire is perceptual. It cannot be argued that mind, which is an important instrument for perceptual knowledge, serves also as an aid for inference, and therefore both perception and inference are of the same nature. Mind serves as an aid for all types of knowledge including *smṛti* (memory) and not exclusively for perception. If on this basis inferential knowledge is considered perceptual, then even *smṛti* would have to be accepted as perceptual. *Anumiti* or inferential knowledge is therefore distinct from perception.

That *anumāna* is a separate *pramāṇa* becomes clear if we analyse the process of inference. The syllogistic argument is expressed in the form; 'The hill has fire because it has smoke (*parvato vahnimān, dhūmavattvāt*).' In this premise, the hill (*parvata*) is technically known as *pakṣa* (subject); the smoke (*dhūma*) is regarded as *hetu* (probans). In the first instance, we see only smoke on the hill, that is, *hetu* in the *pakṣa*. At this stage there is no possibility of observing the fire as invariably connected with smoke (*dhūma-vyāpaka-vahni*). After seeing the smoke, one remembers the invariable association of the smoke with the fire. With the mere recollection of the association of smoke with fire, it cannot be determined that there is also fire on the hill. Even the knowledge of the general principle that the *hetu* as concomitant with *sādhya* is present in *pakṣa* does not establish the presence of fire on the hill. The positive conclusion that there is fire on the hill is to be deduced on the basis of the observed facts. The inferential knowledge is therefore neither perceptual nor a case of memory.[30]

The Cārvākas question the validity of *anumāṇa* as *pramāṇa*. Why is it invalid? asks Vedānta Deśika. Four alternatives are possible for affirming its invalidity. It may be invalid because it is negated by another valid knowledge. Secondly, even though it is not negated, it is still invalid (by its very nature). Thirdly, it is of doubtful character. Fourthly, it is of the nature of memory.

With regard to the first alternative, we should find out whether it is negated by perception or an inference or by verbal testimony. It cannot be by perception. When fire is inferred on the basis of smoke, fire is not actually seen and as such there is no scope for its negation by another perceptual *jñāna*. If it be by *anumāna*, then that *anumāna* will have to be proved as valid, and the invalidity of the inference in question cannot be contradicted by another invalid *annumāna*. Verbal testimony cannot negate it. Verbal testimony depends on inference for the comprehension of meaning (*śakti-grahaṇa*) and in the absence of it verbal knowledge (*śābdabodha*) cannot take place. If it be argued that inference by its very nature is invalid, then the same argument would apply even to perception. Inference cannot be dismissed as invalid on the ground that it is of doubtful character, because the men of wisdom have accepted it as a valid means of knowledge without entertaining any doubt about its validity.

It is not even a case of memory because we get to know

[30]TMK IV-39.

something new through inference, whereas knowledge by memory is restricted to what is already experienced.[31] Vedānta Deśika therefore concludes that inference is a valid and distinct source of knowledge like *pratyakṣa*.

A dialectical argument is put forward to disprove the validity of inference. The presence of fire is inferred from the observation of smoke on the hill. It is questioned whether, by means of this inference, fire in general (*vahni-sāmānya*) is inferred from the smoke in general or a specific case of fire is inferred from a specific case of smoke. If it be the former, it is already known to us that there is a close association between smoke and fire as observed in the kitchen and as such nothing new is established by the inference. If it be the latter, the same smoke along with the fire as seen in the kitchen is not found in the hill. In the absence of not being aware of the concomitance between the specific smoke seen on the hill with fire, how is it possible to prove the presence of fire on the hill? It is not possible to assert that wherever there is smoke there is fire, because no one has seen all the instances of smoke and fire all over the universe and at all times. One might have seen a few cases and on that basis it is not possible to make a universal statement. Even though the association of fire with smoke has been noticed a number of times, there may be exceptions which may be unknown to us.[32]

This dialectic is refuted by Vedānta Deśika. Logic (*tarka*) is based on certain principles and every school of thought which adopts logic have to accept them. Otherwise, logic would become meaningless. Even to disprove the validity of *anumāna*, one has to resort to logic. If the basic principles of *tarka* are not accepted, there is no place for *anumāna*. It may be possible to doubt the soundness of the logical arguments but whenever such doubts arise, they have to be cleared by proper reasoning. If one goes on entertaining a doubt for which there is no end, all human endeavour leading to practical activities would cease. If doubt arises, it needs to be removed by adopting supporting argument. Thus, for instance, one may doubt the presence of fire even though smoke is observed. In such a situation, proper reasoning helps to overcome the doubt. As

[31]TMK IV-40. *vaiśiṣṭyānna smṛtiḥ*. [32]TMK IV-41.

fire and smoke have a causal relationship, it is to be reasoned out that where smoke exists, fire also must exist. This is known as *anukūla tarka* or supporting argument. It is not therefore appropriate to question the validity of *anumāna* on the basis of some unjustified doubt.[33]

Method of Establishing Logical Concomitance

The validity of the inference depends on the soundness of the concomitance (*vyāpti*) between the probans (*hetu*) and the probandum (*sādhya*) as, for example, between the smoke and fire. How do we ensure that in each case the concomitance has been established correctly? The Naiyāyikas maintain that *vyāpti* is comprehended by observing numerous instances (*bhūyo-darśana*). According to another view held by a section of Visistādvaitins, it should be possible to grasp the correlation between the *hetu* and *sādhya* by the observation of one single instance (*sakṛd-darśana*).[34] Repeated observance of several cases is useful in removing the dobut that may arise as a result of certain exceptional circumstances in respect of *hetu*. Thus, for instance, fire and smoke are seen together but we cannot come to the conclusion that fire is invariably associated with smoke since we find an exception to this rule in respect of molten iron ball. Such doubts in respect of the comprehension of concomitance are removed by repeated observation. Vedānta Deśika does not agree with this view. In his opinion, it is not possible to establish a universal proposition or the unconditional and invariable concomitance between two particulars on the basis of one single observation. It is therefore essential to observe several instances before formulating the *vyāpti*. The repeated observation helps to remove the doubt arising as a result of exceptional circumstances. Besides repeated observation, *tarka* or reasoning is also to be adopted for eliminating the doubt arising on account of *upādhi* or certain limiting condition associated with the *hetu*. *Upādhi* is a technical term used by Indian logicians. It is defined as a characteristic which is not extensively applicable to the *sādhana* or *vyāpya*, but which applies extensively to the *sādhya* or *vyāpaka*, being in itself different from the *sādhana*.[35] To put it in simple words,

[33]TMK IV-42. [34]TMK IV-47. This seems to be the view held by Parāśara Bhaṭṭa. See NP, p. 99.

[35]See NP, pp. 99-100. *sādhanāvyāpakatve sati v sādhya-samavyāptaḥ*. See also TMK IV-43. *sādhana-dharma-vyatiriktadharma upādhiḥ*.

it refers to the limiting condition or qualifying adjunct associated with the probans (*hetu*) on account of which the concomitance becomes established. In the syllogism that there is smoke because of fire (*dhūmavān vahneḥ*), the association of fire with smoke is not universal because the molten iron ball which is fire is devoid of smoke. In order to prove the concomitance between smoke and fire, we stipulate the condition that only fire that is associated with wet wood is concomitant with smoke. The association of wet wood with fire is therefore the *upādhi* for *hetu*. Such doubts which may arise on account of *upādhis*, while determining the invariable association of *hetu* and *sādhya*, have to be overcome by adopting proper reasoning or *tarka*.[36]

It may be argued that no one is able to observe all the instances of smoke and fire in this vast universe and in view of this, what is seen once is to be accepted as the basis for determining the *vyāpti*. This is not a correct view. When an object is seen once and when the same is seen again at a later period, we get the experience that it is the same as was seen before. Though the object is seen for a second time, the judgment that it was seen before implies that it is of the same class (*jāti*). It is through the *jāti* which is common to all such objects in the universe, we derive the knowledge of all of them. In the same way, if the *vyāpti* existing between two particular entities is comprehended by seeing a few instances, it would amount to seeing all such entities in the universe since they all belong to the same class of entities observed earlier. In this sense, it is claimed by logicians that *bhūyo-darśana* or observation of numerous instances helps to determine the universal proposition or the unconditioned, invariable concomitance between *hetu* and *sādhya*.

Types of Syllogism

On the basis of the nature of *vyāpti*, the Naiyāyikas have made a formal distinction of three types of *anumāna*—*kevalānvayi*, *kevala-vyatireki* and *anvaya-vyatireki*. When *hetu* exists, the *sādhya* too should be invariably present. For instance, if there be smoke, there should also be fire. This is known as *anvayavyāpti* or a positive concomitance established on the basis of agreement

[36]For further details regarding the types of *upādhis* and how doubts are to be overcome, see TMK IV-44-45.

between the *hetu* and *sādhya.* If *sādhya* does not exist, *hetu* too should be absent; if there be no fire there is no smoke. This is known as *vyatireka-vyāpti* or a negative concomitance based on agreement in the absence of *sādhya* and *hetu.* A syllogism may be formulated with *hetu* and *sādhya* admitting both the *anvaya-* and *vyatireka-vyāpti* or either of the two. A syllogism in which both types of *vyāpti* are found is classified as *anvaya--vyatireki.* In the syllogism 'The hill has fire, because it has smoke', we find an invariable concomitance between the presence of smoke and presence of fire as well as absence of fire and absence of smoke. If in a syllogism the *hetu* adopted admits only an agreement in the absence of *sādhya* and *hetu,* it is regarded as *kevala-vyatireki.* Take, for instance, the following syllogism adopted by the Naiyāyikas: 'Earth is different from other elements such as water, etc. because it is characterised by odour.'[37] In this syllogism it is not possible to have a positive concomitance, viz. whatever possesses odour, that is different from other elements, because other than earth which is the very subject (*pakṣa*) of the syllogism there is nothing else which possesses the odour. Only a negative concomitance is possible in the following form. 'Whatever is not different from other elements such as water does not possess odour.' Such a syllogism in which the *hetu* is based on a negative concomitance is regarded as *kevala-vyatireki.* The third type of syllogism is the one which contains *hetu* based only on a positive concomitance. As an example of this, the following syllogism is cited: 'Pot is definable, because it is knowable' (*ghaṭaḥ abhidheyaḥ prameyatvāt*). Here a negative concomitance, viz. 'whatever is not definable is not knowable' does not hold good because there is nothing in the universe which is not knowable. The *hetu* in this syllogism admits only a positive concomitance expressed as follows: 'Whatever is knowable is definable.' It is therefore known as *kevalānvayi.*

Though there are three types of *anumāna,* some logicians accept only *anvaya-vyatireki* and *kevalānvayi* as sound ones and reject the *kevala-vyatireki.* According to some other logicians,

[37] According to the Nyāya-Vaiśeṣika, odour (*gandha*) is an exclusive attribute of earth and the other four elements—water, air, fire and ether—do not possess it.

only the *kevala-vyatireki* is the sound one. Vedānta Deśika subscribes to the former view. He contends that a syllogism based on *hetu* admitting pure negative concomitance is not logically tenable for the main reason that *sādhya* or probandum in such a syllogism does not have a factual foundation, and as such it is difficult to comprchend the invariable concomitance between the *sādhya* and the *hetu.*[38] According to him, the probans based on positive concomitance (*anvaya-vyāpti*) is sound, while the negative concomitance (*vyatireka-vyāpti*) strengthens it.

The Components of Syllogism

When an inference is adopted to determine the truth for oneself, it is called *svārtha*, as for example, the establishment of the fact that there is fire on the hill. After having known something, if the same truth is to be conveyed to another person, for the purpose of convincing him, the syllogistic form of inference is adopted. This is known as *parārthānumāna.*[39] Such an inference is called *nyāya*. When an inference is used for convincing another, it has to be stated in a logical form. For this purpose five propositions are regarded as necessary: (*a*) *pratijñā* or the statement asserting something;(*b*) *hetu* or the probans for proving it; (*c*) *udāharaṇa* or illustration;(*d*)*upanaya* or the application of the general rule to the specific case; (*e*) *nigamana* or the conclusion.

A full form of syllogism with the five component parts may be illustrated thus: (*a*) yonder hill has fire; (*b*) because it has smoke; (*c*) wherever there is smoke there is fire as for instance in the kitchen; (*d*) yonder hill has smoke such as is invariably associated with fire (*vahnivyāpya dhūmavān*); (*e*) therefore yonder hill having smoke also has fire.[40]

[38]TMK IV 53. *tasya sādhyāprasiddheḥ vipakṣe sādhyābhāvaḥ kathamiva viditaḥ.*

[39]Though a distinction is drawn between two types of inference, Vedānta Deśika is of the view that all inferences are *svārtha* for the reason that self-comprehension of the invariable concomitance is the basis for advancing an inference. See NP, p. 107.

The early Nyāya literature makes mention of three kinds of inference: *pūrvavat, śesavat* and *sāmānyato-dṛṣṭa*. These terms are ambiguous and there is no uniform description of the nature of these in Nyāya literature. Vedānta Deśika does not give much importance to this classification.

[40]If we leave out the first two members of the syllogism, it is comparable to the Aristotelian syllogism. The third part of the syllogism

There is difference of opinion among the logicians with regard to the components of the syllogism. According to the Buddhists, illustration and *upanaya* are important parts of the syllogism. Vedāntins hold the view that *pratijñā*, *hetu* and *udāharaṇa* are important. The Mīmāṁsakas divide the five into ten parts. Vedānta Deśika takes the view that there is no harm if one adopts more than three components if it is required for the purpose of conveying the truth to the other person.

Some argue that there is no scope for the adoption of *parārthānumāna* because of the difficulty in formulating the *pakṣa* or the subject matter to be determined. The formulation of *pakṣa* requires an agreed view among both the disputants, the *vādi* and *prativādi*. If there be no agreed view, then *pakṣa* cannot be formulated. Thus, it is futile to advance *parārthānumāna*.

This is not a correct view. It is not necessary that there should be complete agreement between the disputants for formulating the *pakṣa*. Even if there be some common understanding with regard to some aspect of the subject, it should be possible to formulate the *pakṣa*. Take, for instance, the argument that *śabda* or sound is *anitya* because it is produced. According to one view, *śabda* is a substance (*dravya*), and, according to another, it is a quality (*guṇa*). But *śabda*, in general as an object to be grasped by the auditory organ, is accepted by both the parties. Even though there may be difference of opinion with regard to the actual nature of the entity, it should be possible to formulate the *pakṣa* on the basis of certain commonly accepted notion. Otherwise, there would be no room for discussion.

Logical Fallacies

The validity of an inference depends upon the soundness of the *probans* (*hetu*). The syllogistic argument adopted should be free from logical defects. The logicians have enumerated a large number of fallacies, which are technically known as *hetvābhāsas*. Without going into the details of the various fallacies (which may be found generally in Nyāya literature), Vedānta

stands for the major premise of Western Logic supported by an example. It is the universal proposition on the basis of which reasoning proceeds from the particular to particular through the universal. Such a reasoning is not purely deductive but it is inductive-deductive. See OIP, p. 257.

Deśika mentions how to determine what is a valid *hetu* and what is a fallacious *hetu.* Wherever *vyāpti* is well established and the probans is present in *pakṣa*, it is regarded as *sad-hetu* or valid probans. Where these conditions are not fulfilled it becomes a fallacious *hetu*. The various logical fallacies[41] arise in the latter case.

Rules Governing the Logical Argument

Some Naiyāyikas hold the view that while presenting an inferential argument in the formal way with all the five steps, one should also state that his syllogistic argument is free from any of the logical fallacies. Formulation of such a statement is technically known as *ābhāsoddhāra* or *kaṇṭakoddhāra*. Vedānta Deśika is of the view that there is no need for making such a statement after formally putting forward the syllogistic argument. Making such a statement on one's own accord gives room for doubt in the mind of the opponent. If the purpose of such a statement is to remove the doubt, then the *upanaya-vākya* and the concluding statement (*nigamana*) are primarily intended to remove the possibility of logical fallacies. If only the opponent raises objections, it is then appropriate to answer them properly and prove that one's own argument is free from logical defects. If even after answering the objections the disputant expresses doubt, then one has to resort to counter-argument (*tarka*) to silence him.

Tarka or counter-argument is intended to point out that if the concomitance existing between the *hetu* and *sādhya* is questioned, it would lead to an unacceptable conclusion.[42] Thus,

[41]According to Vedānta Deśika there are five kinds of *hetvābhāsas*. These are: *asiddha*, *savyabhicāra* or *anaikāntika* *viruddha* *bādha* or *kālātyayāpadeśa* and *prakaraṇasama*. *Asiddha* means a *hetu* which is unproved. *Savyabhicāra* refers to the inconclusive reason which may lead to more than one conclusion. *Viruddha* is the reason which contradicts the proposition to be established. In *bādha*, the *hetu* asserts something the opposite of which is ascertained to be true by other evidence. *Prakaraṇasama* means a *hetu* which is equivalent to the proposition and as such leads to no conclusion.

[42]SS, IV-60, p. 224 *vyāpyāṅgīkāre aniṣṭa-vyāpaka-prasañjanaṁ tarka iti lakṣaṇam*. The word *tarka* is used here in the sense of counter-argument leading to a conclusion as opposed to the premise. It is *reductio ad absurdum* in terms of Western logic. This is the technical meaning of *tarka*. *Tarka* in a general sense means reasoning or argument adopted to prove one's

for example, we say that there is fire on the hill because of the presence of smoke. One may question this premise and say that even though there is smoke, there need not be fire. As against this, it is to be argued that if there be no fire, smoke also should not be present. There is a causal relationship between the two, and, as such, since smoke is observed, the presence of fire also should be admitted. Such a type of counter-argument is known as *tarka.* It thus serves the purpose of defending the validity of the argument. It also brings to the attention of the opponent that the rejection of what is a valid argument would lead tc the acceptance of what is invalid. There are five types of counter-arguments (*tarka*). These are known as *ātmāśraya* or self-dependence, *anyonyāśraya* or reciprocal dependence, *cakraka* or circular reasoning, *anavasthā* or infinite regress and *pratibandi* or *counter-argument.* These are actually five types of logical fallacies involved in the argument.[43]

The counter-argument advanced against the opponent tends to land him in five types of absurdities. These constitute the subsidiaries or *aṅga* of tarka. The first one is to press the opponent to accept a position which is opposite of what is sought to be established. Thus, for instance, if the presence of fire is doubted while accepting the presence of smoke, the counter-argument takes the form : 'If there be no fire, then let smoke too be not present.' Absence of fire implies that the presence of smoke which is evident to one is false. This is technically termed *viparyaya.* Secondly, as a consequence of this there would be no room for the opponent to advance any further counter-argument. This position is known as *pratitarka-parāhatiḥ.* Thirdly, it forces the opponent to accept an undesirable position (*para-aniṣṭatvam*). To say that there is no smoke while smoke is actually seen would amount to accepting what is not desired. Fourthly, the *tarka* advanced against the opponent does not serve any useful purpose to him (*anānukūlyam*). Finally, it would lead to position in which a concomitance will

---

theory. It also refers to the Science of Logic (*Tarka-śāstra*). *Tarka* understood in the technical sense is distinct from *anumāna,* according to the Naiyāyika. Vedānta Deśika considers *tarka* is also a kind of *aumāna.*

[43]In the refutation of the arguments, advanced by the rival schools of thought Vedānta Deśika refers frequently to one of these logical defects.

have to be accepted between absence of fire and absence of smoke. That is, the opponent will have to accept that wherever there is absence of fire, there should also be absence of smoke.

Rules Regulating Philosophic Debate

Indian logicians have laid down rules to regulate not only the method of conducting a debate but also the eligibility of a person to enter it. According to Vedānta Deśika, who closely follows the Nyāya system in this regard, a person who does not accept the *pramāṇas*, *prameyas* and the distinction between one's own stand and that of the opponent, is not eligible for a debate.[44] It is futile to hold a discussion on philosophic issues with such a person, because, in the absence of norms laid down and accepted for meaningful discussion, no truth can be decisively established. If a person is not eligible for a debate, how could anyone enter into a meaningful discussion with him? Whether or not one is eligible for a debate is to be decided by an impartial person who presides over the debate (*madhyastha*). If the presiding person takes side without being impartial, discussion must be terminated forthwith. In fact one should not even enter into an argument with the opponent. The point to be noted is that if a discussion is held with the other party, who is considered ineligible for the debate, then it would amount to his being accepted for debate, and as such the disputant gains eligibility for debate. That such a disputant is ineligible for debate is to be communicated to him only through a disciple.[45]

When two persons or parties having a difference of opinion on a philosophic topic agree to hold a discussion, it is called *kathā* or philosophic debate.[46] This is of three types: *vāda, jalpa* and *vitaṇḍā*. *Vāda* is a philosophic discussion undertaken not so much for the selfish purpose of achieving victory for oneself but

[44]This criticism is, mainly directed against the Mādhyamika Buddhist. See *Vedārtha-saṁgraha*, p. 53. *na vāde śūnya-vādinaḥ adhikāro anupāyatvāt.*

[45]See *Śatadūṣaṇī*, *Vāda* 9. In this *vāda* known as *kathānadhikāra-vāda*, Vedānta Deśika states the *prima facie* view but does not offer any counter reply to it for the reasons explained above.

[46]SS IV-62, p. 225. *paraspara-viruddha-vādinor vyavahāraḥ kathā.*

with the sole object of ascertaining the truth by adopting the mutually accepted canons of logic and *pramāṇas*. *Jalpa* is the discussion directed towards establishment of one's own position by refuting the view of the opponent with the purpose of achieving one's own victory in the discussion. *Vitaṇḍā* is an argument adopted solely to refute the opponent's views without bothering to establish one's own position. *Jalpa* itself is *vitaṇḍā* except that in the latter type of argument no attempt is made to establish anything with regard to the opponent. *Vitaṇḍā* discussion is again subdivided into two: (*a*) *vītarāga-vitaṇḍā* or discussion carried on without passion for the purpose of right cause; (*b*) *vijigiṣu-vitaṇḍā* or discussion aimed at the mere refutation of the views of the opponent. Even those who resort to *vitaṇḍā* type of *vāda* are required to accept certain principles though the disputants are not concerned with the establishment of their own theories. Otherwise, they would not become eligible for a discussion.[47]

While conducting the discussion, the opponent is to be defeated by disclosing to him the various fallacies involved in the argument. Gautama, the exponent of Nyāya system, has outlined twenty-one kinds of fallacies which are known as *nigrahasthānās* or points of opponent's defeat.[48] These are aimed at exposing the lack of proper understanding of the topic under discussion. Of these, the most serious defect consists in not having the capacity to understand the fallacy, and, if even one had such a capacity, not being able to raise any criticism (*asiddhi*). The former is also known as *jāti* and the latter as *chala*. *Jāti* is also defined as making a statement as against one's own words (*svavyāhatā vāk*). This may assume many forms depending upon the difference in *upādhi*. The self-contradictory statements may imply either the rejection of what is essential (*yukta-tyāgaḥ*) or acceptance of what is unimportant (*ayukta-grahaṇam*) or attempting to prove what is impossible (*aviṣaye vṛttiḥ*). All the three have a common element, viz. self-contradiction.

Chala is described as an attempt to impute a different meaning to the words expressed other than the intended one and on that basis criticise the argument. Thus, for instance, the expression *nava-kambalo'yam* actually means the person wearing a new

[47]TMK IV-63. [48]See NP, pp. 111-18 for details.

blanket. The word *nava* also means nine, and, by attaching that meaning, it is argued that there are no nine blankets but one only. There are various types of *chalas* but Vedānta Deśika does not go into the details as these are generally found in Nyāya literature.

The most important principle to be observed is that in conducting the discussion everyone should accept authoritative *pramāṇas*.. If there be doubt with regard to *pramāṇas*, it would neither help to prove one's own position nor refute that of the opponent. Whatever is stated would have to be authoritative. These are the prerequisites of a *vāda*.

There are other principles laid down for conducting the debate. The two disputants should be careful about the statements they make. If one makes a mistake by making an erroneous statement, the other party should quickly bring it to his attention. If, on the contrary, the other party remains silent, it will be treated as a lapse on his part. If both make mistakes, then they are allowed three chances each to correct themselves. This is technically called *ṣaṭpakṣī* or six chances, three for each. Within these three chances, whoever corrects himself earlier becomes victorious. If both do not correct themselves within the three chances, the presiding person will have to suspend the discussion.[49]

III. VERBAL TESTIMONY

Śabda as a Valid and Independent Pramāṇa

Śabda or verbal testimony is the third and most important source of knowledge. As mentioned earlier, it is of two kinds: empirical (*laukika*) and non-empirical (*alaukika*). The latter is known as Śruti or Āgama, the revealed scripture which is accepted by the Vedāntins as the most authoritative *pramāṇa* in respect of spiritual matters.

The very first question that needs to be considered is whether verbal testimony is a separate *pramāṇa*. The Buddhists and some Vaiśeṣikas do not accept it as an independent *pramāṇa*. According to them, verbal testimony is a special type of

[49]TMK IV-66.

inferential knowledge. Just as fire is inferred on the basis of the observation of smoke, the knowledge of the person who utters the words is inferred on hearing his words.[50]

Vedānta Deśika criticises this view and affirms *śabda* to be an independent *pramāṇa*. When we hear the words, we derive a new knowledge from them. We cannot regard this knowledge as inferential. Inferential knowledge is based on the invariable concomitance between *hetu* and *sādhya* and there is no such correlation between words and their meaning. The only relation that exists between them is that of *vācya* and *vācaka*. That is, words have the power to denote, whereas objects are denoted by them. In the absence of well-established invariable correlation between words and their meanings, it would not be correct to say that the knowledge of a person is inferred from hearing the words uttered by him.

According to some Buddhists, verbal testimony and inference which constitute indirect experience are of the nature of *smṛti* (memory). That is, the knowledge which is generated by inference and verbal testimony is caused by the recollection of past experience. This is explained by an illustration. One has seen individual trees on past occasions, and on the basis of this experience, one gets the knowledge of the forest consisting of a vast cluster of trees (*senā-vanādi-smaraṇa*). Though the cognition of a forest is a piece of new knowledge, it is caused by the memory of what was observed earlier. In the same way, knowledge derived from inference and verbal testimony is of the nature of what had been experienced earlier.

This is not a correct theory, according to Vedānta Deśika. We do get the knowledge of something more than what was not already experienced earlier by means of inference and verbal testimony. In the case of the sentences uttered by a person, we get to know the relationship between the different words which in fact was not known to us earlier. In *anumāna* it becomes established that *sādhya* is present in *pakṣa* as, for example, that fire is present on the hill. Since some additional new factor is known both in inference and verbal testimony,

[50]Though the Vaiśeṣikas do not admit *śabda* as a separate *pramāṇa*, they have accepted the Vedas as authoritative as these are utterances of an infalliable *Īśvara*.

the two cannot be treated as mere cases of memory.[51]

It may be asked : if *śabda* be a *pramāṇa*, why should it not generate knowledge by itself without the need for one's knowing its import, in the same way as sense organs generate knowledge? This is not a correct view. Take the case of the inferential knowledge of fire derived from the observation of smoke. Unless one has known that there is concomitance between smoke and fire, one does not get the knowledge of the fire on merely seeing the smoke.

Sense organs such as eyes do not by themselves generate knowledge of an object. They need other accessories such as light. In the same way words by themselves do not generate knowledge. They cause knowledge in the person only when he is aware of the meaning of the words. That is, words convey knowledge only in respect of a person who is aware of the meaning of the words.

The validity of *śabda* as a source of knowledge depends on its capacity to convey meaning. Does it have such a capacity and if so, how does it perform this function? There are several answers to this question and by way of explaining this issue several theories are put forward. According to some ancient Mīmāṁsakas, *śabda* has the innate capacity to convey its meaning just as fire has the intrinsic capacity to burn. The Naiyāyikas hold the view that all words convey their meaning on the basis of certain accepted convention (*saṁketa*). There is another view advanced by the Prābhākara school of Mīmāṁsā, according to whom words convey their meanings only as related to specific action. The implication of it is that only injunctive statements are meaningful. Any discussion of these theories involves consideration of several other important issues relating to the function of words in a sentence or the connotation and denotation of the terms in a judgment, the logical import of a sentence in general and, in particular, the import of a sentence in which the terms are found in apposition (*samānādhikaraṇa-vākya*). There are divergent views on these topics. We shall examine them separately in the next chapter. It will suffice to observe here that, according to the Viśiṣṭādvaitin, *śabda* or

[51]TMK IV-68. See also SS, p. 228. *saṁskāre satyapi apūrvārtha-pratipattau na smṛtitvam.*

word has a dual function. Firstly, when words are heard we get the connected meaning of the different terms(*ānupūrvi-pratyakṣa*). Its second function is to cause in us a knowledge of the objects denoted by these words. Verbal testimony is a valid source of knowledge insofar as the words and sentences convey the meaning.

Authoritativeness of the Veda

After having accepted verbal testimony as a valid source of knowledge, Vedānta Deśika proceeds to prove on rational grounds the validity and authority of the Veda or the revealed scripture Following the line of arguments advanced by the Mīmāṁsakas, he affirms that Veda is to be admitted as a valid source of knowledge in the same way as perception is accepted as a valid source of knowledge.[52] We consider a particular perceptual knowledge as invalid, if either its source is found to be defective or when it is negated by another knowledge opposed to it. In the absence of these factors, we accept the perceptual knowledge as valid. On the basis of the same principle, we should also admit Veda as valid because it is free from defective factors that would vitiate its validity. In the first place, Vedic knowledge is not contradicted by knowledge derived from any other source. Perceptual knowledge cannot contradict it because perception has its own limitation and it cannot extend its scope to matters which are beyond our sense experience. Inference too cannot negate it because when a conflict arises between inference and śruti, the latter is admitted by the Vedāntins as of greater validity than the former. The inference which is of lesser validity cannot therefore contradict the scriptural knowledge. There may not be any negation by another knowledge, but if the source is defective, it could become invalid. Even this possibility is ruled out in the case of the Veda because it is regarded as *apauruṣeya*, that is, not ascribed to any human authorship and as such it is free from the defects to which the author (*vaktā*) is normally subjected.[53] Knowledge can also be defective if its content is defective. This possibility also does not hold good in respect of the Veda. The knowledge

[52]TMK IV-101. *bādhādyabhāvāt nigamaḥ itaravat mānam.*
[53]*Ibid. asmin vaktṛ-doṣastu na.*

which arises from the Veda is not of doubtful character. Nor can it be said that it does not arise at all from the Veda. Once it is admitted that knowledge arises from the Veda, it would then follow as a general rule (*utsargāt*) that the Veda is self-valid. As will be shown later,[54] all knowledge in general is intrinsically valid (*svataḥ-prāmāṇyam*). Vedic knowledge is self-valid, and it therefore enjoys supreme authority.

The Naiyāyikas seek to establish the authority of the Vedas on the supposition that the Vedas are the utterances of the trustworthy God. This means that it is divine in origin. The reason for holding such a view is that for Naiyāyikas validity of knowledge is derived from extraneous factors (*parataḥ*). Perceptual knowledge, for instance, is considered valid if the sources such as sense organs are free from defects. If the sources are defective, that knowledge becomes invalid. On the same principle, Naiyāyikas seek to prove the validity of the Veda by means of the trustworthy character of the *vaktā* or the speaker. If the Veda is to be authoritative, it must have been taught by one who is most trustworthy. Such a person is God. In this way both the validity of the Veda and indirectly the existence of God is proved. In support of this view the following syllogistic argument is advanced: 'The validity (of *Īśvara-jñāna*) is caused by an extraneous factor other than the generally accepted accessory causes of *jñāna*; because it is a specific knowledge subject to its being caused, such as the invalidity (of knowledge).'[55]

Vedānta Deśika rejects this argument on the ground that probans (*hetu*) used in the syllogism is fallacious. The argument presupposes the existence of *Īśvara*. If God is admitted to exist, His knowledge and its validity being eternal, it connot be regarded as being caused by an extraneous factor (*kāraṇa-janyā*). If *Īśvara* did not exist, there is no sense in saying that His knowledge is being caused by extraneous factor.

The main point of the criticism is that it is not possible to prove the validity of the Vedas by any other means than the criterion of the self-validity. That it is self-valid is established on

[54]See Section 'Self-Validity of Knowledge' in Chapter V. This is also the position of the Mimāṁsakas.

[55]SS IV-102, p. 246. *pramā, jñāna-sāmānya-sāmagry-atirikta-kāraṇajanyā, kāryatve sati jñāna-viśeṣa-rūpatvāt, apramāvat.*

the basis of the fact that knowledge as a general rule is valid by virtue of its own intrinsic nature. Knowledge reveals an object as it is and it possesses this intrinsic power just as fire has a natural power to burn.[56] It is therefore self-valid (*svataḥ-pramāṇam*). According to the epistemological position of Viśiṣṭādvaita, even in the case of illusory knowledge the knowledge aspect is valid, because no one can deny that there was knowledge. What is invalid is the object aspect (*viṣayāṁśa*) since it is negated by a later knowledge. Since all knowledge by its very nature is valid, the knowledge generated by the Vedas too is valid. Thus, on the basis of self-validity the revealed scripture is upheld as authoritative.

If the Veda is taken as valid, should we accept every scriptural statement as authoritative? We have, for instance, the Vedic texts which describe that Agni or the Fire God wept and his eye drops became silver, etc. ! Again there are statements which describe the sun as a sacrificial pillar (*āditya yūpaḥ*)! Such statements being in direct conflict with our ordinary experience, how can we possibly take these statements as valid?

Two different explanations are offered by Vedānta Deśika to these objections. There are many incredible things happening in the universe which are unbelievable, but nevertheless we accept them as facts. The snakes, for instance, have their organs of hearing located in their eyes. We hear of wondrous things happening in some far off places. What we cannot see or know may be present elsewhere. In the same way, if there are statements in the Vedas describing something of an unusual character, we should not doubt their validity simply because we have no experience of them. As regards the Vedic texts which are in direct conflict with our experience, like the statement treating the sun as pillar, we have to adopt the secondary meaning. If, in matters beyond the scope of our common experience, the Vedas have something to say, we should not question their authority on the basis of our limited empirical knowledge.

The second important reason for accepting unquestionable authority for the Veda is that it is *apauruṣeya*. That is, the Veda is self-existent and is not written by any human being. As against

[56]TMK IV-103. See also p. 183.

this view, it is argued that Vedic statements must have been written by somebody because they are in the form of sentences.[57]

Vedānta Deśika rejects this argument as fallacious. On the basis of the fact that the Vedic statement is in the form of a sentence it is not possible to assert that it is written by somebody. If something is in the form of a sentence, why should it necessarily be *pauruṣeya*? This question calls for a suitable counter-reply in defence, in accordance with the principles adopted for syllogistic arguments. The only possible counter-reply is that if it were not *pauruṣeya*, then it would not be in the form of sentences. This reply will defeat the very basic premise of the syllogism and runs counter to the thesis of the opponent. The point of criticism is that mere *vākyatva* or being a sentence cannot be an adequate justification to deny the impersonal character of the Vedic statements. For the Vedāntins and Mīmāṁsakas, Vedic statements, though they may be in the form of sentences, can be *apauruṣeya* because they are being transmittted orally in a particular sequence from generation to generation, without anyone being its written author. There are śruti and smṛti texts which declare the Veda as *nitya* and *anādi* (beginningless).[58] As against such scriptural evidence an inference loses its validity. Further, we do not have any idea of its author. As it is a very important document, one should have had in the past some knowledge of its author. In the absence of any such information, the Vedas are to be admitted as *apauruṣeya*.[59]

According to the Viśiṣṭādvaitin, even *Īśvara* is not its author. *Īśvara* is only the exponent of the Veda. He teaches it in each *kalpa* (epoch) in the same order as it has existed from time immemorial. It is in this sense considered *nitya* or eternal[60] and *anādi* or beginningless. As Rāmānuja has explained, the Veda is *nitya* in the sense that the particular order (*ānupūrvi*) in which it is being recited remains intact and in the same fixed order of words its recitation is carried on from generation

[57]SS IV-111, p. 250. *vedavākyāni sakartṛkāṇi, vākyatvāt.*

[58]*Taittirīya Saṁhitā*, 276-71. *vācā virūpa-nityayā.* See also *Manu-smṛti, anādi-nidhanā hy-eṣā.*

[59]TMK IV-111 *kartuḥ asmṛteśca.* See also SS, pp. 251.

[60]Eternity is conceived in the sense of *pravāha-nitya*, or the continuous flow of river water.

to generation.[61] The Mīmāṁsakas believe that the letters (*varṇa*) of which words are formed are eternal, and the Veda as a collection of such letters in a particular order is eternal. The Viśiṣṭādvaitin does not agree with this view. *Varṇas* which are mere articulation of sound are non-permanent, because *śabda* itself being only an evolute of *ākāśa* is non-permanent.[62] When dissolution takes place all the words and letters may disappear. But the sequence in which the Veda is recited is not lost, because it can remain in the mind of the omniscient *Īśvara*. At the beginning of the world-creation, *Īśvara* teaches the Veda in the same order in which it was being recited in the earlier epoch. The question of *Īśvara* forgetting it does not arise because He is omniscient and His knowledge is eternal and not dependent on the past memory.

It is said that the Veda in the beginning was one whole unit, and later on it was divided into four parts. We also come across statements that there are different branches of the Veda (*śākhā-vibhāgaḥ*). Some portion of the Veda is attributed to specific personality such as *kāṭhaka*. There are also references in the Vedas to individual sages such as Vasiṣṭha and Viśvāmitra. All these indicate that the Veda was brought into existence at certain points of time.

Against these objections, Vedānta Deśika explains that at one time people were reciting the entire Veda but with the passage of time as the capacity of the people to recite the entire Veda diminished, it was divided into four parts and allocated to four groups of people for recitation and preservation. In the same way, division into different branches was introduced. The names such as *kāṭhaka* came into vogue, because the sage *kaṭha* was teaching it. Similarly, the *mantras* which were already in existence were rediscovered by a few sages through penance who were called *mantra-kartā*. This does not mean that *mantras* contained in the Veda were produced afresh. The reference in the Vedas to such personalities as Vasiṣṭha and Viśvāmitra do not mean that these persons composed parts of the Vedas. The Veda

[61]RB, I-3-29, p. 364. *pūrva-pūrvoccāraṇa -krama-janita-saṁskāreṇa tameva krama-viśeṣaṁ smṛtvā tenaiva krameṇa uccāryatvam*. See also *Vedārtha-saṁgraha*, p. 180.

[62]For further details see Section 'Viśiṣṭādvaita Theory of Attributes' in Chapter X.

is *nitya*, eternal. It is *anādi*, without beginning. It is *apauruṣeya*, not authored by man.

The Vedas and Āgamas of Other Schools

The Vedas are regarded by the *mahājanas* as of greater authority than the Āgamas or the sacred texts of other schools of thought.[63] By *mahājana* is meant men of proven wisdom who have acquired philosophic knowledge through austerities. The Āgamas of other systems are not held in such high esteem. Further, the Āgamas of the atheists or those who do not accept the authority of the Vedas stand contradicted by the Vedas which are free from defects because of their impersonal character. Insofar as these Āgamas are in conflict with Vedic teachings, they are regarded as invalid. There is also mutual conflict between the different Āgamas of Buddhists, Jainas and Cārvākas. Such a conflict between these Āgamas affects their validity. One may claim that the Āgama of a particular school is expounded by a trustworthy person (*āptimūla*) and hence must be accepted valid. But it is possible to make a similar claim for another Āgama of a different school. One may assert that the exponent of the Āgama of a particular school is subject to ignorance (*moha*). A similar charge could also be levelled against the other exponent. Since these defective factors are common to all the Āgamas of the atheists, or those who do not accept the authority of the Vedas, it becomes difficult to determine which one is valid and which one is invalid, and, in the absence of well-established criterion for validity, the conflicts found in their teachings cannot be resolved. It may be claimed that some of the teachings of these Āgamas are in consonance with the teachings of the Vedas and that such portions could be accepted as authoritative. Thus, for example, the teaching of *ahiṁsā* or non-violence in the Buddhāgama is similar to what is taught in the Vedas. Vedānta Deśika points out that such little similarity in respect of a few doctrines is of no use. In fact, he argues that such teachings were taken from the Vedic lore and included in their Āgamas in order to give credibility to their religion. It is safer to rely upon the Vedas in respect of such teachings than resorting to the secondary source of doubtful *prāmāṇya*.[64]

[63]SS IV-114, p. 252. [64]TMK IV-115.

Authoritativeness of Smṛtis and Purāṇas

The Viśiṣṭādvaita Vedānta, unlike some of the other Vedāntic systems, accepts besides the revealed scripture the various smṛtis, purāṇas and the Pāñcarātra Āgamas as equally authoritative and valid *pramāṇa.* The justification for such an acceptance is that the teachings contained in the smṛtis and purāṇas are based on the Vedas. Among the smṛtis, *Manu-smṛti* occupies a very important place. The teachings of Manu correspond to what is taught in the Vedas. In view of this it is stated that all that is said by Manu is like medicine (to the sick) implying that it is beneficial to humanity.[65] Its teachings are free from delusion and deceit. They are not expounded on the basis of perception, inference and verbal statements of ordinary human beings. They owe their origin to the Vedas.

In the same way, the other smṛtis ascribed to different sages enjoy unquestionable authority. It is possible that a particular statement which is mentioned in a smṛti text may not find a corresponding śruti text in support of it. Thus, for example, the *aṣṭakā-śrāddha,* a *śrāddha* ceremony which is to be performed on the eighth day of a particular month to propitiate the manes, is prescribed in the smṛti text but there is no corresponding reference to it in the Vedas. In such cases, it is to be understood that the Vedic texts referring to it must have existed elsewhere at one time, and based on such Vedic authority, its observance has come down to us from generation to generation. It would not be correct to deny Vedic authority to such a smṛti text on the ground that there is no corresponding reference to it in Vedic text.[66]

When a conflict arises between a śruti text and smṛti text, which one should be accepted as of greater authority? In cases of such conflicts, it is laid down by Mīmāṁsaka that smṛti text must be rejected. Śruti obviously enjoys a greater authority and validity. The same rule applies when there is a conflict between śruti texts and purāṇas. It is acknowledged that the authors of Purāṇas are liable to make errors since they are also influenced by *karma.* If conflicts arise between the different purāṇas, we have to determine the relative strength of the statements on the

[65]*Yajur-veda* I-3. *yad-vai kiñca manur avadat tad bheṣajam.* [66]TMK IV-117.

basis of the nature of the purāṇas. The purāṇas are classified into three groups as *sāttvika*, *rājasa* and *tāmasa*. The *Matsya Purāṇa*, which is in consonance with the teachings of the Vedas, has enunciated the relative importance of the different purāṇas. *Tāmasa* purāṇas speak of the greatness of Śiva and Agni; *rajasa* of Brahmā; *sāttvika* speak of the greatness of Viṣṇu. Among these, the teachings contained in the *sāttvika* purāṇas are considered to be of greater authority. Whenever conflicts arise between the different purāṇas, the teachings of *sāttvika* purāṇas are to be accepted as of greater authority.[67]

Authoritativeness of Pāñcarātra Āgama[68]

According to the Viśiṣṭādvaita Vedānta, Pāñcarātra Āgama occupies a unique position, because it is considered to have been taught by *Īśvara* out of compassion towards the humanity.[69] It is therefore regarded as free from the defects common to texts written by human beings. There is also no room for doubt or disbelief in the teachings contained in it.

The validity of Pāñcarātra Āgama is questioned on the ground that it speaks of the origin of *jiva*, a view which is opposed to the teaching of the Veda. In one place in the Pāñcarātra it is said that *jiva* designated as Sankarṣaṇa originates from Vāsudeva, the Supreme Brahman.[70] But *jiva*, according to Vedic teaching, is eternal and is not subject to birth.

This objection is utenable, argues Vedānta Deśika. The very Pāñcarātra texts describe *jīvas* as beginningless and that they are not subject to any destruction. In view of this, the text referring to the birth (*utpatti*) of Sankarṣaṇa *Jiva* is to be interpreted to mean *āvirbhāva* or manifestation of what existed as unamnifest. The Vedic text too says that Brahmā created the *jīvas* (*prajāpatiḥ prajāḥ aṣrjata*), but it is not to be taken as the creation of *jiva*. Here *sṛṣṭi* or creation is understood to mean manifestation of what already existed in a potential form.

[67]TMK IV-119. *anyonyaṁ virodhe tu, sāttvikatvādibhedāt bala-niyatiḥ*

[68]Pāñcarātra Āgamas or Saṁhitās constitute a body of religious treatises dealing with the various aspects of Vaiṣṇava religion and philosophy including mode of worship of God and other sacraments.

[69]SS IV-121, p. 235. *pañcarātrasya kṛtsnasya vaktā nārāyaṇaḥ svayam.* See also RB II-2-49, p. 560.

[70]*Paramasaṁhitā. paramakāraṇāt parabrahmabhūtāt vāsudevāt saṅkarṣaṇo nāma jīvo jāyate.*

The Mahābhārata describes Pāñcarātra as a text of the highest order and as one intended for our highest good (*parama śreyaḥ*) and that Manu teaches *dharma* on the basis of it. Thus Pāñcarātra Āgama is in full agreement with the Vedas. If in some places conflicts arise between śruti texts and the Pāñcarātra texts, these have to be reconciled in the same way as between the affirmative and negative statements appearing in the Vedic texts.[71]

IV. OTHER PRAMĀṆAS

So far we have considered three major *pramāṇas*—*pratyakṣa*, *anumāna* and *śabda*. Besides these, a few other *pramāṇas* are admitted by other schools of thought. These are: *upamāna* or comparison, *arthāpatti* or presumption and *anupalabdhi* or non-apprehension. According to the Viśiṣṭādvaitin, these are not independent *pramāṇas* but form part of either inference or verbal testimony.

Smṛti

Before we examine each one of these, we have to consider whether memory (*smṛti*) is a valid source of knowledge. The Viśiṣṭādvaitin agrees with the Naiyāyikas that smṛti is not a separate *pramāṇa*. However, unlike some other thinkers, he claims validity for knowledge derived from memory. Smṛti is that form of knowledge which is generated by the recall of the latent impression (*saṁskāra*) of an object previously seen. The revival of the *saṁskāra* is caused either when one sees an object similar to what one had experienced earlier or by the influence of the unseen potency (*adṛṣṭa*). The *saṁskāra* may even be revived by seeing an object which was seen along with the object experienced earlier (*sahamita*). The earlier experience (*anubhava*) which is the cause of smṛti may be of three kinds : *pramā*

[71]TMK IV-122. There is a controversy between Śaṁkara and Rāmānuja on the question of accepting Pāñcarātra Āgama as authoritative. The view taken by Śaṁkara is that the *Vedānta-sūtras* (II-2-39 to 42) do not accord authority to Pāñcarātra. Ramānuja, on the basis of the proper interpretation of these *sūtras*, establishes that the *sūtras* 41 and 42 are explicitly in favour of the authority of Pāñcarātra. See RB II-2-41 and 42. See also Yāmuna's *Āgama-Prāmāṇyam*, pp. 50-62.

or valid knowledge, *bhrama* or erroneous knowledge and *saṁśaya* or doubtful knowledge. Accordingly, memory is also of three kinds : valid memory, false memory and memory of doubtful character.[72]

Some hold the view that all knowledge based on memory is false (*ayathārtha*). This is not correct, according to Vedānta Deśika. Its validity or invalidity depends upon the nature of the previous experience. If what was experienced earlier is a valid one, the memory that arises on the basis of the *saṁskāra* of the previous experience should also be regarded as valid. If the earlier experience is a false one, the memory based on the *saṁskāra* of that experience also becomes false. Further, the smṛti knowledge is not without content. That is, the knowledge based on memory has for its content the object once seen. It can also lead one to action, the effort being motivated by a desire to obtain the object recollected. In view of this, the knowledge arising from memory is a valid one.

An objection may be raised against this conclusion. Memory is related to an object which has ceased to exist at present (*naṣṭaḥ*) and whatever is not present or cannot be experienced should therefore become false (*asat*). How could we regard the knowledge of what does not exist as valid? The reply to this objection is that even inferential knowledge as well as verbal testimony are related to an object of the past experience or of future experience; even so, they are accepted as valid despite the fact that their content does not exist at the present moment. In the same way, smṛti is also valid even though its content belongs to the past.

If smṛti is regarded as invalid, then even *pratyabhijña* or knowledge by recognition would have to be invalid, since the latter too depends on the recollection of what was seen earlier. Merely because smṛti depends on past experience, it cannot be treated as invalid. All other sources of knowledge including perception depend on something or the other. The fact that Akṣapâda, the exponent of Nyâya system, does not acknowledge smṛti as a *pramāṇa* does not mean that it is invalid. Vedic texts do recognise that smṛti also is a source of knowledge.[73]

[72]SS IV-124, p. 257. *sā ca svakāraṇa-vaividhyāt triprakārā.*

[73]TMK IV-125. *vede mānais sahoktā smṛtir api.* The *Taittirīya Āraṇyaka* makes mention of *pramāṇas* which include smṛti: *smṛtiḥ pratyakṣam aitihyam*

Vedānta Deśika therefore concludes that though smṛti is not accepted as an independent *pramāṇa*, it is no doubt a valid experience in so far as it is based on previous valid experience.

Upamāna

Upamāna or knowledge derived by comparison is considered as a separate *prāmaṇa* both by the Mīmāṁsakas, and Naiyayikas, though they offer different explanations. After critically examining both the views, Vedānta Deśika holds that it cannot be an independent *pramāṇa* but a part of either inference or verbal testimony.

The Mīmāṁsaka gives the following explanation. A person who is familiar with cow (*go*) casually comes across a wild ox (*gavaya*); he notices the similarity of the wild ox with the cow and discovers that the cow is also similar to the *gavaya*. The cow at this time is not within the purview of his perception. This cognition of similarity of the recollected object to the one seen is due to comparison. In other words, the recollected cow as characterised by the similarity of *go* in the *gavaya* is called *upamāna*. It is regarded as a separate *pramāṇa*, because by means of comparison one apprehends the similarity existing in a thing which is not perceived at that moment. It is not a case of inference, because the factor required for inference, viz. invariable concomitance is not involved here. Nor is it a case of memory, because at the time the cow was seen, the wild ox was not seen, and as such the similarity between the two was also not known earlier.

Vedānta Deśika does not agree with this theory. When a person sees a *gavaya*, does he remember the cow by means of similarity? Or does he remember the cow in the form of the judgment 'the cow is similar to *gavaya*?' If it be the former, it can only become a case of recollection (*smṛti*), because by seeing one object the recollection of another object similar to it arises.[74] If it be the latter alternative, it would mean that he remembers the cow as similar to *gavaya*. In that case, it would be an inferential knowledge, because the judgment that *gavaya*

anumānaṁ catuṣṭayam. Though it is accepted as a valid source of knowledge, it is not regarded as an independent *pramāṇa* as it is generated by the latent impression based on previous experience.

[74]TMK IV-127. *tulyāt tulyāntare dhīḥ smṛtiḥ*.

is similar to cow arises on the basis of the fact that cow is similar to *gavaya*. When we make a judgment that *gavaya* is similar to cow, it conversely means that cow is also similar to *gavaya*, just as when we say that the right palm is similar to the left, it also follows that the left palm is similar to the right. Such a knowledge derived by means of comparison can either be regarded as a case of memory or as a case of inference.[75]

According to the Naiyāyika, *upamāna* consists in associating a thing unknown before with its name later with some other known object by virtue of its similarity with it. A man of the city who has never seen a wild ox goes to the forest and asks the forester: 'what is a *gavaya*'? and the latter replies that it is like a cow. With this knowledge, he happens to see sometime later a *gavaya*, and, finding that it is similar to the cow, comes to know that it is the animal which bears the name *gavaya*. This knowledge of an unknown object by virtue of similarity to a known object is *upamāna*. It is generated by means of association of the unknown animal with its name which is conveyed to the observer on the basis of the similarity of the unknown animal to a known one. What is emphasised here, unlike the view of the Mīmāṁsaka, is the connection between a name and the object that forms the sole sphere of *upamāna*.

Vedānta Deśika says that this method of deriving knowledge by means of comparison falls within the ambit of verbal testimony. When a person who has known the *gavaya* animal describes to the observer what gavaya is, the observer hearing the statement understands the nature of that animal by means of its description. It is similar to the method of knowing the nature of an object by means of its definition.[76] Knowledge arising from description or definition of an object is a case of verbal testimony insofar as the statements are made by a trustworthy person. If such a possibility were not accepted, it would not be possible to understand the nature of the metaphysical categories or of things which are supersensuous by means of description. Insofar as the knowledge of an unknown object is conveyed through verbal testimony, the case of *upamāna* explained by the Naiyāyika does not stand as a separate *pramāṇa*. It becomes part of verbal testimony.

[75]TMK IV-127. *yattulyaḥ yaḥ so ca etatsamaḥ.*

[76]TMK IV-127.

Arthāpatti

Arthāpatti or presumption is the postulation of something to account for what apparently conflicts with experience and is therefore in the nature of a hypothesis. It is a way of reconciling two facts which appear mutually incompatible. Thus, for instance, if we know that Devadatta is alive and do not find him in his house, we draw the conclusion that he must be elsewhere.

Vedānta Deśika states that this method of discovering the unknown from the known is not different from inference. There is a correlation between the two facts, viz. that Devadatta who is not at the house is alive and that Devadatta must be elsewhere. When it is already known that the person is alive, his not being present at home would naturally lead to the conclusion that he is somewhere outside the house. *Anumāna* is the deduction of a particular fact on the basis of another fact. The presence of fire is proved on the basis of the smoke, because there is concomitance between smoke and fire. In the same way, there is a correlation between Devadatta who is alive not being in the house and Devadatta being elsewhere. On the basis of such a concomitance, we deduce that Devadatta is elsewhere. Obviously, this is a case of inference.

Anupalabdhi

Anupalabdhi or non-apprehension is admitted as a separate *pramāṇa* by the Kumārila school of Mīmāṁsā. It is argued that the non-existence (*abhāva*) of an object, as, for example, that there is no pot on the ground, cannot be perceived by the senses, for there is nothing with which the senses can have contact in order to perceive the non-existence. The senses can apprehend only positive entities. Nor can non-existence be apprehended by other *pramāṇas*. *Anupalabdhi* is the only means by which the non-existence of an object is known. *Abhāva* in this system is not a positive content of knowledge.[77]

According to the Viśiṣṭādvaitin *anupalabdhi* is not a separate *pramāṇa*. The same sense organs which apprehend an entity

[77]The Prābhākara school of Mīmāṁsā do not accept *anupalabdhi* as a separate *paramāṇa*, because they recognise non-existence or negation as a positive content of knowledge.

can also cognise its *abhāva* or the non-existence. There is no need to admit a separate *pramāṇa* for this purpose.

It is contended by the Mīmāṁsaka that there cannot be any direct contact of sense organs with non-existence. Besides, there are instances where the knowledge of non-existence of perceivable objects arises. Thus, a person who had been to a market place in the morning did not notice the presence of an elephant. When somebody asked him in the afternoon whether he saw an elephant, his reply was that there was no elephant. This knowledge of the absence of an elephant is not caused by sense perception, because the market place is out of the purview of his perception in the afternoon. Nor is it a case of memory, because he had not thought of the elephant in the morning when he was at the market place. The cognition of the non-existence of an elephant in the market place is therefore caused by the non-apprehension of the absence of an elephant.

In reply to this argument, Vedānta Deśika says that the non-existence of the elephant in the market place can be easily inferred. If one had seen the elephant, he would have recollected it. Because he did not recollect it, he did not see the elephant. When we can infer the absence of an object, there is no need to resort to a separate *pramāṇa* for proving the non-existence of an object. Besides, it is also possible to know the *abhāva* or non-existence of an object through perception in the same way as positive entities are apprehended.

Besides the six *pramāṇas*, some schools admit other minor sources of knowledge such as tradition (*aitihya*), subsumption (*sambhava*), hand-sign (*ceṣṭā*) and script (*lipi*). All these are considered by them as valid sources of knowledge.

Aitihya refers to the statements of an elderly person about matters which are being passed on from generation to generation, their origin being shrouded in the mist of antiquity. Should we accept them as valid? Vedānta Deśika takes the view that such statements may be accepted as valid verbal testimony provided they conform to the facts; otherwise they have to be rejected as invalid.

Sambhava or subsumption is the cognition of a part from the whole of which it is a part. Thus, when we speak of ten thousand, the number one hundred is understood to be a part of it because the former includes in it the latter. That which causes the awareness of number one hundred is known as *sambhava* and as such it is a means of knowledge. As this is strictly a numerical inclusion and there is a definite concomitance between one hundred and ten thousand, it is a case of deductive inference and not a separate *pramāṇa*.

Ceṣṭā or gesture of hand is regarded as a source of knowledge, because by observing the sign made by a person we understand the needs of the person such as his desire for food or drink. This is again a case of inferential knowledge. We infer from the sign what one seeks to convey.

The script or *lipi* causes the knowledge of letters and thereby of words. Even this is a deductive inference and cannot constitute a separate *pramāṇa*.

V. RELATIVE VALIDITY OF PRAMĀṆAS

After examining the nature of other *pramāṇas*, Vedānta Deśika comes to the conclusion that *pratyakṣa*, *anumāna* and *śabda* are the only three *pramāṇas* and the additional ones accepted by the other schools form part of these. All the three *pramāṇas* reveal the truth and are therefore equally valid. Of the three, *pratyakṣa* is an important *pramāṇa* because it serves as the basis for the other two *pramāṇas*.[78] Inference depends on perception for establishing the logical concomitance. Verbal testimony also depends on the hearing of the sound of the words and the comprehension of their meaning. In view of this, *pratyakṣa* is regarded as *upajīvya* or that which offers subsistence, and *anumāna* as well as *śabda* as *upajīvaka* or that which subsists on another. This means that inference and verbal testimony cannot contradict what is proved by perception. According to Vedānta Deśika, if the knowledge that arises from *anumāna* and *śabda* is opposed to perceptual experience, the former cannot be taken as valid.[79]

An objection may be raised against this conclusion. It cannot be said that *upajīvya* is stronger and more valid than the *upajīvaka*. We have an instance in which we find that the inferen-

[78]TMK IV-133. *akṣajanyā manīṣā iha sarvopajīvyā prathamam mānam bhavet.*
[79]*Ibid. mūlam ko'pi na bādhyam.*

tial cognition negates the perceptual experience. Thus, for instance, the perceptual cognition of the flame of a lamp as one (*jvālaikya-pratyakṣa*) is sublated by the inferential cognition that proves that there is a succession of different flames (*jvālābhedānumāna*). The flame of the lamp, as long as it burns, appears to the perception as one and the same; but on the basis of the observation that the different particles of the wick and the oil are consumed in succession it is inferred that there are many distinct flames succeeding one another. Thus, the perceptual cognition which is sublated by the inference becomes invalid.

Vedānta Deśika controverts this argument. In the instance under consideration there is no opposition between the *upajivya* and *upajivaka*. The cognition of the oneness of the flame is not the *upajivya* of the inference referring to the difference of the flame of the lamp. On the contrary, it is the perception which cognises the concomitance between the particles of the wick, the oil and the flame of the lamp that actually constitutes the *upajivya* of the inference, and this particular perception is not sublated by the inference proving the difference of the flame. The present illustration does not prove the fact that inference as *upajivaka* is stronger than perception as *upajivya*. In case of the conflict between perception and inference, the former is definitely of greater validity than the latter.[80]

In cases of conflict between perception and scripture, which is to be regarded as of greater validity? This is an important issue having certain ontological implications. The Advaitin maintains that if a conflict arises between the two, scripture is to be accepted as stronger and of greater authority than perception. According to him, there is a direct conflict between perception and scripture. Perception apprehends a world of plurality and difference, whereas the main purport of scripture is non-dualism or non-difference. On the basis of the principle determining the relation of the sublated to the sublator (*bādhya-bādhaka*), the Advaitin takes the view that the cognition of difference by perception is due to the defective source, viz. *avidyā*, whereas scriptural knowledge is free from all possible defects. Hence scripture is stronger and of greater authority than perception.[81]

[80]See SS IV-133, p. 261. See also SD, Vāda 29.

[81]For details of arguments advanced by Advaitin, see SD, Vāda 29.

Vedānta Deśika does not accept these arguments. He seriously questions the Advaitin's assumption that there is a conflict between the scripture and perception on the basis of the fact that non-dualism is the only purport of scripture. Secondly, it is not possible to prove that perception rests on a defective source, because even scripture, according to the ontological position of Advaita, is a product of *avidyā*. All these issues have certain ontological implications and are discussed separately. The important point to be taken note of for the present is that, in cases of conflict between scripture and perception, the latter is definitely stronger than the former. It does not mean that scriptural statements which conflict with perceptual experience have to be rejected as invalid. But, on the contrary, they have to be accepted but interpreted in such a way as to overcome the conflict. Thus, the Viśiṣṭādvaitin gives equal importance to all the three *pramāṇas* through which we can get to know the reality.

CHAPTER THREE

Logical Import of Words and Sentences

IN THE previous chapter we considered *śabda* or verbal testimony as a valid source of knowledge. In this connection, we referred to a few issues with regard to the manner in which words and sentences convey the meaning. Do the words have the capacity to convey meaning? And if so how do they perform this function? Do they denote the individual objects or their generic character? Do the words in a sentence convey the meaning in isolation or as connected together? What is the import of the sentences or judgments in which the terms are found in apposition? Are all scriptural statements purportful? All these are issues of far-reaching importance, and a fuller discussion of these is called for in order to determine the validity of *śabda* as a *pramāṇa*. The present chapter deals with these matters.

It is generally admitted that words convey their meaning, and through the understanding of the meaning we derive the knowledge of the objects denoted by them. Thus, words have two important functions. First, when we hear the sound of words, we get an awareness of the connected meaning of these words. This is known as *śakti-jñāna*. The second function is to cause the knowledge of the objects denoted by them. This is called *artha-prakāśakatva*. Without knowing the import of the words, the knowledge of the objects denoted by them is not possible.[1]

Some ancient Mīmāṁsakas maintain that *śabda* has an innate capacity to convey the knowledge of objects denoted by them directly without the need of *śakti-jñāna* or the comprehension of the connected meaning of the words. This amounts to the acceptance of only one function of the words and rejection of

[1]SS IV-70, p. 229.

the other function mentioned above. This is not correct, argues Vedânta Deśika. If without the *śakti-jñāna*, knowledge of the objects denoted by the words is possible, then even infants and deaf persons should get it. This is not so. Therefore, both the functions of the words described above have to be accepted.[2]

According to the Naiyâyikas, all words convey their meaning by accepted convention (*saṁketa*). That is, we get to know the meanings of the words through popular usage. There are certain specific words which are known as *saṁjñā-pada*, and these refer only to specific individuals. In the same way, Vedic words convey special meanings on the basis of certain accepted conventions.

This theory is in direct conflict with the śruti texts which declare Vedas as *anâdi*. If some one had authored the Vedas, it would be possible to conceive that words have certain conventional meaning. But this is not so. Even though it is admitted that *Īśvara* taught the Vedas (*upadeṣṭā*), He is not the one who wrote them (*kartā*). If the Vedas are beginningless (*anâdi*) and eternal (*nitya*), there is no scope for any one to have fixed a conventional meaning to Vedic words.[3] Words of non-Vedic language may have conventional meaning, but it is not possible to admit it in respect of words of Vedic language since the Vedas were not written at any particular point of time.

1. CRITICISM OF MĪMĀṀSĀ THEORY

According to Prâbhâkara Mīmāṁsā, words convey their meanings only as related to specific action. The process by which the meanings of words are derived is explained by an illustration. An elderly person asks a younger person to bring a cow and take it back. A child nearby observes the younger person carrying out the command, and comes to understand that the word 'cow' mentioned in the statement refers to the animal 'cow'. From this it is concluded that in the first stage words convey their meanings through such injunctive statements of

[2]TMK IV-70. See also SS, p. 229.
[3]TMK IV-71.

elderly persons involving action.[4] On the basis of this, the Prābhākaras uphold the theory that all words convey their meanings only as related to specific action. The implication of this theory is that only Vedic statements of injunctive character are purportful, whereas those which refer to the existents (*siddhapara*) cannot be taken as valid except as complemental to the injunctive statements.

Following the criticisms offered by Rāmānuja in his *Śrī-bhāṣya*, Vedānta Deśika refutes this theory. Words are meaningful even in respect of existents. The meaning of the words in the initial stage may be determined with reference to the activity caused by the words as in the illustration cited above. But it is not necessary that it should have reference only to action in order to be meaningful.

When we hear words, we are able to derive their meaning because there is some connection between words and the meanings conveyed by them. This connection is technically called *vṛtti* or import. *Vṛtti* is of two kinds: *śakti* or primary import and *lakṣaṇā* or secondary import. Some words bear primary import (*mukhya*); some have a secondary import (*gauṇa*); in respect of some words, we have to adopt a suitable meaning with reference to the context (*lākṣaṇika*); and in some cases we have to accept the general sense of the words (*tātparya*). How do we determine which word conveys which specific meaning? This is to be known through usage (*vyavahāra*). All our empirical usages have bearing on some activity (*pravṛtti*) or cessation from activity (*nivṛtti*). Words therefore derive their specific meaning with reference to such activity or cessation from activity. This is the argument of the Mīmāṁsakas.

The Vedāntins contend that words derive their meaning even in respect of existents and without any reference to activity. Thus, for instance, one asks the question: 'Who is that person?' And the reply comes that he is Pāñcāla (name of the person). The statement that he is Pāñcala refers to an existent and it has no reference to any activity. Nevertheless the word Pāñcāla conveys a meaning. It is evident from our common experience that even the words referring to a *siddha-vastu* convey meaning.

[4]TMK IV-72. *vyutpattiḥ kārya eva prathamasamuditā vṛddhavākyāt pravṛttau.*

As against this, the Mīmāṁsakas hold that words may bear meaning in respect of existents in the case of non-Vedic statements, but with regard to Vedic texts they are meaningful only insofar as they are related to activity (*kāryapara*). Accordingly, the ritualistic portion of the Vedas which contain statements of injunctive character are purportful as being related to activity, whereas the Upaniṣadic portion of the Vedas which refer to Brahman, an existent, are not meaningful.[5]

Vedānta Deśika points out that the above position amounts to the acceptance of half truth (*ardha-ramya*), i.e. that one portion of the Veda is valid, whereas the other portion is only partially valid. This is not correct. The statements appearing in the Upaniṣadic portion of the Vedas are equally meaningful insofar as they teach us about the existence of the supreme goal. The very knowledge of the Supreme Being conveyed by the Upaniṣadic statements is sufficient to bestow validity on them. This is explained by an illustration. A person makes a statement to another person to the effect that there is a hidden treasure in his house. The statement is purportful insofar as it conveys the information which delights the person hearing it. The Upaniṣadic texts teach us that the realization of the Supreme Being is the ultimate goal. They are meaningful insofar as they convey knowledge about the supreme goal.[6] If this position were not accepted there would be direct conflict between the *pūrva-kāṇḍa* or the earlier portion of the Veda devoted to the ritualistic practices and the *uttara-kāṇḍa* or the later portion dealing with the knowledge of Brahman.

Vedānta Deśika explains how even at the initial stage words derive their meanings without any reference to activity in respect of existents. Thus, a person pointing his finger at a cow tells his child that it is called a cow, and the child learns to associate that word with the object 'cow'. The child then understands the meaning of words without those words having any reference to activity. To give another example, an individual, who is aware of the fact that the news about the birth of a child causes pleasure, conveys such news to the father of the new-born child, and the latter feels very happy after hearing the

[5]SS IV-72, p. 230. *ataḥ kārya eva śabdānām vyutpattiḥ; tasmāt na siddharūpe Brahmaṇi vedānta-vākyānām prāmāṇyamiti.*

[6]SS, IV-73 p. 230. *puruṣārtha-paryavasāyitvam hi vākyasya prāmāṇye tantram.*

statement of the former. It is obvious that the statement of the first individual conveys the meaning to the second individual, and as such he reacts with joy. It is not therefore necessary that, in order to be meaningful, statements should have a direct bearing on activity.

After having shown that words convey their meanings even in the initial stage in respect of existents, Vedānta Deśika points out that, in the subsequent periods too, words convey their meaning in respect of existents. A person, who is already acquainted with the meaning of certain words, understands on the basis of previous experience that such and such words have specific meanings or vice versa. With the knowledge of limited number of words, he also learns the meaning of more connected words. Whatever meanings are attached to the words in our ordinary experience, the same also hold good in respect of Vedic vocabulary. When however there are Vedic words which do not bear the meaning current in our ordinary experience, their meaning is to be understood with the help of *Nirukta*, the treatise containing etymological interpretation of Vedic words.

How do we understand the meaning of words such as Indra (a Vedic deity) about whom we do not have the faintest knowledge? It is difficult to know the meaning of words which refer to entities with which we are not familiar.

It is possible to understand the meaning of such words on the basis of the description provided by the Vedic texts. Thus, for instance, a person living in a city has not seen a lion; nevertheless, on the basis of the description provided by a preson dwelling in a forest, he gets an idea of the lion, and, on that basis, he understands that the word 'lion' refers to a specific animal. After having understood the meaning of the word, the same person can communicate the meaning of the word 'lion' to another. In the same way, even if one has not seen Indra, on the basis of the description and comparison to other similar entities, one can derive the meaning of the word. To give another example, one has not seen the river Thames or the Alps mountain. But by means of reading the description of the river and the mountain and also on the analogy of similar known objects, it is possible to get an idea of such remote things not seen earlier. In terms of Western philosophy, this is knowledge of the meaning by description in contrast to knowledge by acquaintance.

II. CONNOTATION AND DENOTATION OF WORDS

The main issue to be considered is whether words denote the generic character (*jāti*) or the individual objects as qualified with generic character (*jati-viśiṣṭa vyakti*). According to Mīmāṁsakas, all words denote the generic character of the objects referred to and not the individuals. When it is said 'bring the cow', what is intended is not a particular cow but any animal possessing the characteristic of a cow. According to another view, words denote only the individuals concerned. If words do not refer to the individual objects (*vyakti*), then there would be no relation between the words and the objects referred to by them. In the statement 'bring the cow', if the word 'cow' means only the generic character of the cow, how would it be possible to bring a particular cow? Actually on hearing the statement, one brings a particular cow, and the word 'cow' therefore has reference to a specific cow. The relationship that exists between the word 'cow' and the object 'cow' is in respect of *vyakti* and not in respect of *jāti*.

The Viśiṣṭādvaitin does not agree with either of the views. According to him, a word such as cow denotes the individual as characterised with the generic character of that individual object (*jāti-viśiṣṭa-vyakti*). The word 'cow' does not refer only to the *vyakti*. If it were so, there being an infinite number of cows we should be able to comprehend all the cows including those which have yet to be born and those which are elsewhere. But it is not so and it is against our experience. It cannot be said that the reference is to one particular entity in which *jāti* and *vyakti* are identical, because substance and attribute are distinct as is well established by experience. Nor can it be said that *jāti* and *vyakti* are both different and non-different because of self-contradiction involved. Since they are distinct, the word 'cow' should refer to the individual cow as characterised by the generic character of cow (*gotva-viśiṣṭa gau*).[7]

It may be argued that *jāti* cannot exist by itself except as inherent in *vyakti*. Mind cannot comprehend *jāti* alone devoid

[7]TMK IV-78. *padāni tadviśiṣṭāmtāmabhidadhati.*

of *vyakti*. In view of this, even if a word refers to *jāti*, it would also refer to *vyakti* indirectly. But such a view, Vedānta Deśika urges, does not support the Mīmāṁsa theory. It only amounts to saying that words refer to objects as characterised by *jāti*.

An importat point to remember is that, according to the Viśiṣṭādvaitin, *jāti* and *vyakti* are inseparable (*apṛthaksiddha*). That is, *jāti* does not exist independently except as inherent in the substance. Similarly, *jāti* cannot be comprehended directly by the sense organs except as related to the substance, because the sense organs do not have direct contact with the qualities but only with the substance. Unless the substance is cognised, *jāti* cannot be known. Therefore, a word denotes an object as characterised by *jāti*.

Mīmāṁsakas raise another objection against the Viśiṣṭādvaitin's theory. Though it is admitted that the knowledge of *vyakti* is needed for understanding *jāti*, it need not necessarily follow that the reference to *vyakti* should be through *jāti* only. Such a reference to *vykti* can take place by adopting a secondary meaning of the word (*lakṣaṇā*). The following argument is put forward in support of the view. There are infinite number of individuals, and, instead of admitting that the word refers to all such individuals, it is more appropriate to accept the reference to *jāti* only, which is one and common to all. Therefore, all words can have direct reference to *jāti* only.[8] If it is asked what then is the difference between the word *gotva* and the word *go*, the reply is that the former is a specific term referring to *gotva jāti* only, whereas the latter is a general term referring to cow in general which is the substratum (*ādhāra* for *gotva*). That is *gotva* to which the word has direct reference also implies indirectly *go*, the individual cow (*vyakti*), because *gotva* depends on *go*.

Vedānta Deśika refutes this view by adopting a counter-argument. The above explanation should also hold good in respect of words such as *pācaka* (a cook), which is technically known as *upādhi-śabda*. *Pācakatva* or the quality in the form of capacity to cook belongs to *pācaka* or the person who cooks. Though it is not a generic character (*jāti*) like *gotva* in the case of cow, it is still a quality belonging to the individual cook. If, according to the Mīmāṁsa theory, the word *pācaka*

[8]TMK IV-80. *jātau śaktiḥ laghutvāt, bhavati ca vacasām bhāṣaṇaṃ jātimātre.*

does not have direct reference to the *vyakti*, it should denote only *pācakatva*, the capacity to cook. *Pācakatva* is not a generic term unlike *gotva*, because the act of cooking (*pāka-kriyā*) is unlimited. It is therefore appropriate to accept a reference of the word *pācaka* to the individual cook rather than to his capacity to cook (*pācakatva*).

Words are classified into three types: (*a*) *jāti-vācaka*, referring to the generic character such as cow; (*b*) *guṇa-vācaka*, referring to qualities such as 'white' or yellow; and (*c*) *kriyā-vācaka*, referring to activity such as *pācaka*. Just as the words which refer to jāti invariably denote the objects to which it is inseparably related, the words referring to qualities (*guṇa-vāci-śabda*) also denote the objects to which they belong. Thus, for example, the expression 'white cloth' (*śuklo paṭaḥ*), the term 'white' which is a *guṇa-vāci-śabda*, denotes the cloth as qualified by whiteness. There is however some exception to this rule. If a term referring to a quality is used in a specific sense to mean a *guṇa* only, as in the example 'whiteness of cloth' (*paṭasya śuklaḥ*), it denotes only the quality and not a substance as qualified by a quality. The important point to note is when two terms are found in apposition (in the same *vibhakti*), one referring to a substance (*viśeṣya*) and the other to a quality (*viśeṣaṇa*), as for example, *paṭaḥ śuklaḥ* (white cloth), the term referring to the *guṇa* invariably denotes the substance as qualified by the quality because the two are inseparably related.[9] On the basis of the above logical principle, the Viśiṣṭādvaitin maintains that the words which refer to body (*śarira-vācaka-śabda*) such as *deva*, *manuṣya* denote ultimately the *jivas* or souls within the body. As there is an inseparable relationship between the body and the soul,[10] the word referring to the body denotes the *jiva* as

[9]This point has been discussed in detail by Rāmānuja in *Śri-bhāṣya* while examining the Vedic statement *aruṇayā ekahāyanyā pingākṣyā gavā somaṁ kriṇāti* (he buys the *soma* juice by means of a one-year old cow of brown colour, etc.). The issue involved here is whether the quality of browness connoted by the term *aruṇayā* applies to *gau* (cow) or not. The *prima facie* view is that it does not extend to the substance. This is criticised by the Mimāṁsakas, and it is established that the quality denoted by the term extends to the substance also. The *Mimāṁsā Sūtra* (3-1-12) says : *arthaikatve dravya-guṇayoḥ aikakarmyānniyamḥ syāt*. Rāmānuja adopts this principle. See RB I-1-13, pp. 231-39.

[10]That body and soul are inseparable is discussed in the Chapter I.

associated with the physical body. Thus, for instance, in the statement 'man comes', the word 'man' does not mean only the physical body but the *jiva* associated with the body. Taking a Vedic statement 'the Brāhmaṇa offers the sacrifice' (*Brāhmaṇo yajeta*), the word 'Brāhmaṇa' does not merely mean the body but the *jiva* associated with the Brāhmaṇa body. In all such cases, the agent for action is the *jiva*, and hence the words though they refer to the body of a human being as *manuṣya* or of a divine being as *deva*, should bear the primary import to the *jiva* within. Here also there is an exception to this general principle. When the word *śarira* bears a determined denotation (*niṣkarṣaka śabda*) as in the example *manuṣya-śarira* (human body), it only denotes the body and not the *jiva*.

In support of the above theory a philosophical explanation based on the Upaniṣadic text is offered. The Upaniṣad says that *Paramātman* or the Supreme Being enters into all entities in the universe through the medium of *jiva* and gives names and forms to them.[11] The implication of this statement, as explained by Rāmānuja, is that Brahman is immanent in all the things in the universe and is also their inner controller, and, in view of this, it is held that there is an inseparable relationship between the Supreme Being and the universe consisting of individual souls and all material entities. *Jiva* exists in all the material entities including human body. The relation is one of body to the soul (*śarirātma-sambandha*). The theory of body-soul relation is discussed in a later chapter.[12]

Arising out of this metaphysical position, the Viśiṣṭādvaitin advances the theory that all words which refer to the individuals denote the *jivātman* which is the soul for the body and through that *jiva*, the *Parmātman* for whom *jiva* is a *śarira*. All entities in the universe, both sentient as well as non-sentient, constitute the body or *śarira* of *Iśvara* insofar as they subsist on *Iśvara* and are also controlled by Him. *Iśvara* is the *śariri* or *Ātman* for all sentient and non-sentient entities. All words referring to them therefore denote ultimately *Iśvara*. Keeping this philosophic truth in mind, the sages describe that all words

[11]Ch UP VI-3-2. *anena jivenātmanā anupraviśya nāmarūpe vyākaravāṇi.*
[12]See Section 'Universe as an Integral Part of Brahman in Chapter VIII.

rest on *Paramātman.*[13] Laymen who are not aware of this truth believe that words denote empirical objects in the universe with restricted meaning and not *Paramātman.*[14]

It may be argued that according to our common experience, words only denote empirical objects in the universe. No one means by these words *Īśvara*, since He is beyond our apprehension. Words in common usage either refer to a material object or a living being or a divine Being. The word 'pot' refers to a material object, *caitra* (name of a person) to a living being and Brahman to a divine Being. This is how the denotative power of words is determined. If such a distinction is not maintained, then all words would convey the same meaning which is absurd. Further, if a particular word does not bear a specific meaning, it is to be understood only in its secondary sense. Thus, for instance, the expression 'The King is Kingdom' (*Rājā-rāṣṭra*) does not mean, taking its primary import, that King himself is Kingdom but is understood in a secondary sense to mean that there is a close affinity between the two. It is in the same way that the statement *Sarvaṁ Brahma* is to be understood. It is not therefore appropriate to say that all words denote *Paramātman.*

Vedânta Deśika does not agree with this view. It is true that words *prima facie* refer to the objects in the universe, but their fuller import must be understood on the basis of Vedântic knowledge. From a purely common sense point of view, words no doubt denote objects of our common experience. To this extent the primary import of words is objects denoted by them. But from the standpoint of a Vedântin, the primary import of words is in respect of *Paramātman.*[15]

[13]*Viṣṇupurāṇa* I-14-23. *natāḥ sma sarva-vacasām pratiṣṭha yatra śāśvati. Tait. Āraṇyaka* 31-11. *sarve vedāḥ yatraikam bhavanti.*

[14]TMK IV-85. *pākaiśca jagati tasya apratīteḥ bhaṅktvā prayogaḥ.* See RB II-3-17, pp. 572-73.

[15]TMK IV-86. *vyutpatteḥ pūraṇam hi śruti-śirasi kṛtam.* See SS, p. 238. *vedāntaśravaṇena hi vyutpattiḥ pūryate.* It is on the basis of this principle that the famous Upaniṣadic text 'That Thou Art' is interpreted by Rāmānuja to mean that 'thou' ultimately refers to 'that' or *Paramātman* and the two are one in the sense that the individual as *Īśvara* associated with the soul (*jīva-śarīrako paramātmā*) is same as *Īśvara,* the primary cause of the universe.

Taking the stand on Nyāya theory, it may be said that *śarīrī* means one who is the master of the body (*adhipati*) and that reference to *Paramātman* should be understood in a figurative sense as in the example, 'King is Kingdom'. The Viśiṣṭādvaitin does not accept this view. *Śarīrī* in his system means more than being a lord of *śarīra*. It implies the organic relationship between the *śarīra* and *śarīrī*. For Nyāya school, it is just the association of the body with the soul. In view of the inseparable relation that exists between *Paramātman* and the universe, the Viśiṣṭādvaitin upholds the view, unlike the Naiyāyika, that all words denote ultimately *Paramātman*.

III. CRITICISM OF SPHOṬAVĀDA

As against the commonly accepted theory that words convey meaning and through the knowledge of the meaning denote the objects, there is a school of thought ascribed to Grammarians, which maintains that words as such do not directly produce the knowledge of the thing. The letters, a group of which constitute a word, generate the essence of sound known as *sphoṭa*[16] which produces the knowledge of the thing. The following argument is advanced in support of this theory. A word has several letters. Do these letters convey the meaning individually or collectively? If it be the former, then the very first letter should convey the meaning. This does not happen. If the letters convey the meaning in a collective form that power not being found in the first letter, how can all the letters combined together have such a power to convey the meaning? Therefore, words as such do not convey the meaning. A special potency or essence becomes manifest in letters when they are combined in a particular form to produce the meaning.

Vedānta Deśika refutes this theory on the ground that there is no proof for the existence of anything like *sphoṭa* or word essence. All that we know on the basis of our experience is that words convey their meaning directly. As regards the dialectical

[16] *Sphoṭa* means that from which the meaning becomes explicit (*sphuṭati asmāt arthaḥ*). According to the advocates of this theory, there are eight kinds of *sphoṭa*: *varṇa, pada, vākya, akhaṇḍa pada, akhaṇḍa vākya, varṇa-jāti sphoṭa, pada-jāti sphoṭa* and *vākya-jāti sphoṭa*.

argument advanced by the *sphoṭa-vādin*, it is pointed out that several causal factors are required for the production of an effect. The question may be raised whether the power (*śakti*) to bring forth the effect exists in each of these causal factors or in the collective totality of these. If it be the former, then the effect is to be brought about by that single causal factor. It is not so. If it be the latter, how could the power to generate the effect which is ineffective in one causal factor be found in the collective totality? In the circumstance, we have to admit that the combination of all the accessory factors has the power to cause the effect. This is known as *sāmagraikya-nīti*. On the basis of this principle, it should be possible to explain that the letters in a word collectively convey the meaning. In the same way, the sentence which is a collection of words produces the meaning of the sentence. This apart, it is not appropriate to postulate that any additional supernormal sound power (*sphoṭa*) generates the meaning of the words.

There is another argument advanced in support of *sphoṭavāda*. It is no doubt true that the word essence is not known by means of perception. Even so, its postulation becomes necessary because letters are not permanent (*anitya*) and it is not possible to explain, except through sphoṭa, that the same letters always do convey the same meaning (*śābda-bodha*) of the words. The reply to this argument is that whatever causes the manifestation of *sphoṭa*, the same should be able to convey the meaning of words.[17] If the *varṇas*, though non-permanent, produce the sphoṭa, the same *varṇas* can as well cause the *śābda-bodha*. There is no need to postulate a new concept like *sphoṭa* for the purpose.

There is a mention of *śabda-brahma* by the sages in the Āgamas and some hold the view that this may imply that *sphoṭa* is a Reality. But this is not a correct interpretation of the concept, according to Vedānta Deśika. *Śabda* here refers to the evolute of *ahaṁkāra-tattva* which is material in character (*acit*). It may be said that the *śabda* which is material refers to the gross sound (*sthūla śabda*), but there is a subtle sound (*sūkṣma śabda*) which is eternal and which causes the knowledge of the meaning of words. Even this contention is untenable,

[17]TMK IV-88.

because no such subtle sound is known to convey the meaning of the words. The mere existence of such a sound cannot generate the meaning of the words. It is only through the knowledge of words that we derive their meaning. The subtle sound is not therefore the cause of *śābda-bodha*.

IV. BUDDHIST THEORY OF VĀKYĀRTHA

After discussing the import of words, Vedânta Deśika takes up the question whether or not a sentence conveys directly its meaning. According to some Buddhists and Grammarians, sentences and the meaning they convey do not really exist but they are just the projection of the mind or mere mental processes. The following argument is adopted in support of this theory. Is the meaning conveyed by a sentence different from the meaning of the individual words of the sentence or is it nondifferent from it? If it be different, then the meaning conveyed by each sentence being different, there would be infinite number of meanings (*akhaṇḍa*). From this it would follow that in the expressions 'bring the cow', and 'bring the horse', the meaning of the word 'bring' in each case should be different. This is opposed to our experience. If, on the contrary, it is said that the meaning of words remains the same as the meaning of sentence, then the meaning of those words should be restricted to that particular sentence. When the same words occur in a separate sentence, the knowledge of the meaning of the sentence should arise without the knowledge of the meaning of the words. This would be logically fallacious (*vyabhicāra*). In the same way, even with regard to the words, the question arises whether the letters convey meaning individually or collectively. As already pointed out, these issues when analysed lead to the conclusion that words do not really convey the meaning. Therefore, the advocates of this theory canclude that both the sentences as well as the meanings they are supposed to convey are not real but are simply mental fabrications. This theory is known as *pratibhā-vākyārtha-vāda*.[18]

Vedānta Deśika rejects this theory on the ground that it is against our experience. Knowledge or *buddhi* is an internal

[18]SS IV-90, p. 239.

entity whereas sentences and their meanings are external phenomena. The two cannot therefore be one and the same thing. Whatever criticisms are levelled by Buddhists against the opponent, the same would equally apply to their own theory. It cannot be said that as there is no connecting link between that which is regarded as a sentence and that which is considered as its total meaning, the projection of knowledge itself is to be admitted as the basis of identity. Empirical usages such as that it is a sentence and that this is its meaning, etc. are made on the basis of the group of words conveying a connected meaning.[19] Whether the words convey the meaning individually or collectively is to be determined with reference to the nature of the sentence and on the basis of our experience.

V. FUNCTION OF WORDS IN A SENTENCE

Do the words in a sentence convey the meaning in isolation or as connected together? There are two different views offered by the two schools of Mīmāṁsā regarding the function of words in a sentence. According to one view, known as *anvitābhidhāna-vāda*, held by the Prābhākaras, words convey their own sense not in isolation but as connected together. In a sentence no word gives by itself any clear meaning but only as related to other words.[20] According to the other view, known as *abhihitānvaya-vāda*, held by the Bhāṭṭas, words primarily signify their own senses; but the meaning thus derived conveys the combined meaning of the sentence (*vākyārtha*).[21] Vedānta Deśika regards the first view as a sounder one.

By way of elucidation of the first theory, it is stated that a word is a combination of two elements—the root and a suffix—and the two, though they have different meanings by themselves, convey a combined meaning. This is clear, for example, from the word *daṇḍi* or one who is holding a stick. The word *daṇḍi* conveys the sense that the person is having a stick. Here the root as well as the suffix of the word combined together convey a unitary meaning. In the same way, the words in a

[19]TMK IV-90.

[20]SS IV-91, p. 240. *padajātaṁ śrutaṁ sarvaṁ smāritānanvitārthakam.*

[21]*Ibid. padair abhihitāḥ padārthāḥ vākyārthaṁ bodhayantīti abhihitānvayaḥ.*

sentence convey the combined meaning of the words as related to each other.[22] When we hear a sentence, we get the meaning of all the words in it as connected together. The words as related to each other cause the memory of the objects to which they refer and thereby convey their meaning.

According to the *abhihitānvaya-vāda*, words primarily convey their own meaning and the meaning thus conveyed produces in us a knowledge of mutual connection existing between the words. It is the knowledge of such a connection (*anvaya*) that causes the connected meaning of the sentence. If such a position is accepted, one has to postulate several functions or powers (*śakti*) for the words: (*a*) the power to convey their meaning; (*b*) the power of the meaning of words to convey their inter-connection; (*c*) the power to connect the combined meaning with the objects referred to. Why can we not admit, asks Vedānta Deśika, that all the three functions are done by the words themselves simultaneously. If it is held that words convey only their meaning without accepting the capacity of words to convey their interconnection, then the function of the words would cease with the first act and then they become powerless to perform the other two functions. According to the Viśiṣṭādvaitin, words first cause the memory of the objects denoted by them and not the knowledge of the meaning; then we try to understand the relationship of the different senses conveyed by the words on the basis of the memory, and thereafter we get the collective meaning of the entire sentence. If we accept Bhāṭṭa's position, words primarily convey their meaning only; the meaning thus conveyed by words in the sentence will remain unrelated. In the absence of a connected sense, the total meaning of the sentence does not take place. *Anvitābhidhāna-vāda* of Prabhākara is therefore sounder than the *abhihitānvaya-vāda* of the Bhāṭṭas.[23]

[22]TMK IV-91. *anyonya-smāritārthānvitam abhidadhati svārtham evaṁ padāni.*

[23]Though this is the conclusion reached by Vedānta Deśika, he seems to justify in a way the Bhāṭṭa theory because of the acceptance of this view by Rāmānuja. There are some instances where the Bhaṭṭa theory holds good. Thus, for instance, in statements such as 'this is a cow' addressed to a child who is being instructed initially about a cow, the words as unconnected convey the meaning through which the object is identified. The Bhāṭṭa theory is not therefore totally rejected by Vedānta Deśika.

VI. IMPORT OF SAMĀNĀDHIKARAṆA-VĀKYA

While considering the logical import of a sentence, Vedânta Deśika discusses the issue whether a sentence or judgment in which the terms are found in apposition (*samānādhikaraṇa*) imply identity or difference. There are two kinds of sentences. In a sentence such as 'jar exists on the ground' (*bhutale ghaṭo vartate*), the words convey that the two entities, ground and jar, are different but are related to each other as *ādhāra* and *ādheya*. Such a sentence which indicates the difference between the two objects is known as *vyadhikaraṇa-vākya*. As a contrast to it there are sentences such as 'blue jar exists' (*nilo ghaṭaḥ vartate*) in which the two terms convey a sense of oneness, viz. that the jar as qualified by blueness exists. Such a sentence in which the two terms are found in apposition (that is, in the same *vibhakti*) is known as *samānādhikaraṇa-vākya*.

Jainas, who uphold the doctrine of *anaikānta*, argue that the *samānādhikaraṇa* sentence conveys difference as well as non-difference. In the judgment 'blue jar', the two terms 'blue' and 'jar' have different connotations and they indicate difference between blueness and the jar. At the same time, as the two terms are in apposition and refer to an attribute and the substance (*viśeṣaṇa* and *viśeṣya*), they convey a sense of identity (*abheda*) or non-difference between the substance and attribute.

This is not a correct view. Actually, blueness as a quality and pot as a substance are distinct. If the sentence conveys an import different from what it should be, it cannot become valid. But the sentence is a valid one and as such it is not correct to say that what is denoted by it is difference and non-difference. The doctrine of *saptabhaṅgi* is not acceptable to the Viśiṣṭādvaitin. The terms therefore convey the sense of difference only (*bheda*).

The Advaitin maintains the view that a *samānādhikaraṇa* sentence conveys a sense of identity. In the judgment 'blue jar' (*nilo ghaṭaḥ*), there are two elements: the entity characterised by blueness (*nilatva*) and the entity qualified by jarness (*ghaṭatva*), and the two cannot be identical. Therefore, we have to exclude the attributive aspect (*viśeṣaṇāṁśa*), viz. the *nilatva* and *ghaṭatva* and accept identity of the substance (*viśeṣya*) which is the basis for both. To illustrate this point the Advaitin cites the example of *pratyabhijñā* or knowledge by recognition. In the judgment 'He is the same Devadatta' which is based on recognition, an identity of the earlier time when Devadatta was seen elsewhere and the present time when he is again seen here is not possible because of self-contradiction. We therefore overlook the time as well as the place factors which are the qualifications, and by accepting only the personality aspect affirm the identity in the sense that the person seen then and now is one and the same. On the same principle, the sentences where terms are found in apposition as in the example of blue lotus, we should admit that their import is identity. The Advaitin extends the same logic to the interpretation of the famous Upaniṣadic text *Tat-tvam-asi*, and affirms the identity of the individual self and the Absolute.

Vedānta Deśika rejects this theory for more than one reason. In the first instance, the interpretation offered by the Advaitin is in direct conflict with our experience. The qualities connoted by the terms are so obvious that it is a self-contradiction (*bādha*) to say that the entity denoted by the terms is devoid of them. Secondly, if the entity denoted by the terms is not regarded as one qualified by the attribute, it would follow that such judgments as 'the person is holding a stick' (*daṇḍi puruṣaḥ*) denote an identity or non-difference between stick and person. This is absurd and even the Advaitin does not accept it. Thirdly, the Advaitin does admit that the terms connote the qualities, but in the same breath he asserts that the object denoted by them is devoid of the qualities. This amounts to contradiction of one's own statement (*svavacana-virodha*). Finally, the illustration offered in support of his theory is faulty. When we say that he is the same Devadatta, we do not mean that the earlier and later times are identical. What we mean is that the person seen earlier (i.e. the person qualified by the earlier time) is the same as the one seen at a later period (i.e. the person qualified by the later time). If this interpretation were not admitted, it would lead to the Buddhist tenet that everything is momentary. Treating two different time units as identical or two space situations as one and the same would involve self-contradiction. But there is no contradiction if we conceive two different time units or two different space situations in succession (i.e. as succeeding events).[24]

The Advaitin puts forward another argument. If *samānādhikaraṇa-vākya* does not denote identity, it ceases to be *samānādhikaraṇa*. The definition of *sāmānādhikaraṇya*, as provided by the Grammarians, is that words which have different connotations denote one entity.[25] If what is connoted by each term in the sentence is separately applied to the object referred to (*viśeṣya*), the object or *viśeṣya* will have to be different because of the difference of the qualities. The assumption here is that each quality connoted by the term distinguishes the object from that qualified with another quality.[26] Thus, for instance, when we say Devadatta is *śyāma* (dark-complexioned) and *yuvā* (young), Devadatta as qualified by dark complexion is different from Devadatta as qualified by youth. This is not correct. It would therefore be appropriate to consider the *samānādhikaraṇa-vākya* as indicative of identity (*ekārthabodhaka*) as per the definition. Take, for instance, the judgment 'blue lotus' (*nīlam utpalam*). The word *nīla* means that which has the colour of blueness (*nīlatva*); *utpala* or lotus refers to that which has the characteristic of *utpalatva*. If both the terms denote the one and the same entity, then the blueness which is a *guṇa* (*nīlatva*) as well as the characteristic of *utpala* (*utpalatva*) which is a *jāti* would have to be identical. This is not so. The Advaitin therefore contends that we have to exclude the quality aspect and accept the identity of the substance aspect.

This interpretation of the Advaitin is not considered correct by Vedānta Deśika. The definition of *sāmānādhikaraṇya* is to be understood in such a way that it would not go against our experience. The correct implication of such a definition is that the terms connoting the different qualities of an object denote that the object as characterised by the qualities is one (*viśiṣṭa-vastu*). Taking the example of 'blue lotus' (*nīlotpala*), the two terms have different connotations: blue meaning that

[24]TMK IV-95. *desabhedaḥ kramāt syāt.*

[25]*Mahābhāṣya* on *Pāṇinisūtra*. *bhinnapravṛttinimittānāṁ śabdānām ekasmin arthe vṛttiḥ sāmānādhikaraṇyam.*

[26]SS IV-97, p. 244. *viśeṣaṇabhedāt viśeṣyabhedaḥ.*

which has the quality of blueness; lotus means that which has the characteristic of lotusness. Though the terms have different connotations, they imply that the substance which is the basis for the qualities (in which the two qualities inhere) is one and the same as characterised by them. It does not mean, as Advaitin believes, that lotus as devoid of its quality of blueness is one.

The above explanation holds good in respect of all *samānādhikaraṇa-vākyas* where the qualities connoted by the terms inhere in the same substance as in the statement that Devadatta is *śyāma* (dark-complexioned) and *yuvā* (youthful). But there are statements in which the qualities connoted by the terms apply to different objects. Thus, for instance, in the statement 'the cow with horn and the cow without horn' (*khaṇḍo muṇḍo gauḥ*), the attribute of being with horn and being without horn does not inhere in the same cow but in two different cows, because the two qualities are mutually opposed (*viruddha-viśeṣaṇa*). In such examples, the terms in the statement denote two different entities.[27] We have to take into consideration whether the qualities connoted by the terms inhere in the same object (*ekāśraya*) or in different objects (*bhinnāśraya*), and on the basis of this it is to be determined whether or not the *samānādhikaraṇa-vākya* denotes one object as characterised.

There are two strong objections raised by the Advaitin against the view held by the Viśiṣṭādvaitin. The first one which we have already considered is that if all the *viśeṣaṇas* mentioned in the *samānādhikaraṇa* sentence apply to one entity as the Viśiṣṭādvaitin claims, then the *viśeṣaṇas* too would become identical. Thus, in the example of 'blue lotus' the quality of blueness and the quality of lotusness would have to be identical. This is not so. Hence it is appropriate to admit that identity is in respect of substance only. The second objection is based on the assumption that if the different attributes are applicable to the same one entity, one attribute will become the basis for another (*anyonya-samavāya-prasaṅgaḥ*). The question is asked whether the attributes are applicable to the substance in succession or together. If together, then

[27]TMK IV-97. *kvāpi tu vihateḥ viśeṣyam bhinnaṁ bhavati.*

it would amount to the identity of the attributes (*anyonyaikya*); if it be in succession, then one quality of the substance would become the basis for the second. Thus, for example, in the statement that Devadatta is dark complexioned and young, it would mean that the characteristic of Devadatta (*Devadattatva*) should become the basis for the quality of dark complexion (*shyāmatva*). Thus it is argued that one attribute becomes the *ādhāra* for the second. This is also absurd. It is therefore appropriate, contends the Advaitin, that attributive aspects have to be overlooked and identity of the *viśesya* or substance only is to be maintained in accordance with the definition of *sāmānādhikaranya*.

The first objection is already answered. It is not necessary that the qualities which refer to the one entity should also become identical. Regarding the second objection in the judgment 'jar on the ground' (*bhūtale ghaṭaḥ*), only the ground is the *ādhāra* for the jar but not the characteristic of ground (*bhūtalatva*). This is borne out by experience. In the same way, the substance denoted by the terms is the *ādhāra* for the qualities connoted by the different terms in so far as these qualities inhere in the same substance. What is implied by the *samānādhikaraṇa-vākya* is that the substance as characterised by the qualities which are not mutually opposed to each other is one. It does not imply that all the other qualities which do not inhere in the substance are also applicable to it. In other words, all that *samānādhikaraṇa-vākya* means is that the substance as the basis of the qualities referred to is one. It does not mean that the substance denoted by the terms is devoid of the qualities. If the words do not have connotation, they would be meaningless (*nirnimitta*). Terms devoid of proper connotation cannot even denote the substance.[28]

There is another type of *samānādhikaraṇa-vākya* in which both the terms are found in apposition but its import is the negation of what is implied by one term by the other (*bādhārtha*). This is explained by an illustration. A person who sees a broken pillar at distance mistakes it for a thief. Another person who knows the truth makes a statement to the effect that the thief seen by

[28] TMK IV-98. *nirnimitte anupākhye svarūpe tātparyaṁ kvacidapi na bhavet.*

you (i.e. what you saw as thief) is only a broken pillar (*tvad-dṛṣṭaḥ coraḥ sthāṇuḥ*). In this statement the two terms 'thief' and 'pillar' stand in apposition, but its import is not identity but the negation of being a thief (*coratva*) in respect of the pillar. This is known as *bādhārtha-sāmānādhikaraṇya*. That is, it is a *samānādhi-karaṇa* statement in which what is implied by one term is negated in respect of the other. On the basis of this analogy, the Advaitin interprets the Upaniṣadic statement that all this (the entire universe) is Brahman (*sarvaṁ khalvidam brahma*) to mean that universe stands negated in Brahman. The implication of this argument is that such *samānādhikaraṇa* statements refer only to the *svarūpa* or the pure substance devoid of all attributes.

The Viśiṣṭādvaitin, who refutes this theory, points out that the negation of one *dharma* in another does not lead to the conclusion that the object referred to is devoid of all other characteristics. Thus, in the instance cited above, the negation of *coratva* (being thief) in respect of the pillar does not imply the negation of other *dharmas* or characteristics of the pillar. Though the pillar being a thief is denied, the pillar possesses other characteristics such as its shape, height, etc.[29] Let us examine the statement: 'The thief seen by you is only a broken pillar.' In this statement, the word thief refers to an entity which possesses certain characteristics common to a human being such as shape, height, etc. which cause the delusion. The words *sthāṇu* or pillar refers to the object possessing the characteristic features of a broken pillar (*sthāṇutva*). The combined meaning of the statement is that what you consider as a thief is only a broken wooden pillar. There is no room for negation of one characteristic in respect of the other. On the contrary, the statement indicates the relationship that exists between the two entities as substance and its attribute.

It may be argued that the word *sthāṇu* refers only to the *svarūpa* of the object and not to an object as qualified by *sthāṇutva*. Similarly, the word *cora* means one being devoid of *coratva* (*coratvābhāvavān*). Thus, there is no reference to a qualified object (*saviśeṣa-vastu*). In reply, it is pointed out that if only *svarūpa* of *sthāṇu* without its characteristics is seen, there is no

[29]TMK IV-100. *yat bādhārthaṁ samānādhikaraṇa-vacanaṁ tat aviśiṣṭam na vadet.*

possiblity of mistaking it for a thief. In the absence of not knowing the object without its characteristic features, there is no scope for saying that it is not a thief. Illusion takes place only when the special character of the object is not known. If the special character is not known, then the illusion also cannot be removed. Therefore, it is to be admitted that the pillar as characterised by *sthāṇutva* in the form of its structure, etc. is known. If this position is accepted, it cannot be said that the import of *samānādhikaraṇa-vākya* is pure substance devoid of characteristics. On the contrary, its import is that it is a qualified entity (*saviśeṣa*).[30]

VII. IMPORT OF LAKṢAṆA-VĀKYA

Before this chapter is concluded there is one other important issue to be discussed in connection with the logical import of sentences. There are verbal statements which are in the form of definition of a concept or a thing. Such statements are commonly found both in the Upaniṣads as well as in our ordinary usage. The issue to be considered is whether such statements purporting to offer definition (*lakṣaṇa-vākya*) denote the very *svarūpa* of the object or the object as characterised. The problem which assumes great importance in Vedānta arises in connection with the interpretation of the famous *Taittirīya Upaniṣadic* text *Satyaṁ Jñānam Anantam Brahma* (Brahman is Truth, Knowledge and Infinitude) which is regarded as a statement offering the definition of Brahman. This text, according to the Advaita Vedānta, refers to the very *svarūpa* of Brahman and not intended to describe Brahman as characterised with the three attributes. It conveys an undifferentiated and non-relational sense (*akhaṇḍārtha*). According to the Viśiṣṭādvaita Vedānta, this text defines Brahman as qualified by *satyatva*, *jñānatva* and *anantatva*. We take up the interpretation of the Upaniṣadic text and the fundamental issue whether Brahman is *nirviśeṣa* or *saviśeṣa* in a later chapter. We confine here to the discussion of the underlying principle whether a *lakṣaṇa-vākya* refers to a qualified entity.

In support of the Advaitin's theory, the statement 'the moon is that which is luminous' (*prakṛṣṭa-prakāśaḥ candraḥ*) is cited.

[30]TMK IV-100.

A person who cannot identify the moon in the sky asks another person: which is the moon (*kaḥ candraḥ*)?' And in reply he is told that that which is very luminous in the sky is the moon. This statemnet, according to the Advaitin, refers to the very *svarūpa* of the moon and is not intended to give a descirption of the moon in terms of its characteristics. The main argument in support of this view is that it is a statement offering the definition. All statements which aim to provide a definition of a thing denote only the *svarūpa* of the object.

According to the Viśiṣṭādvaitin, the argument advanced by the Advaitin is untenable. The definition is primarily intended to bring out the essential characteristic of a thing. In fact a thing can be defined only in terms of its essential characteristic. The contention that the definition refers to the *svarūpa* of an object as devoid of all its characteristics amounts to a self-contradiction (*svoktibādha*).[31] Taking into consideration the definition of the moon as a luminous object, Vedānta Deśika explains that it does not refer to a moon as devoid of any characteristics but to an object as characterised by luminosity. If a person is not aware of the *prakāśa* or luminous character of the moon, he would not be able even to identify the moon. An object is identified only with reference to its essential character. The question 'what is moon?' does not refer to the very *svarūpa* of the moon devoid of luminosity but, on the contrary, to a moon shining with luminosity. This is obvious from the nature of the reply which is in the form of a description of the moon as a luminous object The person who asks the question about the moon should have had some general idea about the moon, viz. that it is a planet appearing at night in the sky; otherwise he should have asked this question even in a day time. While he is asking the question, he must be certainly seeing the shining object; otherwise he would not have grasped the meaning of the statement made in response to his query. Soon after hearing it, what he needs to know is the relation between the word 'moon' and the object denoted by it. This is known as *saṁjñā-saṁjñi-sambandha* or a relation of what is denoted to what denotes it. What is therefore intended to be conveyed by the statement is that the word 'moon' denotes the luminous object in the sky. Under no circumstance

[31]TMK IV-96.

is it intended to point out the *svarūpa* of the object as devoid of characteristics. Thus, the import of *lakṣaṇa-vākya* is not *nirviśeṣa svarūpa*.

The foregoing discussion of the theories relating to the logical import of words leads to the conclusion that the words referring to the *guṇa* or *jāti* or *śarira* denote the entity or the individual as qualified by them as the two are inherently related. Similarly, in the case of judgments or statements where the terms are found in apposition, the import of the statement is in respect of the object or the entity as qualified by the qualities connoted by the terms. The ontological implication of this theory is that scriptural statements that describe or define the nature of ultimate Reality convey the fact that Brahman is *saviśeṣa* or qualified with attributes. Verbal testimony in general and scriptural statements in particular do not support the theory of undifferentiated reality.

CHAPTER FOUR

Theory of Knowledge

THEORY of knowledge occupies an important place in *Tattva-muktā-kalāpa*. One entire part of the text known as *Buddhisara*, is devoted to a comprehensive consideration of this subject. The main reason for giving such a great attention to this matter is to remove the confusion caused by various theories advanced by rival schools of thought.[1] After a critical evaluation of these theories, the Viśiṣṭādvaita system seeks to present a theory of knowledge which is in conformity with the Upaniṣadic teaching and common experience. It attempts to overcome the defects found in the radical theories advocated by the idealists as well as some of the realists.

In examining theory of knowledge, there are three important points to be taken into consideration. The first and most important one is the nature of knowledge, that is, knowledge in relation to the subject. The second point is knowledge in relation to external objects. The third one is the means of knowledge (*pramāṇas*) and their validity. We have already dealt with the *pramāṇas* in the previous chapters. We shall consider in the present chapter knowledge in relation to the subject. The second point, viz. knowledge in relation to the external object will be discussed in the subsequent chapter.

I. KNOWLEDGE AS AN ATTRIBUTE OF JĪVA

According to the Viśiṣṭādvaita system, knowledge which is known as *jñāna*[2] is an attribute of *jiva*. It is therefore described

[1]TMK IV-134. *udvelāpārtha-jalpān apahasitum*. Vedānta Deśika has mentioned ten different theories of knowledge.

[2]The other terms used for knowledge are *buddhi, saṁvit, dhīḥ, prajñā, mati, anubhūti, śemuṣī, medhā, dhiṣaṇā* and *manīṣā*. All these are synonymous words and mean the same thing in Viśiṣṭādvaita system.

as ***dharmabhūta-jñāna,*** attributive knowledge, as distinct from the *jiva* or the knowing subject which as a permanent spiritual entity is also of the nature of consciousness (*jñāna-svarūpa*). *Jñāna* is understood as that which reveals an object (*artha-prakāśaḥ*).[3] This is an important character of knowledge which is not found in a material object. Knowledge reveals an object, whereas a material object cannot do so. The function of knowledge is therefore revelation or manifestation of something outside it. To whom then does it reveal? It reveals the object to a knowing subject or a conscious self. The self knows what is revealed to it by knowledge, whereas knowledge only *shows* but cannot *know* it. Knowledge is comparable to a light which reveals the presence of an object but does not know it. That which knows but does not reveal the objects outside it except itself is technically known as *pratyak* or *svasmaibhāsamānatva.* This is the characteristic feature of the self. That which only reveals to the self but does not know what it reveals is described as *parāk or parasmāevabhāsamānatva.* Knowledge is of this kind. Knowledge, in other words, reveals the object always for the knowing subject; the self or *jiva*, on the other hand, cannot reveal the objects but knows what is revealed to it by knowledge. This is the fundamental distinction between the self and the knowledge. Knowledge thus belongs, on the one hand, to a subject and, on the other, as is implied in the judgment 'I know this', has reference to an object. As an essential attribute of the *jiva*, it necessarily pertains to the self. In view of this, knowledge is known as *dharma-bhūta-jñāna*. The word *dharma-bhūta* is appended to *jñāna* in order to distinguish it from the *dharmi-jñāna* or knowledge which constitutes the very essence of *jiva*.[4]

There is a logical justification for maintaining *dharma-bhūta-jñāna* as distinct from *svarūpa-jñāna*. The *jiva* is eternal and

[3]The fuller definition of knowledge, as offered by Rāmānuja, is that which reveals an object to its subject by virtue of its intrinsic capacity. RB I-1-1, p. 65. *sva-sattayaiva svāśrayam prati kasyacit viṣayasya prakāśanam ḥi samvedanam.*

[4]*Jiva* is regarded as *jñāna-svarūpa* in order to emphasise the fact that it is spiritual in character (*ajaḍa*). The *svarūpa-jñāna* is not knowledge as ordinarily understood, because it is not functional as revealing the external objects to a subject.

immutable, as established by śruti texts and as such it cannot undergo any modification; whereas, knowledge is subject to constant modification, as is warranted by our experience. Knowledge manifests itself when it comes into contact with objects through mind and sense organs and it ceases to function whenever it is not in contact with any object. If *svarūpa-jñāna* alone is accepted, then the modifications that take place in respect of knowledge will have to be credited to the *jiva* and this would militate against its immutable character.

Some schools of thought such as Sāṅkhya-yoga and Advaita attempt to uphold the immutable character of the self by conceiving the internal organ (*antaḥkaraṇa*) as the ego to which all mental modifications are attributed. As will be shown in the chapter on *jiva*, the theory of *antaḥkaraṇa* as the empirical ego is philosophically untenable.

Rāmānuja finds the justification for advocating the above theory of knowledge on the basis of the Upaniṣadic teaching and the *Vedānta-sūtra*. The Upaniṣadic text states that the self is the knower (*boddhā*).[5] Based on the Upaniṣad the *Vedānta-sūtra* also affirms that *jivātman* is a knower (*jñātā*).[6] *Jñātā* means that which is the substrate or subject of knowledge. Accordingly, knowledge is regarded as an attribute (*dharma*) of *jiva*. According to Rāmānuja, the relation of *jiva* to knowledge is comparable to the flame (of a lamp) and its luminosity (*prabhā-prabhāvat*). They are distinct but not physically separable. As in this system substance and attribute are distinct but inseparable, it is logically justifiable to regard *jñāna* as an essential and inseparable attribute of *jiva*. This point is also discussed further in the chapter on the nature of *jiva*.

II. KNOWLEDGE AS SELF-LUMINOUS

Another very important character of knowledge is that it is self-luminous. That is, knowledge reveals itself as well as the object. This is described as *svayam-prakāśa*. It means, according to the Viśiṣṭādvaitin, that *jñāna*, at the time of revealing an

[5]*Praśna Upaniṣad*. IV-9. *eṣa hi draṣṭā...boddhā....*

[6]VS II-3-19. *jño'ta eva*. See RB. *ayam ātmā jñātṛsvarūpa eva, na jñanamātram.*

object does not require to be manifested by another *jñāna*. The common example given to illustrate this point is the light (*dipa*). Light reveals the object around it but does not require another light for it to be revealed.

The existence of external objects becomes known to us through knowledge. How do we know that there is a knowledge about these objects? The Naiyāyikas explain that this is known through mental perception. In the first instance the cognition of an object arises in the form 'this is a pot'; after this cognition takes place, it is related to the self by the mind as 'I know this pot'. The second reperception is described as *anuvyavasāya*. According to the Viśiṣṭādvaitin, knowledge, when it reveals an object, does not require another knowledge to reveal itself. If that were so, it would lead to the fallacy of infinite regress. *Vyavasāya* and *anuvyavasāya* are therefore identical.

Vedānta Deśika advances a logical argument in support of the theory. The knowledge in question is self-luminous because it is of the nature of knowledge (*dhītvāt*); just like the knowledge that arises from the definition of the term *jñāna*; or as in the case of the knowledge of the omniscient *Īśvara*.[7]

The implication of the argument is that self-luminosity is the very nature of *jñāna*. When cognition of an object arises, it simultaneously reveals both itself and the object. The cognition in the form 'I know this object' reveals not only the object but also itself. This is possible because such a cognition is of the nature of knowledge. In other words, knowledge possesses the intrinsic character of self-revelation. Two illustrations are provided to explain this point. The first one is the definition of the term 'knowledge'. Knowledge is defined as that which is the cause of the empirical usage in respect of an entity. This definition of knowledge also includes in itself the knowledge that arises from the definition. The second illustration is the *jñāna* of *Īśvara* who is omniscient. It cannot be said that *Īśvara* knows everything other than His own knowledge. *Īśvara* should have known His own *jñāna*; otherwise He would not be omniscient. In order to know His own *jñāna*, another *jñāna* is not needed. If it were so, then there should be two different *jñānas*.

[7]TMK IV-1. *itaramatiḥ dhītvāt, buddhilakṣmādi-dhīvat svayaṁ-siddhā; yadvā sarvajña-dhīvat.*

This is not acceptable even to the Naiyāyikas. *Īśvara-jñāna* is therefore, admitted to be self-luminous. In the same way, the knowledge which arises in us is to be regarded as self-luminous.

Is it not a contradiction to say that knowledge cognises itself? We can touch another object by the tip of a finger but the same finger cannot touch itself. In the same way, knowledge which manifests the objects cannot reveal itself. This objection does not hold good, because knowledge has the capacity to do two functions simultaneously, viz. revelation of itself as well as the object. As already pointed out, there are instances such as the *Īśvara-jñāna*, definition of knowledge and light (*dipa*), which are capable of revealing themselves as well as others. This is technically known as *svaparanirvāhaka*. On the basis of the same principle, self-luminosity of knowledge is justified.

According to the Advaita Vedānta, what is self-luminous cannot be an object of another knowledge. Knowledge or *anubhūti* as it is termed, which refers to the transcendental consciousness, is self-luminous in the sense that it can never at any time become an object of another cognition.[8] If knowledge were the object of another cognition, it would be no better than a physical object. Hence the essential nature of knowledge should consist in its not being an object of cognition.

The Viśiṣṭādvaitin refutes this theory. The self-luminosity as conceived by the Advaitin is in direct conflict with our experience. We find in our ordinary experience that the knowledge of one person may become the content of the cognition of another. Thus, for instance, the experience of another individual is the object of the inferential knowledge based on the person's friendly or unfriendly appearance. Even in the case of the same individual, his past states of experience become the object of his cognition as expressed in the judgment: 'At one time I knew.' If knowledge were not admitted to be the object of another cognition, there would be an end to all empirical usage depending on speech.[9] All empirical usage takes place through the understanding of each other's thoughts.

[8]See *Tattvapradīpikā*, p. 9. *avedyatve satyaparokṣa-vyavahāra-yogyatā*. See also RB I-1-1, p. 38. *sā ca svatas siddhā, anubhūtitvāt; anyataḥ siddhau ghaṭādivat ananubhūtitva-prasaṅgaḥ*.

[9]TMK IV-2. *vedyatve sā jaḍā syāt iti vihatimat*.

The criticism of the Viśiṣṭādvaitin is based on the assumption that *jñāna*, as generally understood, is that which is related to a subject and an object. Such a knowledge is regarded by the Advaitin as empirical knowledge or the knowledge of the psychosis (*vṛtti-jñāna*), which could be the object of another cognition. The concept of self-luminosity (*svayaṁ-prakāśatva*) as understood in his system is applicable not to the empirical knowledge but to the transcendental knowledge which does not admit the subject-object distinction. It is identical with the Absolute Reality and is self-evident (*svatas-siddha*) in the sense that it is never the object of any empirical thought (*avedya*).

This theory is refuted by the Viśiṣṭādvaitin. As will be discussed presently, it is impossible to prove the existence of such a transcendental, undifferentiated consciousness. Even if it be assumed that such a consciousness exists, it is logically untenable to assert that consciousness is not an object of knowledge in the strict sense of the term. Thus, in the premise 'consciousness is self-luminous', does the term consciousness denote something or does it not? If it denotes something and if that be the Reality, then that becomes manifested insofar as it is the object of knowledge, conveyed by that term. If it be said that the nature of the Reality which is self-luminous is only restated by the term, even then the manifestation of it is inevitable inasmuch as it is the object of that cognition conveyed by the restatement. Thus, in some sense or other, consciousness is to be admitted as an object of thought, even though it is self-luminous in character.

Regarding the main contention that if consciousness becomes an object of cognition it would be no better than a physical object, Vedānta Deśika points out that this is based on a wrong conception of the nature of consciousness. The essential nature of knowledge does not consist in its not being an object of cognition; on the contrary, it consists either in that it manifests its own object by virtue of its intrinsic nature or it manifests itself to its substrate.[10] If knowledge possesses either of these characteristics, it does not cease to be knowledge even if

[10]RB I-1-1, p. 57. *anubhūtitvaṁ nāma vartamāna-daśāyāṁ sva-sattayaiva svāśrayaṁ prati prakāśamānatvaṁ; sva-sattayaiva sva-viṣaya-sādhanatvaṁ vā.*

it be an object of another cognition. In other words, the concept of self-luminosity does not necessarily imply that knowledge is a pure subject without in any form being an object. But, on the contrary, it means that knowledge when it manifests an object does not require itself to be manifested by anything else; and when it manifests, it also manifests itself to its own substrate, the self.[11] There is no correlation between *vedyatva* and *jaḍatva*; nor between *avedyatva* and *jñānatva*. This means whatever is *vedya* need not necessarily be *jaḍa*; in the same way what is *avedya* need not be *jñāna*. The sky-flower is *avedya* but it is not *jñāna*. Similarly, a pot is not *jñāna*, not because it is the object of knowledge but because it does not possess any of the characteristics of knowledge.

As against the theory which regards knowledge as self-luminous, there is a view ascribed to the Bhāṭṭa school of Mīmāṁsaka which maintains that knowledge is neither self-luminous nor is it known by means of mental perception. On the contrary, its presence is inferred on the basis of its function, viz. revelation of objects. According to Kumārila, cognition is inferred from the fact that it reveals the objects.[12] Just as we infer the presence of fire on the basis of the presence of smoke, *jñāna* whose function is to reveal the objects is inferred on the basis of the cognisedness of the object(*jñātatā*) caused by knowledge. The justification for holding such a view is that cognition of an object cannot itself be cognised by some other cognition because we do not experience any such double cognition; besides, it would lead to a *regressus ad infinitum*. If a cognition could be the object of another cognition, then it would not be self-valid. Nevertheless, the presence of the cognition is inferred from the fact that the objects are revealed.

This theory is rejected by Vedānta Deśika. The main premise of Mīmāṁsaka is that knowledge is to be inferred because of the 'cognisedness of object' (*artha-prakāśa*). The cognisedness of object itself is *jñāna* and it is absurd to say that on the basis of it *jñāna* is to be inferred. Both the *sādhya*, what is sought to be proved and the *hetu*, probans are the same.

[11] *Ibid.* p. 65.

[12] TMK IV-3. *arthaprakāśāt buddheḥ anumitiḥ*

It may be argued that cognisedness of an object is a characteristic of the object and it is different from *jñāna* which is the *dharma* of *ātman*, and as such the *sādhya* and *hetu* are not the same. This distinction will not hold good. Knowledge, according to the Mīmāṁsaka, is generated by certain accessories such as sense organs, objects, etc. The same accessories which produce the cognition could as well produce the 'cognisedness' of the objects (*jñātatā*). Then there would be no need to accept *jñāna* other than the accessories such as sense organs. Further, if *jñāna* were to be inferred all the time, it would amount to its denial as it becomes a questionable postulate.[13] But *jñāna* actually exists, and it is therefore appropriate to subscribe to the theory that it is self-luminous.

III. KNOWLEDGE AS ETERNAL

According to the Nyāya-vaiśeṣika system, knowledge is generated by the contact of the sense organs with the objects. Thus, it is an adventitious quality or a phenomenon which is not permanent. As against such a commonly accepted view, the Viśiṣṭādvaitin maintains that knowledge as an essential attribute (*dharma*) of the self is also permanent (*nitya*). The logical justification for such a view is that an essential attribute which is inseparable from its substrate will have to be admitted as permanent insofar as the latter to which it belongs is also permanent. The individual self (*ātman*) is *nitya* and so also the *jñāna* which is inseparably related to it.[14] The śruti and smṛti texts also support the theory. In fact, Vedānta Deśika upholds the eternal character of knowledge primarily on the strength of the śruti and smṛti texts.[15] Thus, the Upaniṣadic text says : *na hi vijñātuḥ vijñāteḥ viparilopo vidyate.*[16] The meaning of this statement, according to the interpretation of Rāmānuja, is that the knowledge of the *vijñātā* (the self) does not have destruction.

[13]TMK IV-3. *sā yadi nityānumeyā, tadā buddhitattvāpalāpaḥ.*

[14]*Śrutaprakāśikā* II-2-33. *svarūpeṇa nityasya vastunaḥ nirupādhika-dharmatvāt.*

[15]TMK IV-4. *nigamaḥ jñātuḥ jñapter alopaṁ kathayati.*

[16]Br VI-3-30.

The two terms used in the statement, *vijñātuḥ* and *vijñāteḥ*, refer to the self and its knowledge respectively signifying the relation that obtains between a substance and an attribute. Because of such a distinction made between the self and its knowledge, it cannot be said that the text in question refers only to the *svarūpa* of *ātman* which is indestructible. Nor could it be said that the text refers to the knowledge of *Īśvara* which is also eternal, because the context in which it appears has reference only to *jivātman*.

The smṛti text is more explicit in reiterating the eternal character of *jñāna*. Thus the *Viṣṇudharma* says: 'Just like the lustre of a diamond which is covered with dirt is not created but only made manifest by removing the dirt, knowledge which is *ātmaguṇa* is not created, it exists eternally as an inseparable *dharma* of *ātman*.'[17] If *jñāna* is an inseparable *dharma* of the *ātman*, it has to be admitted as permanent insofar as the substance to which it belongs is *nitya*. The lustre of the diamond remains permanently with the diamond since the two are inseparable. Even if it is eclipsed temporarily due to dirt, it is not lost but only eclipsed. In the same way, knowledge is not something which arises as a product as the Nyāya-Vaiśeṣika believes but it exists as a permanent attribute of the self.

An objection may be raised against the above theory. Knowledge arises in an individual and it also ceases to function. There are also variations within the knowledge of the same individual, such as mediate and immediate knowledge, memory and perceptual knowledge, earlier and later knowledge, etc. When knowledge is one and permanent, how do we account for its variation?

In reply to this objection, Vedānta Deśika says that though knowledge is one and permanent for each individual, the knowledge of each person is different from that of others because the *jivas* to which they pertain are different. Once it is established that each individual possesses a permanent knowledge which only pertains to him, the variations in respect of knowledge as well as the origin (*utpatti*) and cessation of knowledge are to

[17] *yathā na kriyate jyotsnā malaprakṣālanāt maṇeḥ; doṣaprahāṇāt na jñānaṁ ātmanaḥ kriyate tathā...prakāśyante na janyante nityā eva ātmano hi te.*

be regarded as the various modifications of that particular knowledge.[18] The modifications which come and go are non-permanent but the *jñāna* to which they belong and which is the substrate for them is permanent (*nitya*). As will be shown later, it is possible to conceive that knowledge as a permanent substance (*dravya*) could also have modifications (*avasthās*). While the *avasthās* are non-permanent, what serves as a substrate for them is permanent.

Another objection may be raised against the eternity of *jñāna*. If *jñāna* is regarded as eternal, it follows that it should be present at all times. But during deep sleep (*suṣupti*), knowledge does not exist.

In reply to this objection, Vedānta Deśika says that knowledge does exist even in the state of deep sleep but in an unmanifest form. There is no proof to establish that knowledge does not exist at all during deep sleep. An entity which is capable of being known by perception should have been seen if it existed. If it is not seen, then we say that it does not exist. A jug is capable of being seen and its non-cognition on the ground is a proof of its absence on the ground. This is known as *yogyānupalabdhi* which is a *pramāṇa* for proving non-existence of an object. Such a proof is not available in the case of knowledge in deep sleep, because knowledge cannot be known in the state of deep sleep for the reason that it does not then manifest. According to Viśiṣṭādvaita epistemology, knowledge manifests itself only at the time of revealing an object.[19] In the absence of its non-manifestation, there is only non-awareness of its presence (*anupalabdhi*) in deep sleep. Merely on the ground of its non-awareness, it cannot be said that knowledge does not exist at all. In our ordinary experience, we find instances where an object may not be perceived because of darkness or such other factors but still we do admit that it exists. The fact that knowledge is not apparent in sleep does not therefore prove its non-existence. In fact it exists in a quiescent form. It may be asked why was it not known if it existed in deep sleep. The answer is, as already explained, that knowledge becomes manifest only when it is related to an object. Since it is not related

[18] TMK IV-4. *tasmād ekatvasiddhau, ekatra puṁsi prasaraṇa-bhidayā tadbhidā.*
[19] RB I-1-1, p. 56.

to any object in deep sleep, it does not become manifest even though it exists.[20]

The view that knowledge is eternal has certain important implications. It signifies that knowledge persists in all the states of our experience including the state of *suṣupti*. In the waking state as well as the state of dream, it is functioning insofar as it is related to an object and reveals it to the knowing subject who experiences it. But in the state of *suṣupti*, it does not function as it does not have any content. Nevertheless, it exists in a quiescent form as an inseparable quality of the *jiva*.

Another important implication is that *jñāna* endures as in the state of bondage of *jiva*, even in the state of *mokṣa*, unlike in the Nyāya system. During the state of bondage, *jñāna* is causally determined by the moral law of *karma* and as such its function is restricted. In the state of *mukti*, it is infinite and all-pervasive (*vibhu*). This is not a newly created form of knowledge. According to Viśiṣṭādvaita, knowledge by virtue of its intrinsic nature is infinite in its scope, but due to the influence of *avidyā-karma* its power is restricted.[21] When once the soul becomes free from bondage, knowledge regains its infinite character. The *jiva* then becomes omniscient (*sarvajña*). The analogy of the diamond covered with dirt to which we have referred earlier illustrates this point. This matter is discussed in the chapter 'Sādhana and Muki'.

IV. KNOWLEDGE AS SUBSTANCE

Knowledge which is an attribute (*dharma*) of *jīva* is also regarded as a substance (*dravya*), it being one of the six *dravyas* reckoned in this system. *Dravya*, according to the Viśiṣṭādvaitin, is that which serves as the substratum of modifications (*daśāvat*). Since knowledge undergoes modifications in the form of contraction and expansion, it is regarded as a *dravya*. Vedānta Deśika advances two arguments in support of this view. First, knowledge is a *dravya*, because it undergoes modification (*vikāravattvāt*) as, for example, a lump of clay. Secondly, it is a *dravya*,

[20]TMK-iv-4. *tattad-vastu-prakāśa-kṣaṇa-virahavatī na prakāśeta buddhiḥ.*
[21]TMK V-60. *karmabhiḥ tannirodhaḥ.*

because it is self-luminous (*ajaḍatvāt*), as in the case of the individual self.[22]

The modifications that take place in knowledge in the form of contraction and expansion are warranted by experience. These cannot be attributed to knowledge, if the latter were not admitted as a *dravya*. The *avasthās*, according to the Viśiṣṭādvaita logic, should necessarily inhere in a substrate. That is, they cannot exist independently except as belonging to a substance. This is the significance of the first argument.[23]

The significance of the second argument is that if *jiva* is admitted as a *dravya* on the basis of the fact that it is *ajaḍa* (self-luminous), knowledge also is to be accepted as a *dravya* on the same ground because it is also self-luminous in character. This implies that whatever is self-luminous should also be a *dravya*.[24] Though both the *jiva* and its attributive knowledge are *dravyas* and are self-luminous in character, there is, however an important distinction between the two. As already explained earlier, the former is conscious of itself (*pratyak*), whereas the latter reveals itself to the self (*parāk*). The *jiva* is categorised as *cetana*, meaning that it has consciousness as a quality (*caitanya-viśiṣṭa*) and it is therefore self-realised or knows itself (*svasmai bhāsamāna*). On the other hand, the attributive knowledge is categorised as *acetana*, meaning that it is not self-conscious, unlike the *jiva*; it only reveals the objects to the knowing self (*parasmā eva bhāsamāna*). The term *acetana* is not to be confused with the term *jaḍa*. The latter is absolutely non-intelligent like the physical object and does not possess the characteristic of revealing itself to others, whereas the former has the character of *jñāna* or the power of revealing the objects but not the power of knowing itself or the objects unlike the *jiva*.

If knowledge is regarded as a *dravya* or substance, would it be appropriate to consider it as a *dharma* or attribute of the *jīva*? According to the Naiyāyikas, knowledge or *buddhi* is a *guṇa* of the soul, which is a *dravya*. What is a *guṇa* can never

[22]TMK IV-7. *buddhiḥ dravyaṁ, vikārānvayataḥ, itaravat; ajaḍatvācca bodhṛvat.* *Vikārā* here is understood in the sense of *avasthā* or accidental modification and not actual transformation.

[23]*Śrutaprakāśikā* I-1-1. *jñānaṁ hi dravyaṁ, tasya svarūpātirekeṇa saṅkoca-vikāsātmakam avasthādvayaṁ abhyupetam.*

[24]There are four ontological entities which are admitted in the system as ajaḍa dravya, *Īśvara*, *jīva*, *jñāna* and *nitya-vibhūti*.

be a *dravya*. Knowledge is thus included among the twenty-four *guṇas* accepted in the Nyāya-Vaiśeṣika system.

Vedānta Deśika explains that knowledge being a *dravya* does not rule out the possibility of its being a *dharma*. According to Viśiṣṭādvaita, *guṇa* is a quality or a characteristic of an entity (*dharma-svabhāvaḥ*), unlike in the Nyâya system which understands it in a technical sense as applicable to the twenty-four qualities. Even in our ordinary experience a quality of an object is taken to mean *guṇa*. *Jñāna* is a quality of *jīva*, just as luminosity (*prabhā*) is the quality of the flame of a lamp (*dipa*). It is not therefore inappropriate to consider *jñāna* as a *dharma* of *jīva*, even though it be a *dravya*.[25] Though the acceptance of *jñāna* as both *dravya* and *guṇa* is justified on the basis of the special sense in which the terms are understood, it may be noted that *jñāna* in this system is primarily a substance (*dravya*). However, it is treated as a *guṇa* insofar as it is an essential *dharma* of *ātman*. It is not to be regarded as a *guṇa* in the sense of the *adravyas* or non-substance such as *rūpa*, *rasa*, *gandha*, etc. which can never be the basis for another quality.

Even among the Viśiṣṭādvaitins, some hold the view that *jñāna* is not a substance but it is only an attribute (*guṇa*). They argue that if *jñāna* were a *dravya*, its relation with external objects should take place by direct contact (*saṁyoga*), as in the case of two physical objects. This is not so. Actually, relationship of knowledge with objects is caused by other accessory factors. Therefore *jñāna* is to be regarded as a *guṇa*.

Vedānta Deśika does not subscribe to this view. What is a *guṇa* cannot undergo modification. If *jñāna* were a mere *guṇa* it should not have any modification. If it is admitted that knowledge is related to the external object, even though such a contact is caused by other accessory factors, it would amount to its admission as a *dravya*. According to the definition offered by the Viśiṣṭādvaitin, that which is the substrate of modification is a *dravya*. In the case of knowledge, modification takes place only to the extent of it being subject to expansion and contraction. Insofar as *jñāna* is the substrate for such a modification, it is regarded as *dravya*.

[25]RB on VS 2-2-27, p. 540. *prabhā-dravyasya pradīpaguṇa-bhūtasyeva jñānasyā'py-ātmaguṇa-bhūtasya dravyatvaṁ aviruddhaṁ iti.*

V. THE THEORY OF TRANSCENDENTAL KNOWLEDGE

Is knowledge identical with the ultimate Reality? According to the Advaita Vedânta, knowledge or consciousness which is described as *saṁvit* or *anubhūti* is identical with Brahman and constitutes its very *svarūpa*. Such a knowledge is eternal (*nitya*), one, infinite, undifferentiated and non-relational. It is transcendental knowledge which is beyond all speech and thought. As it is the ground of all experience and being, it does not require to be proved by any *pramāṇas*. It is, in other words, self-established (*svatas-siddha*). The so-called knowledge which is apparent in the usual distinction of knower, known and knowledge, as described by the Viśiṣṭādvaitin, is not ultimately real but is real only from the empirical standpoint. It is the psychosis of the inner organ (*antaḥkaraṇa-vṛttiḥ*) and is regarded as knowledge because of its being the determinant of the transcedental, infinite knowledge.

The Viśiṣṭādvaitin does not accept this theory. The criticism of this doctrine takes us to the examination of the ontological issue whether or not such an undifferentiated, transcendental Being is logically conceivable and metaphysically tenable. Râmânuja has critically examined this matter in great detail in the introductory portion of his *Srī-bhāṣya* and has come to the conclusion that the existence of such a transcedental and undifferentiated consciousness as the very Reality cannot be proved by any of the *pramāṇas*. All that we know of is a *jñāna* which is relational in character as pertaining to a knowing subject and having reference to an object.

Transcendental knowledge which is contentless and which does not admit subject-object relation is of no use for explaining the process of knowing, the way the external objects are known and the variegated nature of experience as well as the different types of knowledge. All these points are no doubt accounted for by the Advaitin on the basis of the empirical ego or knowing subject which functions through the mind and sense organs. The empirical ego in his system is the consciousness as conditioned by the internal organ (*antaḥkaraṇa*). The soundness of this theory depends on the soundness of the doctrine of *avidyā* which causes all the apparent distinction between the subject and object. But the doctrine of *avidyā* is proved to be untenable by the critic. Consequently, the Advaitin's theory that the psychosis of the internal organ as the determinant of the consciousness is knowledge also falls to the ground. These issues are discussed at the appropriate places. We take up here the points which have a direct bearing on epistemology.

The first important point to be noted is that knowledge is to be admitted as different from one individual to another in order to account for the variation of our experience. Unless each one has a knowledge of his own as different from the other, communication of ideas or thoughts is not possible. If knowledge is one infinite, ubiquitous entity, then it would not be possible to distinguish one's experience from that of the others. The Viśiṣṭādvaitin therefore rejects the theory that knowledge is one.

The Advaitin puts forward the following argument to prove the oneness of knowledge: '*Saṁvit* or knowledge is not manifold, because it is devoid of either origin or destruction; that which has either origin or destruction is not one as, for example, a pot.'[26]

The Viśiṣṭādvatin does not accept the above argument. Taking his stand on the common experience, he points out that knowledge arises and also ceases to exist. It is subject to modifications in the form of contraction and expansion. Every individual knows that he is aware of something and not aware of something else. It is not therefore correct to say that knowledge is devoid of origin and destruction.

Further, *avidyā* for the Advaitin is without a beginning (*anādi*) but it is not without an end. The probans (*hetu*) in the syllogism becomes fallacious. That is, on the basis of the probans adopted in the syllogism the oneness of an entity cannot be conclusively established. According to some Advaitins, *avidyā* is not one but manifold on the basis of the multiplicity of *jivas* in which *avidyā* is located. The multiplicity of *jiva* is explained on the basis of the multiplicity of *avidyā*. What is beginningless is thus regarded as manifold too. Either way, oneness of *saṁvit* cannot be proved on the basis of the arguments advanced by the

[26]TMK IV-5. See also SD Vāda 23. *saṁvit na nānā anutpannatvāt, nāśarahitatvāt, yathā ghaṭaḥ.*

Advaitin. In fact, the Viśiṣṭādvaitin asserts that the individual souls are infinite in number and knowledge which belongs to them cannot be one and the same for all of them. It differs from person to person. If all individuals have the same *jñāna*, how could there be any difference between the learned and the ignorant ? As pointed out by Rāmānuja, the difference in knowledge is proved by means of the difference of objects of cognition which is established by valid knowledge, in the same way as the difference of acts of cutting is proved by the difference of the objects cut.[27] It should be admitted, Vedānta Deśika urges, that cognition which is reciprocally related to objects is by its very nature manifold as in the example cited by Rāmānuja.

In support of the theory of oneness of knowledge, the Advaitin advances the view that knowledge is undifferentiated (*nirdharmaka*). Two arguments are put forward to prove this theory. Knowledge is undifferentiated because it is knowledge. To express the same negatively, whatever is differentiated is not knowledge as in the case of a pot. The second argument is that the characteristics (*dharma*) do not apply to knowledge because they are objective, as for example, qualities such as colour, etc.[28] The argument is based on the assumption that the characteristics which are objective insofar as they are knowable (*dṛśya*) cannot be attributed to knowledge which is a pure subject. Subject and object are contradictory, like light and darkness. Therefore, what is pure subject (*dṛk*) cannot be object (*dṛśya*); in the same way whatever is objective (*dṛśya*) can never become a subject, If any *dharma* is admitted in *dṛk* or pure knowledge, it becomes a *dṛśya* or objective in character and as such it ceases to be knowledge.

Both the arguments are refuted by Vedānta Deśika. The main point of the criticism is that it is not possible to deny totally all characteristics in respect of knowledge or *dṛk* even as conceived by the Advaitin. The Advaitin himself admits that knowledge is eternal. Vedānta-Deśika asks whether or not eternity is denied as a characteristic of knowledge. If it be denied, it would then conflict with his own position. If it were not denied, the

[27]RB I-1-1, p. 64.

[28]SS IV-6, p. 178. *vigītā dharmā na saṁvidi vartante, dṛśyatvāt, rūpādivat. anubhūtidharmarahitā, anubhūtitvāt.*

argument would be inconclusive. The Advaitin may however argue that eternity as a characteristic of knowledge is illusory, and as such even if it be attributed to consciousness it will not involve any logical difficulty. In that case, Vedānta Deśika replies that the Advaitin's attempt to establish that knowledge is eternal against those who deny it is futile. To avoid this difficulty, eternity may be regarded as the very *svarūpa* of knowledge. Then the Advaitin should have no dispute with those Buddhists who also admit it as the *svarūpa* of *vijñāna*.[29]

The premise that knowledge is undifferentiated involves self-contradiction. In a judgment, the predicate should be admitted to be related to the subject. If it is not related in anyway, then the judgment has no meaning. If, on the contrary, the predicate is admitted to be related to the subject, it would follow that the subject is differentiated or determinate. Hence it is not possible to assert that knowledge is undifferentiated. *Jñāna*, in fact, possesses such characteristics as *satyatva nityatva*, *ekatva*, etc. and denial of these amount to denial of one's own position (*apasiddhānta*).

Against this criticism the Advaitin may argue that these characteristics are illusory and as such they do not really belong to *jñāna* which remains undifferentiated. This will not hold good, contends Vedānta Deśika. If *satyatva* of *jñāna* is regarded as *mithyā*, then *jñāna* will not be *satya*; if *nityatva* is *mithyā*, then *jñāna* becomes non-eternal. Such a conclusion will militate against the Advaitin's position.

To escape all such criticisms the Advaitin may contend that these *dharmas*, though accepted as real, are the very *svarūpa* of *jñāna* and as such they do not become objective (*dṛsya*). Even this will not improve the position. If these *dharmas* be regarded as *jñāna-svarūpa*, there would be no dispute between the Advaitin and the Viśiṣṭādvaitin as far as *jñāna-svarūpa* is concerned. According to the Viśiṣṭādvaitin, the ultimate Reality, Brahman, is also of *jñāna-svarūpa*. The dispute arises because the latter maintains the view that what is of *jñāna-svarūpa* is also characterised with such *dharmas* as *nityatva*, *jñānatva*, etc. Vedānta Deśika therefore concludes that *jñāna* is to be admit-

[29]SD Vāda 24.

ted as differentiated or relational (*sadharmaka*) in character. There is no such transcendental absolute consciousness deviod of all differentiation, because it is impossible to prove the existence of such an entity by any of the *pramāṇas*. If it be claimed that it is beyond all *pramāṇas* and thought, it would amount to a metaphysical abstraction or a non-entity.[30] Hence the only knowledge we know of is that which is related to a subject on the one hand and has a reference to an object. Such a knowledge can never be idential with the self or Reality.

[30]SD Vāda 33. *tasyāḥ sarva-māna-anāghrātatvena kha-puṣpāyamāṇatvāt.*

CHAPTER FIVE

Knowledge and External World

WE HAVE examined in the previous chapter the nature of knowledge in relation to the knowing subject. We shall now consider knowledge in relation to an external object. According to Viśiṣṭādvaita, there can be no knowledge which does not point to a corresponding object outside it. As explained earlier, knowledge is relational, and therefore it necessarily implies a subject to which it belongs and an object to which it refers. Knowledge functions only in relation to objects, and cognition devoid of content is inconceivable.[1]

This theory presupposes above all the reality of the external object and its existence independent of knowledge. The Viśiṣṭādvaitin, like the other Realists, admits that the objects exist even before they are known, and so their reality is not merely relative but also absolute. It is the function of knowledge to reveal the external world to the knowing subject. *Jñāna* radiates from the *jīva*, comes into contact with the object through the manas and sense organs, and reveals it. The knowledge of the object thus arises when *jñāna* comes into contact with an object through the inner and outer senses.

The above theory of knowledge has been open to criticism at the hands of certain schools like the Buddhists and Advaitins. In the first place, the reality of external objects is seriously questioned by some Buddhists. According to the Yogācāra school of Buddhism, external objects have no reality of their own. For the Mādhyamika Buddhists. what does not exist at all appears as existent. The Advaitin does not admit absolute reality for the external world. Even granting that objects exist,

[1]RB II-2-29. *na kevalasya arthaśūnyasya jñānasya bhāvaḥ sambhavati; kutaḥ, kvacidapi anupalabdheḥ.*

the question arises: how does the subject which is a pure spiritual entity knows the material object which is external to it? Is any relation between the two which are radically different in their nature possible at all? If so, what is the nature of such a relation? This is the fundamental epistemological problem relating to the subject-object relation and needs detailed consideration to prove the soundness of the Viśiṣṭādvaita theory of knowledge.

I. SUBJECT-OBJECT RELATION

The main criticism against the subject-object relation is based on two suppositions. Firstly, the very concept of relation is logically unintelligible. Secondly, even granting that the concept is intelligible, it is hardly possible to understand its nature. The first argument is discussed at length in the chapter on metaphysical cotegories, and it is established that the concept of relation is logically sound and is to be accepted. Regarding the second point, it is contended that there cannot be an external relation (*saṁyoga*) between the subject and object for the obvious reason that the former is not a corporeal thing. Nor can it be an internal relation. For consciousness which is an essential attribute of the subject cannot be inherent in the object. Nor can the object be inherent in consciousness since it is external to it and is also opposed to its nature. Nor is a relation of identity possible inasmuch as the two are opposed to each other and identity between them is inconceivable.

There are other theories to explain the subject-object relation. These account for knowledge by relating consciousness with the object by way of representation (*sārūpya*), causation (*saṁsarga*) or a unique relation. All such explanations are considered unsatisfactory by the Advaitin because one or the other end of the relation is unknown and unknowable. By placing consciousness on an equal footing with the object and relating the former to the latter, consciousness is reduced to the position of a material object. Its unique nature lies in its not being related to anything. The assumption here is that true consciousness is transcendental in character. Thus, on the basis of the unintelligibility of subject-object relation, the Advaitin draws the conclusion that object is illusory in character.[2]

Theory of Viśiṣṭādvaitin

The Viśiṣṭādvaitin does not accept the theory that subject-object relation is unintelligible. According to Rāmānuja, who follows the view of Nāthamuni, the consciousness or knowledge is related to the external object which exists independent of knowledge. The relation that obtains between the two is of the nature of *saṁyoga* or compresence.[3] Cognitive relation, in other words, is external, conjunctive and direct. The fact that there is a knowledge of an object shows that knowledge is related to an object. It is the intrinsic nature of knowledge to reveal an object and such a function is possible only when knowledge becomes related to an object outside it. If this were not admitted, then it would not be possible to maintain a distinction between consciousness and the material object on the ground that the former is self-luminious (*ajaḍa*), whereas the latter is non-sentient (*jaḍa*). The Advaitin claims that object is *jaḍa* because it depends on knowledge for its existence to be known, whereas knowledge is not so as it is self-evident. If this be the position of the Advaitin, then he must admit, Vedānta-Deśika urges, that the object is related to knowledge. If the object were not dependent on knowledge for its manifestation then it would also become self-evident like consciousness. Such a relation should also be regarded as real. If it were illusory, as Advaitin claims, then both the relata should be illusory. There is no justification to say that one of the relata, viz. object is illusory, while the other (knowledge) is real.

As regards the name of this relation, VedantaDeśika states that it may be described as subject-object relation or *viṣaya-viṣayi-bhāva sambandha*. *Viṣaya* means the object and *viṣayī* means the subject or consciousness. By the fact that the two are related whenever cognition arises, the relationship is described as one of subject-object. It is a unique relation or *svarūpa-sambandha*.

[2]See SD Vāda 17 for more detailed arguments in favour of the logical untenability of subject-object relation.

[3]SS V-59 p. 290. *bhāṣyakārāḥ nyāyatattvānusārāt buddheḥ viṣayais-saha saṁbandhaṃ saṁyogam akathayan.*

Relation is defined as that which causes the empirical usage or gives the notion that the two relata are related.[4] The subject and object—the two relata—in the present case cause the empirical usage that knowledge is related to the object. Therefore, it is justifiable to regard the very *svarūpa* of the relata as a *sambandha* or relation. If something is evident to our experience, it cannot be denied even if it cannot be specifically defined. Thus, for instance, the difference in the taste of sugar-cane juice and that of milk cannot be defined in words, but all the same the difference is undeniable inasmuch as it is evident to one's own experience. The same explanation should hold good also in respect of subject-object relation.[5]

It may be noted here that when the Viśiṣṭādvaitin is speaking of subject-object relation, he does not mean by subject the individual self or the *jīvātman*. Though the *jīvātman* is the subject which cognises the object presented to it by knowledge, the fomrer does not have a direct relation to the external object. The direct contact or *saṁyoga* takes place between knowledge and the object outside it whenever the former is in contact with the latter through *manas* or the internal cognitive organ and the senses. The cognitive relation is thus temporal and direct. A *saṁyoga* or external relation is possible, because in this system knowledge is also a *dravya* or substance.

Criticism of Yogācāra Buddhist Theory of Knowledge

The Yogācāra School of Buddhism denies the reality of the external object. According to it, knowledge which is described as *vijñāna* is the sole reality and its content is false. There is neither subject nor object but only a succession of ideas. The specific form which cognition at any particular instant assumes is determined not by an outside object presented to it as the realists believe but by the latent impression (*vāsanā*) left behind by past experience, which in turn goes back to another impression, that again to another earlier experience and so on indefinitely in a beginningless series. Only these ideas (*vijñāna*) are real and the external objects have no reality of their own. The latter are just projections of the internal ideas.

[4]SD Vada 17. *vastunor viśiṣṭa-vyavahāra-janana-svabhāvatvam.* [5]*Ibid.*

In support of this theory, a few arguments are advanced by the Buddhists. These are examined and finally refuted by Vedānta Deśika. The main point of the criticism is that knowledge which manifests as 'I know' is an internal entity, whereas the object which manifests as 'This is' is an external entity and the two which are distinct can never be one and the same. That is, knowing and being can never be identical.

The most important argument put forward by the Yogācāra in support of his theory is that there is an invariable association between knowledge and its content (*sahopalambha-niyama*). Thought and things always appear together and neither can appear without the other. It is not therefore appropriate to assume that they are distinct, and they may well be regarded as different phases of one and the same factor.

Vedānta Deśika refutes this argument. The fact that knowledge and object are found together does not establish that knowledge and object are one and the same. There is invariable concomitance or association between smoke and fire, but nevertheless it does not follow that they are the same. In fact, the very concept of 'invariable association' is meaningful only when two separate entities exist.[6]

There are other problems in assuming that knowledge and object are the same. If the external object is unreal (*mithyā*), as the Yogācāra believes, then *jñāna* too would become *mithyā* since the two are identical in the system. For the same reason, if *jñāna* which is identical with the object is real (*satya*), the latter too would become real.

When a cognition of another individual becomes the content of one's knowledge, the two will have to be the same insofar as *vijñāna* and external object are the same. It cannot be said that the thought of another person does not become the object of one's own cognition. If the thoughts of others are not understood, no communication becomes possible. When we reply to a person, we are supposed to understand his thoughts through his words or facial expression or gesture.

Further, if all external objects are unreal, there would be no difference between the content of shell-silver cognition and that of the real silver cognition. If the two objects—shell-silver and

[6]TMK IV-20. *sahamati-niyamādyanyathaiva. atra siddham.*

real silver—are alike illusory, how could a distinction be drawn between the valid cognition of true silver and the erroneous cognition of shell-silver? It may be argued that all such distinctions are accounted for by means of *saṁvṛti* which causes the variegated appearance. But this will not hold good because *saṁvṛti* itself being unreal in character cannot be the determinant of the distinction between the real and the unreal. According to the Viśiṣṭādvaitin, what is unreal cannot be the cause of what is real.[7]

Another argument is advanced by the Vijñānavādin to prove the unreality of the external objects. In the cognition that 'this is blue' we experience only the blue colour. Does the colour belong to the object or knowledge? If it belongs to the object, then knowledge which becomes devoid of any content cannot manifest itself. If knowledge does not manifest, the object too would become unrevealed, because an object, according to Yogācāra, depends on knowledge. Therefore, the colour which is being experienced should be admitted as belonging to knowledge. In view of this, it is asserted that knowledge and object are identical. That is, what is known is identical with what knows (*ekākāra-pratītiḥ*).[8]

This view, Vedānta Deśika contends, is opposed to our experience. As already mentioned, objects appear as external to our knowledge, whereas knowledge manifests within. The qualities such as blue or yellow cannot belong to cognition. Only after the external objects are perceived, knowledge comprehends the qualities and assumes the character of the objects. Knowledge reveals objects as presented to it and objects become revealed by the former. This is a fundamental distinction between the two, and it is undeniable as it is warranted by experience. If *jñāna* is described as *prakāśa-svarūpa* or that which reveals the external object may be defined as *prakāśya-svarūpa* or that which is revealed by *jñāna*. What is revealed (*prakāśya*) and what reveals (*prakāśa*) are two distinct concepts and they can never be identical.[9]

One other argument is put forward by the Vijñāvādins to prove the unreal character of external objects. If the objects of external world were real, they have to exist always in the

[7]See Section Jñāna as the Means to Mokṣa' in Chapter IX.
[8]SS IV-23, p. 196. [9]TMK IV-23.

same unchangeable form. But this is not so. For instance, the words used to denote the same object are found in different genders as, for example, the words *patni*, *dārāḥ* and *kalatra*. Though all the three mean wife, they are in different genders according to Sanskrit Grammar—the first is feminine, the second masculine and the third is neuter. An object seen by us is considered small but the same is described as large when we see something else smaller than it. If the objects were always of uniform nature, such variations should not arise. Objects are seen to impress different persons differently and even the same person at different times. Thus, for instance, a lady is described by her lover as *kāmini* (beloved); an ascetic regards her as a corpse (*śava*); for a wild dog, she is an object of food. If objects were real, each having its own defined character, such different descriptions should not be possible.

This argument is not sound. The words, used to denote the same object, have no bearing on the intrinsic nature of an object. The words and the objects denoted by them are distinct. The word may belong either to masculine or feminine gender but the gender of the word does not apply to the person referred to by it. An object is regarded as small or large from different standpoints. The description of an object as small or large does not affect in any way its intrinsic character. Similarly, objects are experienced differently by different persons, because an object which has several characteristics admits itself of different descriptions. Each person is attracted by a particular aspect of an object in accordance with his mental disposition and he describes the object emphasising that aspect only.[10] It is not necessary that an object should be comprehended in the same way by everybody. Individual variations in the matter of perception do not therefore necessarily mean the non-existence of external objects.

The Vijñānavādin adopts another important argument based on the analogy of dreams where experience arises without corresponding objects and internal thought appears as external. This is expressed in the form of a syllogism : 'The knowledge in dispute is devoid of any content other than itself, because it is knowledge; as, for instance, the dream experience.'[11] In dream,

[10]TMK IV-23. *ekam nānākṛti syān nijaguṇa-bhidayā.*

[11]TMK IV-24. *vimatamatiḥ svānyārthaśūnyā, dhītvāt, yathā svapnādipratyayaḥ.*

though we experience the objects, the latter do not actually exist. In the same way, though our ordinary experience may refer to external objects, the latter do not really exist.

Vedânta Deśika rejects this argument on the ground that it contradicts one's own words and also experience.[12] Does this inference refer to something or not? If it be the former, then the inference contradicts its own premise, insofar as it has reference to a content. If not, then nothing becomes established by it. It cannot thus prove that external objects do not exist. The inference also suffers from other logical fallacies. *Vijñāna* in this system is a series of cognitions each lasting for a moment only. In such a series, the later cognition has for its content the earlier one. Though it is a *jñāna*, it has for its content another cognition, and as such the probandum (*sādhya*), viz. that *jñāna* is devoid of the content other than itself does not hold good. The illustration given in the inference is also fallacious. According to the Viśiṣṭādvaitin, even the dream objects are real for the duration of the dream since these are considered, on the strength of scripture, as creations of *Īśvara*.[13] The probandum will not be present in the illustration, leading to the fallacy of unproved illustration (*dṛṣṭāntāsiddhi*).

To escape from this difficulty, the illustration of shell-silver may be cited. For the Buddhist, shell-silver does not exist but it becomes the object of cognition. But the Viśiṣṭādvaitin does not accept this explanation. For him, an object which does not exist anywhere and at any time cannot appear as the content of erroneous cognition. This point is discussed later. The silver seen sometime ago in a shop is cognised in shell due to the similarity, eye defect and other factors. It is not therefore a totally non-existent entity like the sky-flower. Even granting that there may be a few instances of illusory objects, it would not follow that all other objects in the universe are false (*mithyā*).[14]

Vedānta Deśika further observes that knowledge which arises only in relation to objects cannot be devoid of a content. There are three sources of knowledge—perception, inference and verbal testimony. Perception takes place only when there is sense contact with objects that exist; even *smṛti* or memory

[12]TMK IV-24. *svoktibuddhyādibhagnam.* [13]RB III-2-3. [14]TMK IV-24.

occurs with regard to an entity or event already experienced. Inference is possible only when concomitance (*vyāpti*) is established between two particular objects. Cognition through verbal testimony (*śābda-bodha*) depends on the relation between the words and the objects denoted by them. If objects denoted by the words do not exist, the words cannot convey any meaning. Even illusory cognition presupposes previous experience of an object. If there were no previous experience of an object, illusion would not arise. Besides, the knowledge of the substrate (*adhiṣṭhāna*) is also required for illusion. If shell did not exist, it could not have been mistaken for silver. Thus, all our knowledge depends upon the existence of objects. The admission of the reality of external objects is therefore absolutely essential for the functioning of knowledge. If knowledge has no relation to any object other than itself, it ceases to be knowledge.

Further, it is a matter of common experience that knowledge is variegated, and this diversity is possible because of the differences in their contents. If existence of objects is denied, the diversity of knowledge cannot be accounted for. The Vijñānavādin may say that all the variegated experiences take place on account of the influence of beginningless *vāsanā* or latent impressions. But this does not help because even *vāsanā* which is a mental impression is not different from cognition (*vijñāna*), since in this system nothing other than *vijñāna* exists.[15]

The Buddhist tries to explain the diversity of experience on the basis of the variegated *vāsanā*, which are in the form of a continuous series like the flowing river from a beginningless time. *Vijñāna* is also a series of momentary mental processes, and the *vāsanas* which are associated with them influence *vijñāna* and thereby cause the diversity of experience.

Such an explanation does not hold good, contends Vedānta Deśika. *Vijñāna* for the Buddhist is *kṣaṇika*, that is, it changes every moment. In the series of cognitions, when the earlier cognition ceases to exist, the *vāsanā* associated with it is also erased and as such it cannot influence the next momentary cognition. If the series of cognitions is admitted as one continuous cognition, it may be possible to account for the continuation of *vāsanā* and its influence on the cognition. Alternatively

[15]TMK IV-26. *vāsanā buddhyātmā*.

reality of external object is to be admitted to account for diversity of experience. Neither is accepted by the Vijñānavādin and his theory is therefore untenable.[16]

Criticism of Sautrāntika Buddhist Theory of Knowledge

The Sautrāntika School of Buddhism admits the reality of both the internal knowledge and the external object, though both are momentary (*kṣaṇika*). However, the external object is not directly perceived but is to be inferred on the basis of the cognition of the object that takes place. The justification for such a view is that objects, being momentary, cannot be present at the time they are perceived. If they were present, they should endure for at least two moments—that when they served as the cause of perception and that when they were actually perceived. If things have only momentary existence, then it is only a past thing that can be perceived. So what is present externally when perception takes place is only the successor in the object series in question of the member that served as its cause. The previous member leaves its impression on the percipient mind before it disappears, and it is from impression (*ākāra*) that we infer the prior existence of the corresponding object.[17]

This theory is criticised on the ground that it is impossible for an object to transfer its image or impression to *jñāna*. The Sautrāntika adopts the analogy of the reflection of the face in the mirror in support of his theory. Though we do not see our face, it is perceived when it is reflected in a mirror. This is what is meant by *ākāra-samarpaṇa*, transference of its image. Such an explanation does not hold good in respect of knowledge and object. *Jñāna* by its nature is devoid of any form (*nirākāra*). How could there be any reflection in it?[18] In the case of the mirror, reflection is possible in the glass even if it is clean, because it is tainted with mercury. There is no such conditioning factor (*upādhi*) in respect of *jñāna*. Besides, *jñāna* as well as the object, according to the Sautrāntika, are momentary. By the time the object transfers its image to *jñāna*, the former would have changed. The object to be reflected and the recipient of the reflection are not of the same temporal order. Therefore, the reflection of objects is not possible.

[16]TMK IV-26. [17]SS IV-27, p. 200. See also OIP, p. 202.

[18]TMK IV-27. *svacche parasmin chāyā na bhavati, asau rūpaśūnye na ca syāt.*

The possibility of *jñāna* and object coming together is explained on the analogy of a lump of black powder getting mixed up in a heap of black gram (*māṣa-rāśi*). When the black powder is mixed with the black gram, the two become almost indistinguishable, though they are distinct entities. In the same way, knowledge and object come into such a close contact that the two are not distinguishable.

Eevn this explanation does not hold good, argues Vedānta Deśika. There should be some similarity and proximity between the two entities in order to come together, as in the case of black powder and black gram. There is no scope for such a possibility in the case of *jñāna* which is internal and the external object. It may be possible to explain the transference of the quality of one entity to the other by way of proximity as in the example of white crystal placed next to the red rose. But this will not be applicable to *jñāna* and an object as conceived by the Buddhist since there is no common feature between the two.[19] As already pointed out, knowledge is devoid of any form (*nirākāra*) whereas *ākāra* is found only in the external object. Thus, it is not possible to prove in any manner that object becomes known, because it is reflected in *jñāna*.

There is one other view held by a section of Sautrāntikas to account for the relation of *jñāna* to object. Neither the object nor *jñāna* has any separate *ākāra*, but nevertheless when the two come together an *ākāra* is produced. This is explained on the analogy of betel leaf and lime. The betel leaf is green and lime is white, but when the two are combined and chewed along with arecanut red colour is produced. In the same way, *jñāna* and object coming together (*saṁsarga*) causes the cognition of object with its characteristics.[20]

Even this theory is untenable. What does *saṁsarga* or togetherness imply? Does it mean that they come together at one place (*deśa*) or at one time (*kāla*) or is it the placement of one in front of the other (*ābhimukhya*) as in the case of magnet and an iron piece? Or is it the subject-object relationship

[19]TMK IV-27. *dvayamapi ekākāroparaktaṁ na.*

[20]SS IV-28, p. 201. The Vaibhāṣika Buddhist also holds a similar view. According to him, objects are known directly but perception takes place like fire produced by the rubbing of two sticks, which implies direct causation. See OIP, p. 202.

(*viṣayi-viṣaya-bhāva-sambandha*)? Spatial conjunction is ruled out as the Buddhists do not accept space as a separate category. Nor is it possible to explain *saṁsarga* on the basis of their appearing at the same time, as this would lead to the position that all objects should become presented at the same time to knowledge. We cannot even speak of their relation on the basis of one being placed in front of the other (*ābhimukhya*). Only two entities having physical form could be juxtaposed, but in this system both are formless.[21] It is also not possible to explain *saṁsarga* on the basis of subject-object relationship. Unless knowledge assumes the form of the object, it cannot be said that knowledge is related to object.[22] Besides, all objects are momentary, and at the time knowledge arises the particular momentary object ceases to exist. How then is the *ākāra* of the object passed on to knowledge? The analogy of betel leaf and lime is not applicable here. Only when two entities come together, either at one place or at any one time, is it possible to explain their relationship. As both subject and object are momentary, the subject-object relation is inconceivable.

Criticism of the Theory of Mādhyamika Buddhist

According to another extreme view advanced by the Mādhyamika School of Buddhists, the objects of the external world do not have real existence. Though it is a non-existent (*asat*), it manifests itself as existent (*sat*). This is justified on the basis of their metaphysical position. No entity in the universe is of the nature of *sat* or Being. If something is *sat*, it should not be sublated; it should always exist everywhere in the same form. It cannot be otherwise, since any change in its *svarūpa* is not possible. Nothing in the universe is of the form of *asat*. What is *asat* should not appear to cognition. It is not so, because at some time or some place or in some manner it appears to cognition. Further, it cannot be both *sat* and *asat* because of the defects pointed out in respect of the first two alternatives. Besides, it involves self-contradiction. Nor could it be said that it is devoid of *sat* and *asat* because of the same objection stated with regard to the third alternative. These are the four possible

[21]TMK IV-28. *vyaṁśe naivābhimukhyam.*

[22]*Ibid. ākṛteḥ prāk viṣaya-viṣayitā asiddhā.*

modes of predication, and *tattva* cannot be characterised by any of these predicates taken singly or in combination. That is, reality is neither real nor unreal, nor real-unreal, nor different from both real and unreal but different from all the four alternatives (*catuṣkoṭimuktam ca tattvam*).[23] It is absolutely indeterminable (*śūnya*). If this be the nature of reality, then objects of this universe including the categories of thought do not exist as such.

Vedānta Deśika summarily rejects this theory on the ground that it is riddled with contradiction (*vyāghāta*). If it be argued that there is no contradiction, then how can the Mādhyamika justify his own criticism of the Jaina doctrine of *saptabhaṅgi* or any other doctrine which is opposed to his tenet. The Mādhyamika criticises the Jaina theory on the ground that it is riddled with contradiction. The same argument holds good even in respect of Mādhyamika doctrine.

It is impossible to conceive *tattva* as absolutely indeterminable (*śūnya*). Even such terms as *śūnya* (void), *alika* (false) and *tuccha* (non-existent) which are in common parlance and which appear to mean total negation (*sarva-śūnya*) do not imply absolute non-existence. Negation necessarily presupposes its counter-correlates. It does not deny total non-existence at any time or at any place. When we say that an object does not exist, it only means that it exists at some other place or at some other time, but not that it is absolutely non-existent like a sky-flower. Absolute non-existence (*sarvathā śūnyatva*) is not logically tenable. What does not exist here and now, does exist elsewhere and at some other time.

Though the upholders of *śūnyavāda* do not accept a total negative concept, it would eventually end up in total negation when the concept is subjected to logical analysis. If every thing in the universe is described as *alika* (false), it should mean that objects are non-existent. In defence of their theory, the Mādhyamikas speak of two types of non-existence: positive non-existence (*vidhyalika*) and negative non-existence (*niṣedhālika*) The silver in the shop is of the former type and the illusory

[23]SS. IV-18, p. 188. *na sannāsanna sad-asanna cāpyanubhayātmakam catuṣkoṭi-vinirmuktam tattvam mādhyamikā viduḥ.* See also T.R.V. Murti's *The Central Philosophy of Buddhism*, p. 228.

silver is of the latter type. It should therefore be possible to use the expression existence and non-existence.

Vedânta Deśika does not accept this explanation. What does not exist is *alika* or false; what exists is the existent having an objective reality. To make a distinction of non-existent as *vidhyalika* and *nisedhālika* amounts to making assertions about a barren woman's son (*vandhyā-putra*). That a non-existent exists is self-contradiction.[24] It is not therefore correct to deny the reality of the external objects on the basis of *śūnya-vāda.*

The Advaitins also do not admit absolute reality for the external world. On the basis of degrees of reality, the objects of the external world are regarded as empirically real, as compared to the dream objects or shell-silver which are illusory in character. From the transcendental point of view, even the physical objects are *mithyā* or illusory in character. The Viśiṣṭādvaitin does not accept this doctrine. The objects of the external world are not illusory but real. The criticism of this doctrine is taken up in the chapter on Brahman and universe.

II. THEORY OF TRUTH AND ERROR

The foregoing critical evaluation of the theories of knowledge advocated by the Buddhists leads to the conclusion that knowledge, if it were at all to function as knowledge, should have a reference to an object that should exist independently of it. In fact, according to the Viśiṣṭādvaitin, only that which exists is cognised and that knowledge in the absence of a real object corresponding to it is inconceivable. In view of this, Rāmānuja asserts that all knowledge is of the real (*yathārtham sarva-vijñānam*), a fundamental tenet of Viśiṣṭādvaita epistemology which is traced back to the ancient teachings of the Vedas.[25]

If all knowledge is valid, how do we make a distinction between true and false knowledge? It is an admitted fact that in our common experience we come across cases of error. Thus a rope is mistaken for a snake; the white shell is taken for a piece of silver; the mirage is mistaken for water; in the dream

[24]TMK IV-18. *vidhyalīkādi-vādaḥ vandhyā-putrādi-śabdaiḥ samātām bhajati.*

[25]RB I-1-1, p. 132. *yathārtham sarvavijñānam iti vedavidām matam.* This is also the view of the Prābhākara School of Mīmāṁsā.

state, we experience things which do not actually exist. Then, if all knowledge is valid, how do we account for such experiences as are generally considered to be invalid?

There are various answers to this fundamental question of epistemology. Different theories are formulated on the basis generally of the metaphysical position of the concerned school of thought. These are known as *khyāti-vādas* or theories of truth and error. According to the Naiyâyika, the error is caused by misapprehending one thing for another. The shell is mistaken for silver. This is known as *anyathā-khyāti*. According to the Mīmāṁsaka, error arises as a result of non-apprehension of the distinction between what is presented (shell) and the object (silver) seen elsewhere. This is known as *akhyāti*. According to the Advaitin, the object seen in error is inexplicable (*sadasadvilakṣaṇa*) and is caused by *avidyā*. This is described as *anirvacaniya-khyāti*. The Buddhist schools offer different explanations. For the Mādhyamika, the object of error is non-existent but it appears as existent due to *samvṛiti*. This is known as *asatkhyāti*. For the Yogâcāra, error is the superposition of the mental idea on the external object. This theory is named *ātma-khyāti*.

These are the main theories of error. Which one of these is a sound theory that explains error satisfactorily? *Prima facie*, the Nyāya theory appears plausible because of the simplicity of explanation. Recognising this fact Rāmānuja states that the advocates of other theories of error have to resort in one way or the other to *anyathā-khyāti*.[26] That is, whatever explanation one may offer for the error, one has to admit in the last resort that in error one thing is mistaken for another. Keeping in mind this statement of Rāmānuja, Vedānta Deśika also says that all have to accept *anyathā-khyāti* and it conforms to the principle of parsimony (*laghiyasi*).[27] But this does not mean that *anyathā-khyāti* is the accepted theory of error by Viśiṣṭādvaitin as is evident from the fact that he criticises it. According to Vedānta Deśika, *akhyāti* or the non-apprehension of the true nature of the object presented is definitely a much simpler and sounder theory of illusion than *anyathā-khyāti*.[28] In his

[26]RB I-1-1, p. 130. *khyātyantaravādinām ca sudūramapi gatvā anyathāvabhāso avaśyāśrayaṇiyaḥ.*

[27]NP. p. 91. *sarvairapyanyathākhyātiḥ dustyajatvāt laghiyasī.*

[28]*Ibid. tadvādinā'pi avarjyatvāt tato'pi akhyāti-lāghavam.*

opinion, even the upholders of *anyathā-khyāti* have to accept *akhyāti* because the former is based on the latter insofar as misapprehension is due to non-apprehension of what is presented. This does not mean that he rejects the *sat-khyāti* propounded by Rāmānuja. Keeping his allegiance to Rāmānuja he upholds the view that *yathārthakhyāti* as combined with *akhyāti* (*akhyāti-saṁvalita yathārthakhyāti*) is the sound theory of error.

Criticism of Buddhist Theories of Error

The above conclusion is made after a critical examination of the theories of other schools. Let us first take the extreme view of the Mādhyamikas who regard the object of illusion as a non-existent (*asat*). According to their metaphysical position to which we have referred earlier, everything in the universe is void (*śūnya*) implying that its nature is indeterminable. If the material objects are of such a nature, the shell-silver is a non-existent but it appears as existent due to the influence of *saṁvṛti*. Hence the theory is known as *asat-khyāti*. As already pointed out the description of the *tattva* as devoid of all description as *sat* or *asat* or both, etc. is untenable. A total negation does not imply total non-existence at any time or at any place. When we say that an object does not exist, it only means it exists at some other time or some other place. If shell-silver is a non-existent like the sky-flower, then to say that it appears as existent amounts to a self-contradiction. This theory does not therefore explain the cognition of silver in shell, unless it is admitted that what is perceived (the silver) exists somewhere or seen at some other place or time. That is, what never exists anywhere, such as sky-flower, cannot become the object of cognition.

It is contended by some Buddhists that illusion could take place even without an objective basis (*adhiṣṭhāna*). In the illusory cognition in the form 'this is silver', the term 'this' does not refer to the shell as such but it is the idea of silver caused by the experience of silver earlier (*saṁskāra*) that manifests itself as silver devoid of any objective basis.[29]

This theory is unsound, contends Vedānta Deśika, because an object is seen right in front of us at the time of illusion. Besides,

[29] SS IV-29, p. 202.

illusion does not arise at all the time but only when an object is presented. If illusion takes place only on account of the latent impression in our mind (*saṁskāra*), then it should happen even when shell is not seen.

It may be argued that there are some cases of illusion which arise without an objective basis. As an example of this, the illusion of a cluster of curly hairs in the sky (*keśa-guccha*) or the one of castle in the sky is cited. Such a thing has no objective basis. In the same way, it should be possible for the illusory cognition of shell-silver without shell being present as its substrate.

Even in this instance, Vedānta Deśika urges that the illusion is not without a substrate. In this particular case, the darkness (*tamas*) which emanates from the eyes due to some eye defect such as cataract causes the illusion of the cluster of black hair. This dark shade constitutes the *adhiṣṭhāna* or the substrate for the illusion. Similarly in the case of the illusion of a castle in the sky, the moving clouds in the sky form the basis for the illusion.[30] In the case of shell-silver illusion, the Buddhists accept the judgment 'this is silver'. The term 'this' here obviously refers to an object, though silver may not be present. Admission of *adhiṣṭhāna* or the presence of the objective basis is essential for explaining illusion.

There is one other theory of illusion, held by some Buddhists, according to which the illusory cognition does not have a content (*nirviṣaya*). In support of this view, it is stated that sometimes when the mind is deeply absorbed in something, the objects are not seen at all even though they are present right before the person. In the same way, illusion of silver may arise even without taking cognisance of the shell.

Vedānta Deśika rejects this view as it is opposed to our normal experience. Knowledge, whether it be valid or invalid, cannot arise unless it has a reference to some object. The nature of knowledge is to reveal the objects (*vastu-viṣayaka-prakāśa*). In the absence of its being related to any objects, it does not function. Even though the mind is considered to be empty, it is not totally empty but it is only absorbed in one particular thing or idea.[31]

[30]SS IV-29, p. 202.
[31]TMK IV-30. *khyātiḥ kasyāpi puṁsaḥ kvacidapi viṣaye siddharūpā hi siddhā.*

According to the Yogācāra school of Buddhism who deny the reality of the external world and accept *vijñāna* or the mental series as the only reality, error is caused by the super-position of the mental idea (*jñānākāra*) on the external object. The *vijñāna* creates the illusory percept.

This theory is based on the metaphysical position that it is the inner knowledge that appears as coming from outside and that the external object as such does not exist. We have already examined this doctrine in detail and shown its untenability. Knowledge is an internal entity and the object is external and the two cannot be identical. If knowledge itself, irrespective of any external condition, imposes upon itself the knower and illusory percept, then the illusory cognition should assume the the form 'I am silver' and not 'this is silver'. This theory which is based on a wrong hypothesis becomes untenable.

Criticism of Advaitin's Theory of Error

The Advaitin maintains that the object cognised in illusion is neither real nor unreal, but it is different from real and unreal (*sad-asad-vilakṣaṇa*). If it were real, it would be valid. Since this is sublated by the later cognition, it cannot be real. If it were unreal, it would not appear as an object for cognition. Since it appears, it cannot also be unreal. Nor can it be called both real and unreal as this would amount to subsistence of two contradictory qualities in one and the same entity.[32] Taking the example of the familiar shell-silver illusion, if the shell-silver is real then the contradictory cognition that it is not silver cannot arise. If it be unreal like the sky-flower, it cannot appear as silver. However, it does appear but it is also negated. Therefore, shell-silver is neither *sat* nor *asat*. It is therefore described as *sad-asad-vilakṣaṇa*. This is the meaning of the term *anirvacaniya*, that is, indefinable or indescribable either as *sat* or *asat*. The inexplicable object seen in illusion as silver is caused by *avidyā* with the help of the residual traces of a past-cognition of the object revived by the similarity of silver with the shell with which the defective sense organ is in contact.

Vedānta Deśika refutes this theory on the ground that the concept of *sad-asad-vilakṣaṇa* is a self-contradiction (*vyāghāta*).

[32]SS IV-16, p. 185 (quoted from *Iṣṭasiddhi*, p. 47). *sattve na bhrāntibādhau stām, nāsattve khyātibādhane; sad-asadbhyām anirvācyā.*

Sattva and *asattva* are mutually opposed. They are contradictory like light and darkness. If it is not *sattva*, it has to be *asattva*; if it is not *asattva*, it has to be *sattva*. The two cannot coexist. It is therefore a contradiction to describe the object of illusion as different from *sat* and *asat*.

The Advaitin holds the view that the shell-silver is produced by *avidyā*. If the silver is actually produced at the time of illusion, then the cognition of silver should be true and not false. The assumption here is that which is a product should be real and also serviceable.[33] Against this the Advaitin may say that the silver seen in illusion, unlike the silver in the shop, is not serviceable and therefore it is to be regarded as illusory (*mithyā*). This explanation will not hold good, replies Vedānta Deśika. The fact that a piece of silver is not usable as an ornament at a particular time should not render it *mithyā*. If that were so, the lump of silver which is not being used as an ornament would have to be regarded as illusory.[34]

What is the cause of the production of the indefinable silver at the time of illusion? Is it the *avidyā* which is the cause of the appearance of the universe? Or the sense organs (*indriyas*)? Or the very cognition of shell-silver?

As regards the first alternative, *āvidyā* is *anādi*, that is, it exists from time immemorial and so why should it not have caused the shell-silver even earlier? Regarding the second alternative, the sense organs cannot produce the objects. They only serve as means to knowledge. The third alternative also is equally untenable since the cognition of shell-silver does not produce the shell-silver. The appearance of shell-silver actually causes its cognition; what serves as a cause of cognition cannot produce itself.[35] *Anirvacanīya-khyāti* cannot therofore be a sound theory of error.

Theory of Sat-khyāti

Coming to Rāmānuja's theory of *sat-khyāti*, Vedānta Deśika tries to explain its fuller ontological and epistemological significance with a view to removing the possible misunder-

[33]See *Śrutaprakāśikā* I-1-1. *paramārthasyaiva arthakriyākāritvāt utpattimattvācca.*
[34]TMK IV-17. *karyāsāmarthyamātrāt tad apramā iti kathanāmatiprasaktyai na kalpate*
[35]*Ibid.*

standing of the theory by the critics. Rāmānuja, following the tradition, held by the eminent thinker such as Nāthamuni, upholds that all knowledge is of the real.[36] This view is described as *yathārtha-khyāti* or *sat-khyāti*. *Khyāti* means knowledge and *yathārtha* or *sat* means that the object which is the content of knowledge is real. The first question that arises is: if all knowledge is of the real, then how do we account for the cases of illusion such as shell-silver, mirage, dream, etc. where we do not seem to have a corresponding real object? Rāmānuja acknowledges the commonly accepted cases of error and offers explanation consistent with his realistic position. In the case of the illusions of shell-silver and mirage, he adopts the Vedāntic doctrine of quintuplication (*pañcikaraṇa*), according to which objects of the visible world, which are all compounds, contain all the five elements (*bhūtas*), though in varying proportions. Thus in the case of the mirage, the heated sand particles contain not only the elements of *pṛthivi* and *tejas* which are preponderating but also some aspect of *ap* or water element. The apprehension of water is therefore of what is really present. The shell-silver illusion is also accounted for on the basis of the presence of some aspect of silver in the shell, though infinitesimal as compared to the predominant shell part. When it is said that some aspect of silver is present in the shell, what is intended is not the very silver itself but the glitter or brightness of silver.[37] There is similarity between the shell and silver in respect of the lustre. This similarity is regarded by Rāmānuja as the presence in the shell, though only to an extremely limited extent of the very basic substance, viz. aspect of *tejas* (*tejo'ṁśa*) which constitutes silver. Likeness is another term for partial identity of material and so what is perceived even here is what is actually presented.[38] As regards the dream experience, a different explanation is offered. Taking his stand on the authority of the Upaniṣads, Rāmānuja explains that the dream objects are created by *Īśvara* to provide suitable means for the individual to experience pain or pleasure according to his past *karma*.[39] The objects thus experienced in the dream are also

[36]TMK IV-10. *nāthair-uktā yathārthā vimatamatiḥ nyāyatattve.*

[37]SS IV-10, p, 180. *śuktau sādṛśyāt rajata-sadbhāvaḥ.*

[38]See *Śrutaprakāśikā* I-1-1. *sampratipanna-rajatādy-avayava-susadṛśākāratvameva teṣām rajatādyavayavatvaṁ, na tu rajatādibhya ānīya niveśitatvam.*

[39]RB I-1-1, p. 135. Also RB III-2-3.

real, although they last only as long as they are experienced by the particular individual. The reality of the objective content in all these cases is justified on the basis of a metaphysical stand taken on the strength of the Upaniṣadic teaching.

There are other instances of illusion such as the white conch which is seen yellow by a person with a jaundiced eye; the firebrand-circle (*alātacakra*) where a point of light, owing to its rapid movement, is mistaken for its locus; the white crystal appearing as red when juxtaposed with a red flower; the appearance of double moon is seen with a squinted eye; the reflection of the face in the mirror; the illusion about the direction (*dig-moha*) as to whether it is east or west, etc. Rāmānuja offers varying explanations to account for these different types of illusion.[40] But in all these cases he maintains that what is seen is real, and as such he asserts that knowledge is of the real.

Though all knowledge is of the real, a distinction is however made between the right knowledge and wrong knowledge on the basis of a two-fold criteria of truth. Knowledge to be true should fulfil two conditions: first, it should have agreement with the outside reality (*yathāvasthita*); secondly, it should be adapted to the practical interests of life (*vyavahārānuguṇa*). Truth, in other words, means not merely correspondence to reality but also adaptability to the practical needs of life.[41] If the silver seen in the shell is considered false, it does not mean that some aspect of it is not present there as otherwise we could not have mistaken the one for the other. But the silver we see in the shell cannot be put to any practical use because of the slightness (*alpatva*) of silver element. When this fact becomes known, we regard the cognition of the silver in shell as erroneous. The distinction between true and false knowledge lies in the fact that one leads to practical utility, whereas the other does not. That is, the silver in the shop is useful for making ornaments, whereas the silver noticed in shell is of no practical value. On the final analysis, error is due to the non-apprehension of the difference between the silver which has practical utility and the one which does not have it.[42] This is same as *akhyāti* or non-apprehension of the differ-

[40]RB I-1-1, pp. 136-38.

[41]NP, p. 90. *yathāvasthita-vyavahārānuguṇam jñānam pramā.*

[42]TMK IV-10. *yogyāyogyādibhedāgraha iha caramāṁ saṁpratiṣṭhāṁ gāhate.* See also SS, p. 180.

ence between the two. So even in the theory of *sat-khyāti*, *akhyāti* is involved as one of the factors for causing error. In view of this fact, Vedānta Deśika describes the Viśiṣṭādvaita theory of error as *akhyāti-saṁvalita-yathārtha-khyāti*.

The justification for accepting *akhyāti* besides *sat-khyāti* advocated by Rāmānuja is that certain cases of error such as the delusion of body as the self (*dehātma-bhrama*) cannot be accounted for on the basis of the metaphysical explanations such as *pañcikaraṇa* theory, because there are no common features between the self and the body as in the case of shell and silver. In such cases, illusion arises due to the non-awareness or non-apprehension of the difference that exists between the self and the body. Non-apprehension is in a sense incomplete knowledge about the object cognised. In all cases of error, non-apprehension of the true nature of the object presented to the cognition is to be admitted as one of the important causal factors for error. As already pointed out, even though the content of the wrong cognition (say, the apprehension of silver in shell) may be denied as real insofar as it is not serviceable, the cognition of it is not negated. That is, no one says that the silver in shell was not seen, as otherwise illusion would not occur. The knowledge aspect is valid, and it has a reference to a content which exists as real, if not here, elsewhere. In the light of the above explanation, the theory of *sat-khyāti* of Viśiṣṭādvaita is justified as a sound theory of truth and error.

Theory of Akhyāti

Is *akhyāti* which is accepted as the basis for *sat-khyāti* a sound theory? The Naiyāyikas who uphold *anyathā-khyāti* have raised some objections against it. Error, according to Prabhākara, is due to the non-apprehension of distinction between two cognitions. When we mistake the shell for silver, we make the judgment 'this is silver'. Here 'this' refers to the object perceived, viz. the shell with its certain qualities. The knowledge of these qualities revives in one's mind the impression of an earlier experience, and one remembers silver immediately. The error here consists of the non-awareness of the distinction between the two cognitions—perception immediately followed by memory—and as a result we fail to notice the separateness of their respective contents.

Against this view, the Naiyāyikas urge that mere non-apprehension of the distinction cannot cause the illusion of silver in the shell. When shell is mistaken for silver, it also leads to activity like one stretching the hand to pick it up. When the illusion is removed, there is a cessation of such activity. The mere non-apprehension of the difference between the shell and silver cannot cause such an activity. If that were so, the absence of such a non-apprehension (*bhedāgraha*) should also stop one from moving forward to pick up the silver. This is not so. What actually causes the activity is the perception of silver in the shell. That is, unless the shell is misapprehended for silver, the illusion cannot induce action. This is *anayathā-khyāti*, and this is to be accepted to account for the error satisfactorily.

Vedānta Deśika does not agree with this view. It is not the mere apprehension of the difference between the shell and silver that is the cause of non-activity. On the contrary, what stops one from proceeding to pick up the silver is the awareness of the fact that it is a shell only which is not what is desired (*aniṣṭa-bheda-graha*).[43] That is, if one apprehends the true nature of shell, there is no room for illusion of silver in it and consequently any inducement for action. When the true nature of the shell, which is the substrate for the illusion of silver, is not known and when the silver seen earlier is remembered—illusion arises as a result of non-apprehension of the difference between the shell and silver. It is not necessary that there should be the actual perception of silver in the shell for the purpose of activity. This point is made clear in the following criticism of *anyathā-khyāti*.

Criticism of the Theory of Anyathā-khyāti

According to Nyāya-Vaiśeṣika, error is the apprehension of an object as other than what it is. The shell is mistaken for silver. It is normally found in our experience that unless one has a knowledge of the desired object, one will not make any effort to secure it. When the individual mistakes the shell for silver, he stretches his hand to pick it up and such an activity is explicable if only he had the perception of silver in the shell. The mere non-cognition of the true nature of shell is not sufficient to induce a person to pick up the silver, but, on the contrary, he should know that it is silver. The Naiyāyikas therefore urge that, besides non-apprehension of difference between shell and silver, the perception of

[43]TMK IV-11.

silver in shell is also needed for the illusion to arise. That is, unless one misapprehends the shell for silver, one cannot have the illusion of silver. The Naiyāyikas therefore contend that the theory of *anyathā-khyāti* is justified.

The above argument is refuted by Vedānta Deśika. It is not necessary that one should have the cognition of the object in order to secure it. Thus, for instance, a person who sees only the lustre of a shining gem mistakes it for the gem itself, stretches his hand and happens to pick it up. In this case, he has not actually seen the gem except its lustre. What prompted him to make an effort to look for the gem is not actually the knowledge of the gem but the illusion caused by the lustre of gem. Even though the knowledge which prompted activity is false insofar as it is a mistaken notion for the gem, the activity itself as well as the result obtained are true. Even if *jñāna* be true, its content need not be true.[44]

The Naiyāyika's argument is based on the assumption that a person who is prompted by activity should have the knowledge of the object desired by him. Unless the silver is seen in the shell, one would not stretch his hand to pick it up as this is the case in the case of real silver. In support of this point, the following syllogistic argument is put forward: 'The shell as qualified by silverness is the content of (illusory) cognition; because it induces activity in the individual desirous of silver as in the case of real silver.'[45]

This argument is fallacious, contends Vedānta Deśika. A person, who wants milk, drinks it which is mixed with water without being aware of the presence of water in it. He has however fulfilled his desire. In the same way, the knowledge which has prompted a person to pick up silver need not necessarily be related to silver. It is not therefore necessary to adopt *anyathā-khyāti* to account for error.[46]

Vedānta Deśika advances a counter-syllogism to refute the Naiyāyika's argument: 'The shell is not the content of the cognition of silver, because it has the characteristic of shellness; or, to give another reason, because it is different from silver, just like true shell.' When the shell is known as such, that is, when there

[44]TMK IV-12. *ratnāṁśau ratnabuddhyā anavagate ratna eva pravṛttiṁ viduḥ.*

[45]*Śuktiḥ rajatatva-prakārakajñāna-viṣayaḥ, rajatārthi-pravṛtti-viṣayatvāt, satya-rajatavat.* [46]TMK IV-13.

is the cognition of real shell, there is no possibility of its being cognised as silver; in the same way, even in the case of erroneous knowledge of silver, shell cannot be the content of that cognition. In the illusory experience 'this is silver', 'this' aspect refers to *śukti* which is a separate cognition and perceptual in character; *silver* aspect is a separate cognition and is a case of memory. The two cognitions with different contents being distinct, the possibility of *śukti* appearing or being apprehended as silver does not arise.[47]

Further, Vedānta Deśika observes that for the Viśiṣṭādvaitin the cognition of shell-silver is true knowledge (*yathārtha-jñāna*) because it is of the nature of knowledge and not *anyathā-jñāna* or wrong knowledge, as Naiyāyikas say, because knowledge itself is not invalidated. Even, according to *anyathā-khyāti*, the cognition aspect is true, and only the content aspect is false. No one says that knowledge did not arise. Knowledge insofar as it is related to some content is true.

This raises another issue. If the knowledge of shell-silver is also true, how does the later knowledge which contradicts it (*bādhaka-jñāna*), viz. that it is not silver, arise? In reply, Vedānta Deśika explains that the function of *bādhaka-jñāna* is to show that the silverness, which was wrongly attributed to the shell, does not exist in the shell.[48] Nobody admits that silver really belongs to the shell. It is the silver, seen elsewhere, that is being remembered and apprehended in the shell. The later cognition which negates the silver determines that the silverness is not related to the shell. For this purpose it is not necessary to adopt *anyathā-khyāti*. On further analysis, it may be observed that the element of silver, which is supposed to manifest in the shell as claimed by the Naiyāyikas, does not actually exist there, and as such the *anyathā-khyāti* would end up in the theory of *asat-khyāti*, that is, the apprehension of what actually does not exist.[49]

If the shell-silver cognition is also true (*yathārtha*), what is the meaning of the term *bhrānti* or erroneous cognition? This is a question which is raised against the Viśiṣṭādvaitin who regards even the shell-silver cognition as real. Vedānta Deśika replies to this by pointing out that the same two factors which are considered by the Naiyāyikas as responsible for illusion, viz. the cognition of the substrate (*adhiṣṭhāna-jñāna*) and the recollection of

[47]TMK IV-13. [48]SS IV-13, p. 183. [49]TMK IV-13.

silver seen elsewhere, are regarded as *bhrānti-jñāna* by the Viśiṣṭādvaitin.[50] That is, the non-awareness of the difference between these two cognitions is itself *bhrānti*. Instead of accepting such a simple explanation for error, the Naiyāyikas bring in an additional factor as responsible for illusion; this is known as *viśiṣṭa-jñāna*, that is, the cognition of shell as qualified by silver (*rajatatva-prakāraka śukti-jñāna*). Vedānta Deśika argues, taking his stand on the principle enunciated by Rāmānuja and also the evidence of common experience, that it is more appropriate to account for illusion on the basis of commonly accepted factors rather than postulating any additional factor not warranted by experience. Accordingly, *bhrānti-jñāna* is not a single cognition as the Naiyāyikas believe but it comprises two cognitions—perception and memory. What causes illusion is the non-apprehension of the difference between the two. This is the same as *akhyāti* and not *anyathā-khyāti*, the apprehension of an object as something else.

III. SELF-VALIDITY OF KNOWLEDGE

The critical evaluation of the different theories of truth and error leads to the conclusion that all knowledge including the so-called erroneous cognition is valid, and has a reference to an object outside it. Knowledge, by virtue of its intrinsic nature, reveals the object as it is, and, in view of this, it is admitted in the system as self-valid (*svataḥ prāmāṇya*). Revelation of object is the natural character of *jñāna* in the same way as the capacity to burn is the natural character of fire.[51] As a general rule knowledge being revelatory in character is self-valid. Whether the object revealed by knowledge is true or false is to be known after knowledge arises. The invalidity of knowledge is therefore caused by certain extraneous factors (*upādhi*) such as defective eye sight, darkness, etc. (*parataḥ aprāmāṇya*).

According to the Naiyāyikas, both validity and invalidity of knowledge are caused by extraneous factors (*parataḥ*). When knowledge arises, we do not know whether it is valid or not. Its validity or invalidity is known only subsequently depending on

[50]TMK IV-14. *yo'asau bodhaḥ anyathā-dhī-janaka iti jage, asau bhrāntir ityucyate.*

[51]TMK IV-103. *saṁvittīnām yathāvasthita-nija-viṣayollekha autsargikaḥ syāt.*

whether it leads to fruitful activity or not. We require an additional means, viz. fruitful activity, to ascertain its validity. Validity is thus known on the basis of the extraneous factor.

Vedānta Deśika rejects this view. As already pointed out, knowledge by its very nature is valid, and it does not require any extraneous factor to determine its validity. Even the Naiyāyikas have admitted self-validity in respect of *Īśvara-jñāna* which is eternal and not caused by any external accessories. If *Īśvara-jñāna* is self-valid because it is free from defects, then the same argument would hold good in respect of Vedic knowledge.[52]

Further, the released souls (*muktātma*) are omniscient as declared by the śruti, and their knowledge which is free from the influence of any extraneous factors is admitted to be self-valid. On the basis of the same principle, the knowledge of other bound souls is to be accepted as self-vaild. No one has illusion in respect of *ātman*, which is the substrate for *jñāna*, and also with regard to *jñāna* itself or its object as far as their intrinsic nature is concerned. No one doubts whether the knowing self exists, whether or not knowledge arose. Similarly, no one questions whether an object was revealed or not. In other words, there is no illusion in respect of the very *svarūpa* of these entities.[53] Illusion does not arise in respect of the *substrate*—the 'this' aspect of cognition which is actually perceived; but it does arise with regard to the characteristic it possesses. Insofar as cognition reveals the *substrate*, it is self-valid.

The Buddhists maintain that all knowledge by its very nature is *invalid*, and only the cognition of the bare particulars (*svalakṣaṇa-jñāna*) is valid. This is also not a sound theory, argues Vedānta Deśika. It is not possible to prove that all knowledge is *apramāṇa*. At least this one statement 'that *aprāmāṇya* is self-established' would have to be admitted as valid in order to prove their theory. Further, if all determinate knowledge (*vikalpa*) is false, then the objective basis (*adhiṣṭhāna*) for illusion is to be admitted as real. As we have observed earlier, no illusion can take place without an objective basis. If something is accepted as true, how could the Buddhists assert that all knowledge is false? Further, there is no *pramāṇa* to prove that invalidity is the very nature of

[52]TMK IV-103. [53]TMK IV-104.

knowledge, and that validity is dependent on extraneous factors. The Buddhists themselves admit that *vijñāna* in the state of release becomes free from all vāsanās. If that knowledge in the state of release is also invalid, then the concept of *mukti* would become meaningless.[54]

The Sāṅkhyas maintain the view that both validity and invalidity are self-established (*svataḥ*). Vedānta Deśika rejects this theory. He asks whether both validity and invalidity are found in different entities or in the same entity ? If it be said that they are found in different entities, then some criteria have to be laid down to determine what is valid and what is invalid. This would amount to the acceptance of the Nyāya position. If they are found in the same entity, then it would involve a self-contradiction as the two opposed to each other cannot coexist.

The self-contradiction can be overcome by maintaining the view that knowledge in respect of some aspect of the object is valid, while in respect of some other aspect it is invalid. This would lead to the position that all knowledge is both valid as well as invalid. This is not a sound view. It is therefore more appropriate to accept that knowledge is valid by its very nature, and its invalidity is only caused by extraneous factors.[55]

One objection may be raised against the Viśiṣṭādvaitin's view. If all knowledge by its very nature is valid, there should be no room for doubt as to the validity or invalidity of a particular knowledge. In the absence of doubt, there is no need for any kind of philosophic enquiry.

This is not a valid objection, argues Vedānta Deśika. Doubt may arise due to some reason or other even after the ascertainment of the truth. No school of thought admits that doubt will not arise after determining the validity or truth of a theory. It is natural even for a philosopher to question his own conclusion even after it is well established. The possibility of such a doubt, which is natural and common in the matter of philosophical discussion, does not affect the intrinsic character of knowledge as self-valid.

The validity of knowledge is self-revealed. The validity of knowledge of God is known by *Īśvara* Himself; otherwise He would not be omniscient. In the same way, the definition of know-

[54]TMK IV-105. [55]TMK IV-107.

ledge, viz. 'uncontradicted knowledge is valid' includes in itself its own validity. Valid knowledge, as repeatedly pointed out, reveals an object as it is.[56] Validity means that something is revealed in its true form. It is not correct to say that when knowledge arises it does not manifest its validity. Vedānta Deśika therefore concludes that knowledge is self-valid.

[56]TMK IV-109. *māne arthaḥ svātmanaiva sphurati.*

CHAPTER SIX

The Doctrine of Jīva

THE Viśiṣṭādvaita Vedānta presents a distinctive doctrine of *jiva*.[1] Based on the teachings of the Upaniṣads, the *Vedānta-sūtras* and the *Bhagvadgītā*, it establishes that *jiva* or the individual self is an eternal spiritual entity and is distinct from the Supreme Self or Brahman. Even in the state of *mokṣa*, it does not lose its individuality. *Jivas* are infinite in number and they are essentially of the nature of knowledge (*jñāna-svarūpa*). Though *jiva* is of the nature of knowledge, it is also the substrate of knowledge, emphasising the fact that it is the knowing subject (*jñātā*). It is thus the agent of action (*kartā*), and enjoyer of pleasure and pain (*bhoktā*). It is monadic in substance (*aṇu*).

In order to establish the soundness of this doctrine, Vedānta Deśika takes up for critical examination the other theories of *jiva* which are opposed to it. The more important of them discussed in *Tattva-muktā-kalāpa* are : the Cārvāka view that body itself is *jiva*; the Nyāya theory that *jiva* is not of the nature of consciousness; the Advaitin's view that *jiva*, which is pure consciousness, is identical with Brahman; the Vaiśeṣika view that *jiva* is all-pervasive (*vibhu*); the Jaina view that *jiva* is of the size of the body which it occupies. The section related to *jiva* (*jivasara*), also deals with the eligibility of *jīva* for *mokṣa*, the means to attain *mokṣa*, the status of *jiva* in *mokṣa* and other allied issues. These topics will be discussed in a separate chapter under the title 'Sādhana and Mukti'. In the present chapter,

[1]The word *jiva* means that which lives or sustains life (*jīvati iti jīvaḥ*). It is also known as *ātman* or that which pervades the body (*āpnoti iti*). It is described as *jīvātman* to distinguish it from *paramātman*, the supreme self. The other terms used for *jīva* are *cit*, *cetana* or that which has consciousness, *kṣetrajña*, the knower of the field of knowledge and *ahampadārtha*, the entity denoted by 'I'. All these terms are synonymous in Viśiṣṭādvaita. The words Mind, Spirit, Soul, etc., used in the Western philosophy do not convey the same meaning of *jīva* or *ātman* as conceived in Vedānta.

we shall deal with the important issues relating to the nature of the individual self.

I. JĪVA AS DIFFERENT FROM BODY AND MIND

The Cārvākas, the Indian materialists, do not admit the existence of *jiva* as different from the body. While criticising this view, Vedānta Deśika points out that *jiva* is not only different from body but also the sense organs, the mind and *prāṇa* (vital breath) and intellect (*buddhi*).[2]

When we say 'my hand', 'my leg', the hand, the leg, etc. appear to be different from 'myself'. In the same way when we get the experience in the form 'my body', the body which is the aggregate of the various organs should be considered as distinct from the self. In other words, the entity which manifests itself as different from the body is the self or *jiva*.[3] If it be argued that body itself is *jiva*, then it is asked whether or not each part of the body possesses *jiva*. If *jiva* exists in each part, then it would amount to saying that there are several *jivas* in the same body. In that case conflict among the different *jivas* is inevitable, as in the case of the several rulers ruling the same kingdom and there would be no unity of purpose and action. It cannot be said that there is no scope for such disputes because anyone who is born as a human being cannot be totally free from the passions arising from the ego. Further, if *jiva* exists in each part of the body, with the removal of any one of the limbs the experience belonging to it cannot be recollected by another as there is no transmission of such experience from one limb to the other.

It may be possible to overcome the above difficulty by assuming that *jiva* is present not in each part of the body but in the aggregate of the parts (*avayavi*). But this would lead to another difficulty. If *caitanya* or *jivahood* is not found in the parts, it would not also be present in the aggregate. A quality which does not exist in the parts cannot be found in the aggregate of the parts. Besides, the physical body being an aggregate of several parts or limbs would only be a non-intelligent entity

[2]See *Ātmasiddhi*, p. 8. *dehendriya-manaḥ-prāṇa-dhībhyo anyaḥ.* The arguments advanced by Yāmuna have been adopted by Vedānta Deśika. [3]TMK II-1.

(*acit*) like a pot and as such it cannot possess consciousness. The Cārvākas argue that consciousness or the spiritual principle emerges as a result of the combination of the four physical elements like the intoxicating quality that arises by the mingling of certain ingredients such as yeast which separately do not possess it. This view is also rejected as unsound. In the illustration cited by the Cārvākas, the element that produces the intoxicating quality is present in the ingredients in a potential form, and it therefore causes the emergence of a new property. In the case of the physical body, there is no evidence to show that consciousness is present in each of the physical parts of the body.[4]

How do we explain the expression 'myself' (*mama-ātmā*) ? Would it mean that *ātman* is different from the self? As self and *ātman* cannot be different, such an expression has to be understood in its secondary sense. That is, the *ātman* here means the mind and not the self. Alternatively, the word 'mine' in the genitive case means non-distinctness as in the example *rāhoḥ śiraḥ* or Rāhu's head.[5] Though the terms indicate that head is distinct from Rāhu, actually the two are the same. It is a linguistic usage in which the genitive case is to be explained in the sense of their being one and the same.

For a layman the experience arising in the form 'I am fat', 'I am beautiful', etc. may only mean that body itself is soul in the same way as a molten iron ball can be mistaken for a fire ball due to the non-awareness of the difference between the two. But for those who have unquestionable faith in the revealed scripture, the self is different from the body as it is evident from the various scriptural texts. Our ordinary experience may not reveal that the self is different from the body. In a matter which is supersensuous, we have to rely on the evidence of scriptural texts. The śruti says that a person who has performed meritorious deeds will be reborn with merit. Similarly, a person who has done wicked deeds will be reborn into evil. Such scriptural statements would become meaningless if the self is not admitted to be different from the body. In order to explain such statements

[4]SS II-1, p. 72.

[5]Rāhu is the name of a demon who, according to Indian mythology, possesses only the head, his trunk having been severed from the head by Lord Viṣṇu for committing a fraud.

satisfactorily, we have to admit the difference between self and body. The śruti as well as smṛti texts[6] also declare that the self is eternal, that it is neither born nor does it die, and that it is of the nature of consciousness and bliss (*saṁvidānanda-rūpaḥ*).

The self is also different from the sense organs (*indriyas*). When an object is perceived through the visual organ and the same is also cognised through the organ of touch, we make the judgment that what is seen is also touched. It is evident from this that the same individual who sees also touches the object. This recognition of the object as one and the same (*pratyabhijñā*) arises in respect of the same individual. If sense organs were the *jiva*, then the organ of touch should be separate from the organ of vision and the experience of the same object by two different sense organs which are supposed to be *jivas* would not be one and the same. The recognition (*pratyabhijñā*) of what is already experienced points out that it is one and the same individual self that sees as well as touches the object. Again during sleep the external sense organs do not function but still we experience dream-objects. *Jiva* is therefore different from sense organs.[7]

Jiva is also different from mind (*manas*) because it is established by *pramāṇas* that *manas* serves as an instrument[8] (*karaṇa*) for recollection of past experience by *jiva*. Just as the organ of vision serves as an instrument for the *jiva* to see colours, mind serves as an instrument for the *jiva* to recollect what is previously experienced. What is a *karaṇa* for an agent cannot itself be the agent (*kartā*).

The vital breath (*prāṇa-vāyu*) cannot be the *jiva*. There are five *prāṇas* and the question would arise whether *jiva* is present in each *prāṇa* or in the aggregate of the five *prāṇas*. If *jiva* is present in each *prāṇa*, there would be several *jivas* and conflict between them is bound to arise. If, on the contrary, *jiva* is found in the aggregate of the *prāṇas*, what is not found in one *prāṇa* cannot exist in the aggregate of the *prāṇas*.

Nor is it possible to say that *buddhi* or knowledge itself is the *jiva*. As explained in the previous chapter, knowledge is a *dharma* or attribute of the *jiva*, whereas *jiva* is the *jñātā* or the substrate

[6]Ka Up 2-18. *na jāyate mriyate....ajo nityaḥ śāśvato'yam.* Svet Up 6-13. BG II-30. *dehī nityam avadhyo'yam.* [7]TMK II-3.

[8]See the section 'The Nature of the Sense Organs' in Chapter X for discussion.

of knowledge. Therefore, the two are different. Further, according to Buddhists, *jñāna* which is known as *vijñāna*, is momentary (*kṣaṇika*) and what is momentary cannot be the same as the *jiva* which is admitted as the permanent spiritual entity. Thus, *jiva* is different from the physical body, *indriyas*, *manas*, *prāṇa* and *buddhi*.

II. JĪVA AS THE SUBJECT OF KNOWLEDGE

Coming to the nature of *jiva*, the Viśiṣṭādvaita Vedānta maintains the view that *jiva* is an eternal spiritual entity and the subject of knowledge (*jñātā*). Unlike the Vaiśeṣikas, the Viṣiṣṭādvaitin regards *jiva* as of the nature of knowledge (*jñāna-svarūpa*). The implication of it is that *jiva* is not a non-sentient entity (*jaḍa*) with knowledge as its adventitious quality. It is, on the contrary, a spiritual substance. In order to bring out the spiritual character of *jiva*, it is regarded as *jñāna-svarūpa*. Further, it is not merely *jñāna-svarūpa*, as Advaitins believe. It also possesses knowledge as an essential attribute (*jñāna-guṇaka*). It is the substrate for knowledge, which means that *jiva* is also the knowing subject. Thus, the Viśiṣṭādvaitic concept of *jiva* differs from that of the Advaitin for whom it is mere transcendental consciousness, and also from that of Nyāya-Vaiśeṣika for whom it is not of the nature of consciousness. As will be shown presently, both these aspects of *jiva* are supported by the Upaniṣadic texts and are also justifiable on logical ground.

The Vaiśeṣikas question the soundness of accepting a separate entity as *jivātman*, besides *jñāna*. If according to the Viśiṣṭādvaitin, *jñāna* is *nitya* and is capable of functioning through the sense organs, where is the need to admit a separate entity known as *ātman* as its substrate? For the Vaiśeṣikas, *jñāna* is not permanent, and they find it necessary to assume a separate permanent entity as its substrate. They therefore contend that the *dharma-bhūta-jñāna* should suffice and there is no need to postulate *ātman* as a separate permanent entity.

In reply to this objection, Vedānta Deśika points out that the argument of Vaiśeṣikas is tenable if the theory of *ātman* is formulated mainly on the basis of logic. The Viśiṣṭādvaitin does not advance his theory on the limited basis of logic. On the contrary, he holds the view on the strength of the scriptural texts that both *jñāna* as a *dharma* of *ātman* and that *ātman* as its *dharmi* (substrate) are *nitya*. As explained in the chapter on 'Theory of Knowledge', the Upaniṣadic text asserts that both the *ātman* and its knowledge are not subject to destruction.[9] Further, *ātman* is *nirvikāra*, as śruti declares and in order to uphold the unchanging character of *ātman*, the attributive knowledge is to be admitted. The modifications take place only in respect of the attributive knowledge, while *ātman* remains unaffected by them.

If *ātman* is distinct from knowledge, is it necessary to admit that it is also of the nature of consciousness (*jñāna-svarūpa*)? If it be *jñāna-svarūpa*, could it also be a substrate of knowledge? How can knowledge be substrate of knowledge? In determining the nature of *jīvātman*, the Viśiṣṭādvaitin contends that one has to rely on the teachings of the scriptural texts. The śruti categorically states that the self is the knower (*boddhā*). The same text also describes self as *vijñānatmā* which means that it is of the nature of knowledge.[10] Thus, the scriptural texts do not speak of *ātman* as merely *jñāna-svarūpa* but also as *jñānāśraya*. Based on the teaching of the Upaniṣads, the *Vedānta-sūtra* also states that *ātman* is a knower (*jño'ta eva*). Commenting on this *sūtra*, Rāmānuja says that *jīvātman* is essentially a knower and not either mere knowledge or non-sentient in character.[11]

Vedānta Deśika seeks to justify on logical ground that *ātman* as *jñāna-svarūpa* could become the substrate for *jñāna* as *dharma*. *Jñāna* is defined in this system as that which manifests something (*artha-prakāśaḥ*). This characteristic feature of *jñāna* is common to both the substrate (*ātman*) and its *dharma* (*jñāna*). The former reveals itself and the latter manifests objects. As both reveal something, the term *jñāna* is applicable to both. Nevertheless, it is possible to conceive two entities of the same nature as substance and attribute. Thus, for instance, the flame of a lamp (*dipa*) and its luminosity (*prabhā*) are of the same character insofar as the element of fire or brightness (*tejas*) is

[9]Br Up VI-3-30. *nahi vijñātuḥ vijñāteḥ viparilopo vidyate, avināśitvāt.* See Section 'Knowledge as Eternal' in Chapter IV for interpretation of this text.

[10]Praśna Up IV-9. *eṣa hi draṣṭā, spraṣṭa, śrotā, ghrātā, rasayitā, mantā, boddhā, kartā vijñānātmā puruṣaḥ.*

[11]RB II-3-19. *ayam ātmā jñātṛsvarūpa eva. na jñānamātram, nāpi jaḍasvarūpaḥ.*

common to both, but the two are nevertheless distinct as substance and attribute. They are also different functionally; flame illumines itself, whereas its luminosity illumines itself as well as other objects.[12] In the same way *jiva* and its attributive knowledge, though they may have a common characteristic feature, are distinct as substance and attribute. They are also different in respect of their functions. The *jiva*, constituted of knowledge which is known as *dharmijñāna* or substantive-knowledge, reveals itself and not the external objects; it knows what is revealed to it. On the other hand, knowledge as the essential attribute of the self known as *dharma-bhūta-jñāna* or attributive knowledge reveals itself as well as the external objects to the self and does not know them. *Ātman* exists by and for itself (*pratyak*) and its *dharma-bhūtajñāna* exists for the *ātman* (*parāk*).[13] The former is categorised as *cetana* or that which has consciousness, and the latter is regarded as *acetana* or that which is devoid of consciousness. It is not therefore inappropriate to regard *jīva* as *jñānāśraya.*

Then, how about some śruti texts which describe *ātman* as only of the nature of *jñāna*? Thus, the *Bṛhadāraṇyaka Upaniṣad* states: *vijñanaghana eva,*[14] that is, *ātman* is only knowledge. Vedānta Deśika explains that such texts are intended to mean that there is no element of *jaḍatva* or non-sentience in it but they do not deny that *ātman* is the substrate of knowledge. To illustrate this point, the same Upaniṣad gives the example of salt crystal (*saindhava-ghana*). In the salt crystal there is no part which is free from salt element. When we describe the salt crystal as constituted of salt only, we do not rule out the possibility of its possessing some other qualities. In the same way, the description of *ātman* by the Upaniṣads as *jñāna* does not exclude its other characteristics such as knowership.

III. JĪVA AS SELF-LUMINOUS

According to the Viśiṣṭādvaita Vedānta, *jiva* is self-luminous because it is of the nature of knowledge. Vedānta Deśika puts

[12]See NS, p. 213. See also RB I-1-1, p. 69.

[13]TMK II-5. *ātmā tu svasyaiva siddhim anubhavati, matiḥ svānyayoh siddhi-bhāvam anubhavati.*

[14]Br Up VI-5-13 and IV-4-12.

forward the following argument in support of it: '*Ātman* is self-lunminous because it is of the nature of *jñāna* like the *dharma-bhūta-jñāna.*'[15] We have observed in the earlier chapter that knowledge is self-luminous in the sense that while revealing an object it does not need another knowledge to reveal it. In the same way, *ātman* is also self-luminous because it does not require another knowledge for its manifestation. It is known by itself and is not in need of another knowledge to know it. It manifests itself always as 'I' (*ātmā aham iti svenaiva siddhyati*). According to the Viśiṣṭādvaitins, the entity denoted by 'I' (*ahamartha*) is the true self.[16] It is not the same as the *ahaṁkāra* or the ego which is caused by the delusion of the physical body as the soul. Nor is it the product of the *mahat-tattva*, the evolute of *prakṛti*.

This view is also supported by the scriptural text. Thus, the *Bṛahadāraṇyaka Upaniṣad* says: '*Atrāyam puruṣaḥ svayaṁjyotir-bhavati*'.[17] The meaning of this text, taken in the context in which it appears, is that the *jiva* becomes self-luminous even in the state of deep sleep.

Self-luminosity or *svayaṁprakāśatva* of *ātman* is not to be understood in the sense that *ātman* reveals itself as 'I' to all and at all time. It reveals itself as 'I' to each individual, whereas for others it is known through their knowledge as 'he' or 'you.' The fact that it becomes known (*vedya*) does not affect its self-luminosity. As we have already discussed in the chapter on 'Theory of Knowledge', the concept of self-luminosity as absolute unknowability (*avedyatva*) is logically untenable. Even though knowledge or *ātman* becomes the object of another knowledge, it is self-luminous insofar as it is not dependent, unlike a material object, on another knowledge for its revelation.

If *ātman* which is *nitya* is self-luminous, it should manifest itself always. But in the state of deep sleep we do not have the experience of anything, and it is not therefore possible to assert that *ātman* reveals itself in that state. Against this argument the Viśiṣṭādvaitin maintains that even during the state of deep sleep *ātman* reveals itself as 'I'. This is evident from the experi-

[15]NS, p. 213. *ātmā svaprakāśaḥ, jñānatvāt dharma-bhūta-jñānavat.*

[16]That the entity denoted by 'I' is the individual self is proved with elaborate arguments by Rámānuja in *Śrī-bhāṣya.* See RB I-1-1, pp. 68-69. See also Śatadūṣaṇi vāda 27. Also AV, pp. 62-65. [17]Br Up VI-3-9.

ence which arises in the form 'I slept happily' soon after waking up. Because the self reveals itself in deep sleep the experience of having slept happily remains unsublated soon after waking. It cannot be said that this experience in the form 'I slept happily' is a mental state, that is, an experience caused by the mind, because mind cannot generate any experience without the aid of other accessories of knowledge. During deep sleep none of the accessories which cause knowledge is present. If they were present, there should have been an experience of them. If there be some experience, then it would not be regarded as a state of deep sleep. The experience 'I slept happily' is not one generated by the mind. On the contrary, it is an experience of the self in the form of enjoying its own bliss (*sukha*).[18]

It may be still argued that mind needs the accessories of knowledge for the purpose of experiencing the external objects. It does not need such accessories for experiencing internal states such as grief or joy. The absence of grief during the sleep gives the feeling of happiness. Such an experience of happiness during deep sleep could therefore be a mental state, and in view of this it cannot be claimed that the *ātman* is self-luminous during deep sleep.

This argument is refuted by emphasising the self-luminous character of the self. It is well established by the Upaniṣad that the self is of the nature of knowledge. On the basis of inference also it is possible to prove that *ātman* is self-luminous. Because it is of the nature of knowledge, it reveals itself, unlike a physical object, without the aid of another knowledge. It is, in other words, self-luminous and it remains as such in all the states of experience including deep sleep.

IV. JĪVA AS ETERNAL

Are *jivas* eternal? There is a view ascribed to Brahmadatta,[19] according to which Brahman alone is eternal and all else includ-

[18]*Sukha* or happiness experienced by the self in the state of deep sleep is not of the type of sensual pleasure (*vaiṣayika-sukha*), the happiness that is generated by the experience of external objects or any internal mental ideas, because knowledge through which experience takes place is not then operative. It is therefore admitted that *sukha* in the state of deep sleep is only the experience of the bliss of the *ātman* by itself. According to Viśiṣṭādvaita, the self is of the nature of bliss (*ānanda-svarūpa*) and it experiences its bliss. See NS, p. 213.

[19]Brahmadatta is referred to by name by Vedānta Deśika as the upholder

ing the *jivas* originate from Brahman and dissolve in it. In support of this he quotes the famous *Chāndogya Upaniṣadic* text which says that in the beginning there was Being, one only without a second. Accordingly, it is believed that *jivas* come into existence or are produced at the time of evolution, in the same way as *acit* or matter is brought into existence.[20]

Vedānta Deśika sets aside this view as one based on imperfect study of sacred texts (*anadhyetṛcodyam*). Numerous scriptural as well as smṛti texts speak of *ātman* as *nitya* and that it is not subject to any origin or destruction. There may be a few stray scriptural statements which appear to mention the birth of *jivas*. Thus, for example, the *Puruṣasūkta* text says: Prajāpati (the creator) created the individuals.[21] Such texts have to be understood to mean that *jivas* are born in the sense that they become associated with the physical bodies. As it is made explicit in the *Bhagavadgitā*, the birth of a *jiva* is only its association with a physical body and death is its dissociation from it. If śruti texts are properly understood, there would be no room for any conflict between one text and another. If there be any apparent conflict, it should be possible to reconcile it by interpreting the texts in their appropriate context and also with reference to other important and related statements whose import is indisputable.

If *jivātman* is not admitted to be *nitya*, several problems arise. The Buddhists hold the view that at each moment *jiva* undergoes change. This would mean that *jiva* which is constantly in a state of flux cannot be a permanent entity. If such a theory is accepted, there would be no scope for human endeavour to achieve something at a later period. All human effort is directed towards achieving something. If an individual changes at every moment, there would be no continuity of his existence and consequently what is done in one moment disappears with the person of that moment. What is done in the next moment becomes the achievement of another person. Why should the *x* moment person make any effort at all as an *x* individual if at the *y* moment he cannot enjoy its result?

To overcome this difficulty, it may be postulated that *ātman* continues in the body for the duration of that one life. In that

---

of this peculiar theory of *jiva*. We do not have any information about him or any of his works. [20]TMK II-16. [21]*Prajāpatiḥ prajā asṛjata.*

case, the religious activities pursued by an individual for the purpose of achieving higher spiritual goals in the life after death would become futile. As the soul ceases to exist after the end of the present life, the achievement of any higher goals after death would be out of the question.

To meet the above objection, it may be argued that *ātman* lasts till the end of the dissolution of the universe (*ākalpa-sthāyi*). If we accept such a view, all *jivas* would cease to exist at the time of dissolution and thus there would be no individual souls left to seek *mokṣa*. Consequently, the teaching of Vedānta for the purpose of achieving *mokṣa* would become futile.

It may be said that *jivas* continue to exist till they achieve *mokṣa* and that thereafter they would cease to exist. If we concede this view, it would imply that *jivas* do not exist in the state of *mokṣa*, and as such they would be non-eternal. The Viśiṣṭādvaitin does not accept this view because the *jivas*, according to Viśiṣṭādvaita, do not lose their individuality even in the state of *mokṣa*. Taking the stand on śruti texts, he maintains that *jivas* do exist in the state of *mokṣa* without losing their individuality. When *jivas* become free from the shackles of *karma*, they manifest themselves in their true nature in the state of *mokṣa*. This point is discussed in detail in the chapter on Sādhana and Mukti.

V. JĪVA AS KARTĀ AND BHOKTĀ

We have already observed that *jiva* is a knowing subject (*jñātā*). It is not merely of the nature of knowledge but is also the substrate of knowledge (*jñānāśraya*). The individual self which is the knower is also the agent of action (*kartā*) and enjoyer of pleasure and pain (*bhoktā*). The same *ātman* which performs *karma* also enjoys the fruit of action. This truth, Vedānta Deśika asserts, is well established by all the *pramāṇas*, *pratyakṣa*, *anumāna* and *āgama*.[22]

The Advaitin however does not admit that the true self which is pure undifferentiated consciousness is the knower inasmuch as knowership involves change, while the self must be immutable. The functions such as knowing, feeling and willing are the characteristics of the empirical ego, the consciousness conditioned by

[22]TMK II-8. *pratyagarthaḥ boddhā kartā bhoktā ca pramāṇaiḥ dṛḍham avagamitaḥ.*

the internal organ (*antaḥkaraṇa-avacchinna caitanya*). The cognisership (*jñātṛtva*) actually belongs to the internal organ. The self appears to be the knower because of the superimposition of the internal organ on it.

This theory has serious limitations. Both Rāmānuja and Vedānta Deśika have shown with convincing arguments that superimposition of cognisership on the self is an impossibility. Superimposition is possible either when there is some similarity between two things or where the distinction between the two objects is not distinctly apprehended. As consciousness for the Advaitin is devoid of all determinations, it does not admit similarity with any other object and consequently the question of non-apprehension of distinction does not arise. The possibility of reflection of consciousness in the internal organ, as the Sāṅkhyas believe, is also ruled out since consciousness does not have any form (*rūpa*) for purposes of reflection. There are other arguments to account for the cognisership in the self but all these are rejected as untenable. We need not go into these details. The important point to be considered is whether or not the act of knowing involves change or some modification in respect of the individual self, which according to the śruti is immutable (*nirvikāra*).

Vedānta Deśika points out that the admission of cognisership in *jīvātman* does not affect its immutable character. If an entity transforms itself from one state to another, as in the case of the lump of clay, then the immutable character of the self becomes affected. No such transformation takes place in respect of the self. Whatever modifications take place, these apply to attributive knowledge, which is distinct from the self and the latter remains unaffected by them. By mere admission of cognisership, which is warranted by the scriptural texts as well as experience, it cannot be said that the self undergoes change.[23]

It may be noted that *jīva* is regarded as *jñātā* or knower in the sense that it is the *āśraya* or substrate for knowledge through which all experiences take place. By being *āśraya* for *jñāna* which is subject to modifications, *jīva* is not subjected to any change. In the same way, *kartṛtva* and *bhoktṛtva* admitted in *jīva* do not involve change in it. *Jīva* is *kartā* or doer in the sense that it is the

[23]SD, Vāda 27. See also AV, pp. 65-69.

āśraya or substrate for *kṛti* or effort.[24] Effort is caused by a desire (*icchā*) to do an act. It is therefore a mental modification or an *avasthā* of *jñāna*. It is not to be confused with the actual physical activity which follows subsequent to the desire to do an act. Insofar as *jiva* is the *āśraya* for the *kṛti* which is a particular state of knowledge, *jiva* becomes the *kartā*. The change involved in the physical activity does not affect the *jiva*.

The same explanation holds good for *jiva* being the *bhoktā*.[25] *Bhoga* is an experience in the form of pleasure or pain. Pleasure and pain are different states (*avasthās*) of *jñāna*. Pleasure is an agreeable disposition of the mind (*anukūlatva-jñāna*) and pain is the disagreeable disposition of the mind (*pratikūlatva-jñāna*). As *jiva* is the *āśraya* for such states of experience, it is regarded as *bhoktā* or enjoyer of pleasure and pain. The change involved in such mental dispositions applies to the attributive knowledge and not to *jiva*. Such an explanation is logically tenable in the Viśiṣṭādvaita system because of the admission of *dharmabhūta-jñāna* as distinct from *jīvātman*. The modifications apply to the former, while the latter remains unaffected.

If the *jivātman* is not admitted as both the agent of action (*kartā*) and the enjoyer of the result (*bhoktā*), the scriptural texts which enjoin the performance of Vedic rites by an individual would become meaningless. Thus the *Vedānta-sūtra* says : 'The *jiva* is an agent on account of scripture (thus) having a purport.'[26] Commenting on this *sūtra*, Rāmānuja explains that when sacred texts (*śāstra*) enjoin the performance of *upāsanā* for achieving *mokṣa* or the performance of a *yāga* or sacrifice for the attainment of heaven, these are intended to be done by one who himself is the enjoyer of the fruit. *Śāstra* means to command (*śāsanācca śāstram*). A command is to induce one to do a thing, and it is meaningful only in respect of an intelligent agent and not one who is non-intelligent (*acetana*). In other words, the Vedic command is meaningful only in respect of one who is an agent of action.

Against this theory a view is held that *ātman* is not really the agent of action but the doership belongs to the *prakṛti*, the physical body constituted of the three *guṇas*—*sattva*, *rajas* and *tamas*. This means that all activities are caused by the three *guṇas*, and the

[24]See RB on BG XIII-20. *śarīrādhiṣṭhāna-prayatna-hetutvameva hi puruṣasya kartṛtvam*. For explanation see *Tātparya Candrikā*, p. 373.

[25]*Ibid. sukha-duḥkhānubhavāśraya iti.* [26]VS II-3-33. *kartā śāstrārthavattvāt*.

individual self is only the enjoyer but not the agent of action. It is stated in the *Bhagavad-gītā*:[27] '*Prakṛti* is said to be the cause of body and sense organs which serve as the basis for activities (*kriyākāri*); *puruṣa* is said to be the experiencer of pleasure and pain.' In another place the *Gītā* says : 'All action being caused by the *guṇas* of *prakṛti*, one clouded with ignorance thinks "I am the doer".'[28]

These verses apparently give the impression that *puruṣa* or the *jīvātman* is not the *kartā* but the *guṇas* of *prakṛti* are responsible for action. These ideas expressed in the *Gītā* appear to be in conflict with the teaching of the *Vedānta-sūtra* which says that *jīva* is *kartā*. Following the commentary of Rāmānuja on the *Gītā*, Vedānta Deśika does not accept this view and asserts that there is no conflict between the teachings of the *Vedānta-sūtra* and the *Gītā*. The apparent conflict is reconciled by the author of the *Gītā* himself. It is made clear in a later verse of the *Gītā* that all that is meant by it is that *jīva* caught up in bondage functions under the influence of *guṇas*. Though *jīva* is primarily the agent for action, it can act only when it is associated with a body, mind and sense organs while in the absence of these it cannot function. In view of this, emphasis is laid on the influence of the *guṇas* of which the body, mind, sense organs are constituted. Keeping this truth in mind, it is stated in the *Gītā* that one's attachment to *guṇa* is the cause of his birth in a good or bad family.[29] In another place in the *Gītā*,[30] it is stated explicity that there are five factors which are responsible for all action : the body (*adhiṣṭhāna*), the agent (*kartā*), the different organs (*karaṇa*), the fivefold vital breath and their modifications (*vividhā ceṣṭā*) and lastly, *Īśvara* (*daivam*). Though according to this verse *Īśvara* is an important cause for action of an individual because He is the controller of the universe including the human souls, equal importance is also given to the *kartṛtva* of the *jīva*.

From this it follows that though *jīva* is the *kartā*, its action is controlled by *Īśvara* as pointed out in the *Vedānta-sūtra*—'*parāttutat śruteḥ*'.[31] Commenting on this *sūtra*, Rāmānuja explains that *jīva's* action (*kartṛtva*) is caused by *Paramātman* (*paramātmana eva hetoḥ bhavati*), because it is stated so in the śruti and smṛti texts. Thus, the śruti says : 'He (*Īśvara*) controls all individuals by residing

[27]BG XIII-20. [28]*Ibid.* III-27. [29]BG XIII-21. [30]XVIII-14.
[31]VS II-3-40.

within their bodies.[32] The *Antaryāmi Brāhmaṇa* of *Bṛhadāraṇyaka Upaniṣad* repeatedly says that *Paramātmā* as the indweller of all beings controls them. The *Gitā* also reiterates that *Īśvara* resides in the hearts of all beings and thereby controls their activities by his divine power.[33]

Theory of Free-Will and Determinism

If the action of *jiva* is controlled by *Paramātman*, does the *jiva* have any freedom at all to act? If *jiva* has no freedom to act, the scriptural injunctions enjoining duties to be performed by the individual can have no significance. This is the familiar ethical problem of free-will versus determinism. Based on the *Vedānta-sūtra*, Rāmānuja answers this objection by providing an explanation. A distinction is drawn between the initial action of the individual and the subsequent activity. In all human effort, the individual initially wills to do a thing. To this extent he is free to do what he desires. Based on this initial action, the subsequent activity which follows it is approved by *Īśvara*. By according such an approval, *Īśvara* prompts the individual to proceed further (*pramātmā tadanumatidānena pravartayati*).[34] If it were not so, the Vedic injunctions in this regard would become futile. This is explanied by an illustration. A property is held jointly by two individuals. One of them desires to donate a part of it to some other person. In order to do so, he needs and seeks the consent of the other partner. With such a consent he gives away his share. Though the approval of the other partner is there, the act of giving it away in charity belongs to the individual who so desires to donate it and the fruit derived from such charitable act is also enjoyed by him. In the same way, even though *Īśvara* gives his approval to the activity initiated by an individual, He does not become the *kartā*—the doer. The real *kartā* is the individual. It is in this sense that *Īśvara* is considered to be the controller of human action and only to this extent the human freedom is not affected. Therefore the individual self is the *kartā* in this restricted sense.

One may well ask whether *Īśvara*, by according His approval to the subsequent activity of the individual, can escape the moral responsibility for the consequences of the act whether they are

[32]*Taittirīya Āraṇyaka* 3-11-10. *antaḥ praviṣṭaḥ śāstā janānāṁ sarvātmā.*
[33]BG XVIII-61. [34]RB II-3-41.

good or evil. Thus, for instance, if an individual indulges in a sinful activity such as murder, does not God too become a participant in it insofar as He remains neutral and does not stop the person from doing so? The Viśiṣṭādvaitin's answer to this is in the negative. In all these cases the initial action is important and that alone determines the moral responsibility of the individual. God has endowed each individual with the mental faculty to think and act rightly. He has also given the ethical code (*śāstra*) as a guide to act in the right way and avoid what is considered to be sinful. To this extent God is the general cause (*sādhāraṇa-kāraṇa*) for the activities of all human beings, in the same way as rain water is a common cause for the growth of all plants. An individual is expected to exercise his thinking power and make use of the guidelines in initiating his activity. In this respect he becomes the specific cause (*viśeṣa-kāraṇa*) for the results accruing from them, like the special effort made by one to cultivate the land with the help of the rain water for better yield. Neglecting the common factors, if one indulges in sinful activities, God cannot be responsible for the consequences. If God remains neutral by merely according His approval to an act already initiated by an individual, it is due to the fact that the individual who primarily acts under the influence of the past *karma* should be allowed to reap the consequences of the *karma*.

This raises another issue. If one is bound by the past *karma*, where is the freedom for him to act independently? The Viśiṣṭādvaitin does not believe that everything is determined by the past *karma*. An individual as the primary agent of action (*kartā*) is free to act independently even though the past *karma* may have influence on him. He is free to overcome the good or bad effects of the *karma* by making a sincere effort in the right direction with the exercise of the mental and physical powers given to him by God and the guidance provided through the sacred texts.

Another issue is raised in this connection. If *Īśvara* is the cause of all actions, is there any need for individual effort? If it is the will of God that something should happen, then it is bound to happen even if we remain passive. If it is the will of God that something should not happen, then despite our endeavour it will never happen. Therefore, in either case it is futile for a human being to make an effort.

This is not correct, argues Vedānta Deśika. There is a third alternative which calls for human effort. If it is the will of God that effort is to be made in order to achieve a result, there is need for human effort.[35] If it is the will of God that something should happen without human effort, in such a case there is no scope for human effort at all. Similary, if it is the will of God that something should not happen in spite of human effort, human effort may be futile. But where, according to the will of God, effort is called for to achieve a result, human effort is justified. We may not be aware of this fact until we see the final outcome of the effort. A human being should therefore make an effort spontaneously as he cannot know in advance how the will of God is operating at any given moment.

VI. PLURALITY OF THE INDIVIDUAL SELVES

According to Viśiṣṭādvaita, the *jivas* which are eternal spiritual entities are infinite in number. They are not only different from one individual to another but are also distinct from Brahman, the Supreme Self (*paramātman*). This is established on the basis of experience as well as the authority of scriptural texts. As the knowledge, memory, desire, happiness and suffering, birth and death pertaining to each individual differ from one another, *jivas* by their very nature are different (*svataḥ bhinnāḥ*). If *jivas* were not different from one another, then everybody would be conscious of the feelings and thoughts of everybody else. It is not possible to account for the differences in the experience on the basis of the mere physical body and the sense organs which are no doubt different for each individual, because these are non-intelligent in character and as such cannot have any experience. The phenomena of recollection of the past life cannot also be explained on the basis of physical body, because it is not the same body that endures in the next life after death. In the same way, it is not possible to account for these differences purely on the basis of mind (*manas*) which is only an internal sense organ.[36] Besides, the scriptural text categorically states that *jivas* are eternal and also many (*nityānām bahūnām cetanānām*).[37]

The Advaitin does not admit that the individual selves are

[35]TMK II-9. *yat yatnenaiva bhavyam tat. . .yatnataḥ bhavati.* [36]TMK II-10.
[37]Ka Up 5-13.

ultimately real. True self is one only but it appears as many. The plurality of *jivas* which is apparent to our ordinary experience is accounted for on the basis of limiting adjuncts (*upādhi*). Thus, for example, *ākāśa* or space is all-pervasive and one; when the same is conditioned by pots, we call them as different *ākāśas*. In the same way, there is only one self or *ātman*, and the same when conditioned by different internal organs (*antaḥkaraṇa*) are regarded as different *jivas*. This is the view upheld by one school of Advaita, ascribed to the author of *Bhāmati*.[38]

This view is untenable, contends Vedānta Deśika. Such *jivas* which exist as a result of the different *antaḥkaraṇas* conditioning the one Absolute Self cannot be real ultimately. They are also not eternal, because with the removal of the limiting adjuncts they cease to exist. The śruti, on the contrary, describes *jivas* as *nitya* and also as many (*bahūnāṁ nityānām*). Thus, the Advaitin's theory goes counter to the scriptural teaching.

The plurality of the selves is accounted for in another way. The self which is one appears as many because of the difference of the bodies, the internal organs, etc. This is explained on the analogy of the reflection of the single moon in the waves. Just as the single moon appears as many being reflected in the waves, likewise the self also appears as many being reflected in the numerous internal organs. This is the theory of *bimbapratibimbavāda* associated with the name of Prakāśātman, the author of *Vivaraṇa*.

Even this theory is most unsound (*atyanta duḥstham*). On this view, *mokṣa* would amount to the destruction of the *jiva* (*jiva-nāśa*), as *jiva* is only a reflection in the internal organ like the reflected moon in the watershed. When the watershed which is the basis for reflection is removed, the reflection also disappears. In the same way, if *avidyā* which is the cause of reflection of the Absolute Self in the internal organs is removed, the individual selves cease to exist. It may be argued that *jiva* is not destroyed but it becomes one with Brahman, the Absolute. But this does not hold good, because the *bimba*, the object, which reflects and the *pratibimba*, the reflection, do not become one.[39]

It may be said that reflection is a mere appearance. *Jiva*

[38]This is also the view of Bhāskara except for the difference that *upādhi* in this system is real.

[39]TMK II-15. *chāyāchāyāvato aikyaṁ na bhajati.*

appears to be different from Brahman due to *avidyā*. With the attainment of *mokṣa* such an appearance of *jiva* as separate from Brahman ceases to exist. This is the implication of *jiva* becoming one with Brahman (*jivaikya*). It does not therefore mean the destruction of *jiva*.

This explanation does not improve the situation. If Brahman is pure and undifferentiated (*nirviśeṣa*), as Advaitin believes, there is no scope for Brahman experiencing the appearance of *jiva* as distinct from it. If the theory of *avidyā* were sound and logically tenable, it would be possible to account for the plurality of selves. According to the Viśiṣṭādvaitin, the doctrine is riddled with contradictions, and on that account the plurality of *jiva* cannot be proved in Advaita. That the doctrine of *avidyā* is untenable is discussed in a later chapter.[40]

According to Yādavaprakāśa, *jivas* are parts (*aṁśa*) of Brahman which is pure Being (*sanmātra-Brahman-bhāgaḥ*). Just as the atoms in the universe are many and differ from *pṛthivi* or the physical matter and also differ from one another, in the same way the *jivas* are different from Brahman and also differ from one another. On this view there is no problem in accounting for the difference that exists between the happiness or suffering of different individuals and also their emancipation.

This theory is also unsound. In fact, it is worse than that of Advaita. In Advaita Vedānta, the defects found in the *jivas* and universe do not affect Brahman since these are illusory in character. In the case of Yādavaprakāśa, both the *jivas* and universe are real and they are also non-different from Brahman. Thus, all the defects found in the universe and *jivas* would apply to Brahman.

Criticism of Ekajivavāda

According to some Advaitins, *jivas* are not many but there is only one *jiva* or *ātman*. This is known as *ekajivavāda*. There are two views regarding this theory. According to one, there are different bodies but in all bodies only one single *jiva* exists. *Jiva* is actually Brahman as associated with *avidyā*, and as such it is one and the same in all bodies. According to the other, there is only one *ātman* found in one body and all the other bodies are mere appearances similar to the objects seen in a dream.

[40]See Chapter VIII.

In support of the first view, the following syllogistic arguments are advanced : the bodies in question (that is, all bodies in the universe) possess my own self as their selves because they are bodies just like my own body.[41] The self of all is my own self, because it is sentient like my own.[42] If this were not admitted, there would follow the prolixity of assumptions (*kalpanā-gaurava-prasaṅgaḥ*).[43]

These theories are unsound, because they are opposed to our experience and they also conflict with several śruti texts. When it is so obvious to our common experience that selves are different from one another, it would be absurd to deny it on the basis of logic. Ignoring what is apparent to experience, if logic alone is adopted to prove the identity or oneness of all *jīvas*, one could as well argue on the basis of logic that all pots are one and the same because all of them possess the characteristic of potness. One could as well say that there is no difference between the two disputants—*vādi* and *prativādi*. The syllogistic arguments are fallacious and, on that basis, it is not possible to establish the identity of selves and deny their plurality.[44]

According to the second theory, Brahman as associated with *avidyā* is *jīva* (*sāvidyam Brahma jīvaḥ*) and that *jīva* has only one body. The plurality of individuals is only an appearance like the dream objects. Just as in the dream the same one individual sees several persons, in the same way the one self sees several bodies or individuals in the universe. In such a view there is no real emancipation, nor is anyone in bondage. The so-called release and bondage become mere illusions. This theory is summarily dismissed as absurd, because it is opposed to all *pramāṇas*.[45] If only one *jīva* exists, the teaching of Vedānta by a teacher to his pupil becomes untenable. The concept of teacher-pupil relation involves the existence of two separate individuals. If there is no self in anybody other than his own self in his own body, it is not possible to say that one individual teaches another individual. As Rāmānuja points out, the relationship between the teacher and taught is inconceivable unless the two are admitted

[41]TMK II-12. *vigītāni śarīrāṇi mayaiva ātmavanti, śarīratvāt, sampratipannamat-śarīravat.* [42]*Ibid. sarve jīvāh aham syuḥ, puṁstvāt.* [43]SD, Vāda, 36.

[44]See SD, Vāda 36 for more detailed criticism.

[45]TMK II-13, *Sarvam mānoparodhāt asat.*

to be really distinct. Similarly, the possibility of bondage and release of souls cannot be explained satisfactorily.

VII. JĪVA AS AṆU

Another distinctive aspect of *jīva* which has been brought out by Viśiṣṭādvaita is that it is *aṇu* (monadic in substance). The main justification for accepting such a view is that the scriptural texts describe *jiva* as infinitesimal. Thus, the *Śvetāśvatara Upaniṣad* says that the self is infinitely smaller than the hundredth part of the point of a hair divided a hundred times and yet it is infinite in range.[46] Another Upaniṣadic text clearly states that this *ātman* is *aṇu*.[47] Further, the śruti texts also describe that *jiva* like *prāṇa* or the vital breath departs from the body after death.[48] Such a movement or motion is possible only if *jiva* is of atomic size. The Upaniṣad also speaks of the movement of *jiva* within the body. Thus, it is stated that during deep sleep the *jiva* rests in the *puritat-nāḍi*[49] (a specific nerve centre).

The monadic character of *jīva* is its natural form. That is, it is not caused or conditioned by any physical limitation. *Īśvara* is *vibhu* or all-pervasive but he is described as infinitesimal in the inner recess of the heart (*antar-hṛdaye aṇiyān*). Here the *aṇutva* of *Paramātman* is not His natural character but is caused by the physical limitation (*aupādhika*). No such limitation is mentioned in respect of *jivātman*. Therefore *aṇutva* of *jiva* is its natural state.

While describing *jiva* as infinitesimal, the Upaniṣad uses the expression that *jiva* is *ananta* or infinite.[50] In another place, *jiva* is described as *nitya* and *sarvagataḥ*, that is, it is eternal and pervades everywhere. This gives the impression that *jiva* is *vibhu* or all-pervasive. Vedānta Deśika points out that such descriptions of *jiva* as pervading everywhere are to be understood to mean that *jiva* as a spiritual entity (monad) could enter into any material substance without obstruction. Even though *jiva*

[46]Svet V-9. *vālāgra-śatabhāgasya śatadhā kalpitasya ca; bhāgo jivasya vijñeyaḥ.*
[47]Mund 3-1-9. *eṣo aṇur-ātmā cetasā veditavyaḥ.*
[48]Br 6-4-2. *tena pradyotena eṣa ātmā niṣkrāmati.* See also RB II-3-20.
[49]Br II-1-19. *tābhiḥ pratyavasṛpya puritati śete.*
[50]Svet V-9. *sa ca ānantyāya kalpate.*

is not all-pervasive, its attributive *jñāna* is infinite and all-pervasive like the light of the sun.[51] The infinite character (*ānantya*) applies not to *jīva* but to its attributive knowledge. This means that *jīva* is *aṇu*, whereas its knowledge is capable of becoming infinite. In the state of *mukti*, when the *jīva* is totally free from *karma* it becomes omniscient.[52]

Criticism of Jaina Theory of Jīva

The importance of Viśiṣṭādvaita view of *jīva* as *aṇu* could be better appreciated if we consider the theories of Jainas and Naiyāyikas. According to the Jainas, *jīva* is of the size of the body of the individual it occupies, whereas for the Naiyāyikas it is *vibhu*. Both the views suffer from serious defects. Vedānta Deśika therefore examines these theories critically and brings out the significance of the atomic character of *jīva*.

The Jaina view, it is contended, conflicts with the śruti texts which declare that *ātman* is not subject to any modification (*nirvikāra*). Jainas argue that the judgment 'I am fat' and also the experience of pain in the leg and of pleasure in the head prove the fact that *jīva* is in all parts of the body. Vedānta Deśika points out that neither *ātman* is fat, nor the experience of happiness and suffering which are the characteristics (*dharma*) of *jīva* are present in the head and leg respectively. Nevertheless, such usages are current because of the delusion of *ātman* as body itself. Further, if *jīva* is of the dimension of the body, it would follow that *jīva* would be broken into parts when it assumes different bodies out of yogic power. Similarly, in the state of *mukti*, *jīva* would be without any dimension because in this state it gets rid of its physical body. Such a position is unacceptable to the Jainas. *Ātman* being a substance (*dravya*), it cannot remain without some kind of dimension.[53]

It may be said that in the state of bondage the size of the *jīva* is determined by the size of the body it occupies, whereas in the state of *mukti* it becomes *vibhu*. This will not hold good. According to the Jainas, *mukti* is a continuous upward movement towards the higher region (*satata ūrdhvagamanaṁ*). If the released soul (*muktātmā*) becomes *vibhu*, then what is *vibhu* cannot have activity in the form of upward movement. In order to overcome this

[51]TMK II-22. See also RB, II-3-26.

[52]Ch 7-26-2. *sarvam ha paśyaḥ paśyati.* [53]TMK II-23.

difficulty, if it be said that, in the state of *mukti*, *jiva* assumes some kind of body, then such a body would be limited in size, and it cannot be said that *jiva* is *vibhu* in the state of *mukti*. It cannot be held that *jiva* acquires a body by will-power in order to retain the same dimension. *Jiva* needs a body for the purpose of experiencing pleasure and pain. In the state of *mukti*, Jainas do not admit the possibility of any experience of pleasure or pain. It is therefore absurd to say that *jiva* assumes a body in *mokṣa*. Vedānta Deśika therefore concludes that it is more appropriate to admit, as Viśiṣṭādvaitin does, a dimension for the *jiva* which remains unchanged both in the states of bondage and *mokṣa*.[54]

Criticism of Nyāya Theory of Jiva as Vibhu

The Naiyāyikas reject both the Viśiṣṭādvaitin's view and that of the Jainas and maintain that *jiva* is *vibhu* or all-pervasive.

The argument advanced in support of this theory is that *jivas* experience pleasure and pain both at a distant place as well as nearby. This is possible because *jivas* are all-pervasive. It may be said that, as individuals move from place to place along with both the respective bodies and the *jivas*, the *jivas* experience the pleasure and pain in those places. If by means of the movement of the body of an individual from place to place, the experience of pleasure and pain could be accounted for, it is a prolixity of assumption (*gaurava*) to accept the movement of both the body and the *jiva*. It is therefore more appropriate to admit that *jiva* is *vibhu* and on that basis explain the experience of pleasure and pain at distant places. This theory is untenable, argues Vedānta Deśika. The *Chāndogya Upaniṣad*[55] dealing with the topic relating to the life after death refers to the movement of *ātman*. These scriptural texts cannot be totally ignored. If the movement of *ātman* is accepted, it cannot be regarded as *vibhu*. What is *vibhu* cannot have any movement. Even though the soul is not all-pervasive, it is possible for it to experience pain and pleasure in distant places through the medium of its attributive knowledge which, according to the system, is capable of expansion and contraction. As already pointed out, though *jiva* is monadic in substance, its *jñāna* is infinite and all-pervasive. *Jiva* can control the activities of the different parts of the body through

[54]TMK II-24. [55]Ch V-3-4.

the *jñāna*. In the same way, even if an individual assumes different bodies through yogic power as in the case of Saubhari, a mythological personality, the same individual soul functions in all the bodies through the pervasive character of its knowledge.[56]

The Vaiśeṣikas put forward the following syllogistic argument to prove the *vibhutva* of the self. 'The unknown potency causes its effects in respect of other places or individuals only as connected with its locus (the self); because it is a *guṇa* or quality that produces action, as, for example, the quality of weight (*gurutva*).' The implication of this argument is that the *adṛṣṭa* of an individual in the form of merit and demerit (*puṇya* and *pāpa*) are responsible for the events causing happiness or suffering to the person. The events which may take place in a distant place in the shape of good fortune or misfortune are caused by the *adṛṣṭa* of that person. Wherever effect takes place the cause also should be proximate to it. *Adṛṣṭa* in the form of potency is located in *jīva*. If *jīva* were atomic, the *adṛṣṭa* would become restricted with that *jīva* within the fold of the body, and it could not operate or cause its influence in respect of an event in a far-off place. If, on the contrary, *jīva* is *vibhu* or all-pervasive, the *adṛṣṭa* which is associated with the *jīva* becomes coextensive with the distant places, and thus can cause the events. In other words, merit and demerit associated with a *jīva* cannot produce their effects in a different place unless the *jīva* which is their locus is coextensive with those places.

In reply to this argument, Vedānta Deśika states that the syllogism supports the Viśiṣṭādvaitin's position, and as such it suffers from the fallacy of proving what is already accepted by the opponent (*siddha-sādhana*). For the Viśiṣṭādvaitin *adṛṣṭa* is *anugraha* and *nigraha* of *Īśvara*, that is, the pleasure and displeasure (favourable and unfavourable disposition) of *Īśvara*. *Īśvara* is *vibhu* and He acts as the medium for both the self and the *adṛṣṭa*. Even if *jīva* be atomic and the *puṇya* and *pāpa* inhere in it, the *anugraha* and *nigraha* of *Paramātman* could cause the events in distant places. On this account it is not necessary to accept *vibhutva* for *jīva*.[57]

[56]TMK II-19. *avyāpitve'pi puṁsaḥ abhimata-bahu-vapuḥ-preraṇe yaugapadyaṁ jñāna-vyāptyā upapannam.* [57]TMK II-19.

Let us assume that *jiva* is *vibhu*. According to the metaphysical position of Vaiśeṣikas, knowledge which arises in *jiva* is confined to one limited area of *jiva* just as *śabda* or sound in *ākāśa* is restricted to a limited area in *ākāśa*. In the same way, the operation of *adṛṣṭa* should be restricted to a limited area. If that were not the case, the pleasure which is caused to the individual should have been experienced not only within that individual but also outside by somebody insofar as *jivas* are all-pervasive. This is not so. On the same basis, we have to admit that *adṛṣṭa* has its influence for that individual and causes pleasure and pain only to him, and that it cannot have influence on other persons who are away from him. In other words, *adṛṣṭa* located in the *ātman* with the particular body causes pleasure and pain only to that individual and it cannot cause pain to an enemy or pleasure to a friend who are away from him. Thus the assumption of *vibhutva* to a *jiva* does not serve any purpose.

The acceptance of *jiva* as *vibhu* leads to other difficulties. If *jiva* is *vibhu*, then all *jivas* being *vibhu* should be pervasive in all bodies. Then how could one determine that *x* body is of *x* only and not of *y*. The reply to this is provided by the Vaiśeṣika thesis that the specific *adṛṣṭa* of the individual is responsible for that particular body.

The above explanation also does not hold good. Just as *jiva* is all-pervasive, the *adṛṣṭa* belonging to that *jiva* could also be all-pervasive and as such the *adṛṣṭa* could cause other bodies as well and not one specific body for a particular individual. From this it would follow that all *adṛṣṭas* should cause pleasure and pain to all individuals.[58]

The Viśiṣṭādvaitin holds that *jiva* is atomic, but nevertheless *Paramātman* dispenses pleasure and pain to individuals in accordance with their *karma*. An objection may be raised against this view. As *Paramātman* is common to all individuals, why is there great disparity in the enjoyment or suffering between different individuals? Why does *Īśvara* cause such a variation in the pleasue or pain dispensed to the different individuals?

In reply to this objection, it is pointed out that *Īśvara* confers the good or bad effects in accordance with the *karma* of each individual for which He has no responsibility. The disparity in

[58]TMK II-21.

the enjoyment and suffering of the individual is due to one's own *karma*, and as such *Īśvara* cannot be regarded as being partial in conferment of the different results. This is explained by Vedānta Deśika on the analogy of a king and his attendants. A king allocates different duties to different individuals and also prescribes the forms of rewards for those who perform the prescribed duties and punishment for those who disregard the same. Those who perform the duties properly are rewarded suitably, and those who don't are punished. A king cannot be considered as partial because he dispenses different treatment to different attendants. In the same way, *Īśvara* cannot be regarded as partial because of the variation in pleasure and pain of different individuals.[59]

VIII. JĪVA AND BRAHMAN

Before we conclude this chapter we may consider another important aspect of *jiva* in relation to Brahman which is discussed in detail by Rāmānuja in the *Śri-bāṣya*. We have already observed that, according to the Viśiṣṭādvaita Vedānta, the *jivas* which are infinite in number are not only different from one another but also from Brahman or *Īśvara*. *Īśvara* and the *jiva* are two spiritual entities which are absolutely real and also distinct. This truth is established primarily on the strength of the scriptural texts. The Upaniṣadic texts referring to the nature of Reality speak of Brahman as different from *jiva*. They also describe that they are of different nature. Thus, the *Śvetāśvatara Upaniṣad* says: 'There are two, the one knowing, the other not knowing, both unborn, the one a ruler, the other not a ruler.'[60] The *Muṇḍaka Upaniṣad* describes *jiva* as one caught up in bondage, whereas *Īśvara* is free from it.[61] The Antaryāmi Brāhmaṇa of the *Bṛhadāraṇyaka Upaniṣad* refers to Brahman as the indweller of *jivātman*.[62] There are several such passages which emphatically assert the distinction between the two realities expressed in terms of the ruler and the ruled, the all-knowing and the ignorant, the independent and the dependent, the pure and the impure, etc. *Īśvara* is *vibhu* (all-pervasive), whereas *jiva* is monadic (*aṇu*). In

[59] *Ibid. yathākarma bhoga-pradānāt bhogasāmyam na hi bhavati.*

[60] Svet 1-9. [61] Mund 3-1-1; also Svet. 4-6. [62] Br V-7-22.

view of these facts, the *Vedānta-sūtra* also states cotegorically that Brahman is different from *jiva* which is subject to *karma*.[63]

The scriptural texts also speak of non-difference between Brahman and *jiva*. Thus says the *Chāndogya Upaniṣad* : 'Thou art that' (*tattvamasi*). The *Bṛhadāraṇyaka Upaniṣad* equally asserts the identity : 'This self is Brahman' (*Ayam ātmā Brahma*). How do we account for such texts which emphasise non-difference or identity of Brahman and *jiva*? If absolute difference is maintained, as Naiyāyikas and Madhvas believe, the texts speaking of non-difference would have to be considered as unimportant or invalid and monism given up . If, on the other hand, non-difference is upheld as the true purport of the Upaniṣads, as Advaitins do, the texts speaking of difference would be unimportant or invalid. It may be possible to overcome both these difficulties by subscribing to the theory of *Bhedābhedavādin*, according to which Brahman and *jiva* are both different as well as non-different.

Rāmānuja does not accept the *Bhedābheda* theory because it would amount to the admission of the defects of *jiva* in Brahman. Nor does he subscribe either to the view of the pluralist emphasising only difference or to that of Advaitin upholding only non-difference, because in either case the validity of all the Upaniṣadic texts cannot be maintained. He attempts to reconcile the conflict and uphold the validity of all the texts by advancing the theory that *jiva* is an *aṁśa* or mode of Brahman on the basis of the śruti texts and *Vedānta-sūtra*. Thus, the author of the *sūtra*, who acknowledges the two conflicting views about *jiva* and Brahman as different (*nānā*) and also non-different (*anyathā ca*), uses the expression '*aṁśa*' to explain the relation of *jiva* to Brahman.[64] While commenting on this *sūtra*, Rāmānuja states that *jiva* is to be accepted as an integral part (*aṁśa*) of Brahman in order to account for its non-difference as well as difference from Brahman.[65]

What is meant by *aṁśa* and how is it logically and ontologically justified to regard *jiva* as part of Brahman? *Aṁśa* or part does not mean a spatial part of the whole, because soul as a spiritual entity does not admit of any spatial division. Nor is Brahman a

[63]VS II-1-22. *adhikaṁ tu bhedanirdeśāt.*

[64]VS II-3-42. *aṁśo nānāvyapadeśāt anyathā ca....*

[65]RB II-3-45, p. 595.

quantitative infinite of which soul is a part. The term '*aṁśa*' is therefore defined by Rāmānuja as that which constitutes an integral part of an entity (*eka vastu eka deśatvam hy aṁśatvam*). What is meant by part of a whole is that it is an essential attribute of a complex whole (*viśiṣṭasya ekasya vastunaḥ viśeṣaṇaṁ aṁśa eva*).[66] This is explained by a few illustrations. The luminosity radiating from a luminous body such as fire or sun is part of that body; the generic characteristic of cow (*gotva*) as an essential attribute is part of the substance in which it inheres. In the same way, *jiva* is regarded as part of Brahman. By adopting the metaphysical category of substance and attribute and the concept of *apṛthak-siddhi*, Rāmānuja explains the relation of *jiva* to Brahman. The doctrine of substance and attribute as well as the concept of *apṛthak-siddhi* have been discussed at length in an earlier chapter.[67] Substance and attribute, according to the Viśiṣṭādvaitin, are distinct but are inseparable. On the basis of this theory, Rāmānuja justifies the admission of both difference as well as non-difference in respect of Brahman and *jiva*. Brahman and *jiva* as *aṁśi* and *aṁśa* or substance and attribute are distinct, in the same way the luminosity radiating from the flame is distinct from the latter. It is on the basis of this fact that the Upaniṣadic texts speak of difference between the two. But at the same time, substance and attribute being inseparable, they constitute one entity as an integral and complex whole. Brahman as integrally related to the *jivas* is a *viśiṣṭa* entity and as such it is one. It is in this sense that the texts speak of non-difference between *jiva* and Brahman. Thus, the validity of both the *bheda-śrutis* and *abheda-śrutis* is upheld by Rāmānuja.[68]

Rāmānuja also adopts the logical principle of co-ordination (*sāmānādhikaraṇya*) in determining the relation of *jiva* to Brahman. The two crucial Upaniṣadic statements which speak of the non-difference between *jiva* and Brahman are : 'That thou art' and 'The self is Brahman'. These are regarded as propositions or judgments in which the two terms are found in apposition. They are technically called *samānādhikaraṇa vākya*. According to the Advaitin, the logical import of such statements is absolute identity. The Viśiṣṭādvaitin does not accept this view. We have discussed this matter in detail elsewhere[69] and have shown that the

[66]*Ibid.* [67]See pp. 43-47. [68]See RB II-3-45, p. 595.
[69]See Section 'Import of Samānādhikaraṇa Vākya' in Chapter III.

import of *samānādhikaraṇa vākya* is that though the two terms connote different characteristics, the substance denoted by them is one as characterized by the attributes. On the basis of this principle, both these Upaniṣadic texts are interpreted to mean that *jiva* and Brahman are non-different only in the sense that Brahman having *jiva* as his body (*jiva-śariraka paramātmā*) is the same as Brahman, the primary cause of the universe. Thus, in the text 'That thou art', the term 'that' connotes *Īśvara* as the cause of the universe as is evident from the context in which it occurs. The term 'thou' refers to the same *Īśvara* in a different aspect as the indweller or the inner controller of the *jiva* associated with the body. The identity implied by the text in question is of these two complexes—God as the source of the universe and God as the indweller of *jiva*. According to the Viśiṣṭādvaitin, all terms ultimately refer to *Paramātman.*[70] It is therefore justifiable to say that the term *jiva* also connotes Brahman.

From an ontological standpoint Rāmānuja explains the relation of *jiva* to Brahman on the basis of the concept of body-soul relation (*śariraśariri-bhāva*) which we have discussed in the chapter on Metaphysical Categories. Brahman as the material cause of the universe and ground of all existence is the *ādhāra* and the *jivas* are described as *ādheya*, that which depends on it for its existence. Brahman as the immanent spirit and the inner controller of the universe of *cit* and *acit* is the *niyantā* and *jiva* is the *niyāmya*, one which is controlled by *Īśvara*. From the ethical and religious standpoint, *jiva* is described as *śeṣa*, as one who subserves God, and God as *śeṣin*, the Master of all. This threefold relationship is described as *śarira-śariri-sambandha*, or the relation of the body to the soul. A detailed discussion of this theory is reserved for a later chapter. For the present it may be noted that *jiva* is an integral part (*aṁśa*) or mode (*prakāra*) of Brahman and it is therefore distinct but inseparable from it.

[70]See Section 'Connotation and Denotation' in Chapter III.

CHAPTER SEVEN

The Doctrine of Īśvara

THE SECTION dealing with *Īśvara*[1] or the *Nāyakasara* in the *Tattva-muktā-kalāpa* is devoted primarily to a discussion of certain major issues connected with the doctrine of God in Vedānta. The foremost issue to be considered is whether or not the Absolute of metaphysics or Brahman described in the Upaniṣads as the ultimate Reality is the same as *Īśvara* or the personal God of religion who is conceived as the creator and controller of the universe. The second important issue is whether Brahman which is regarded as the material cause of the universe (*upādāna-kāraṇa*) by the Upaniṣads undergoes any transformation or does it appear itself as the phenomenal universe owing to cosmic ignorance (*avidyā*). The third issue is whether it is possible to prove the existence of God by means of logical arguments without resorting to scriptural testimony. The first issue is related to a crucial problem in Vedānta metaphysics which raises the question whether there are two realities, the one higher which is pure Being, the Absolute of metaphysics, and the other lower which is of lesser reality. This involves the question whether Brahman is *nirguṇa*, the undifferentiated transcendental Being or *saguṇa*, a God endowed with attributes. The second issue is related to the major controversy in Vedānta as to whether *vivartavāda* or the theory of the illusory appearance of Brahman as the phenomenal universe is sound and tenable. This involves a critical examination of the doctrine of *avidyā* as formulated by the Advaita Vedānta in all its aspects including the issue whether the universe is illusory in character. The third issue refers to the controversy between Naiyāyikas and Vedāntins whether or not the existence of God can be proved by means of logical arguments. While Naiyāyikas

[1]In Viśiṣṭādvaita the words *Īśvara*, *Nāyaka*, *Paramātmā*, *Parameśvara*, *Sarveśvara* and *Bhagavān* mean the same as God. Even the term Brahman used in the Vedānta also bears the same meaning.

hold that the existence of God can be proved by means of logic, Vedāntins maintain that revealed scripture (śruti) is the sole authority for understanding the nature and existence of God. All these issues are discussed in detail in the present chapter.

I. PROOFS FOR THE EXISTENCE OF GOD

The very first question that arises while considering the nature of God is whether it is possible to know the existence of God. It is argued that if God existed, He should have been perceived; since we do not see Him, He does not exist. This argument is not valid because God is not an object of perception. If an object which is capable of being perceived (*yogya*) is not apprehended, then its non-existence becomes established. This is called *yogyānupalabdhi*, a separate *pramāṇa* to prove the non-existence of an object. In the case of God, He cannot be known through perception because God is a supersensuous entity. For the reason that He cannot be known by perception, it does not follow that His existence can be questioned.[2] The self or *ātman* of another individual is not seen by oneself. But still one accepts its existence. In the same way, the existence of God cannot be questioned even though He is not perceived. Nor can the existence of God be negated by inference, because such an inferential argument advanced to disprove God can be negated by another inferential argument such as the one adopted by Naiyāyikas. Besides, such an argument to disprove God also stands contradicted by scripture. When a conflict arises between inference and scripture, the latter is accepted by Vedāntins as of greater validity than the former.

Those who do not accept the existence of God argue that the concept of God as the creator of the universe is untenable, because God does not possess a body for the purpose of creating the universe. Such arguments are also not valid, says Vedānta Deśika, because, as stated in the śruti, *Īśvara* can create the universe by His will (*saṁkalpa*) without the aid of a body. Neither inference (*anumāna*) nor the statements of the atheists can disprove the existence of God. Śruti or revealed scripture is the sole authority for knowing the existence of God.

[2]TMK III-2.

The Advaitin questions the view that Brahman is to be known through revealed scripture. According to him, Brahman as the transcendental Reality is self-established (*svatas-siddha*) and is beyond all speech and thought. It cannot be grasped by the intellect. Thus, the Upaniṣadic text which is quoted in support of this says that Reality is unperceivable and ungraspable.[3] Another text states that all speech recedes from it along with the intellect.[4] Brahman is therefore *avedya*—beyond all empirical *pramāṇas* and cognition.

Vedānta Deśika criticises this view. It is not correct to say that Brahman cannot be known by means of scriptural texts. The very Upaniṣads say that Brahman is only knowable by means of śruti. Thus the *Kaṭha Upaniṣad* states : 'All Vedas speak of His nature.'[5] There are several texts which say that Brahman is describable by words and also knowable.[6] The Upaniṣadic text which speaks of Brahman as beyond words and thought can only mean that Brahman which is infinite cannot be described adequately by words, and that it cannot also be known in all its fullness by our finite mind. The true implication of *avācyatva* or indescribability is that words are inadequate to describe the infinite nature of Brahman and that mind also cannot comprehend its nature. If this interpretation were not accepted, there would be conflict with both the earlier and the later statements made in the same Upaniṣadic passage. Thus, the passage which discusses the blissful character of Brahman commences with the statement that he who knows Brahman (*brahmavit*) attains the Supreme (*āpnoti paraṁ*); the concluding statement says that Brahman is comprehended as *ānanda* (*ānandaṁ brahmaṇo vidvān*). These statements clearly imply that Brahman is capable of being known. In fact, all the Upaniṣadic passages dealing with Brahman have a direct reference to Brahman, and all these would be meaningless if it were held that Brahman is *avedya* or unknowable.

It is contended by the Advaitins that the terms Brahman, *ātman*, etc. mentioned in the Upaniṣads do not have a primary

[3]Mund 1-1-5. *yattad adreśyam agrāhyaṁ.*

[4]Tait *yato vāco nivartante aprāpya manasā saha.*

[5]Ka II-15. *sarve vedāḥ yatpadam āmananti.*

[6]Ch I-6-7. *tasyoditi nāma.* Br 4-3-6. *atha nāmadheyam satyasya satyam.* Tait *yo veda nihitaṁ guhāyāṁ. Taittirīya Āraṇyaka* III-11. *Sarve vedā yatraikam bhavanti.*

import (*mukhyārtha*) in respect of Brahman, but they have only a secondary import (*lakṣaṇā*). That is, these words do not refer to Brahman directly but indirectly. This is explained on the analogy of the moon seen through the branch of a tree (*śākhā-candra-nyāya*). The moon visible as if close to the tree branch is made use of to identify the real moon which is far distant from us in the sky. Though there is no connection between the bough and the moon, the former serves the purpose of identifying the moon in the sky. In the same way, the term Brahman in the Upaniṣads serves to convey the knowledge of Brahman without having any direct reference to Brahman.

Such an explanation will not hold good, according to the Viśiṣṭādvaitin. If a term is devoid of primary import, its secondary import is also not possible. If there is to be a secondary import, this would necessarily have to be grounded on the primary import. In the absence of primary import, a secondary import is unimaginable.[7] It is not appropriate to regard the secondary import of the term as primary import, since logicians do not accept such a position. Further, we do not find anywhere and at any time a difficulty in accepting primary import in respect of *Para Brahman*, the higher Reality postulated by the Advaitin. The word Brahman, *ātman*, etc. and all the Upaniṣadic texts related to the discussion on the nature of Brahman refer directly to the higher Brahman. If it be argued that direct reference is only to the lower Brahman (*Apara-Brahman*), then the statements related to the higher Brahman become invalid, and the very existence of such a Brahman would be questionable. It is impossible to maintain that Brahman is unknowable. Even if Brahman were the content of the indirect reference, it would become the object of knowledge to that extent. It is therefore more appropriate and logical to accept that Brahman is known through the scripture and that scripture is the sole authority for proving its existence.

II. CRITICISM OF NYĀYA ARGUMENTS FOR THE EXISTENCE OF GOD

The Naiyāyikas attempt to prove the existence of God by means of inference (*anumāna*). The Vedāntins seriously question this

[7] SD, Vāda 1.

and uphold the view that it is not possible to prove conclusively the existence of God as a Supreme Being as established by the Upaniṣads by adopting logical arguments.

The Naiyāyikas advance more than one argument to prove the existence of God. Of these the most important one is the cosmological argument, based on the idea of causation. The universe is an effect and must have been produced by an agent or creator called *Īśvara*. The argument is expressed in the following syllogistic form : 'The physical universe must have been caused by an agent, because it is an effect just as a pot.'[8] This is based on the assumption that every effect must have a cause and the universe being an effect must have a cause. That cause is *Īśvara*.

The criticism of this argument is very elaborate but we may take note of only the important points. If we take the syllogistic argument as it is together with the illustration cited, it would amount to saying that *Īśvara* as a causal agent is subject to *karma*, as in the case of the potter who is the agent of the pot is subject to *karma*. Obviously, this is not the intention of the Naiyāyikas. What is sought to be established by the syllogism is that the agent who is the cause of the universe should be one endowed with knowledge and capacity to create and not as one subject to *karma* (*karmavaśyatva*) which is irrelevant. Whatever factors are considered essential for the purpose of causing an effect only those are to be accepted. The knowledge and capacity to create are the important factors for the agent and not his being subject to *karma*. *Kartā* or agent here means one who makes an effort (*prayatnavān*) ; effort is caused by *jñāna* which does not have any bearing on *karma*.

Against this argument it is pointed out that knowledge which is considered necessary for making an effort also presupposes the need for the sense organs and a physical body. That is, knowledge cannot function without the sense organs and the body. If these be admitted, then the influence of *karma* is inevitable, because it is only the *karma* that causes the *indriyas* and the body. This point may be countered with the argument that the knowledge of *Īśvara* is eternal and capable of comprehending everything, and as such will not have to depend on *indriyas* for

[8] *pṛthivyādikaṁ sakartṛkaṁ, kāryatvāt, ghaṭavat.*

His functioning. This will not hold good, replies Vedānta Deśika, because it is not possible to prove the presence of such an eternal and omniscient knowledge in the agent on the basis of our common experience and also this particular inference. What we find in our common experience is that knowledge, which is limited in its scope and non-permanent, is related to what is caused by an agent. Thus, the syllogistic argument of Naiyāyikas can only prove the need of effort on the part of an agent for causing an effect, but it cannot establish that the agent should also possess knowledge.

To overcome the above difficulty, the Naiyāyikas argue that effort necessarily involves both knowledge and desire on the part of the agent with regard to the object to be created. If the agent does not have either an idea of the object or a desire for it, he cannot produce it. Therefore the present syllogism should prove that the creator of the universe should be endowed with knowledge and desire for creation.

Even this argument is untenable, according to Vedānta Deśika. It is not necessary to postulate the need for knowledge and desire in respect of *Īśvara*. According to the Nyāya system, knowledge of *Īśvara* is not caused by any extraneous factors but it is self-evident (*svatas-siddha*). In the same way, the effort of *Īśvara* could be regarded as spontaneous and related to object without the need for knowledge. If it be said that such a thing is not warranted by ordinary experience, then even the admission of *nitya-jñāna* for *Īśvara* is opposed to experience. If *jñāna* and *icchā* (desire) are accepted as part of effort in respect of *Īśvara* on the basis of our ordinary experience, then *Īśvara* is also to be admitted as subject to *karma*.

Further, it should be possible to account for the creation of the universe with the influence of *adṛṣṭa* or a potent special power. The Naiyāyikas accept the potent power as responsible for spontaneous effort or action. The same explanation could as well be adopted for the causation of the universe. If it be argued that, since *adṛṣṭa* is non-sentient an intelligent agent is needed to control its operation, then the admission of *jivas* or individual selves associated with *adṛṣṭa* should suffice for the purpose. If it be also necessary to accept *Īśvara* over and above the *jivas*, then there would be two agents for the created objects.

The objections so far raised against the Naiyāyikas, though not very relevant, have been mentioned by Vedānta Deśika to bring out the lacuna in the syllogistic argument adopted by the Naiyāyikas. The main point of criticism is that it is not possible to establish by means of inference that the agent required for the creation of the universe should be omniscient. He raises the question whether *Īśvara,* who is sought to be proved by the inference, possesses some limited knowledge required for the creation of the universe or infinite knowledge. It cannot be the former since such a being with limited knowledge cannot be considered *Īśvara.* In the latter case, concomitance cannot be established between *kartṛtva* and *sarvajñatva.* That is, taking into consideration the illustration cited in the syllogism, viz. the production of a pot, it does not follow that the agent should necessarily be an omniscient being. All that is necessary for the production of the pot is the conception of the pot, a desire to produce it and the capacity to produce it, but certaintly not omniscience.

It may be argued that the nature of the agent should be conceived in accordance with the nature of the object to be created. The capacity needed for the production of the pot should not hold good for the creation of the universe. In a matter like the creation of the universe, the agent or its creator should be one possessing suitable capacity and knowledge for its creation. Such a capacity and knowledge should be all-powerfulness and omniscience respectively. This is what is sought to be established by the inference.

This argument also becomes untenable, contends Vedānta Deśika. All that can be established by the syllogistic argument is that a superindividual (*jīva*) possessing unlimited capacity and knowledge is the creator of the universe and not an omniscient *Īśvara* as distinct from *jiva.*[9] The postulation of the Caturmukha-Brahmā[10] who has unlimited capacity and knowledge could as well be the creator of the universe, but it need not necessarily be an omniscient *Īśvara.*

[9]TMK III-20. *sukṛta-viṣamitā jīva-śaktiḥ siddhā.*

[10]Caturmukha-Brahmā is the first deity of the Hindu Trinity who was brought into existence by the Supreme Lord for the task of creating the physical universe. This Brahmā is different from Brahman referred to in the upaniṣad as the ultimate Reality or Supreme Being (*Paramātmā*) See p. 228.

It may be argued that according to scripture, *Īśvara* is the cause of the universe, and on the strength of śruti texts, the inference is advanced to prove the existence of *Īśvara*. If this be the case, then it would be more appropriate to accept the existence of God on the strength of the śruti text itself. The syllogistic argument would then become redundant. There is no justification to adopt two *pramāṇas*, inference as well as scripture to prove the same truth. In the opinion of Vedānta Deśika, if two *pramāṇas* are adopted to prove a thing, one should supplement the other. Inference is no doubt justified if it is used to support what is taught in the scripture, but it cannot be used as the sole means of proof for the existence of God for the reasons already given. If *anumāna* alone could prove the existence of God, *śāstra* or sacred texts would lose importance. Besides, *anumāna* cannot by itself conclusively prove the existence of the Supreme Being. Apart from the fact that it suffers from various logical fallacies, it is possible for one to advance syllogistic arguments to disprove what is asserted by means of inference. In view of this, the author of the *Vedānta-sūtras* says that *śāstra* alone is the supreme authority for our belief in the existence of God.[11] The implication of this is, as Vedānta Deśika points out, that solely by means of inference it is neither possible to disprove the existence of God nor to prove His existence.[12] Scripture is therefore considered the sole authority in matters which are supernormal.

III. THE NATURE OF ULTIMATE REALITY

According to the Viśiṣṭādvaita Vedānta, the ultimate Reality or Brahman referred to in the Upaniṣads is the personal God of religion. It rejects the theory of two Brahmans admitted by Advaita Vedānta—the higher Brahman (*para*) which is the Absolute Being devoid of all attributes and a lower Brahman (*apara*) endowed with attributes which is of lesser reality. There is only one Brahman which, as the *Vedānta-sūtras* clearly points out, is the creator of the universe and which is qualified with infinite auspicious attributes (*ananta-kalyāṇa-guṇa-viśiṣṭa*). Such

[11]VS I-1-3. *śāstra-yonitvāt.*

[12]TMK III-24. See also VS II-1-11. *tarkāpratiṣṭhānādapi.*

a Reality is no other than the personal God of religion. Thus, Rāmānuja asserts at the very outset of his commentary on the *Vedānta-sūtras* that the term Brahman denotes *Puruṣottama*, the Supreme Person or Self, who is essentially free from all imperfections and possesses infinite auspicious attributes of unsurpassable excellence.[13] The etymological meaning of Brahman as indicated by the śruti and smṛti texts is that which grows and causes to grow (*bṛhattvāt brahmaṇatvāt*).[14] If we take into consideration these two epithets, then the term Brahman is applicable primarily to the Supreme Lord (*Sarveśvara*).[15]

The nature of ultimate Reality is to be determined not merely on the strength of a few Upaniṣadic texts but by taking into consideration all the other relevant Upaniṣadic statements. The Upaniṣadic passages which deal with the creation of the universe refer to *sat*, *ātman* and Brahman as the first cause of the universe. Thus, in one place the Upaniṣad says: '*Sat* alone existed in the beginning.'[16] In another place it says: '*Ātman* alone existed in the beginning.'[17] Yet in another place it says: 'Brahman alone existed in the beginning.'[18] Thus, three different terms—*sat*, *ātman* and Brahman—are used. Since several entities cannot be the cause of the universe, it has to be admitted that one particular entity is the sole cause of the universe. The question to be determined is: what is that entity? The word *sat* is too general and may mean anything that exists. *Ātman* is little more specific than *sat* but it is applicable to both *jivātman* and *Paramātman*. The word Brahman is much more specific but it is applicable to more than one entity; it also means *prakṛti* and *jiva*. Another Upaniṣadic passage describing the creation of the universe mentions Nārāyaṇa as the cause of the universe. Thus, it is stated: Nārāyaṇa alone existed in the beginning—('*eko ha vai Nārāyaṇa āsit*)'.[19] The word Nārāyaṇa is used in this passage in place of the terms *sat*, *ātman* and Brahman, mentioned in other passages as the

[13]RB I-1-1, p. 6. *brahma-śabdena ca svabhāvato nirasta-nikhila-doṣaḥ anavadhi-kātiśaya-asaṅkhyeya kalyāṇa-guṇa-gaṇaḥ puruṣottamo abhidhīyate.* [14]SD Vāda. 1.

[15]The term *sarveśvara* implies, according to Vedānta Deśika, all the essential characteristics of the Supreme Being such as *vyāpakatva* or, all-prevasiveness, *sarvādhāratva* or the ground of all, *sarvaśeṣitva* or the ruler of all, etc., See NS, p. 225.

[16]Ch VI-2-1. [17]AI 1-1-1. [18]Br 3-4-11. [19]*Mahopaniṣad* I-1.

cause of the universe. According to the principle of interpretation laid down by the Mīmāṁsakas, when terms are used in the same context the term having a general meaning should bear the meaning of the specific term. According to the grammatical principle formulated by Pāṇini,[20] the term Nārāyaṇa is treated as a specific proper name (*saṁjñā-pada*) and is applicable to one specific Being only but not to any other entity like the general terms such as Brahman, *sat* and *ātman*. It is therefore concluded that Brahman referred to in the Upaniṣads as the cause of the universe is the same as Nārāyaṇa.[21]

Further, the *Subāla Upaniṣad* describes Nārāyaṇa as *antarātma*,[22] the inner controller of all beings in the universe. Only that which is the creator of the universe could be the *antaryāmin* or inner controller of all beings as is evident from the scriptural text which says : 'After creating it, the same (Brahman) entered into it.' The *Antaryāmi Brāhmaṇa* also reiterates the same truth. On the basis of these authorities it is asserted that Nārāyaṇa is the very Brahman described in the Upaniṣads as the creator of the universe.

An objection may however be raised against this conclusion. In another text it is said that that which is the cause of the universe is to be meditated upon (*kāraṇam tu dhyeyaḥ*) and that Śambhu is to be meditated upon at the centre of *ākāśa*.[23] How then can we claim Nārāyaṇa to be the cause of the universe?

In reply to this objection Vedānta Deśika says that Śambhu in this passage does not mean Śiva but the very Nārāyaṇa. According to the root meaning, Śambhu is one who is the giver of happiness (*śam bhavati asmāt*). The supreme happiness consists in *mokṣa* and the giver of *mokṣa* is Nārāyaṇa.[24] Śambhu therefore means Nārāyaṇa who is to be meditated upon for attaining the goal.

In another place it is said that only Śiva is to be meditated

[20] *Paṇini-sūtra* 8-4-3. *pūrva-padāt saṁjñyāyām*. In a *saṁjñā pada*, the letter *na* (in soft sound) becomes *ṇa* (a hard sound) if it is preceded by a word ending with *ra*. Thus, the word *Nārāyana* becomes *Nārāyaṇa*. In view of this, the term is treated as a specific proper name applicable to one particular Being only.

[21] TMK III-5. Also RB II-1-15, p. 486.

[22] Sub. VII. *eṣa sarvabhūtāntarātmā apahatapāpmā divyo deva eko Nārāyaṇaḥ*.

[23] *śambhuḥ ākāśa-madhye dhyeḥ*. [24] *mokṣam icchet janārdanāt*.

upon (*śiva eko dhyeyaḥ*). Here again Śiva means Viṣṇu or Nārāyaṇa. In the *Viṣṇu Sahasranāma*, the word Śiva is used as synonymous with Viṣṇu.[25] Śivā also means auspiciousness. Nārāyaṇa or Viṣṇu is the personification of auspiciousness (*maṅgalānām ca maṅgalam*). Therefore, the text in question means that Nārāyaṇa is to be meditated upon.

The equation of Brahman with Nārāyaṇa should not be understood to mean that God of a particular religious cult is being imposed on the Upaniṣadic concept of Brahman. All that is meant by Nārāyaṇa is that the Ultimate Reality of philosophy cannot be anything other than a personal Supreme Being who should have the function of the creation of the universe (*jagat-kāraṇatva*). The name given to such a Reality is immaterial insofar as it meets the requirements of the concept of Ultimate Reality. If the name Nārāyaṇa is accepted, it is due to the fact that the term implies the essential characteristics of Brahman as taught in the Upaniṣads. According to the etymological meaning of the word, Nārāyaṇa is one who is the ground of the entire universe of *cit* and *acit* (*nārāṇām ayanam*) and who is immanent in all (*nārāḥ ayanaṁ yasya saḥ*).[26]

One other term which signifies the fuller meaning of the concept of Ultimate Reality is Viṣṇu. It means that which pervades everything (*viṣulṛ vyāptau*). It is therefore used as synonymous with Brahman or Nārāyaṇa. In view of this, the author of the last four sections of the *Mimāṁsā-sūtras* (known as *Devatā-kāṇḍa*) asserts in the concluding *sūtra* that the ultimate deity to be worshipped is Viṣṇu and that the same is described as Brahman.[27] This conclusively establishes that Brahman described in the Upaniṣads is the same as Viṣṇu, the Supreme God of religion as upheld in the Vedas.

That the Ultimate Reality or Brahman is a personal God bearing the name Nārāyaṇa is also emphatically brought out by the *Taittiriya Upaniṣad* (which is a part of *Taittiriya Āraṇyaka*). Thus it says: 'Nārāyaṇa is *para-Brahman* and Nārāyaṇa is also *para-tattva.*' It also describes Nārāyaṇa by such expressions as *para-jyotiḥ*, *paramātmā*.[28] These are the very expressions used in the other

[25]*Sarvaḥ śarvaḥ śivaḥ sthāṇuḥ....* [26]*Rahasyatrayasāra*, Ch. 27.

[27]*Sa Viṣṇur-āha hi, tam Brahmetyācakṣate....* See also SD, Vāda 3.

[28]Tait II-93 (*Taittiriya Āraṇyaka* VI 9). *nārāyaṇa paraṁ brahma, tattvaṁ nārāyaṇaḥ paraḥ, nārāyaṇa paro jyotiḥ, ātmā nārayaṇaḥ paraḥ.*

Upaniṣads to describe the different *upāsanas* on Brahman. The *Puruṣa-sūkta* which is regarded as the most authoritative one because of its inclusion in all the four Vedas also upholds that the Supreme *Puruṣa* or the personal God is the Ultimate Reality.

There are several other *pramāṇas* upholding the supremacy of Nārāyaṇa as the Ultimate Reality. These are: the *Rāmāyaṇa*, the oldest epic; the *Mahābhārata* which is regarded as the fifth Veda; *Pāñcarātra Āgamas*; the *Sāttvika Purāṇas*, *Dharma Śāstra* expounded by the great sages such as Manu, Yājñavalkya, etc. the Mūla-Veda—a branch of Vedas which is considered as the root of the Pāñcarātra. Among the Upaniṣads the most important ones which acknowledge Nārāyaṇa as Supreme Being are *Subāla*, *Kaṭha*, *Nṛsimhatāpaniya*, *Brahma-bindu* and *Nārāyaṇa*.

There are statements found in some Purāṇas extolling the supremacy of Śiva. How then can we regard Nārāyaṇa as the Supreme Being? In reply to this question, Vedānta Deśika says that when conflict arises between the two statements found in the Purāṇas, the issue is to be decided on the strength of the statements made by impartial and neutral Maharṣis such as Manu, Parāśara and Vyāsa. According to the views of these great sages, Nārāyaṇa or Viṣṇu is the Supreme Being and the creator of the universe as described in the Upaniṣads. The Sage Parāśara, who is regarded as one blessed with the intuitive knowledge of *para-devatā*, the Supreme Being, has affirmed in his writings the supremacy of Viṣṇu. Even the *Skanda Purāṇa*, which is classified as Śaiva Purāṇa and which gives primary importance to Śiva or Rudra, declares the supremacy of Viṣṇu. These Purāṇas contain vivid descriptions of the glory of Viṣṇu.

There are other theories about the Ultimate Reality which question the claim of the Viśiṣṭādvaitin. These are briefly stated and rejected by Vedānta Deśika on the ground that they are opposed to what has been established beyond any shadow of doubt by numerous scriptural texts.

These views centre round the Hindu concept of the trinity of Gods—Brahmā, Viṣṇu, Rudra. It is generally believed that Brahmā is the creator of the universe, Viṣṇu the protector and Rudra the destroyer of the universe. The questions usually raised with regard to their relative importance are: (*a*) whether all the three deities together constitute the Ultimate Reality; (*b*) whether Viṣṇu included in the trinity is the same as the

Supreme Being called Nārāyaṇa; (*c*) whether either of the other two, viz. Brahmā or Rudra is supreme; (*d*) whether there is a Supreme Being over and above these. A proper understanding of these issues is necessary to determine the supremacy of Nārāyaṇa as *para* Brahman, as claimed by the Viśiṣṭādvaitin.

After a critical examination of the above views, Vedānta Deśika maintains on the strength of the sacred texts that Brahmā and Rudra are the creations of the Supreme God, Nārāyaṇa. The Purāṇas say : 'Nārāyaṇa is the Supreme Deity, from Him arises Brahmā.' 'Nārāyaṇa is the Supreme Deity, from Him was born Brahmā, the four-faced, and from Brahmā arose Rudra.'[29] Both Rudra and Brahmā are thus subject to origin and also *karma*. They cannot be accepted as the Ultimate Reality. As regards Viṣṇu who is included in the trinity, the Purāṇas say that the Supreme Brahman or Nārāyaṇa assumed the form of Viṣṇu for the protection of all beings.[30] From this it is clear that by His own will, Brahman incarnated himself as the Viṣṇu of trinity. The Viṣṇu included in the trinity is not therefore different from the Viṣṇu or Nārāyaṇa who is described in the sacred texts as the primary cause of the universe and there is no other eternal being in the universe than Nārāyaṇa. On the basis of such extensive scriptural testimony Vedānta Deśika rejects the theories which uphold that (*i*) the three deities of the trinity are all of equal importance; (*ii*) that the three are one and the same; (*iii*) that there is a Being above and beyond the trinity; and (*iv*) that either Brahmā or Rudra among the trinity is the Supreme Lord.[31]

He therefore concludes that the very *para* Brahman or the Absolute of Upaniṣad is the personal God under the name of Nārāyaṇa as described in the Upaniṣads, Purānas, etc. He is the sole creator of the universe; He sustains and controls the universe and He is the one who causes the dissolution of the universe as declared in the *Vedānta-sūtra* based on the *Taittirīya Upaniṣad*.

[29] *Varāha Purāṇa*, 25-26.

[30] *Rāmāyaṇa*, VII-101-26.

[31] TMK III-14. See also *Rahasyatrayasāra*, Ch. 6.

IV. THE THEORY OF NIRGUṆA BRAHMAN

Is there a Brahman higher than the *saguṇa* Brahman or the personal God admitted as Supreme Being by the Viśiṣṭādvaita Vedānta? The Advaitin answers in the affirmative. He advocates the theory of two Brahmans—*para* and *apara* or the higher and lower.[32] The *para* Brahman which is the Ultimate Reality is pure Being devoid of all differentiation, the Absolute of metaphysics. It is transcendental, supra-relational and beyond all thought and speech. That is why it is described as *nirviśeṣa* or *nirguṇa*. When the *para* Brahman becomes conditioned by *māyā* and obscured, as it were, it is called the *saguṇa* Brahman or the lower Brahman (*apara Brahman*). It is the personal God conceived as the creator of the universe and endowed with attributes. The *apara* Brahman is of a lesser reality than the *para* Brahman.

This theory is advanced by Advaita Vedānta primarily on the strength of a few scriptural texts. There are Upaniṣadic statements which describe Brahman as devoid of qualities.[33] There are also statements which speak of Brahman as qualified by numerous attributes.[34] These two kinds of statements are known as *nirguṇa* śrutis and *saguṇa* śrutis, and there is an apparent conflict between the two. Both the texts, the Advaitin contends, cannot be taken to be equally valid in view of the fact that they refer to an existent (*siddha-vastu*). Obviously, one of them has to be negated as invalid. Of the two conflicting śrutis, which one should we consider as of greater validity? The answer of the Advaitin is that the texts which deny all qualities in respect of Reality are later in order than the texts which affirm Reality as qualified, because denial presupposes that which is to be denied. Negation in view of affirmation is later and what is later, according to the principle of subsequent sublating the earlier (*apaccheda-nyāya*)[35] is of

[32]See *Śaṁkara-bhāṣya* on VS IV-3-14. [33]Svet 6-19. *niṣkalam niṣkriyam*... *niravadyam nirañjanaṁ*. Mund 1-1-6. Br V-8-7.

[34]Mund 2-2-7. *yaḥ sarvajñaḥ sarvavit*. Ch. 8-1-5. Tait 1-1-2. Svet 6-8.

[35]The word *apaccheda* means to let go the hold. *Apaccheda-nyāya* is the name of a principle formulated by the Mīmāṁsakas to determine which one is the earlier event and which the later in connection with the expiatory rites. The different priests participating in a *yāga* (sacrifice) are required to go round the sacrificial fire along with the chief priest each one holding the tucked-up waist-cloth of the priest in front. While going round the fire, if any one lets go the hold of the tucked-up cloth, certain expiatory rites are laid down. The

greater force and occupies the position of the sublator (*bādhakam*). The Advaitin therefore considers that the *nirguṇa* śrutis are of greater validity than the *saguṇa* śrutis. Accordingly, the Ultimate Reality is an undifferentiated Being (*nirguṇa Brahman*).

Viśiṣṭādvaita Vedānta does not accept the theory of two Brahmans. Taking its firm stand on scriptural evidence, it asserts that the Ultimate Reality is Brahman as qualified by numerous attributes. It would not be appropriate to accept the validity of a few scriptural texts which speak of Brahman as devoid of qualities and discard the large number of *saguṇa* śrutis as invalid on the basis of *apaccheda-nyāya*. In fact, as Vedānta Deśika points out, the *apaccheda-nyāya* does not hold good for determining the relative validity of *saguṇa* and *nirguṇa* śrutis.[36] The *apaccheda-nyāya* is applicable only where there is no fixed order as earlier and later between two events or two texts (*aniyata-virodha-paurvāparye*). Where there is a fixed order between the two texts coming as earlier and later (*niyata-virodha*), the earlier text is of greater importance than the later ones, according to the principle of the earlier being stronger than the later (*upakramādhikaraṇa-nyāya*). In view of this the question of the later statement being stronger does not arise at all. The *saguṇa* and *nirguṇa* śrutis always remain opposed to each other, like all affirmation and negation, and as such the principle of *apaccheda-nyāya* is inapplicable in this particular case.

The validity of both the *saguṇa* and *nirguṇa* śrutis can be very well maintained and the apparent conflict between them overcome by adopting another principle known as *utsargāpavāda nyāya*. According to this principle, the negative text will have to be interpreted in accordance with the affirmative text. Thus, for instance, there is a scriptural text which says that animals should not be injured, while another text says that a particular animal

---

nature of the expiatory rite varies depending on which particular priest lets off the hold of the waist-cloth. If it is done by the *udgātṛ* (one who chants the hymn), then the entire sacrifice is to be restarted. If it occurs with the *pratihartā* (one of the specific priests), then an amount equivalent to all the materials is to be given as a sacrificial fee (*dakṣiṇā*). If two persons let go the hold, then the expiatory rite is of the second kind and not of the first. The Vedic texts describe all these points. The implication of this is that when a conflict of the nature described above arises, the later text prescribing the expiatory rite becomes stronger than the earlier one.

[36]TMK III-57.

(*paśu*) should be used for a specific sacrifice. According to the Mīmāṁsā principle of interpretation, such a conflict is to be overcome by interpreting the former text to mean that animals other than those enjoined in the scriptural text for sacrificial purpose should not be injured. The same logic should hold good in respect of *saguṇa* and *nirguṇa* texts. If some texts affirm that Brahman possesses qualities, and others deny the same, the latter should be understood to mean the denial of qualities other than those mentioned in the former (*vihita-vyatirikta-guṇa-niṣedhaḥ*). In other words, the implication of the negative texts is that Brahman is devoid of such inauspicious attributes as change, *karma*, etc. but not that it is devoid of all characteristics. Such an interpretation, though it restricts the import of the negative texts to some extent, maintains the validity of both the *saguṇa* and *nirguna* śrutis. As the contents of the two texts apply to different aspects of Reality, there is absolutely no conflict between them. Thus, on the basis of scriptural evidence, it is not possible to establish that Brahman is *nirguṇa* and that it is higher than *saguṇa* Brahman.

There are other arguments advanced by the Advaitin to defend his theory of *nirguṇa* Brahman. A fuller discussion of these would involve not only the detailed examination of the interpretation of the relevant scriptural texts but also some of the fundamental doctrines of Advaita Vedānta. This matter has been discussed comprehensively by Rāmānuja in the *jijñāsādhikaraṇa* of *Śri-bhāṣya* and also by Vedānta Deśika in the *Śatadūṣaṇi* which is primarily devoted to the refutation of Advaita doctrines. For this reason, *Tattva-muktā-kalāpa* does not go into the details of *nirviśeṣa Brahma-vāda*.[37] It may however be noted here, as repeatedly stated by Rāmānuja in his *Śri-bhāṣya*, that the concept of *nirviśeṣa-vastu*, an entity totally devoid of all differentiation, whether it be a physical object or consciousness or even the Ultimate Reality, is untenable both on logical and metaphysical grounds. From the metaphysical angle, the creation of the universe which constitutes an important function of Brahman, as is evident from the Upaniṣads and the *Vedānta-sūtra*, cannot be explained satisfactorily in respect of a *nirguṇa* Brahman. If, in order to overcome this difficulty, saguṇa Brahman or Brahman as conditioned by

[37]This is the expression that Vedānta Deśika uses to describe Advaita. See SD, Vāda I (opening sentence).

māyā is postulated, it also becomes untenable because the doctrine of *māyā* on the basis of which *Īśvara, jiva* and the material universe are explained is riddled with contradictions.

From the standpoint of logic and epistemology, it is impossible to prove the existence of a *nirviśeṣa-vastu* by any of the accepted *pramāṇas*. As discussed in the chapter on *pramāṇas*, all knowledge reveals an object only as qualified. Even the very premise that Brahman is *nirviśeṣa* expressed in the form of a judgment involves the relation of the predicate to the subject. The nature of an object can be conceived or understood only in terms of its essential characteristic. Such an undifferentiated Reality as being beyond all thought and speech is a metaphysical abstraction. The Viśiṣṭādvaitin therefore rejects this concept of *nirguṇa* Brahman and upholds that the Ultimate Reality is only a *saviśeṣa*[38] Brahman which is the same as the personal God of religion.

V. GOD AND HIS ATTRIBUTES

According to Viśiṣṭādvaita, Brahman conceived as *saviśeṣa* implies that it also possesses a bodily form (*vigraha*) and is qualified by attributes (*guṇa*) and the properties (*vibhūtis*) which comprise the transcendental realm as well as the cosmic universe of sentient souls and non-sentient matter. As far as the body of Brahman is concerned, it is not governed by *karma* as the bodies of the bound individual souls are, but is assumed by *Īśvara* out of His free will (*icchā*) for the benefit of His devotees to enable them to offer prayers and do meditation. The bodily form assumed by *Īśvara* in His eternal abode is *nitya*. It is constituted of pure *sāttvika* stuff known as *śuddha-sattva*.[39] There are several *pramāṇas* supporting the existence of a *nitya-vigraha* or unblemished and imperishable bodily form for *Īśvara*. The Pauṣkara Āgama which is considered to have been expounded by Viṣṇu speaks of such a *nitya-śarira* for God. The *ekāyana* śrutis, constituting a branch of Vedas says that body

[38]The term *saviśeṣa* Brahman is a better expression than *saguṇa* Brahman as is commonly used, since the former brings out fully all the important aspects of Brahman—*svarūpa, rūpa* (*vigraha*), *guṇa* and *vibhūti*—as explained by Rāmānuja in his description of Brahman.

[39]The theory of *śuddha-sattva* is discussed in Chapter X.

of *Īśvara* is *nitya* and not caused by any external element but is of a natural form. Brahmānandi, commentator on *Chāndogya Upaniṣad* (accepted as an authority by Śaṁkara) and the Dramiḍa Bhāṣyakāra (accepted as an authority by Rāmānuja), support the existence of non-material body for *Īśvara.*

The Mīmāṁsakas of the Kumārila school do not accept any bodily forms for the divine beings. According to them, the divine beings such as Indra, Varuṇa, Agni, etc. do not possess any body and sense organs. The belief that they are present at several places where sacrifices are offered, that they receive the offerings made to them, that they are pleased by such rituals and that they award good results is based on false notions.[40] On the same basis one might argue that even *Īśvara* does not possess a bodily form.

Vedānta Deśika refutes this view. That divine beings exist and the fact that they possess extraordinary powers is beyond the reach of our ordinary experience. We have to rely on the scriptural texts in understanding the super-normal things. Several śruti and smṛti texts speak of their greatness, the supreme power possessed by such divine beings and the way they function. In the same way we have to concede a bodily form to *Īśvara* on the basis of scriptural testimony.

What are the attributes by which Brahman is qualified? Attributes or *dharmas* are broadly classified into two categories :

(*a*) The essential characteristics which are integrally related to the object and without which the *svarūpa* of an object cannot be determined or defined. These are known, in the Viśiṣṭādvaita terminology, as *svarūpa -nirūpaka-dharma,* that is, *dharma* which determines or defines the *svarūpa* of an object.

(*b*) The secondary characteristics which belong to an object but are externally related to it. They are technically called *nirūpita-svarūpa-viśeṣaṇa,* that is, the qualities which become known only after the *svarūpa* of an object along with its essential attributes is understood.

The first one, which is unique to the object, constitutes its distinguishing feature. It is only on the basis of such a characteristic that the object is differentiated from another class of object which does not possess it.

[40]TMK III-68.

What is the *svarūpa* of Brahman and what are its essential characteristics? Before we answer this question we should understand the concept of *svarūpa* and *dharma* (also known as *svabhāva*) and the distinction between them. *Svarūpa*, according to Vedānta Deśika, is the *dharmi* or substrate which is determined or qualified by its distinguishing characteristics.[41] The essential *dharma* or *svabhāva* is that characteristic which is unique to the object and which determines the nature of that object. According to the Viśiṣṭādvaitin, every entity in the universe, both physical as well as ontological, consists of two aspects: substantive aspect which is *dharmi* and attributive aspect which is *dharma*. The latter cannot exist by itself and it necessarily inheres in the former which is the basis or *āśraya* for the *dharma*. The two by virtue of their intrinsic character are distinct but are inseparable. When an object is cognised, it is comprehended along with its essential attributes. This is a fundamental theory of Viśiṣṭādvaita and it is discussed in detail in the chapter on Metaphysical Categories. The implication of this is that the *svarūpa* of an entity cannot be known or described except in terms of its essential attributes. In the opinion of Vedānta Deśika, a mere *svarūpa* devoid of essential characteristics is a non-entity like the horns of the hare.[42]

In the light of the above explanation, we may now revert to the question : what is the *svarūpa* of Brahman? The *Taittirīya Upaniṣad* defines Brahman in the words : *satyaṁ jñānam anantaṁ Brahma.*[43] Brahman is that which is real, knowledge and infinite. Another text describes Brahman as *ānandaṁ* or bliss.[44] The Upaniṣads also speak of Brahman as free from all imperfections (*amalam*).[45] These five terms are very significant because they bring out fully the *svarūpa* as well as the essential characteristics of Brahman. These are therefore regarded by the Viśiṣṭādvaitin as *svarūpa-nirūpaka dharmas* or attributes defining the essence of Brahman. The word *satyam* means that which has absolutely non-conditioned existence (*nirupādhika sattā-yogi*).[46] *Sattā* means existence and *nirupādhika* implies that it is not

[41]*Rahasyatrayasāra*, Ch. 5. *svāsādhāraṇa-dharma-nirūpita-dharmi.*

[42]*Ibid.* [43]Tait 1-1. *satyaṁ jñānam anantaṁ brahma.*

[44]*Ibid. ānandaṁ brahmaṇo vidvān.*

[45]Br V-8-8. *asthūlam anaṇu ahrasvam adīrgham.* See also Mund 1-1-5. The word *amala* is not used in the Upaniṣads. However, the description of Brahman as not gross (*asthūla*) implies that it is free from all imperfections (*heyapratyanīka* or *amala*). *Heyapratyanīkatva* is considered an essential characteristic of Brahman. See RB III-3-31. [46]RB I-1-2, p. 180.

subject to any kind of modification (*vikāra*). Brahman is *satyam* in the sense that it is never subjected to any kind of modification unlike the non-sentient matter and the bound souls. The word *jñānam* is interpreted by Rāmānuja as that which possesses eternal and non-contracted knowledge (*nitya asañkucita jñānaikākāra*).[47] Though knowledge in this sense means the attributive knowledge of Brahman, it also denotes the *svarūpa* of Brahman insofar as Brahman is the substrate for it. That is, Brahman is *jñana-svarūpa* and *jñāna-gūṇaka*. Brahman as *jñānam* is distinguished from the released souls (*muktātmā*) whose knowledge in the state of bondage was subject to contraction and expansion. The term *anantam* means that which is not limited either by space or time or by any other entity *deśa-kāla-vastu-paricchheda-rahitam*).[48] That is, Brahman is not bound either by space or time because both space and time subsist in Brahman. Nor is it conditioned by any other entity because whatever exists in the universe is pervaded by Brahman. As Brahman is *saguṇa*, the term infinite applies to both the essential nature and the attributes of Brahman. That is, the attributes of Brahman are infinite in number and are also perfect *par excellence*. Brahman as *anantam* is distinguished from the eternally free souls (*nityas*) which are monadic in substance.

The term *ānandam* means that which possesses unsurpassable bliss (*ānandamaya*) as enunciated in the Ānandavalli section of *Taittiriya Upaniṣad*. As in the case of the term *jñānam*, it also signifies that Brahman is also of the essence of bliss (*ānanda-svarūpa*). The term *amala* implies that Brahman is free at all time from imperfections. It emphasises the fact that Brahman is not subject to evil and imperfection like the individual soul. Nor is it subject to mutation like the physical world.

These five distinguishing characteristics determine the *svarūpa* of Brahman. That entity which is characterised by these five attributes is the *svarūpa* of Brahman. In other words, when we speak of the *svarūpa* of Brahman, we describe it as *satyam* or Reality, *jñānam* or knowledge, *anantam* or infinite, *ānandam* or bliss and *amalam* or purity. When we speak of the essential characteristics of Brahman, we describe them as *satyatva, jñānatva, anantatva*, etc.[49]

[47]RB I-1-2, p. 180. [48]*Ibid.* [49]*Rahasyatrayasāra*, Ch. 5.

The *Taittirīya Upaniṣad* offers another important definition of Brahman. Thus it says : 'That from which all things are born, in which they live on being born, and unto which they enter when they perish; that is Brahman.'[50] It refers to three fundamental functions of Brahman, viz. the creation, sustenance and dissolution of the universe. The second *Vedānta-sūtra* which is introduced to answer the question relating to the nature of Brahman states that Brahman is that from which the origin, etc. of this universe proceeds.[51] This characteristic of Brahman as the creator of the universe, though it is an important function of the Supreme Being, does not constitute the *svarūpa-nirūpaka dharma* unlike *satyatva*, *jñānatva*, etc. However, it is the fundamental characteristic of the *viśiṣṭa*-Brahman, that is, Brahman as inseparably related to *cit* and *acit*. According to the Viśiṣṭādvaita Vedānta, Brahman is the Supreme Being as organically related to *cit* and *acit* at all times (*sarvadā*), both in the state of dissolution and even after evolution. Only such a *viśiṣṭa*-Brahman is the material cause of the universe. This truth is determined, as will be explained later, on the strength of the Upaniṣadic text referring to the creation of the universe (*kāraṇa-śruti*). The Sūtrakāra has therefore adopted this definition of Brahman referring to the creative function of the universe. The earlier definition describing Brahman as *satyam*, *jñānam* and *anantam* refers to the substantive aspect of Brahman (*svarūpa*), whereas the one adopted by the Sūtrakāra brings out the functional character of Brahman. The philosophic significance of the definition offered in the Upaniṣads which is reiterated in the *Vedānta-sūtra* is that the Ultimate Reality should be *saviśeṣa* or one qualified with attributes and should also have the functions of creation, sustenance and dissolution.

We may consider in this connection an important issue raised by the Advaita Vedānta. The Advaitin maintains that the Upaniṣadic text in question defining Brahman refers to the very *svarūpa* of Brahman and not to Brahman as qualified by the attributes. The chief argument adopted in favour of this view is that a sentence in which the terms are found in apposition (*samānādhikaraṇa*) conveys an impartite and non-relational sense (*akhaṇḍārtha*).

[50]Tait III-1. *yato vā imāni bhūtāni jāyante, yena jātāni jīvanti, yat prayanty abhisaṁviśanti tad vijijñāsasva tad brahmeti.*

[51]VS I-1-2. *janmādyasya yataḥ.*

Thus, for instance, in the judgment 'He is that Devadatta' the two terms 'He and Devadatta' which stand in apposition do convey the idea of one individual. In other words, a sentence of this type conveys the idea of one entity only when all its constituent terms denote one and the same thing. Accordingly, the Upaniṣadic text in question is understood to mean that Brahman is truth, knowledge and infinitude and not that it possesses these characteristics. If all the terms denote the same sense, would it not follow that they are synonymous? To this the Advaitin replies that the terms can convey a meaning without being synonymous. These terms convey a meaning which is contrary to what is ordinarily implied by them. They have a negative implication and serve to distinguish the entity denoted by them as different from things which possess characteristics other than what are ordinarily implied. In the Upaniṣadic text in question, Brahman is defined as what is contrary in nature to all other things. The term *satya* has the purport of distinguishing what is not real (*anṛta*). Similarly, *jñāna* distinguishes it from things which are non-sentient (*jaḍa*). The term *ananta* distinguishes Brahman from whatever is limited in space, time and object (*deśa-kāla-vastu-paricchinna*). Thus, these terms, though they denote the *svarūpa* of Brahman do not become synonymous insofar as they convey the essential distinction of Brahman from everything else. Brahman as defined by the Upaniṣadic text is one homogeneous Being devoid of all differentiation. This in fact is one of the arguments adopted by the Advaitin to defend the *nirviśeṣa* character of Brahman.

The Viśiṣṭādvaitin does not accept this view. According to him, the text in question does not convey *akhaṇḍārtha*. As we have discussed earlier,[52] a sentence where the terms stand in apposition denotes one entity as qualified by the characteristic connoted by the terms in the sentence. This is the true meaning of *sāmānādhikaraṇya* as defined by the Grammarians. Thus, the *Mahābhāṣya* of Patañjali on Pāṇini sūtras defines: *Sāmānādhikaraṇya* is the power of words which have different meanings to denote only one entity.'[53] To put it in terms of modern logic, *sāmānādhikaraṇya* is that where the terms having different con-

[52]See Section 'Samānādhikaraṇa-Vākya' in Chapter III.

[53]*bhinnapravṛttinimittānāṁ śabdānāṁ ekasmin arthe vṛttiḥ sāmānādhikaraṇyaṃ.*

notations denote one entity. Though the terms of the proposition have different connotations, they can yet denote one and the same entity. Thus, for instance, in the judgment 'blue lotus' the term blue has a different connotation from that of lotus. The connotation of 'blue' is the quality of blueness, while that of 'lotus' is lotusness, and yet the two terms refer to one and the same object. The Viśiṣṭādvaitin therefore asserts that in the Upaniṣadic text Brahman is referred to as qualified by the attributes of *satyatva*, *jñānatva* and *anantatva*.

There is one other argument adopted by the Advaitin in defence of his theory. A statement or proposition which is intended to define an object known as *lakṣaṇa-vākya* denotes only the *svarūpa* of an object. The Upaniṣadic text in question being a *lakṣaṇa-vākya* or a statement defining Brahman is to be interpreted as referring to the *svarūpa* of Brahman. The logical import of *lakṣaṇa-vākya* is discussed in an earlier chapter[54] and it is established that the purport of such a statement is to define the object as qualified by the essential characteristics. The Upaniṣadic text in question therefore defines Brahman as characterised by *satyatva*, *jñānatva* and *anantatva*.

Besides the five distinguishing characteristics, six other important attributes are also admitted in *Īśvara*. These are *jñāna* (knowledge), *bala* (strength), *aiśvarya* (lordship), *vīrya* (virility), *śakti* (power) and *tejas* (splendour). *Jñāna* or knowledge here refers to the *dharma-bhūta-jñāna* of Brahman. It is *nitya* and not subject to any contraction and expansion unlike the knowledge of the bound souls. Through this knowledge *Īśvara* comprehends directly everything in the universe at all times. He is omniscient (*sarvajña*).[55] *Bala* or strength is that quality by which *Īśvara* supports without effort everything in the universe, both sentient beings and the non-sentient matter.[56] *Aiśvarya* or Lordship signifies the quality of being the creator and controller of the universe by means of His unchecked freedom. *Vīrya* or virility refers to that quality of *Īśvara* who, in spite of His being the material cause of the universe, remains unaffected by the changes (*vikāra*). *Śakti* or Power is that special quality through which *Īśvara* causes the

[54]See Section 'Import of Lakṣaṇa-Vākya' in Chapter III.

[55]Nāthamuni describes it thus : *yo vetti yugapat sarvaṁ pratyakṣeṇa sadā svataḥ.*

[56]*Gadya-bhāṣya*: *śrama-prasaṅga-rahitaṁ sarva-dhāraṇa-sāmarthyam.*

evolution of the prakṛti into the manifold universe. *Tejas* or splendour signifies that *Īśvara* does not depend on any external aids for creation, sustenance and destruction of the universe.[57] Of these six attributes, *jñāna* and *śakti* are the most important because all the other qualities are different aspects of these.[58]

The secondary attributes are infinite in number. Some of the important ones are omniscience, omnipotence, etc. which are useful for the act of creation; *vātsalya* (love), *sauśīlya* (friendly disposition) and *saulabhya* (easily approachable) which are useful for providing refuge to the devotees; *dayā* or compassion and other qualities which are useful for the protection of the pious. Vyāsa in the *Mahābhārata* enumerates one thousand names for *Īśvara* and each one of them indicates a particular quality or attribute of god.

Vedānta Deśika does not discuss the nature of these attributes in *Tattva-muktā-kalāpa*. He only raises a few issues connected with the theory of attributes of God and clarifies certain doubts raised in this regard. The first question that arises is whether all the essential attributes abide in God during His different incarnations. According to Viśiṣṭādvaita, God manifests Himself in five forms :

(1) The transcendental form (*para*) ;
(2) *Vyūha* or the divine manifestation as Vasudeva, Saṅkarṣaṇa, Pradyumna and Aniruddha for purposes of meditation and creation of universe;
(3) *Vibhava* or the several incarnations of God in the universal manifestation such as Matsya, Kūrma, Varāha, Rāma, Kṛṣṇa, etc.;
(4) *Archā*, that is, entering into the substance chosen by devotees, as, for example, idols in the sacred temples; and lastly
(5) *Antaryāmi*, that is, residing within the inner recess of our hearts for purposes of meditation.

The purpose of such incarnation, as explained fully in the *Gītā*, is to destroy evil and establish righteousness (*sādhuparitrāṇa* and *duṣkṛtām vināśaḥ*). The question which needs clarification is whether or not *Īśvara* in all His different incarnations functions with His infinite power, omniscience, etc. This question arises

[57] *Ibid. tejastu anyānapekṣatā.* [58] TMK V-97.

because the different descriptions given in the religious literature about the nature and functions of the four *vyūhas* speak of only two qualities except in the case of Vāsudeva who is regarded as possessing all the six qualities. Similarly, when God incarnates Himself in the human or any other form and assumes a corresponding physical body, the question is raised whether He possesses all His qualities. The answer to this question is given in the affirmative. However, depending upon the function to be performed, only certain of His qualities are manifested, while the other qualities exist in latent form. In the same way, even in His role in different incarnations either as Vāmana, Kṛṣṇa or Rāma, some of His attributes become manifested, while others remain hidden. In any case, whenever God incarnates there is absolutely no limitation on His *svarūpa* even as in His original state as Supreme Being (*para*).

With regard to the attribute of *sarvajñatva*, a few queries have been raised. It is an accepted fact that events or objects are subject to temporal variations. What is yet to come is considered future; what is future becomes present when we reach that point of time; and what is present becomes past at a later time. In such a situation, does God know things differently, that is, as of past, present or future or does He know them all in the one form without temporal distinctions? If the former alternative is accepted, then the knowledge of *Īśvara* cannot be regarded as *nitya* or of unchanging character because it is subject to constant change on account of temporal distinctions. If the other alternative is accepted, then it would amount to delusion, since what was a future event is being known as such even after the future has become the present.

This objection is untenable. *Īśvara* sees things as they are, that is, He sees things of the past as past, of the present as present and of the future as future. On that account there is neither any scope for His knowledge becoming non-permanent nor His being subject to illusion. Knowledge remains one and the same but its contents may vary.[59] The correct implication of *sarvajñatva*, as explained by Nāthamuni, is that *Īśvara* comprehends everything simultaneously by means of direct perception. God's knowledge is intuitional as it does not depend upon the sense organs, unlike our knowledge.

[59]TMK III-76.

With regard to the attribute of *sarvaśakti* or omnipotence, one may ask : if God is all-powerful, is it possible for Him to change the blue into red? If it be possible, it could be done only through some magical power, as normally such a feat is impossible. In that case, there will be no settled cosmic order in the universe, because anything could be changed at any time. If, on the contrary, He cannot do the impossibility, how could He be regarded as omnipotent?

This objection is answered by pointing out that the implication of *sarvaśakti* should not be taken to mean that He will disturb the settled order of the universe in a whimsical way. The correct meaning of the concept is that whatever is free from self-contradiction and whatever is difficult to achieve by others, God is capable of achieving it.[60] For instance, sky-flower is a non-existent entity, and it cannot be produced even by God. The creation of a universe is a possibility but it cannot be done by anyone other than God. Only in this sense God's omnipotence is to be understood.

Īśvara is the creator of the universe. He creates the universe in accordance with the *karma* of the individual souls without any bias. The purpose of creation is two-fold: compassion towards the suffering humanity and Divine sport (*krīḍā-kāruṇya-tantraḥ*). Creation of the universe is a divine sport from which *Īśvara* derives *ānanda*. It also serves the purpose of providing the individual souls caught up in the ocean of bondage an opportunity to escape from it and reach the final release. The individual souls cannot strive for the spiritual goal without their being associated with the body, sense organs and intellect. The question which is raised here is : if God is all-compassionate and if the universe is His own creation, why should there be so much suffering in the universe and such wide disparities in the suffering and happiness of individuals? This is explained, as in all other theistic Indian systems, as being due to the *karma* of each individual which varies from one to the other in accordance with one's past deeds. God dispenses good to those who have done good deeds and evil to those who have done wicked deeds. Hence God is free from partiality (*vaiśamya*). He is also free from the defect of being harsh (*nairghṛṇya*).[61]

[60]TMK III-77. *vyāghāta-śūnyeṣu anitara-suśakeṣu asya tādṛktva-siddheḥ.*
[61]TMK III-1. See also VS II-1-34.

If God creates the universe as a divine sport for His own pleasure, it would imply that He has some desire to fulfil. In that case, how could He be regarded as *avāpta-samasta-kāma*, that is, as one whose desires are all fulfilled. In reply, Vedānta Deśika points out that the concept of *avāpta-samasta-kāma* does not mean that God has no desires or that all His desires are already fulfilled, but, on the contrary, it implies that desires of *Īśvara* become fully achieved without any obstruction.[62]

VI. MATERIAL CAUSALITY OF BRAHMAN

One of the major problems of Vedānta is to provide a satisfactory explanation of the material causality of Brahman. The Upaniṣads indicate that Brahman is the material cause (*upādāna kāraṇa*) of the universe on the analogy of the lump of clay being the material cause of pot. On the strength of the Upaniṣadic teaching, all the Vedāntins except Madhva accept that Brahman is the material cause of the universe. If the illustration offered by the Upaniṣad is taken into consideration, it would follow that Brahman itself transforms into the universe. The śruti texts also categorically declare that Brahman is immutable, that is, not subject to any kind of change. The material causality of Brahman thus needs to be accounted for without affecting the *svarūpa* of Brahman. How is this to be done? Each school of Vedānta attempts to offer an explanation in this regard. There are three important theories of material causality of Brahman:

(1) Brahman itself transforms into the universe—a view held by Yādavaprakāśa and Bhāskara. This is known as *Brahma-pariṇāma-vāda*.[63]

(2) Brahman associated with *cit* and *acit* in their subtle form (*sūkṣma-cid-acid-viśiṣṭa*) is the material cause of the universe—a view held by the Viśiṣṭādvaitin. This may be regarded as a modified *Brahma-pariṇāma-vāda*.

(3) Brahman as the basis of the illusory appearance of the universe is its material cause. This is the view of the Advaitin

[62] *Ibid. bhagavataḥ avāpta-kāmatva-vādaḥ svecchāyām sarvasiddhim vadati.*

[63] The earliest exponent of this theory is Bhartṛprapañca, who lived prior to Śaṁkara. According to him, Brahman itself evolves into both the *jīva* and the physical universe.

known as *vivarta-vāda*. Vedānta Deśika rejects the theories of Yādavaprakāśa and the Advaitin as untenable and upholds the soundness of the Viśiṣṭādvaita view.

Criticism of Yādavaprakāśa Theory

According to this school of thought, the very Brahman as associated with three-fold energy (*śakti*)—*acit-śakti*, *cit-śakti* and *Īśvara-śakti*—is the material cause of the universe. That is, Brahman itself through the threefold power it possesses undergoes changes as God, individual souls and matter. That part of Brahman containing *acit-śakti* evolves itself into *acit* or material universe, that part of Brahman containing *cit-śakti* transforms itself into individual souls, and that part of Brahman containing *Īśvara-śakti* transforms itself into *Īśvara*. Just as water of sea turns itself into waves, foam and bubbles, Brahman which is Being (*sat*), manifests itself in the triadic forms.[64] By such an explanation the *svarūpa* of Brahman remains unaffected, because change or transformation takes place only in respect of the *śakti* of Brahman.

This theory is rejected by Vedānta Deśika as unsound. He raises the question whether the *śakti* is different or non-different from Brahman. If it be different, then it cannot be said that Brahman is the material cause, although on this view Brahman remains unaffected by modification. The material causality actually applies to the *śakti* but not to Brahman. If the *śakti* is non-different from Brahman, then it would lead to the position that Brahman itself undergoes transformation but such a view would conflict with the śruti texts speaking of Brahman as immutable and free from all defects. Other than Brahman and the *śakti*, no other third entity is admitted. It may be said that there is difference as well as non-difference between Brahman and its *śakti* (like the ocean and its waves), and such a Brahman could become the material cause even though the *śakti* itself actually transforms. If such a view is held, it would amount to the acceptance of the Jaina theory of *saptabhaṅgi*, which is rejected by Yādava. In other words, acceptance of difference and non-difference amounts to self-contradiction.

[64]This seems to be the view of Yādavaprakāśa as stated by Vedānta Deśika. He quotes a verse in support of it from the *Kātyāyana-kārikā* which is not extant at present). See SS III-28, p. 135. *īśvarāvyākṛta-prāṇair-virāṭ-sindhur ivormibhiḥ yat pranṛtyādivābhāti tasmai sad-brahmaṇe namaḥ.*

Another objection is raised against this theory. If Brahman evolves itself into the universe, then all the elements found in the cause should also be present in the effect. Brahman in this system is constituted of *sat*, *cit* and *ānanda* and these elements, if not all the three, at least the *sat* or consciousness should be found in the universe. But this is not so.

Against this objection, Yādavaprakāśa defends his theory by admitting the presence of consciousness (*cit*) in all things in the universe. If it is not directly experienced, it is due to the fact that it is latent, in the same way as odour, though present in the gem (being a material object), is not cognised. That *cit* or consciousness is present everywhere is proved on the strength of the scriptural texts. The Upaniṣadic text says : 'Everything is Brahman.' Another text points out that Brahman itself is constituted of three—*cit*, *acit* and *Īśvara*.[65] In view of the fact that the whole universe is Brahman, the Upaniṣad regards even the fishermen as Brahman (*brahma-dāśāḥ*). Therefore, Brahman which is capable of undergoing manifold modifications is present in everything in the universe.[66] That is, Brahman which is constituted of *cit*, *acit* and *Īśvara* in an unmanifest form becomes manifest as *cit*, *acit* and *Īśvara*. The example given to explain this is a piece of multi-coloured cloth. The colours present in the three different threads become manifest in the woven cloth.

The above explanation is also untenable, argues Vedānta Deśika. In the first place it is admitted by all that Brahman is beyond our perceptual experience, and the *sat* aspect of Brahman cannot therefore be apprehended in the universe by the sense organs. Further, the scriptural texts declare that Brahman and universe are distinct, and it cannot therefore be said that Brahman is universe. Even if the relationship between the two is conceived in terms of *śarira-śariri* (body-soul relation), distinction is inevitable. As regards the Upaniṣadic texts which speak of non-difference, it is to be understood that Reality is one as a qualified entity. This is discussed separately. Thus, the theory that Brahman itself transforms into the universe is untenable.

[65]Svet I-12. *bhoktā bhogyaṁ preritāraṁ ca matvā sarvaṁ proktaṁ trividhaṁ brahmametat.*

[66]TMK III-29. *anavadhidaśā-citram sat sarvānuvṛttam.*

Criticism of Bhāskara's Theory

Bhāskara, another exponent of the *Bhedābheda* doctrine, presents a modified theory of Brahman as the material cause of universe. According to Bhāskara, Brahman as associated with *upādhi* exists as the one without a second in the state of dissolution (*pralaya*), but when evolution takes place it energizes itself and emanates successively into the manifold of sentient souls and non-sentient matter on account of the *upādhi* or limiting adjunct. This *upādhi* is called *avidyā* but unlike in Advaita system it is real, beginningless and *jaḍa* (non-sentient in character). It is different as well as non-different from Brahman.[67] Brahman is *saguṇa* or endowed with qualities and has a two-fold evolving power, namely, *jīva-pariṇāma śakti* and *acetana-pariṇāma śakti*, by which it becomes the finite individual selves and objects of experience.[68] Like the spider weaving its web, the absolute transforms itself into the relative by its *pariṇāma-śakti* or evolving power. Thus by postulation of a limiting condition (*upādhi*) the transformation of Brahman into *jīvas* and *acit* is accounted for.

This theory is also rejected as unsound. If *jīvas* are non-different from Brahman, the suffering experienced by the latter would also apply to the former. The limiting adjuncts may account for the plurality of *jīvas* as in the case of the different bodies assumed by Saubhari, the mythological personality. But the experience of pleasure or pain of the different bodies belong to that one person who has assumed different bodies. In the same way Brahman cannot escape the suffering of the different individual selves. The omniscient Brahman who has transformed into *jīvas* as a result of the *upādhi* cannot be unaware of the fact that *jīvas* are not different from Him and as such He has to share the suffering of the *jīvas*.

Criticism of Vivarta-vāda

The Advaitin admits on the strength of the scriptural text that Brahman is the material cause of the universe. However, Brahman which is pure Being devoid of any differentiation does not undergo any transformation into universe. In order to account for the material causality of Brahman, the Advaita Vedānta adopts the doctrine of *māyā* or *avidyā*, the cosmic principle which causes

[67]TMK III-31. [68]SS III-27, p. 134.

world illusion. Brahman is eternally self-illumined but owing to *māyā*, it illusorily appears as the universe. In other words, the phenomenal universe is superimposed on Brahman, like the snake in the rope, due to *avidyā*. Insofar as Brahman is the substrate for *māyā* which causes the appearance of the universe, it is regarded as *upādāna-kāraṇa*. All changes in the form of evolution into various modifications apply not to Brahman but to *avidyā*. Brahman thus remains unaffected by change as declared by the śruti, but at the same time, being the basis (*adhiṣṭhāna*) for the cosmic illusion, it is regarded as the material cause of the universe.

The above theory is subjected to severe criticism by the Viśiṣṭādvaitin. The main point of the criticism is that the doctrine of *avidyā*, which is the pivot of Advaita Vedānta, is untenable. As shown by Rāmānuja in his *Śrī-bhāṣya*, the theory is riddled with contradictions. Secondly, the universe is not *mithyā* or illusory, as the Advaitin conceives. It is as real as Brahman, and the possibility of it being an illusory manifestation of Brahman like the appearance of the rope as snake due to *avidyā* is ruled out. All the arguments advanced by the Advaitin to prove the illusoriness of the universe and the theory of *avidyā* are critically examined in detail and shown to be untenable. We will take up this matter in the subsequent chapter. For the present it may be noted that the *vivarta-vāda* or the theory that Brahman itself appears as the universe is untenable.

Viśiṣṭādvaita Theory of Brahman as Material Cause of Universe

According to Viśiṣṭādvaita, the mere *svarūpa* of Brahman as unconnected with *cit* and *acit* cannot become the material cause of the universe. Nor can the non-sentient *Prakṛti* by itself be the material cause of the universe as the Sāṅkhyas believe. It is Brahman as associated with the individual selves and the cosmic matter in their subtle state (*sūkṣma-cid-acid-viśiṣṭa-brahma*) that constitutes the material cause of the universe. In the state of dissolution, the cosmic matter as well as the individual selves exist in Brahman in an unmanifest form as devoid of name and form; when creation takes place, they become unfolded and assume name and form. In other words, Brahman with *cit-acit* in a state of non-differentiation becomes Brahman with *cit-acit* in a state of differentiation with an infinity of distinctions in name and form.[69] What actually evolves or undergoes modification is the *acit* and *cit* but not Brahman directly. Insofar as Brahman is the *ādhāra* or ground for *cit* and *acit*, Brahman is regarded as the material cause.

The above explanation is offered on the strength of the scriptural texts and also the theory of causality accepted by the Viśiṣṭādvaitin. Cause and effect are different states (*avasthās*) of the same substance. Nothing new comes into being in the causation but what already exists in an unmanifest form is made manifest. The earlier state is called *cause* and the later one as *effect*. They are relative terms. *Avasthās* or the states are accidental, that is, they come and go. The lump of clay which is the cause of the pot becomes an effect when it changes into a pot. *Upādānatva* or material causality consists in the association of an entity with a different state (*avasthāntara-yogitvam*). That which serves as the ground or basis for the changed states is regarded as material cause. Thus the clay is the *upādāna-kāraṇa* for pot and vase, which are made of the basic substance clay. It is in the light of this illustration that the material causality of Brahman is to be understood. Both *cit* and *acit* are the modes or *prakāra* of Brahman, whereas Brahman as the *ādhāra* and controller of the *cit-acit* is its *śarīri* or *ātman*. They are organically related to Brahman and as such Brahman is at all times associated with *cit* and *acit* both in the state of dissolution as well as the state of creation.[70] The only difference between the two states is that in the state of dissolution the *cit* and *acit* are unmanifest or indistinguishable by name and form; in the state of creation, they become distinguishable by name and form. When cosmic evolution takes place, change takes place directly in respect of *acit* which actually transforms into the universe of name and form; indirectly change takes place in *jivas* only in respect of its attributive knowledge but not in the *svarūpa*; even with regard to *Īśvara* there is modification to the extent of His becoming the *niyantā* or controller of the *cit* and *acit* in their manifested form.[71] That is, *Īśvara*, prior to creation was *niyantā* or controller of the *cit* and *acit* in their

[69]TMK III-25. *sūkṣmāvyaktādi-dehaḥ sthūlavṛttyā anekadhā pariṇamati.*

[70]RB on VS II-3-18, p. 574. *sarvadā cid-acid-vastu-śarīratayā tat-prakāraṁ brahma.*

[71]*Ibid.*, p. 575. *ubhayaprakāra-viśiṣṭe niyantṛaṁśe tadavastha-tadubhaya-viśiṣṭatā-rūpa-vikāro bhavati.*

unmanifested form; but after creation, He becomes the controller of all the beings created in the universe. In this way, there is the assumption of new *avasthā* even by *Īśvara*. The *avasthās* in this system are adventitious qualities (*āgantuka-dharma*) which may come and go but they do not affect the *svarūpa* of the entity to which they belong for the duration they last. Hence there is no change in the *svarūpa* of *Īśvara* even though he is subject to modification. The *cit* and *acit* are however subject to modification but this change does not affect *Īśvara*, even though He is the *ādhāra* for them. This is illustrated by the analogy of the bodily changes taking place in a personality. A boy grows into a youth, a youth attains manhood and from this stage he grows to be an old man. The different states such as boyhood, youth, manhood, etc. actually apply to the physical body but the *ātman* which is the basis of the body remains unaffected by them. In the same way, though Brahman being *ādhāra* of *cit* and *acit* is the material cause of the universe, it remains unaffected by the evolution of the universe. It is only in the light of this explanation that the material causality is to be understood.

Logically the above explanation sounds convincing. But the problem arises when the Viśiṣṭādvaitin is confronted with the question whether *cit* and *acit* exist along with Brahman even in the state of dissolution. The *Chāndogya Upaniṣadic* text referring to the creation of the universe declares that in the beginning this was *sat* alone which is one only without a second.[72] If one takes the literal meaning of the terms—*sad-eva*, *ekam-eva* and *advitiyam*—as the Advaitin understands, emphasising the absolute identity without any internal or external differentiation, there may be difficulty in assuming that Brahman is associated with *cit* and *acit* in the state of dissolution. This possible objection is met by Rāmānuja by offering the correct interpretation of this Upaniṣadic text. This matter has been discussed in detail in the *Vedārtha-saṁgraha* and also in *Śrī-bhāṣya*[73] and it is conclusively established that the term *ekatva* or oneness applies to Brahman as associated with or qualified by *cit* and *acit* in their subtle form (*sūkṣmāvasthā-*

[72]Ch VI-2-1. *sad-eva saumya idam agra āsīt ekam-eva advitīyam.*

[73]RB I-1-1, p. 89 and II-1-15, p. 483. *Vedārtha-saṁgraha*, pp. 31-35.

viśiṣṭa-brahma). Brahman as associated with such an *avasthā* is one. If such an interpretation is not accepted, it would not be possible to account for the subsequent statement in the same Upaniṣadic passage which says that the one wills to become many (*bahusyām*). The counter-correlate of *bahu* or many is *eka* or one. That is, only the *sat* or Being which is one as associated with *cit* and *acit* in an unmanifest form could become many in a manifested form. According to the *satkārya-vāda*, only what exists in the causal state becomes the effect by assuming a change of state (*avasthāntara*). That the universe existed in an unmanifested form in the state of dissolution is also supported by the *Bṛhadāraṇyaka Upaniṣadic* text which says: 'Now all this was undifferentiated; it became differentiated by name and form.'[74] It is obvious from this text that the cosmic matter and the souls existed in the state of dissolution without name and form, and the same became manifested with name and form after creation. There are other scriptural texts which affirm that cosmic matter assumes the subtle form in the state of dissolution.[75] That *tamas* or cosmic matter is the body of *Īśvara* is also evident from the *Antaryāmi Brāhmaṇa*.[76] Besides, souls and matter which are *nitya* in this system do not become destroyed in the state of dissolution. Therefore, it has to be admitted that they remain in a subtle state along with Brahman. When Brahman wills to become many, what remained unmanifest is made manifest in the form of the manifold universe with names and forms. This is the significance of the material causality of Brahman.

Why should we not say that *Īśvara* is *upādāna-kāraṇa* in a direct way without bringing in a media in the form of *cit* and *acit*? This is not possible for the reasons already explained. The scriptural texts declaring Brahman as material cause have to be reconciled with the texts declaring Brahman as *nirvikāra*. Hence Brahman is *upādāna kāraṇa* only in an indirect sense. All the other systems have to account for material causality only through the acceptance of a media. Bhāskara postulates the limiting adjunct (*upādhi*) in the form of *avidyā* while Yādavaprakāśa admits the concept of *śakti* as associated with Brahman. Śaṁkara postulates

[74]Br-III. 4-7 *taddhedaṁ tarhy avyākṛtaṁ āsīt tannāmarūpābhyām eva vyākriyate.*

[75]*Sub. tamaḥ-pare deve ekībhavati.* The word *tamas* here refers to *prakṛti.*

[76]Br. *yasya tamaḥ śarīram.*

māyā. Viśiṣṭādvaitin explains it on the basis of *cit* and *acit* as associated with Brahman. The advantages and the logical soundness of this theory lie in the fact that the reality of the universe which is so evident to experience is maintained, and the authoritativeness of scriptural texts relating to this matter is upheld and the apparent conflicts are also overcome.

CHAPTER EIGHT

Brahman and Universe

THE fundamental problem of Vedânta is to account for the causal relation between Brahman and the universe. How does the one Absolute become the manifold universe with its infinite variety of names and forms? This is an important metaphysical question to which every Vedântin seeks to provide a satisfactory answer. We have already discussed the explanation offered by the Viśiṣṭâdvaita Vedânta and also the views of Bhâskara and Yâdava. We have also briefly referred to the explanation provided by the Advaita Vedânta. We shall take up in this chapter a detailed and critical examination of the Advaitin's view, and elucidate the Viśiṣṭâdvaita theory that the universe is an integral part of Brahman.

According to Advaita Vedânta, it is owing to *avidyâ* that Brahman appears as the universe. *Avidyâ* is the cosmic principle which causes world illusion. It is not a mere absence of knowledge but a positive entity (*bhâva-rûpa*) and beginningless (*anâdi*) but removed by right knowledge.[1] It cannot be defined either as *sat* or *asat*, and hence its nature is indescribable (*anirvacanîya*).[2]

Does this theory offer a satisfactory solution to the problem? According to the critics of Advaita, it does not. It explains away the problem instead of giving any satisfactory account of the creation of the universe. The critics have therefore subjected the doctrine to critical scrutiny. Râmânuja in his *Śrî-bhâṣya* has levelled a seven-fold objection against this doctrine (*saptavidhânupapattiḥ*).[3] According to him, in the first place its *svarûpa* is riddled with contradictions. Secondly, its description as something inexplicable is untenable. Thirdly, the theory is not supported by any of the *pramâṇas*. Fourthly, neither Brahman nor *jîva* could be

[1]See *Tattva-pradîpikâ*, p. 57. *anâdibhâvarûpam yad vijñânena vilîyate; tad ajñânam-iti prâjñâḥ lakṣaṇam sampracakṣate.*

[2]*Iṣṭasiddhi*, p. 47. [3]RB- I-1-1, pp. 113-40.

its locus(*āśraya*). Fifthly, its function as obscuring the true nature of Brahman (*tirodhāna*) is unintelligible. Sixthly, the removal of *avidyā* by right knowledge is untenbale. Finally, the very conception of the cessation of *avidyā* remains a riddle. These seven criticisms are elaborated by Vedānta Deśika in his *Śatadūṣaṇī* in which he devotes a separate *vāda* for each major point of criticism.[4] In *Tattva-muktā-kalāpa*, he mentions only such of the criticisms as are relevant for the evaluation of the soundness of *vivarta-vāda* on the basis of which Brahman as the material cause of the universe is justified by the Advaitin. We shall give a brief account of these criticisms.

I. CRITICISM OF THE DOCTRINE OF AVIDYĀ

Avidyā, like *jñāna*, implies some person to whom it belongs and some object to which it refers. That is, there must be some person whom it characterises and some object which is misapprehended through it. In the case of the shell-silver illusion, the person who mistakes the shell for silver is its seat (*āśraya*) and shell is its object (*viṣaya*). It is ignorance (*ajñāna*)[5] thus determined that is regarded as the source of error. Now what is the locus and content of cosmic illusion, viz. *avidyā*? Brahman itself is both the locus and content of *avidyā* as there is nothing else beside it. But Brahman in the Advaita system is self-luminous knowledge. It is opposed to *avidyā* like light and darkness. How can it become the seat of *avidyā* which is opposed to its nature and which is avowedly sublated by knowledge?[6]

The Advaitin's answer to this objection is that *avidyā* is not opposed to the knowledge which constitutes the very *svarūpa* of Brahman. What is opposed to *avidyā* is the empirical knowledge of Brahman generated by the study of scriptural texts (*vṛtti-jñāna*) since that alone removes *avidyā*. This argument does not hold good, contends Vedānta Deśika. What is the content of this

[4]See SD, Vādas, 19, 35, 39, 40-44.

[5]The words *avidyā*, *ajñāna* and *māyā* are used in the same sense as the cosmic principle which causes world illusion. However, some Advaitins make a distinction between *avidyā* and *māyā* but such a distinction is not accepted by Vedānta Deśika. See SD, vāda, 42; also ĀV, pp. 136-39.

[6]TMK III-33. *tat-prakāśaika-bādhyā sā svaprakāśe tasmin kathamiva vilaget?*

knowledge? The Advaitin has to say that it is Brahman itself since in his system nothing other than Brahman ultimately exists. If Brahman itself be the content of empirical knowledge, in no way would it be distinct from the knowledge which constitutes the very *svarūpa* of Brahman inasmuch as both refer to the true nature of Brahman. Hence, as in the case of the knowledge that constitutes the *svarūpa* of Brahman, even *vṛtti-jñāna* cannot remove *avidyā*. If the latter could remove it, then the former itself would have to put an end to it. In the case of ordinary illusion, a distinction is drawn between the cognition of the general character of the object and the cognition of its special characteristic. When a rope is mistaken for snake, only the general character of the rope is known but not its specific characteristics. When the latter cognition arises, the illusion of snake disappears. Such an explanation cannot hold good in respect of Brahman-illusion. Brahman, according to the Advaitin, is *nirviśeṣa*, devoid of all characteristics. It is not therefore possible to say that the content of *vṛtti-jñāna* is different from *svarūpa-jñāna*. Both are of the same nature as far as its content is concerned. Therefore neither the illusion could arise nor its removal becomes possible. If it is argued that *vṛtti-jñāna* has the intrinsic power to remove the cosmic illusion in the same way as medicine cures the disease by virtue of its intrinsic potency, then it cannot be said that the cosmic illusion is sublated by *jñāna* alone. What is removed by means other than *jñāna*, as in the case of diseases by medicine, is not illusory but real.

Just as Brahman cannot be the locus of *avidyā*, it cannot also be its content. Brahman is regarded as the content of *avidyā* in the sense that the latter conceals the true nature of Brahman. According to the Advaitin, *avidyā* has two important functions : (*a*) concealment of the true nature of Brahman (*tirodhāna*); and (*b*) projection of the illusion of the universe (*vikṣepa*). Because the true nature of Brahman is concealed or obscured by *avidyā*, Brahman appears illusorily as the manifold universe.

How can Brahman be concealed by *avidyā*? asks Vedānta Deśika. If Brahman which is essentially of the nature of consciousness becomes concealed, it would amount to the destruction of the very *svarūpa* of the Brahman. There are only two ways in which the concealment of an eternally self-luminous entity could be understood. It means either the destruction of the luminosity that already exists (*prakāśa-vilayana*) or an obstruction to the origination of luminosity (*prakāśa-utpatti-rodha*).[7] If it be the destruction of the existing *prakāśa*, Brahman would become perishable. If it be the obstruction of the appearance of *prakāśa*, then Brahman would be subjected to origination. But to the Vedāntin Brahman is eternal, and therefore the possibility of its concealment in any sense is inconceivable.[8]

The other function of *avidyā*, viz. the projection of the illusion of the universe, is also inconceivable. *Avidyā* is illusory in character. The appearance of what is illusory is always due to some defect (*doṣa*), as in the case of the illusion of snake in rope. Now, what is that defect on which illusory *avidyā* depends? If a defect be admitted as the source of manifestation of *avidyā*, then that defect being illusory in character would require another defect for its manifestation and so on *ad infinitum*. If in order to overcome this difficulty we held that Brahman itself causes the manifestation of *avidyā*, then Brahman being eternal the appearance of *avidyā* too would become eternal.[9] It may be argued that *avidyā* is beginningless (*anādi*), and hence there is no need to postulate another defect to account for its manifestation. Even this argument will not do because if *avidyā* be beginningless, it would only mean that it is not caused by anything, and on that ground it cannot be claimed that it is not dependent on a defect. *Avidyā*, insofar as it is illusory in character, must depend on a defect for its appearance even though it be beginningless. If, on the contrary, it could manifest itself without a defect, it would become real like Brahman, insofar as it exists from time immemorial without the need of a defective cause.[10] Further, if *avidyā* could manifest itself without the need of another defective source, then for the same reason it should be possible for the appearance of the universe without a defective cause, viz. *avidyā*.

The crucial argument advanced by the Advaitin in defence of his position is that *avidyā* which is also known as *ajñāna* is not a negative concept but a positive entity (*bhāva-rūpa*). It is not totally opposed to Brahman as the critics suppose, even though

[7]TMK III-34. *bhāvānāṁ chādanaṁ sphuraṇa-vilayanaṁ tasya utpatti-rodho vā.*
[8]TMK III-34. See also RB I-1-1, p. 115. [9]TMK IV-35.
[10]*Ibid. anādeḥ apekṣā na cet, sati syāt.*

the latter is of the nature of knowledge. It is therefore possible for *avidyā* to inhere in Brahman. That *avidyā* is a positive entity is established by means of perception, inference and scripture.

That perception reveals the positive nature of *ajñāna* is proved by such experience as one gets after awaking from deep sleep in the form: 'Then I was not aware of anything.' This is not a case of mere absence of knowledge, because knowledge itself cannot know its absence insofar as the two are incompatible. That is, to know its absence the knowledge itself will have to be first known. If the knowledge of the object whose absence is to be perceived is brought within consciousness, how can its absence be also asserted at the same time? Hence the experience in question is of a positive *ajñāna*. What is positive in character can be known by its own nature, that is, without the knowledge of the counter-correlate.

Vedānta Deśika criticises this view. Even if *avidyā* is regarded as *bhāva-rūpa*, it is still opposed to *vidyā* or *jñāna* and as such it cannot co-exist with Brahman which is of *jñāna-svarūpa*. It may be contended that the *ajñāna* which is supposed to be experienced in the state of deep sleep is not opposed to knowledge. This view is untenable because there is no such experience of *ajñāna* as an entity and also as unopposed to knowledge. The experience, 'I was not aware of anything', only implies that one does not have the knowledge of any external objects. *Jñāna* in the form of the attribute of the self (*dharma-bhūta-jñāna*) exists even during deep sleep, but it is only devoid of content. That is, in the absence of its being related to object it is not functioning. It, however, exists in a quiescent form. If this were not admitted, the recollection that follows soon after sleep cannot be accounted for satisfactorily. Even in such judgment as 'I am ignorant', 'I am a fool', the words *mugdha* and *mūḍha* imply the negative character of *ajñāna*, even though these words do not have negative particle, viz., *non* (*na*). They do not imply a positive character of *ajñāna* but, on the contrary, they refer to the absence of knowledge. It is therefore not possible to prove by means of perception that *ajñāna* is a positive entity.[11]

Nor can it be proved by means of inference. The following syllogistic argument is adopted by the Advaitin to prove *ajñāna* as a positive entity :

[11]TMK III-36. SD Vāda 39.

> All knowledge established by one of the *pramāṇas* is preceded by something else which is different from prior non-existence of knowledge, which obscures the object of knowledge, which is removed by itself and which exists in the same place as knowledge; because knowledge possesses the property of manifesting things not illuminated before, just as the light of a lamp lit in a dark place manifests things.[12]

This significant and well-formulated syllogism is intended to prove that all knowledge is preceded by a positive state of ignorance which is removed as soon as knowledge arises. Ignorance like darkness is a positive entity which hides the nature of things.

The above syllogism suffers from logical fallacies. The probans in the syllogism is inconclusive. The function of manifesting what is not already manifest belongs to knowledge only. Manifestation of an object does not merely consist in dispelling what is opposed to it. On the contrary, it consists in defining the objects. This function belongs only to the knowledge. The light of the lamp serves only as an auxiliary inasmuch as it reveals the object to the sense organs by dispelling the enveloping darkness. If the power of manifestation of what was not already manifest were admitted to the auxiliary factors also, then it should be admitted in respect of sense organs as well. But sense organs are not preceded by anything different from that which is terminated by their activity, and as such the probans would become inconclusive. Inference is ineffective in proving the theory in question.[13] As Rāmānuja points out, it is also possible to prove by the same means of inference the exactly opposite theory, viz. that *ajñāna* is not a positive entity as held by the Viśiṣṭādvaitin.

One other modified syllogistic argument formulated by Citsukhācārya is put forward to prove the positive character of *avidyā*: 'The valid knowledge of Devadatta removes that ignorance which is different from the non-existence of his knowledge and

[12]*Vipratipannaṁ māna-jñānaṁ sva-prāgabhāva-vyatirikta-svaviṣayāvaraṇa-svanivṛttya svadeśagata-vastvantara-pūrvakam, aprakāśitārtha-prakāśakatvāt, andhakāre prathamotpanna-pradīpa-prabhāvat.*

[13]TMK III-37. See SD, Vāda 39 for more detailed criticism of this syllogism. Also RB I-1-1, pp. 126-27.

which is beginningless, because it is a valid knowledge as, for example, the knowledge of Yajñadatta.[14]

Even this argument is fallacious. It does not necessarily follow that a piece of knowledge, because it is valid, should remove such a positive ignorance which is beginningless. If a counter-syllogistic argument is advanced questioning the basis of the syllogism, it cannot be easily refuted. The syllogism cannot therefore be valid.

Further, for the Viśiṣṭādvaitin non-existence (*abhāva*) is not a separate entity. It is only another form of existence (*bhāvāntara*). When we say there is no light, it only means there is darkness. Hence, the term *pramābhāvātirikta* used in the syllogism is meaningless. The main point of criticism is that there is no evidence to prove that a valid knowledge removes positive ignorance existing from beginningless time. All that is known is that the absence of knowledge precedes the valid knowledge. When knowledge arises, it removes its previous state of non-existence.

The scriptural texts also do not support the theory of *ajñāna* as a positive entity. The two important śruti texts which are quoted by the Advaitin in support of his theory are: hidden by the untrue (*anṛta*)[15] and then there was neither non-being nor being, but there was darkness, hidden by darkness (*tamas*).[16] Both these texts, according to the proper interpretation offered by Rāmānuja taking into consideration the relevant contexts and other concerned śruti texts, do not refer to *ajñāna* as conceived by the Advaitin, viz. that it is an inexplicable positive entity. The word *anṛta* in the first text refers to *karma* or such action as stands in the way of the knowledge of Brahman. *Anṛta* means that which is different from *ṛta*. The term *ṛta* denotes such actions which aim at the propitiation of God and thus enable the devotee to attain Him. *Anṛta* in this text is therefore to be understood as actions which come in the way of Brahman-realisation.[17] The word *tamas* in the other text also does not refer to the *avidyā* as understood by

[14]*Tattva-pradīpikā*, p. 58. *devadatta-niṣṭha-pramāṇa-jñānaṁ tanniṣṭha-pramābhāvātirikta-ajñānasya anādeḥ nivartakaṁ, pramāṇa-jñānatvāt, yajñadattīya-pramāṇa-jñānavat.*

[15]Ch VIII-3-2. *anṛtena hi pratyūḍhāḥ.*

[16]*Yajurveda* 2-8-9. *nāsadāsīn no sadāsīt tadānīm, tama āsīt tamasā gūḍham agre praketam.*

[17]See RB I-1-1.

the Advaitin. It means primordial cosmic matter (*mūla prakṛti*). This is established by the Upaniṣadic texts which say that *tamas* becomes one with the Supreme Self and whose body is *tamas*.[18]

Even the scriptural texts which specifically mention the terms—*māyā* and *avidyā*—do not lend support to the Advaitin's theory. These terms in these texts refer to cosmic matter (*prakṛti*) as is evident from those very texts which say that *māyā* is *prakṛti*.[19] Further, the term *māyā* does not necessarily mean what is *anirvacanīya*. On the contrary, the term is also applied to that which produces wonderful effects (*vicitra-sṛṣṭi-karatva*).[20]

Apart from the śruti texts, the very concept of Brahman as *niravadya*, that is, free from all defects abhors the idea of the presence of *ajñāna* in Brahman. The śruti describes Brahman as *niravadya* and this is accepted by all Vedāntins. *Niravadya* means free from defects, such as *avidyā*, *karma*, etc. If it is said that *avidyā* being illusory in character does not become a *doṣa* or defect in respect of Brahman, then why should any effort be made to remove it.

The Advaitin contends that the admission of *avidyā* in Brahman is necessary as otherwise it would not be possible to account for the identity of Brahman and *jīva* as declared by the Upaniṣadic text *Tattvamasi* (That Thou Art). In view of this, the śruti describing Brahman as *niravadya* is to be interpreted as a reference to Brahman that has become free from *avidyā*.

This view is untenable, argues Vedānta Deśika. The scriptural text speaking of oneness of Brahman and *jīvātman* is to be interpreted in such a way as would not conflict with several other scriptural texts, smṛti texts and other *pramāṇas* which support the view that Brahman is qualified by numerous auspicious attributes. When this is possible, it is inappropriate to adopt a meaning implying identity, ignoring several other texts which have a different implication. In order to justify an interpretation adopted by the Advaitin, the postulation of the theory of *avidyā* in Brahman is unwarranted.

The Advaitin attempts to justify the admission of *māyā* in Brahman on different grounds. According to Upaniṣadic teaching, Brahman is the material cause of the universe. But the śruti texts

[18]*Tama ekībhavati yasya tamaḥ śarīram.*

[19]Śvet. 4-10. *māyāṁ tu prakṛtiṁ vidyāt.*

[20]RB I-1-1, p. 140.

also declare that Brahman is *nirvikāra*. How could Brahman be the material cause of the universe without undergoing modification? If this problem is to be solved, *upādhi* or a conditioning principle in the form of *māyā* is to be admitted. *Māyā* is illusory in character. What is illusory should have a substrate which should be real just as the rope is the substrate for the illusion of snake. Without admitting *māyā* as the cause of illusion, the appearance of the universe cannot be accounted for. The second argument in support of *māyā* is based on the theory of causality. The cause and effect should be of the same nature. The universe which is a product of *māyā* is illusory in character in the sense that its nature cannot be determined either as *sat* or *asat*. It is different from *sat* and *asat* or *sadasad-vilakṣaṇa*. This is the meaning of *mithyā*. If the effect is *mithyā*, its cause also should be of the same nature. Such a cause of the illusory universe is *māyā*.

Both these arguments are rejected as unsound by the Viśiṣṭādvaitin. In the first place, the universe is not illusory in character, as the Advaitin believes. Its reality is well established both by our experience as well as śruti texts. It is not therefore appropriate to postulate an illusory cause for it in the form of *māyā*. The *Chāndogya Upaniṣad* dealing with *sad-vidyā* clearly points out that the universe cannot be caused by what is *asat* or unreal.

Further, it is not necessary that cause and effect should be of the same nature. While criticising the Sāṅkhya theory of *prakṛti* as the material cause of universe, the author of the *Vedānta-sūtra* has rejected the view that cause should be of the same stuff as the effect.[21] According to the Sāṅkhya system, the universe is constituted of the three *guṇas—sattva*, *rajas* and *tamas*. The material cause of such a universe is *prakṛti* constituted of three *guṇas* and not Brahman. Sūtrakāra does not agree with this view because there is no rule that cause and effect should be of the same nature. There are examples of cause and effect being of different nature. Thus, for instance, the scorpion is born out of cowdung; the bees come out of the germs (*kṛmi*). It should therefore be possible for Brahman to become the material cause of the illusory universe without the need of *māyā*. If, on the contrary, it is held that the material cause of the universe should be real, then, on the basis of the principle that cause and effect should be of the

[21]VS II-1-6. *dṛśyate tu.* See RB p. 449. *vilakṣaṇayorapi kārya-kāraṇabhāva darśanāt.*

same nature, the universe, which is its effect, should also be real.[22] This is acceptable to the Viśiṣṭādvaitin. There are two alternatives open to the Advaitin: he should either accept that the universe is real on the basis of the above principle or that the real Brahman is the material cause of the illusory universe without *avidyā*. There is no justification to postulate *avidyā* in Brahman for the purpose of accounting for material causality.

II. CRITICISM OF THE THEORY OF UNIVERSE AS ILLUSORY

If the universe is illusory, the acceptance of *avidyā* or *māyā* in Brahman is justified. Is the universe illusory? The Advaitin maintains that it is illusory, and in support of it he puts forward a few strong and well-formulated arguments. The most important argument is in the form of the famous syllogism having for its probans the cognisability (*dṛśyatva*). That is, the phenomenal world is regarded as illusory on the ground that it is presented to knowledge or objective in character (*dṛśya*). The syllogism is thus expressed : 'The universe under dispute is illusory, because it is cognised; whatever is cognised is illusory, like the shell-silver.'[23] The inference is called *dṛśyatvānumāna*, because it establishes the probandum *mithyātva* by means of the probans *dṛśyatva*.

Vedānta Deśika subjects this syllogism to a critical examination. At the outset he raises a general criticism that the syllogism as a whole is defective and does not prove that the universe is illusory. In the premise 'The universe is illusory', is the subject (*pakṣa*), which in this case is universe, established by *pramāṇas* or not? If it is well established by *pramāṇas*, its negation by the predicate amounts to a self-contradiction. If, on the contrary, the *pakṣa* is not established by *pramāṇas*, the syllogism suffers from the fallacy of *āśrayāsiddhi* (proving what is not established).[24] It is not appropriate to advance a syllogistic argument which is defective. It may be said that an argument may be advanced on the basis of certain commonly accepted view. In that case, we have to admit that the universe is real because, according to our common experience, universe is real.

[22]TMK III-44.

[23]*Vigitam mithyā, dṛśyatvāt, yadyadittham tat tathā, yathā śuktirajatam iti.* cp. Ānandabodha's, *Nyāya Dīpāvalī*, p. 1; *Advaita Siddhi*, p. 31 (Nirnayasāgara Edn).

[24]TMK III-45.

The probandum *mithyātva* is subjected to logical analysis. What does it mean? It is resolved into seven alternatives:

(*a*) Absolutely unreal (*tuccha*);
(*b*) Being the content of apprehension otherwise (*anyathā-khyātiviṣayatvam*);
(*c*) Being different from the real as well as the unreal (*sadasad-vilakṣaṇatvam*);
(*d*) Being the counter-correlate of the negation of what is found in a particular locus (*pratipanna-upadhau-niṣedha-pratiyogitvam*);
(*e*) Being cognised in the same locus as its own absolute non-existence *svātyantābhāvā-samānādhikaraṇatayā pratiyamāna-tvam*);
(*f*) Being different from the real Brahman (*satya-brahma-vila-kṣaṇatvam*);
(*g*) Something else (*anyadeva kiñcit*).[25]

The first two alternatives are not of importance as the Advaitin himself does not admit them. By illusoriness, he does not mean either that which is totally unreal (*tuccha*) or that which is the content of apprehension otherwise.

The third alternative is of significance. The term (*mithyā*) is understood as that which is neither real nor unreal but different from both. That is, the universe is illusory in the sense that it cannot be characterised as real or as unreal. Real is that which is not sublated at any time. But the universe is sublated by the Brahman-knowledge, and therefore it is not real. Nor is it unreal because what is unreal is never cognised, while the universe is cognised. It cannot be both real and unreal because of self-contradiction. It is therefore something different from the real as well as unreal. In other words, it is indeterminable (*anirvacaniya*). This is the meaning of *mithyātva*, which is commonly accepted by all the Advaitins.[26]

According to Vedānta Deśika, the concept of *sadasad-vilakṣaṇa* is a self-contradiction.[27] The terms real and unreal being opposed to each other, like light and darkness, are contradictory. A

[25]See *Tattvapradīpikā* (2nd Edn), pp. 32-33.
[26]*Iṣṭasiddhi*, p. 47.
[27]TMK III-48 *sadasaditaratā vyāhatatvādiduḥsthā.*

thing must be either real or unreal and it cannot be both. Nor can it be different from real and unreal. In a sense a thing could be real-cum-unreal from different standpoints but it is impossible to conceive that it could be different from both real as well as unreal. Thus, the probandum *mithyātva* in the syllogism in the sense of *sadasad-vilakṣaṇa* is a non-established qualification (*aprasiddha-viśeṣaṇa*). The concept sought to be proved in the syllogism should be acceptable to both the disputants. But the Viśiṣṭādvaitin does not admit it as it is a self-contradiction.

The Viśiṣṭādvaitin no doubt regards the shell-silver as unreal (*mithyā*) and what he means by *mithyā* is the apprehension of an object as different from its own nature (*anātmanā vedyatā*). A jug as a jug is real but a jug as a piece of cloth is unreal. Brahman as a non-sentient entity is unreal. In the same way the universe as different from what it is may be regarded as *mithyā*. If the Advaitin understands the term *mithyā* in this sense, then the syllogism suffers from the fallacy of proving what is acceptable to the opponent (*siddha-sādhana*).

The universe may be understood to be illusory in the sense that it is different from the real Brahman (*satya-brahma-vilakṣaṇatvam*). This will not do, for the Viśiṣṭādvaitin also admits that the universe is different from Brahman though it is organically related to it. Nevertheless, if it be argued that the universe is illusory because it is different from reality (*satyetara*), the reply is that it need not be so. For, that which is real by its nature would not become unreal because it is different from another real entity. The pot for instance, is different from another real object, say, cloth; but on that account it cannot be regarded as unreal. It may be argued that what is denied in respect of the universe is absolute reality (*pāramārthika satyatva*). But even this view does not improve the position. There cannot be any concomitance between *dṛśyatva* which is the probans and *pāramārthika satyatva*, the probandum, because we do not have any experience of Brahman as absolute reality.[28]

Illusoriness of the universe may mean the appearance of the universe in the same locus where it does not exist at all. The shell-silver, for instance, does not exist in the shell but yet it appears there. It is, in other words, cognised in the same locus as its own

[28]TMK III-46.

absolute non-existence. Similarly, the universe does not exist in Brahman but it appears there insofar as it is superimposed on Brahman. In this sense it is illusory.

As against this argument, it is asked whether it is possible to prove the absolute non-existence of the universe in Brahman. The non-existence of the universe in a place where it appears cannot be comprehended by perception. If there is no perception of it, the inference which is based on perception is also not possible. Nor can it be proved on the strength of the scriptural texts. The scriptural statements which are quoted by the Advaitin in support of his theory have a different import to the Viśiṣṭādvaitin.

Mithyātva may be understood as that which is negated even where it is found to exist. This is termed as *bādhyatva* or being sublated. The silver, which appears to be present in the shell, is negated by the later cognition in the form: 'This is not silver.' The shell-silver is thus the counter-correlate of the negation of what is found to exist in shell. It is, in other words, sublated by the cognition : 'This is not silver.' It is therefore regarded as illusory. On the same analogy, the Advaitin contends that the world-appearance is also negated by the Brahman-knowledge, and hence it is illusory.

Vedānta Deśika refutes this argument. *Bādhyatva*, in the sense that it is negation of what is found to exist in its own place and time, would render the *hetu* or probans fallacious. The *hetu* is *dṛśyatva*, being cognised. That is, whatever is *dṛśya* should also become sublated (*bādhita*). This condition may hold good in the case of shell-silver. The appearance of silver in a place and at a time where it does not exist is negated later. There is concomitance between *mithyātva* of shell-siver and *dṛśyatva*. But this is not so in the case of objects such as a pot. A pot is congnised but it is not sublated. If we take into consideration the universe in respect of which *bādhyatva* is to be proved, the universe as far as our experience goes is not sublated. All *pramāṇas* support the reality of the universe.[29]

Some general criticisms in the form of dialectic are levelled against the syllogism as a whole. Is the illusoriness (*mithyātva*) of the universe illusory or not? If it be illusory, it would follow that the universe is real, a position which is acceptable to the

[29]TMK III-47. *nikhilamapi mānam tadvidhānaikatānam.*

Viśiṣṭādvaitin. Thus, the inference would suffer from the fallacy of the establishment of what is already established. Besides, it would militate against the Advaitin's theory. If, on the other hand, the illusoriness of the universe were not illusory, then it is asked whether it is Brahman or something different from Brahman. Obviously, it is different from Brahman. This would lead to the position of accepting a real entity other than Brahman and as such it goes against the fundamental tenet of Advaita, viz. that everything other than Brahman is *mithyā*.

Again, does the subject of the syllogism 'entire universe' include the *mithyātva*, the probandum? If it does, then the same becomes negated. If it does not include, then the *mithyātva* not being negated becomes real and renders the *hetu* inconclusive.[30]

The concept of *dṛśyatva* which is used as the probans in the syllogism is also subjected to critical analysis. What does it mean? If *dṛśyatva* means being the object of cognition, it is pointed out that the probans becomes inconclusive. If something is illusory merely because it is the object of cognition, then Brahman also would become illusory insofar as it is the object of knowledge in some sense or another. It cannot be argued that Brahman is not the object of knowledge. For Brahman is the object of philosophic enquiry as is evident from the opening *Vedānta-sūtra* and many other Upaniṣadic texts which teach about Brahman. It may be said that the cognisedness of Brahman is only empirical and is not absolutely real. This is inadmissible since the cognisedness accepted in respect of the universe is also empirical and not real.

To overcome the above difficulty, *dṛśyatva* may be interpreted to mean *jaḍatva* or non-sentience. The universe is illusory because it is non-sentient in character. *Jaḍatva* does not apply to Brahman, unlike cognisedness and as such *hetu* does not become inconclusive. Against this, Vedānta Deśika points out that *jaḍātva* is not applicable to the *jivas* which, according to the Viśiṣṭādvaitin, are part of the universe. This leads to the fallacy of *asiddha*, partially unproved *pakṣa* (*aṁśataḥ asiddham*). A *hetu* which is fallacious cannot prove what is sought to be established. Thus, *dṛśyatvānumāna* does not establish the illusoriness of the universe.

One other syllogistic argument is put forward to prove the

[30]TMK III-49.

illusory character of the universe. What is real must be unchangeable. Judged on this basis, the objects of our experience cannot be real because they are constantly changing. They are therefore illusory. To express it in the form of a syllogism: pot and similar things are illusory because they are changing *(vyāvartamānatvāt);* whatever are changing are illusory, as is the shell-silver.[31] In the same way the universe, which is subject to change, is illusory.

This syllogism is also rejected by Vedānta Deśika on the ground that the probans adopted here is defective. What does *vyāvartamānatva* mean? Does it mean (*i*) difference from something or the other (*bhinna*) or (*ii*) being sublated (*bādhyatva*) or (*iii*) being subject to destruction (*naśvaratva*)?

The first alternative is untenable. Brahman is different from the universe but it does not become illusory simply because it is different from the universe. Thus the *hetu* or probans becomes inconclusive.

Nor is the second alternative sound. According to the Viśiṣṭādvaitin, the physical objects in the universe such as pot, cloth, etc. are not sublated at any time insofar as our experience goes. The probans in the sense of *bādhyatva* is unproved (*asiddhi*).

The third alternative is also untenable. Destruction is possible only for such entities as exist or real. No one speaks of destruction of hare's horn. If existence of the universe is accepted, the denial of its reality would militate against one's own position (*apasiddhānta*). Besides, the probans, understood in the sense of being subject to destruction, becomes completely divorced from the illustration cited in the syllogism. No one would say that the snake superimposed on the rope is destroyed. The terms *vināśa* (destruction) and *bādha* (sublation) have different connotations. Destruction is the dissolution of an entity which exists prior to its destruction, whereas sublation or *bādha* is negation of what was cognised as not this.[32] Only when a real snake is killed with a stick, it is considered to be destroyed. If, on the contrary, the illusion of snake in the rope is removed, it is called sublation.

[31]SS III-51. *vimatam mithyā, vyāvartamānatvāt, yaduktasādhanam taduktasādhyam; yathā śukti-rūpyam.*

[32]SD, Vāda 16. *pratipannasya neti niṣedho bādhaḥ; vināśastu labdhasattākasya svarūpa pracyutiḥ.*

There is yet another view of change, viz. manifestation of a thing in some place and at some time and non-manifestation of the same at other place and time, like the shell-silver or rope-snake. Even this view is inadmissible, since it cannot be the determinant of illusoriness. The non-manifestation of an object at other times is due to the absence of the requisite accessories that cause its cognition. If non-manifestation at any particular time be regarded as the criterion of illusoriness, then Brahman also would be illusory since it is not manifest owing to *avidyā* until the time of release. All supernormal objects which are not perceived by us would, by that reason, become illusory.[33]

It may be argued that objects of the physical universe are non-permanent in character and they are therefore illusory. This is based on the following assumption: what really exists should exist all the time permanently like Brahman and what does not exist can never exist anywhere at any time like the sky-flower. This is expressed in the form of an argument: what does not exist earlier and at a later time cannot also exist in the present time. This would mean that the physical objects which exist only at some time or some place but not always are therefore illusory in character.

Vedānta Deśika refutes this view.[34] The fact that an object exists now is proof of its existence at an earlier time and also at a later time. As a matter of fact, it is on the basis of the cognition of the object in the present time that its non-existence earlier and later is proved. Except with reference to the present, the concept of earlier and later has no meaning. Then how does it happen that the object which does exist now, ceases to exist later? And how can the same thing which did not exist earlier happen to exist now? The prior existence and later existence of a thing is determined by the accessory factors which cause their origin and destruction. The accessory factors responsible for the production of an object bring it into existence; in the same way the accessories responsible for its destruction make it non-existent at a later period. The fact that an object is non-permanent does not render it illusory like the hare's horn. In fact, *mithyātva* (illusoriness) and *anityatva* (non-permanence)

[33]TMK III-51.

[34]SS III-52, p. 156. *yat prāg ūrdhvaṁ ca asat tan madhye'pyasat; yathā sampratipannam; vimatam ca tathātvāt mithyā.*

cannot be synonymous terms. In other words, what is non-permanent in character does not become illusory.[35]

Does revealed scripture prove that the universe is illusory? The Advaitin answers this question in the affirmative. In fact, it is on the strength of the scriptural texts that he affirms the phenomenal character of the universe. The crucial Upaniṣadic texts which are quoted in support of his theory are the one in the *Chāndogya* declaring the existence of Brahman as one only without a second and the oft-quoted *Bṛhadāraṇyaka* statement which negates all plurality.[36]

Without directly entering into any controversy on the interpretation of the relevant Upaniṣadic texts, Vedānta Deśika points out that śruti does not say anything that goes counter to what is well established by perception. Perception reveals beyond any shadow of doubt that the universe is real. The scripture cannot contradict this perceptual knowledge. If such a view is not maintained, then there are several scriptural statements like 'The sun is the sacrificial pillar' (*adityo yūpaḥ*), which have to be accepted with their literal meaning as against what is evident to perceptual experience. But in such cases, the practice is to adopt a secondary meaning to avoid the glaring conflicts with perceptual experience. In the example cited, if we were to accept the literal meaning, it would mean that the sun is identical with *yūpa*. But as it is against perception we take it to mean that the sacrificial pillar (*yūpa*) is brilliant like the sun. Perception being the foundational knowledge cannot be overlooked even by scripture.

This raises a fundamental question. When there is conflict between scripture and perception, which should we accept as more authoritative? The Advaitin maintains that, in cases of such a conflict, scripture is stronger than perception, and as such the former is of greater validity than the latter. The main reason for holding such a view is that perception is capable of imperfection as it has for its source the impression of difference

[35]TMK III-52.

[36]Ch. VI 2-1. *sadeva saumya idam agra āsīt ekameva, advitīyam*; Br 6-4-19. *neha nānāsti kiñcana.* According to the Advaitin, these texts deny the existence of everything other than the Absolute Brahman. But, according to Rāmānuja, both these texts assert the existence of Brahman as associated with the universe.

(*bheda-vāsanā*) which is considered to be a defect. Scripture, on the other hand, is absolutely free from defects, because it is impersonal (*apauruṣeya*), and as such there is no room for its being the product of one's delusion, deceit or carelessness of the agent. Scripture is thus of greater force than perception, and it is therefore capable of negating what is revealed by perception.[37]

Vedānta Deśika rejects this argument. The basis on which greater validity is accorded to scripture does not hold good in the case of the Advaitin, because even scripture is of a defective source insofar as it is a product of *avidyā*. It cannot be said that the sacred texts are not the product of *avidyā*, because, according to the ontological position of Advaita, everything else other than Brahman is *mithyā*. Besides, it is also not possible to establish conclusively that the impression of difference (*bheda-vāsanā*) is a defect.[38]

It may be argued that scripture, although it is based on a defect, sublates perception insofar as it generates the knowledge which dispels all plurality apprehended through perception and is thus later than perception (*param*). According to the principle of the Mīmāṁsā, known as *apaccheda-nyāya* (the principle of the later sublating the earlier), what comes later is stronger than the earlier.

The Viśiṣṭādvaitin rebuts the above argument by saying that the defectiveness of the source of the scripture having been once conceded the circumstance of its being later is of no avail. This point is explained by an illustration in the *Śrī-bhāṣya*.[39] If a person is afraid of a rope which he mistakes for a snake, his fear does not cease just because another man, whom he considers to be in error himself, tells him : 'This is no snake, do not be afraid.' That scripture is founded on something defective is known at the very time of studying the sacred texts (*śravaṇa*), for the *manana* (recollection) which follows *śravaṇa* consists in repeated attempts to cognise oneness of Brahman, a knowledge which is destructive of all plurality apprehended through the hearing of the Upaniṣads.

Even if we acknowledge that sacred texts are of greater authority than perception, it would not prove the point of the

[37]TMK III-55. *pratyakṣam doṣamūlam iha śrutiḥ pauruṣeyatva-hāneḥ na tathā.*

[38]See SD Vāda 29 for more details. Also AV, p. 29.

[39]RB I-1-1, p. 85.

Advaitin. The Advaitin's contention is that the revealed scripture teaches non-dualism, whereas perception reveals difference. Scripture which is *apauruṣeya* and free from all defects is of greater validity. This argument does not hold good, because the very scripture also teaches us difference. Thus, the Upaniṣadic texts which are intended to teach the nature of Reality speak of the difference between Brahman and the individual soul. It may be argued that there are scriptural texts which emphasise the identity of *jiva* and Brahman, and between the two conflicting scriptural statements those that emphasise non-difference are stronger and of greater validity than those speaking difference. As negation comes later than affirmation, the texts which negate difference become more authoritative than those affirming difference.

This argument is controverted by the Viśiṣṭādvaitin on the ground that *apaccheda-nyāya* is not applicable in this case. The *apaccheda-nyāya* holds good where the two events do not follow as earlier and later uniformly at all times. Where there is a fixed order as earlier and later as in the case of the two scriptural texts, one affirming and the other negating what is affirmed (*niyatā-virodha-paurvāparye*), the earlier text is predominant, according to the principle of the earlier being stronger than the later (*upakramādhikaraṇa-nyāya*).[40] As the texts emphasising non-difference and those referring to difference are always mutually opposed to each other by their very nature, the texts negating difference do not become more authoritative simply because negation comes later than affirmation. On the contrary, the texts which speak of difference between Brahman and *jiva* are of greater validity than those emphasising their absolute identity.

The Advaitin adopts a different type of argument to defend his tenet. He argues that perception cognises a world of plurality and difference. What is already known by common experience which is empirical in character cannot be the purport of the sacred texts. The revealed scripture becomes purportful only when it teaches something which is other than what is empirically known. On the basis of the six-fold criterion governing the

[40]TMK III-57. *niyatimati atra upakrama-nyāya-siddheḥ, apaccheda-nītiḥ na.* See also SS, p. 161. *aniyata-paurvāparye hy apaccheda-nayaḥ niyame tu upakrama-nayāt parānutpattireva.*

authenticity of interpretation,[41] the Advaitin claims that the main purport of the Upaniṣads is non-dualism. Hence scripture enjoys a greater validity than perception.

This argument is not of much significance. If non-dualism is the purport of the sacred texts according to Advaitin, even transcendental difference is the purport according to the Viśiṣṭādvaitin. The Upaniṣads do not speak of the difference that is ordinarily known to us as between cloth and pot, but they advocate and teach us the ontological difference that exists between Brahman and *jiva*, or that between Brahman and the material universe. The concept of *bheda* in respect of ontological entities is not ruled out by the sacred texts. Thus, it is wrong to assert that only non-difference or non-duality is the purport of sacred texts and on that count regard it as of greater validity than perception revealing empirical difference.

According to some Advaitins, perception does not cognise difference. On the contrary, it apprehends an undifferentiated and indeterminate Being (*nirviśeṣa-sanmātra-grāhi*) and as such there is no conflict at all between perception and scripture since both have the same content. Perception is of the one real, difference being superimposed thereon.[42] The main argument in support of this view is that difference is a relative notion and as such its cognition is dependent upon the knowledge of its substrate and counter-correlate, while 'Being' is not so. Perception which is momentary is capable of cognising only 'Being' while difference is imposed on it later by thought.

According to the Viśiṣṭādvaitin, perception is capable of cognizing both difference as well as 'Being' in that very moment. This is an epistemological problem which is discussed elsewhere. The main criticism of Vedānta Deśika against the above theory is that if Reality or Brahman is cognised by the perception, it

[41]The six criteria followed in determining the purport of the scriptural passages are: *upakrama* and *upasaṁhāra* (the opening and concluding statement), *abhyāsa* (repetition of what is taught), *apūrvatā* (novelty of the meaning), *upapatti* (being reasonable), *arthavāda* (laudatory statements) and *phala* (declared result); on the basis of these principles it is asserted by Advaitin that the *sadvidyā* in *Chāndogya Upaniṣad* speaks of non-dualism. Rāmānuja in his *Vedārtha Saṅgraha* affirms, by adopting the same principles of interpretation, that the *sadvidyā* speaks of Saviśeṣa Brahman.

[42]This is the view advanced by the author of *Brahma-siddhi*.

becomes a *dṛśya* or an object of knowledge. This goes against the fundamental tenet of Advaita, according to which whatever is cognisable is *mithyā*. Further, if Brahman could be known through perception, there is no need for philosophical enquiry through the study of Upaniṣad.

III. UNIVERSE AS AN INTEGRAL PART OF BRAHMAN

With the rejection of *vivartavāda* and the establishment of the reality of the universe, the Viśiṣṭādvaitin is confronted with the problem of finding the causal relationship between Brahman and the universe. The *sadvidyā* in the *Chāndogya Upaniṣad* states this problem in a classical manner: 'What is that by knowing which everything else is known?' If we take into consideration the illustrative instances of common experience cited by the Upaniṣad such as clay and its products, it follows that by knowing the cause the effect too becomes known. This would be possible if only the cause is immanent in the effect and non-distinct from it (*ananya*). The issue to be considered is whether Brahman as the material cause and the universe as its effect are non-distinct. The author of the *Vedānta-sūtra* states on the strength of the Upaniṣadic texts: 'That the two are non-distinct (*ananya*).'[43] The question to be decided is in what sense are the two entities—Brahman and universe—non-distinct.

This matter is closely linked with the concept of the cause and effect. This is discussed in detail in the chapter on Metaphysical Categories. The Advaitin maintains the view, following the dialectic of Buddhists, that the causal relation is logically untenable and as such it is not ultimately real. The implication of this is that only cause is real, whereas the effect is illusory and on this basis it is argued that Brahman as the cause is real and the universe as an effect is illusory. In this sense, the cause and effect are not distinct as there are no two realities.

As against this theory, the Viśiṣṭādvaitin argues that causal relation is logically tenable and that both cause and effect are real. According to him, cause and effect are different modifications of the same substance, as in the case of the clay and its modifications

[43]VS II-1-15. *tad ananyatvam ārambhaṇaśabdādibhyaḥ*.

such as pot, vase, etc. As two different states of the same substance there is unity or non-difference between cause and effect. As explained in the previous chapter, Brahman as associated with *cit* and *acit* in their subtle form becomes Brahman with *cit* and *acit* in their manifested form. This is the significance of how the 'one' becomes 'many'—the fundamental ontological question raised in the *Chāndogya Upaniṣad*.

What then is the relation between the two? Rāmānuja accounts for the relationship both on the strength of scriptural evidence and also on logical grounds. From a logical point of view he adopts the metaphysical category of substance and attribute and the concept of *apṛthak-siddhi* or inseparability that obtains between the substance and its essential attribute. We have discussed this doctrine at considerable length in a separate chapter and shown conclusively that substance (*veśeṣya*) and attribute (*viśeṣaṇa*) are distinct and real. Substance is the basis for attribute and the latter cannot exist by itself except as related to the former. Substance also cannot be conceived without its essential characteristics. The two are inherently related and they are inseparable. The same logical explanation holds good in respect of Brahman and the universe. Brahman is the primary substance, whereas *cit* and *acit* which constitute the universe are its modes or *prakāras*. The universe of *cit* and *acit* is an integral part of Brahman, the former being entirely dependent on the latter for their very existence and also being entirely subject to the control of Brahman.

From an ontological standpoint, the relation is explained on the analogy of the organic relation that obtains between the physical body and soul. This is described as *śarira-śariri sambandha* or *śarirātma-bhāva*.[44] This means that the universe consisting of *cit* and *acit* is organically related to Brahman or *Īśvara* in the same way as our body is related to the soul. *Īśvara* is the *śaririn* or the inner self, whereas *cit* and *acit* are His *śarira* or the body. The term *śarira* does not mean the physical body as ordinarily

[44]The *śarira-śarirī* relation is not different from the logical relation of substance-attribute which is described as *viśeṣya-viśeṣana* or *prakāra-prakārī* or *aṁśa-aṁśī*. Where an integral relation exists between a sentient soul and a substance, it is termed as *śarira-śarirī*. If such a relation is found only between a substance and its essential attribute or even between two substances, then the other terms are used.

understood but it bears a specific and technical sense. It is defined by Rāmānuja as a substance, which a sentient soul or self is capable of completely supporting and controlling for its own purpose and which stands to the self in a subordinate relation. That is called the *śaririn* which is always the ground or basis (*ādhāra*), controller (*niyantā*) and which uses it for its own satisfaction (*śeṣin*). The fuller implication of this definition and the justification for its adoption is discussed in an earlier chapter.[45] All sentient beings and non-sentient matter together constitute the *śarira* of *Īśvara,* for they have their being in Him wholly controlled by Him and exist for His satisfaction. Vedānta Deśika brings out the fuller significance of the *śarira-śariri-bhāva* in a clearer way by using the three concepts of *ādhāra* and *ādheya* (sustainer and sustained), *niyantā* and *niyāmya* (controller and controlled), *śeṣin* and *śeṣa* (self-subsistent and dependent). *Īśvara* is regarded as *ādhāra* and *niyantā* of all sentient beings and non-sentient matter, because from His *svarūpa* or essential nature and *saṅkalpa* or will they derive their existence (*sattā*), continuance (*sthiti*) and activities (*pravṛtti*). Just as *Īśvara* is the basis (*āśraya*) for the essential attributes such as *satyatva, jñāna* and *anantatva* which are inseparably related to Him, in the same way He is also the *ādhāra* for *cit* and *acit*. That is, *Īśvara* who is immanent in *cit* and *acit* sustains them by His *svarūpa* (*svarūpāśrita*). He as the inner self of all beings in the universe also supports them by His will power or *saṅkalpa* (*saṅklpāśrita*). Thus, it is said : 'The heavens, the sky with the moon, the sun and the stars, the different quarters, the earth, the great ocean—all these are supported by the might of the Supreme Being, Vāsudeva.'[46] There is an organic relationship between Brahman and universe similar to the one we find between our physical body and the soul within. The physical body exists from the time of the entry of the soul into it, and it perishes when the soul leaves it. The *jiva* is therefore the *ādhāra* of the body and the existence of the latter is dependent on the *svarūpa* of *jiva*. Similarly, the *jiva* controls the body by its will or *saṅkalpa*. In the waking state when the body is kept from falling, it is sustained by the will of the *jiva*. In the state of dreamless sleep the will of the *jiva* is not operating but

[45]See Section 'The Concept of Body-Soul Relation' in Chapter I.

[46]*Mahābhārata*, Anuśasanika parva, 254-136.

the body which continues to exist without any deterioration is then dependent on the *svarūpa* of the *jiva*. When the existence of the body is dependent only on the *svarūpa* of the *jiva*, it is said to be supported by the latter (*ādheya*); when the existence depends on the will or *saṅkalpa*, it is said to be controlled by the latter (*niyāmya*).

Īśvara is said to be the *śeṣin* of all things, because they exist solely for the fulfilment of His purposes. They are his *śeṣas* or those which exist to subserve the Lord. *Śeṣi-śeṣatva* connotes the absolute self-subsistence of the one and the utter dependence of the other. The entire universe is thus dependent upon *Īśvarasvarūpa* as well as His *saṅkalpa* and also subserves His purpose. In view of this it is described that the universe is *śarira* of Bhagavān. It is in this sense that the organic relationship between *Īśvara* and the universe of *cit* and *acit* is to be understood.

This doctrine has been advocated by Rāmānuja primarily on the authority of the scriptural texts – the *Antaryāmi Brāhmaṇa* of the *Bṛhadāraṇyaka Upaniṣad* or the passage expounding Brahman as the Inner Ruler, which explicitly mentions the *śarira-śariri* relation. The seer Yājñavalkya tells Uddālaka that he knows Brahman, and describes it emphatically and repeatedly as *antaryāmin* and *amṛta*, the indwelling Self as immortal, that abides in all beings as their inner Ruler. The passage makes an exhaustive division of the types of beings that form the *śarira* of Brahman, starting with the five elements that constitute the objective world of space-time and ending with the *jiva* or *vijñāna* which is the subject of all knowledge. The last statement in the passage brings out significantly the main teaching : 'He who dwells in the *jiva* and with the *jiva*, whom the *jiva* does not know, whose body the *jiva* is and who rules it from within, He is the Self, the Inner Ruler, Immortal' (*sa ta ātmā antaryāmy-amṛtaḥ*).[47] These Upaniṣadic statements affirm that Brahman 'is in all', 'dwells in all', but 'the all know Him not', and 'the all constitute His body' and 'He rules from within'. Brahman is the Inner

[47]Br. V-7-22. *ya ātmani tiṣṭhan ātmano antaraḥ yam ātmā na veda yasyātmā śarīraṁ ya ātmānam antaro yamayati sa ta ātmā antaryāmy amṛtaḥ*. This is according to Mādhyandina recension. The Kāṇva recension uses the expression *vijñāna* in place of *ātman*. According to Rāmānuja, *vijñāna* stands for *ātman*.

Self (*śarīri*) of all *cit* and *acit*, while the latter are his body (*śarīra*).

Rāmānuja extolls this as *ghaṭaka* śruti because it reconciles the apparent contradiction between the *abheda* śrutis which emphasise the non-difference or unity or Reality and the *bheda* śrutis which emphasise the absolute difference between *Īśvara*, *cit* and *acit*. By advocating the *śarīra-śarīri-bhāva* on the strength of *ghaṭaka* śrutis, Rāmānuja bridges the gulf between Advaita and Dvaita. The Advaita Vedānta, basing its teaching on the strength of the *mahāvākya* and the *nirguṇa* śrutis, maintains that the ultimate Reality is the Absolute Brahman devoid of all differentiation. In that system, *Īśvara*, *jīva* and universe do not have the same reality as Brahman. On the contrary, the Dvaita Vedānta holds that *cit*, *acit* and *Īśvara* are eternally distinct, and their relation is therefore only external. According to this school, *Īśvara*, who is an external designer and ruler, is also not immanent in creation and *jīva* is also not part of Brahman. Rāmānuja tries to mediate between these two extreme views and maintain that his theory of *śarīra* and *śarīri* provides relevance to all texts and reconciles the apparent conflicts.

Without going into the detailed interpretation of the śruti texts we may briefly mention how Rāmānuja attempts to remove the contradiction found in the Upaniṣadic texts on the strength of *ghaṭaka* śrutis. The *abheda* śrutis, Rāmānuja points out, do not deny all distinctions. The texts denying plurality have to be understood in the sense that the whole universe, formed of the sentient and non-sentient entities, constitutes the body and mode of Brahman and that Brahman alone exists as the *ātman* or *śarīri* of all and has every thing as its mode. The texts which proclaim unity are not to be taken to mean absolute identity, but, on the contrary, they imply that Brahman and the universe as constituting an organic unity is one. Thus the apparent contradictions in the Upaniṣadic texts are reconciled by accepting the theory of *śarīra-śarīri-bhāva* on the basis of the *ghaṭaka* śrutis. While posing a question as to whether the Viśiṣṭādvaitin upholds unity or plurality or both unity and plurality, Rāmānuja replies in a striking way that he upholds all the three views as all these are affirmed in the Veda (*sarvasya veda-vedyatvāt sarvaṁ samarthitam*).[48] Unity or *abheda* is established because Brahman alone

[48]*Vedārtha-Saṅgraha*, p. 90.

exists as the unity of *śarira-śariri* relation in which the *śaririn* is the one without a second that sustains the manifold of *cit* and *acit*. *Bhedābheda* or both unity and plurality is upheld because the one Brahman itself has all the sentient and non-sentient beings as its modes and thus exists as qualified by plurality (*nānātvena*). Plurality or *bheda* is established since all the three entities, sentient beings, non-sentient matter and *Īśvara*, are mutually distinct in their nature and character (*svarūpa-svabhāva-vailakṣaṇya*).

By way of conclusion, it may be observed that *vivarta-vāda* which is adopted to uphold idealistic monism does not provide a satisfactory solution to the ontological problem of *one* becoming *many* except by denying Ultimate Reality of the universe and the individual souls. The only way to account for the causal relationship between the Ultimate Reality and the universe of sentient souls and non-sentient matter is to accept the modified *Brahma-pariṇāma-vāda* as explained by Rāmānuja and the doctrine of organic relationship between Brahman and the universe. Whether or not such a theory is philosophically sound is discussed in the concluding chapter.

CHAPTER NINE

Sādhana and Mukti

THIS CHAPTER is devoted primarily to a discussion of a few important issues related to the nature of *mokṣa* or the final liberation of the soul from bondage, and the *sādhana* or the means to achieve it. Though most schools of Indian thought generally admit that *mokṣa* is the supreme goal of life (*parama-puruṣārtha*), they offer divergent views regarding its nature.[1] Similarly, with regard to the means to be adopted for attaining *mokṣa*, there is no unanimity among the exponents of different systems. The fundamental issue to be considered is whether the individual self, the aspirant for *mokṣa* is annihilated or retains its individuality in the state of *mokṣa*. Taking its firm stand on the scriptural texts, Viśiṣṭādvaita Vedānta maintains that *jiva*, which is an eternal spiritual monad, remains in its true nature in the state of *mokṣa* with infinite knowledge, enjoying fully the eternal bliss of Brahman (*paripūrṇa-brahmānubhava*). In expounding this theory, Vedānta Deśika takes up for critical examination a few of the rival theories which are directly opposed to Viśiṣṭādvaitin's view. As regards the *sādhana* or method of achieving *mokṣa*, the main issue involved is whether *jñāna* is the means to *mokṣa* as the Advaitin contends or whether *bhakti* is the direct means. In this connection, the place of *karma*[2] in the spiritual discipline comes up for detailed examination.

I. ELIGIBILITY OF JĪVA FOR MOKṢA

While considering the nature of *mokṣa*, two basic questions arise. First, is there scope at all for the soul to escape from the so-called bondage? Secondly, if there be, would all souls be eligible for

[1]See Section 'Criticism of Other Theories of Mokṣa' in this chapter.

[2]*Karma* here means the observance of religious duties as laid down by scripture.

mokṣa? The first question arises because of the accepted fact that souls are caught up in a continuous cycle of births and deaths. *Karma*[3] which cause bondage to the soul is beginningless, and it flows continuously like the stream of a river. If *jiva* is caught up in such a constant stream of births and deaths, would there be any scope for its escape from it? There is a view, according to which *karma*, unless it is experienced, does not cease to have its influence on the individual even after millions of epochs.[4] How then can *jiva* escape from bondage?

It is no doubt true that *jiva* is passing through the cycle of *karma-avidyā*. Nevertheless, a stage arises in this long march when a good *karma* becomes ripe to provide for the individual an opportunity to escape from bondage. As a result of the meritorious deed performed in earlier births, the individual comes into contact with men of spiritual wisdom. Through their influence, he earns further merit by doing good deeds and thereby becomes the object of grace of *Īśvara*. As a result of this, he becomes an aspirant for mokṣa (*mumukṣu*) and thereafter he undertakes *Brahmopāsanā* or the meditation on Brahman which is the means to *mokṣa*. The *upāsanā* helps to get rid of the past *karma* as well as the *karma* of the future. Once the *jiva* becomes free from *karma*, it achieves *mokṣa*.[5]

It is interesting to note how *jiva* becomes a *mumukṣu*, an aspirant for *mokṣa*. In the state of dissolution (*pralaya*), *jiva* is almost like a non-intelligent material entity (*acid-vastu*). At the time of creation, *jiva* escapes from this condition and comes back to life being endowed with a physical body and consciousness through the compassion of *Īśvara*. Even as a living individual, the *jiva* has to pass through various states of waking, dream, dreamless sleep, death or half-death in the form of swoon. All these states involve some amount of suffering that the *jiva* has to undergo during its lifetime. What is considered to be happiness during this stage is a misnomer. According to men of philosophic wisdom, happiness is comparable to the firefly (*khadyota-kalpa*). It is highly transitory in character. If one

[3]The word *karma* is used here in the sense of the result of the actions of past lives.

[4]*nābhuktam kṣīyate karma kalpakoṭiśatairapi.*

[5]TMK II-25.

realises through philosophic wisdom that life is nothing but suffering (duḥkha) and the so-called happiness is rooted only in suffering (*duḥkha-mūla*), one naturally looks forward to the permanent and real happiness. Only such individuals who develop a detachment towards worldly pleasures of evanascent character become the aspirants for *mokṣa.*[6]

We now come to the second question, viz. whether all souls are eligible for *mokṣa*? This question arises because some believe that there are eternally bound selves (*nitya-baddha* or *nitya-saṁsāri*),[7] in the same way as there are eternally released souls (*nitya-mukta*). According to the Viśiṣṭādvaita system, *jivas* are classified as *baddhas*, those who are in bondage; *muktas*, those who are released from bondage, and *nityas*, those who are eternally free, that is, those who never had bondage.

There are two divergent views on this matter both in defence of and opposed to the concept of *nitya-samsāri*. By way of defence, it is contended that the existence of eternally bound souls is to be accepted in order to account for the possibility of periodical creation and dissolution of the universe The assumption here is that the creation of the universe is intended for the bound souls to experience pleasure and pain. If all the souls were eligible for *mokṣa*, all of them are expected to be released eventually. When such a situation arises there would be no scope for creation.[8] As against the theory of *nitya-saṁsāri*, it is argued that its acceptance would lead to the possibility of no one aspiring for release. If there are eternally bound souls, a doubt might arise in one's mind whether he could be such an individual, and with such a doubt one would not strive for *mokṣa*.

Counter-arguments are also advanced against both the views. The contention that if all souls achieved *mokṣa* there would be an end to the creation of the universe is not correct, because it contradicts the śruti text which says that the creator created the universe as it had been done previously.[9] Nor is it sound to

[6]TMK II-26.

[7]This view is held by a section of Viśiṣṭādvaitins and Mādhvas. See Ś S, p. 87. *Sayūthyāḥ pare ca kecid āhuḥ*. . . . A few stray smṛti statements seem to lend support to this view. *ekam padam noddharate. . . .kṣipāmi ajasram aśubhān. . . .*

[8]TMK II-27. *sarga-sthityādi-santatyaviratiḥ.*

[9]Tait. *dhātā vidhāta yathāpūrvam akalpayat.*

admit that some individuals would forever suffer bondage as it would go against the all-compassionate character of *Īśvara.*[10] How could the all-compassionate *Īśvara* tolerate the permanent suffering of some individuals?

By way of a direct reply to the arguments of the opponents one may point out that even if the creation of universe comes to an end as a result of all *jivas* being released, it should not matter at all since *Īśvara* is free to do so out of His free will. Similarly, even if we accept the existence of some *nitya saṁsāris*, it would not be a reflection on *Īśvara* because His compassion may remain restricted to some individuals out of His will. Whatever happens out of the free will of the all-powerful and all-compassionate God, one has to accept it as His dispensation.

Vedānta Deśika does not agree with any of these arguments. The *jivas* are infinite in number, and the view that all souls would achieve *mokṣa* is not tenable. The issue to be considered is whether or not everyone is eligible for *mokṣa.* According to the Viśiṣṭādvaita Vedānta, there is no difference with regard to the intrinsic nature of *jivas*, and as such it is not correct to assume that only some will achieve *mokṣa* and others will ever remain in bondage. The correct position is that all are eligible, but, however, only an individual who is desirous of attaining *mokṣa* has to endeavour for it by adopting the prescribed *sādhana* and he will no doubt achieve it with God's grace.[11] God in order to shower His grace looks forward to a sincere desire for release on the part of an individual.

II. BHAKTI AS THE MEANS TO MOKṢA

According to the Viśiṣṭādvaita Vedānta, *bhakti* is the means or *upāya* to *mokṣa*, as this is evident from numerous śruti and smṛti texts.[12] What is *bhakti*? The term *bhakti* is derived from the root word *bhaj* which means *sevā* or meditation (*bhaj sevāyāṁ*).[13] In

[10]TMK II-28. *nirupadhika-dayā-hāniḥ.*

[11]See *Lakṣmītantra* (17-78) quoted in *Rahasyatrayasāra*, Ch. XI. *saṁsāra-tantra-vāhitvāt rakṣāpekṣām pratīkṣate.*

[12]See TMK II-29. *śruti-śata-vihitaḥ mukter upāyaḥ bhaktiḥ.*

[13]According to *Nighaṇṭu* (the Glossary of Vedic Words), *sevā* means *bhakti, upāsanā.* See *Śrutaprakāśikā* I-1-1. *sevā bhakti upāsti iti naighaṇṭukokteḥ*

common usage it is understood in the sense of love towards the respected or elderly person (*mahanīya-viṣaye prītiḥ*). Love or *prīti* is a state of knowledge, a mental disposition. *Bhakti* as a means or *upāya* is therefore defined as unceasing meditation done with love on the Supreme Being (*snehapūrvam-anudhyānam*).[14] It is thus regarded as knowledge (a mental activity) in the form of love for God (*prītirūpa jñāna*). It is generated by scrupulous observance of religious duties as laid down by scripture in accordance with one's *varṇa* and *āśrama*, along with spiritual knowledge. The performance of one's duties and rituals (*karma*) will have to be observed, as explained in the *Gītā*, purely as a divine service for the pleasure of God (*bhagavat-prīti*) and not in expectation of any rewards thereof.[15] This in brief is the Viśiṣṭādvaita view of *sādhana* for *mokṣa*.

The Upaniṣads, while describing the *upāya* for *mokṣa* do not use the term *bhakti* but use other terms such as *jñāna*, *vedana*, *darśana*, *dhyāna*, *dhruvā-smṛti* and *upāsanā*. The question arises whether it would be justified to regard *bhakti* as the direct means to *mokṣa*. After a careful analysis of the various concerned passages in the Upaniṣads and taking into consideration the opening as well as concluding statements of these passages, the explanation offered in the *Bhagavad-gītā*, authoritative statements of the Vākyakāra, one of the earliest commentators on the *Vedānta-sūtras*, and also the statement in *Vedānta-sūtras* itself, Rāmānuja comes to the conclusion that all the terms bear the same meaning, and they all refer to *bhakti*. According to the principle of interpretation laid down by the Mīmāṁsakas, when two terms are used in the same context, the word having a general meaning should bear the meaning of the specific term.[16] As will be shown presently, the terms *vedana*, *jñāna*, *upāsanā*, etc. are general terms; *bhakti* is a term bearing a specific meaning.

An Upaniṣadic text says: 'Having *known* him, he transgresses death (bondage) and there is no other means to attain him.'[17] Another text asserts: 'He who knows Brahman attains the

[14] See S S II-29, p. 88. *snehapūrvam anudhyānaṁ bhaktiḥ iti copāyo viśeṣyate.*

[15] TMK II-29.

[16] *Ibid. sāmānyoktiḥ samāna-prakaraṇa paṭhitā paryavasyed-viśeṣe.*

[17] Svet III-8. *tameva viditvātimṛtyumeti nānyaḥ panthā vidyate ayanāya.*

highest.'[18] These statements indicate that *jñāna* or knowledge of Brahman is the means to *mokṣa*. In fact, the Advaita Vedānta asserts, on the authority of such scriptural texts, that *jñāna* alone is the sole means to *mokṣa*. The practice of *upāsanā* or *nididhyāsana* (contemplation), referred to in other texts as the means to *mokṣa*, is considered by the Advaitin as subsidiary aid to *jñāna*. The Viśiṣṭādvaitin does not question the basic view that *jñāna* is means to *mokṣa*, as evidenced in the above scriptural texts. The issue which he raises is : what kind of knowledge serves as the means to *mokṣa*? Is it the knowledge as generated by the Upaniṣadic texts (*vākyārtha-jñāna*)[18a] as the Advaitin contends, or *jñāna* in some other form? It is pointed out by Rāmānuja and in a more elaborate way by Vedānta Deśika that *vākyārtha-jñāna* cannot be the means to *mokṣa*. On the contrary, it is *jñāna* as developed into the form of steadfast meditation or *bhakti* that constitutes the direct means to *mokṣa*. That *vākyārtha-jñāna* cannot serve as a means to *mokṣa* is discussed in detail later.

The justification for introducing the concept of *bhakti* is provided on the authority of a specific passage in the *Muṇḍaka Upaniṣad* and the relevant verses in the *Bhagavad-gītā* which elucidate the nature of the means for God-realization as implied in the Upaniṣadic text. The Upaniṣadic text says : 'This Self (Brahman) cannot be attained by the study of the Vedas, nor by meditation nor through much hearing. He is to be attained only by one whom the Self chooses. To such a person, the Self-reveals its nature.'[19] The implication of this statement as explained by Rāmānuja is that mere *śravaṇa* (hearing), *manana* (reflection) and even *nididhyāsana* (contemplation) undertaken without intense love to God cannot serve as means to God realisation. Only that individual on whom God showers His grace could attain Him. Whom then does God choose to receive His grace? The answer, according to Rāmānuja, is that one who is beloved to God is chosen by Him (*priyatama eva hi varaṇiyo*

[18]Tait I. *brahmavid āpnoti param.*

[18a] For the meaning and implication of *vākyārtha-jñāna*, see the following section 'Theories of Jñana as the Means to Mokṣa' in this chapter.

[19] Mund 3-2-3. *nāyamātmā pravacanena labhyo na medhayā na bahunā śrutena; yamevaiṣa vṛṇute tena labhyaḥ, tasyaiṣa ātmā vivṛṇute tanūm svām.* The same text is also found in *Kaṭha Upaniṣad* I-2-23.

bhavati).[20] The questions as to who is the one most dear to God and why he is regarded so are answered in the *Bhagavad-gītā*. Thus the *Gītā* says: 'To those who crave for eternal union (with Me) and meditate (on Me), I bestow with love that clear divine vision (*buddhiyoga*) by which they attain me.[21] In another verse it says : 'The one who is devoted to God is the dearest to Him.'[22] God loves him who loves God most intensely. It is also made explicit in the *Gītā* that *bhakti* is the only means to attain God. Thus it says: 'Neither by the Vedas, nor by austerities, nor by gifts, nor by sacrifice can I be seen as thou hast seen me. But by devotion exclusive I may in this form be known as seen in true form, Arjuna, and also be attained.'[22a] This verse is an elucidation of the statement in *Muṇḍaka Upaniṣad* and the fuller implication of it is that without deep devotion to God the mere study of scripture, observance of austerities and performance of rituals will not help to attain God.[23] It is only the unconditional, deep-rooted love for God that serves as a means to know God in His true form, to have His vision and eventually to attain Him. This means that divine vision is possible only through God's grace and in order to earn it one has to be deeply devoted to God. Only to such individual, who loves God and who craves to

[20]RB I-1-1, p. 19.

[21]BG X-10. *teṣāṁ satatayuktānāṁ bhajatāṁ prītipūrvakam; dadāmi buddhiyogam taṁ yena māṁ upayānti te*. *Buddhiyoga* here means *parā-bhakti* or a stage of *bhakti* that has been perfected to the extent of leading to divine vision (*darśana-samānākāra*).

[22]BG VII-17.

[22a] BG XI-53-54. *nāham vedaiḥ na tapasā na dānena na ca ijyayā; śakya evaṁ-vidho draṣṭuṁ...bhaktyā tu ananyayā śakya aham evaṁvidho' rjuna; jñatum draṣṭum ca tattvena praveṣṭum ca parantapa*.

[23]On the face of it this Upaniṣadic text and the *Gītā* seem to contradict what is stated in the *Bṛhadaraṇyaka Upaniṣad* which states that for self-realisation *śravaṇa*, *manana* and *nididhyāsana* are needed (*ātma vā are draṣṭavyaḥ śrotavyo mantavyo nididhyasitavyaḥ* Br. 6-5-6). This is not so. All that is negated in this particular verse is that *mere śravaṇa* (*kevala śravaṇa*), etc. devoid of intense *bhakti* is of no use for God-realisation. It should be observed with deep devotion to God. This explanation is offered on the basis of the principle of interpretation adopted by the Mimāṁsakas. There is a scriptural text (*Yajur-veda* 5-2-7, 35) which states that fire is not to be installed on the ground nor in the sky nor in the heaven *na pṛthivyām na antarikṣe na divi agniḥ cetavyaḥ*: Here what is implied is that fire is not be installed on bare ground but on a platform specially erected for it. Such statements are known as *viśiṣṭa-vidhi*. See *Tātpatya-candrikā* on BG XI-53-54.

have His vision, God showers His grace and reveals Himself. In view of these facts, Rāmānuja maintains that *bhakti* is implied in the Upaniṣadic statement referred to above.

Upāsanā, *dhyāna* and *smṛti-santati* which are mentioned by the Upaniṣads as means to *mokṣa* are the same as *bhakti* referred to in the *Gītā*. The practice of *dhyāna* means contemplation (*cintana*)[24] or meditation. Such meditation will have to be done continuously and repeatedly, as explained in the *Vedānta-sūtra* (*āvṛttiḥ asakṛt*). When it is practised continuously it takes the form of remembrance of the object of contemplation without interruption. This is called *smṛti-santati*, unbroken series of recollection of the object of meditation, comparable to the uninterrupted flow of oil.[25] In other words, it is steadfast contemplation which is enjoined as a means to *mokṣa*. The word *upāsanā* is also used in the same sense, viz. the continuous and steadfast mental concentration.[26] When *upāsanā* or *smṛti-santati* gains intensity by repeated and continuous observance, it assumes the form of vividness similar to that of a direct vision of the object of contemplation (*darśana-samānākāra*). Such a state is known as *darśana*. Thus *dhyāna* leads to *dhruvā-smṛti* which assumes the form of *upāsanā* and *upāsanā* culminates in *darśana* or direct vision.[27] Only such an *upāsanā* or meditation, as perfected to the extent of its becoming similar to the vision of the Supreme Being, is considered as the means (*upāya*) for *mokṣa*.[28] The same is described as *parabhakti*.[29] The words *vedana*, *darśana*, etc. used in the Upaniṣadic texts as direct means to *mokṣa* imply *upāsanā* as explained above.

[24]See VS IV-1-1. *dhyānam ca cintanam; cintanam ca smṛti-santatirūpam.*

[25]RB I-1-1 p. 17. *dhyānam ca tailadhārāvat avicchinna-smṛtisantāna-rūpam.*

[26]*ekāgra-cittai-vṛtti-nairantaryam.*

[27]*vedanam dhyāna-viśrāntam dhyānam śrāntaṃ dhruvāsmṛtau; sā ca dṛṣṭitvamabhyeti, dṛṣṭiḥ bhaktitvam icchati.*

[28]RB I-1-1, p. 19. *evaṁrūpā dhruvānusmṛtireva bhakti-śabdena abhidhīyate; upāsana-paryāyatvāt bhakti-śabdasya.*

[29]According to Rāmānuja, there are three stages or grades of *bhakti* depending on intensity: *para-bhakti*, *para-jñāna* and *parama-bhakti*. When the unceasing meditation on God is perfected to the extent of its becoming similar to a clear vision (*darśana-samānākāra*), it is known as *para-bhakti*. After reaching this stage, if the devotee develops a craving to have the vision of God and if he is blessed with a glimpse of God, it is called *para-jñāna*. When the devotee, not being satisfied with such a temporary vision, wishes to have a permanent vision of God, it is regarded as *parama-bhakti*, the final stage.

How could knowledge (*vedana*) and contemplation (*upāsanā*) mean the same thing? That the two terms have the same meaning is established on the basis of the fact that the expression *veda* and *upāsita* are used as interchangeable words in one and the same passage dealing with the same topic. Thus, the passage in *Chāndogya Upaniṣad* discussing the manner of doing *upāsanā* of Brahman starts with the statement *mano brahmeti upāsita*[30] (Brahman is to be contemplated as Mind), using the expression *upāsita* or to be contemplated. While concluding this passage, it is stated *ya evaṁ veda*, meaning he who knows thus (*veda*). The term *veda* is used here in the place of *upāsita*. Taking into consideration the context of the passage, *veda* at the concluding statement means the same as *upāsita* used at the beginning. In another passage of *Chāndogya*[31] referring to the greatness of the sage Raikva, the opening sentence states *yastadveda yat sa veda*, meaning what Raikva knew and what is to be known, etc. While concluding this narration, it is stated: whatever *devatā* you contemplate (*tvam upāsse*),[32] tell me in detail about the same deity. In this passage, unlike the previous one, the term *veda* is used in the beginning, and at the end the word *upāsanā* is used. Taking both these passages into consideration Rāmānuja comes to the conclusion that *vedana* and *upāsanā* should be taken to mean the same thing. The two are not distinct as is commonly understood.

Thus the terms such as *jñāna*, *dhyāna*, *dhruvānusmṛti*, etc. which are used in the Upaniṣads as means to *mokṣa* are to be understood to mean the same thing. Otherwise it would amount to the admission of different means for *mokṣa*. If the means be different, the goal to be achieved would also be different. Actually, the goal is the same for all, and hence the means should also be the same. Therefore, it is concluded that all these terms, though they appear to have different meanings, should bear the meaning of the specific term *bhakti*, according to the Mīmāṁsa principle of interpretation.[33]

If *jñāna* alone is considered as the sole means to *mokṣa*, as Advaitin contends, all the Upaniṣadic texts referring to *upāsanā* become meaningless. In fact *upāsanā* is enjoined as a means to

[30]Ch 3-18. [31]Ch 4-1-4. [32]Ch 4-2-2.
[33]TMK II-29. *jñāna-dhyānādi-vācāṁ sama-phala-viṣayā saiva yuktā pratiṣṭhā.*

attain *mokṣa*. Vedānta Deśika therefore concludes that *bhakti* in the form of continuous and unbroken process of meditation culminating in the vision of the Supreme Being is the direct means to *mokṣa*.[34]

Bhakti as a *upāya* for *mokṣa* is described in the *Gītā* as *bhakti-yoga*. It is a life-long rigorous discipline involving the acquisition of spiritual knowledge, development of certain ethical virtues and observance of religious duties as laid down by sacred texts. These details are discussed in the *Vedānta-sūtras* and the *Gītā*. It is to be preceded by the practice of *karma-yoga* and *jñāna-yoga* referred to in the *Gītā*.[35] *Karma-yoga* emphasises the disinterested performance of action (*karma*), such as sacrifice (*yajña*), charity (*dāna*) and austerity (*tapas*) as divine service without any expectation of rewards thereof. *Jñāna-yoga* signifies constant meditation upon *ātman*, the individual self with the control of mind and senses. The two are inter-related and the aim of these is self-realization (*ātmāvalokana*). Both these subserve *bhakti*, and as such they are the subsidiary means to *bhakti-yoga*, which is the direct means to God-realization.[36]

Upāsana performed for the purpose of realising Brahman is known as *Brahma-vidyā*. The Upaniṣads refer to thirty-two such *vidyās* and describe them under different names such as *pañcāgni-vidyā*, *vaiśvānara-vidyā*, *dahara-vidyā*, *madhu-vidyā*, *sad-vidyā*, *nyāsa-vidyā*, etc. They are named differently because of the difference in the description of the object of contemplation, viz. Brahman in terms of its different attributes. These *vidyās* are therefore different in character.[37] However, the goal to be achieved in all

[34] TMK II-30. According to the Viśiṣṭādvaita Vedānta, besides *bhakti*, *prapatti* or the absolute self-surrender to God is also laid down as an alternative means to *mokṣa*. *Bhakti* is a rigorous discipline, and for those, who are incapable of undertaking it, *prapatti* is advocated as an alternative easy path to *mokṣa*. This doctrine is adopted on the strength of the teachings contained in the Vedas as well as the Itihāsas, Purāṇas and Pañcarātra literature. It does not come up for discussion in the *Tattva-muktā-kalāpa* except the mention of the term *nyāsa-vidyā* as one of the thirty-two *vidyās* because of the fact that Vedānta Deśika is primarily concerned with the discussion of the fundamental metaphysical doctrines.

[35] *Gītārtha-saṃgraha* (verse 1). *Sva-dharma-jñāna-vairāgya-sādhya-bhaktyaika-gocaraḥ*.

[36] TMK II-31. [37] TMK II-31. See also VS III-3-56. *nānā śabdādibhedāt*.

these *upāsanās* is the same, viz. realization of Brahman. In view of this, these *upāsanās* are considered as alternative means to *mokṣa*, as explained in the *Vedānta-sūtra.*[38]

III. THEORIES OF JÑĀNA AS THE MEANS TO MOKṢA

According to one school of thought ascribed to some ancient Advaitins, *niyoga* generated by *nididhyāsana* as enjoined in the Upaniṣads is the means to *mokṣa*. *Niyoga* is a special potency or power in the form of *adṛṣṭa* and this is generated by the observance of continuous meditation. This potency causes direct intuitive knowledge of *ātman* (*aparokṣa-jñāna*) which removes the cosmic illusion. This view is known as *dhyāna-niyoga-vāda.*

According to another school of thought attributed to some Advaitins who are supposed to be the followers of ancient Mīmāṁsakas, although the universe is illusory, it appears as real in Brahman. In other words, Brahman appears as universe due to the cosmic illusion. Brahman is the *adhiṣṭhāna* or the basis for the illusory appearance of the universe. It is therefore regarded as *saprapañca* or as associated with the universe. *Mokṣa* in this system is the realization of the true nature of Brahman as *niṣprapañca*, that is, Brahman as devoid of the illusory universe. In order to achieve this goal, continuous meditation on Brahman is necessary. The Upaniṣadic injunctions such as that Brahman is to be meditated upon (*nididhyāsitavyaḥ*) are intended to convey this fact, viz. that Brahman is to be realized as acosmic. This view is known as *niṣprapañca-niyoga-vāda*, or the theory which advocates that the continuous meditation of Brahman as devoid of *prapañca* will lead to the realization of Brahman.

The third view which is an important one held by Śaṁkara and his followers emphasises that *jñāna* as generated by *śravaṇa*, *manana* and *nididhyāsana* removes the cosmic illusion and that alone is the means to *mokṣa*. That is, the *jñāna* generated by the hearing of the Upaniṣadic texts referring to the identity of Brahman and *jiva* (*vākyārtha-jñāna*) is the means to *mokṣa*. All the three views are subjected to critical scrutiny by Vedānta Deśika.

According to the first theory, the special unseen potency (*niyoga*) generated by constant and continuous meditation on

[38]VS III-3-57. *vikalpo' viśiṣṭaphalatvāt.*

the identity between Brahman and the individual self as taught in the scriptural text 'That Thou Art' (*tattvamasi*) produces immediate knowledge (*aparokṣa-jñāna*) by means of which cosmic illusion is removed. If this is the position, it is relevant to ask why the knowledge which arises as a result of knowing the meaning of *tattvamasi* does not remove the cosmic illusion. It may be said that the knowledge that arises from the hearing of the scriptural text is mediate in character (*parokṣa*), whereas the cosmic illusion which is of perceptual character needs to be removed only by perceptual knowledge which is immediate in character. The constant meditation upon what is taught by the scriptural text is claimed to produce an immediate knowledge which alone removes the illusion.

This argument is rejected by Vedānta Deśika on the ground that there are instances in which a cognition which is considered to be immediate in character is sublated by a cognition of mediate character. Thus, for instance, the wrong cognition that the flame of a lamp is one is contradicted by the inferential knowledge (which is mediate in character) that the flame is not one but a series of flames. It may be possible to overcome this objection by admitting that *dhyāna* produces some special power (*śakti*) in the form of *adṛṣṭa* which removes the cosmic illusion. But the Advaitin does not accept this position. If the special power generated by *dhyāna* removes *avidyā*, then it is not *jñāna* alone but something other than *jñāna* that is the cause of the removal of *avidyā*. This would then lead to what would be unacceptable to the Advaitin that this universe is real and not illusory.[39]

Regarding the second theory that Brahman is to be realized as devoid of the illusory universe through meditation Vedānta Deśika points out that nowhere in the Upaniṣads we come across an injunction (*vidhi*) enjoining that Brahman is to be meditated upon as dissociated from the universe. It may be argued that the injunction *upāsita* which enjoins that Brahman is to be meditated upon implies that Brahman which is manifesting itself with the universe is to be dissociated from the universe. That is, by means of continuous meditation of Brahman as devoid of universe, Brahman is realised ultimately as devoid

[39]TMK II-43.

of its association with the universe. The *niyoga* is the fruit of *Brahmopāsana-vidhi*.

This argument is also rejected by Vedānta Deśika as unsound. In the *pūrva-kāṇḍa* of the Vedas, rituals are enjoined, as for example, the scriptural injunction which says: 'One who is desirous of *svarga* should perform *agnihotra*'.[40] According to the Mīmāṁsakas, who are the authoritative interpreters of the rituals, *svarga* is the goal and it is attained through *apūrva*, the unseen potency, generated by the performance of the special sacrifice (*agnihotra*). Accordingly, sacrifice or *yāga* constitutes the *sādhana* or the means for *niyoga*. The various preliminaries of the ritual are regarded as subsidiary means (*itikartavyatā*). Thus, in all such injunctions enjoining the performance of rituals, three factors are involved: *sādhya*, what is sought after, *sādhana*, the means to achieve it and *karaṇa*, different preliminaries of rituals serving as subsidiary means. What then is the *sādhya* in the present case and what is its *sādhana*? In the injunction 'Brahman which is associated with the universe is to be realised as dissociated from it', the *sādhya* or goal is realisation of Brahman as dissociated from the universe; and the *sādhana* for it is also meditation of Brahman as dissociated from the universe. Thus both the *sādhana* and *sādhya* are the same. This is not a satisfactory position. If there be no distinction between *sādhana* and *sādhya*, there is hardly any scope for subsidiary means.[41]

Further, if *mukti* in the sense of cessation of the appearance of universe in Brahman is to be achieved by means of an unseen potency (*niyoga*), then the universe sublated by it cannot also be considered as illusory. As already pointed out, what is sublated by means other than *jñāna* cannot be illusory.[42] Besides, what is achieved by *niyoga*, according to the Mīmāṁsaka, is not permanent as, for instance, *svarga*. Thus, *niyoga* as described by the ancient Advaitins cannot be accepted as a means to *mokṣa*.

We now take up for examination the third view as advanced by the Śaṅkarites. According to them, the knowledge which is generated by the hearing of the Upaniṣadic texts which teach the identity of the individual self and Brahman such as the *mahā-vākya* 'That Thou Art' is the sole means to *mokṣa* (*vākyā-*

[40]*agnihotram juhuyāt svargakāmaḥ*. [41]TMK II-44.
[42]*Ibid. muktiḥ naiyogikī cet jagadapi mṛṣā na syāt*.

rtha-jñāna-mātrāt mokṣam). It is asked whether one attains release from bondage by means of the knowledge generated by the mere hearing the Upaniṣadic texts (*śravaṇajanyajñānamātrāt*). This cannot be so because such an assumption conflicts with our experience and cannot also be proved by any of the *pramāṇas*. We find that a person, even after hearing the sacred texts, continues to experience bondage in the same manner as before. If hearing of the sacred texts through the teacher is sufficient for the removal of one's bondage, then *manana* or reflection and *nididhyāsana* or meditation which are enjoined by the Upaniṣad for this purpose would become superfluous. This is not appropriate. Nor is this position acceptable even to the Advaitin.

According to the Advaitin, the knowledge arising by the mere hearing of the sacred texts is not sufficient to remove *avidyā*, which is the cause of bondage in the form of ignorance about Brahman. The impression that the individual self is distinct from Brahman (*bheda-vāsanā*) is beginningless and is deep rooted in the mind, and hence the knowledge of identity of the two (*abheda-jñāna*) arising from the mere hearing is not effective enough to remove it. What is learnt from the teacher as the real meaning of the sacred texts (*śravaṇa*) needs to be reflected upon repeatedly before it is transformed into deep conviction. It is to be meditated upon constantly until one gets a proper knowledge of the identity of the individual self with Brahman (*abheda-jñāna*). Only such a knowledge arising from meditation can remove bondage.

Even this explanation fails to improve the situation, argues Vedānta Deśika. Is there any distinction between the *jñāna* which arises after hearing the sacred texts and the *jñāna* which arises after going through meditation? A difference is possible if it be admitted that certain aspects of Brahman which were not realised earlier become known after the meditation. But according to the ontological position of the Advaitin, Brahman is *nirviśeṣa*, and there are no special characteristics in respect of Brahman. In the absence of any difference in the content of the two types or levels of knowledge, it is not possible to say that the knowledge that arises later after meditation is different from the earlier one and as such it is capable of removing the cosmic illusion.[43]

[43]TMK II-45. There are a few other arguments advanced by the Advaitins to substantiate the view that there is a distinction between the knowledge

There is another view according to which the Upaniṣadic statements such as *tattvamasi* generate knowledge of immediate character (*aparokṣa-jñāna*) which is capable of removing the cosmic illusion. That verbal testimony generates immediate knowledge is explained by an interesting illustration. Ten persons who crossed a river together started counting themselves to make sure that all the ten had safely arrived at the other side of the river. Each one counted the persons present without also counting himself and thought that there were only nine in the group. Someone else who arrived at the spot counted everybody one by one and said to the tenth person that you are the tenth (*daśamastvamasi*). The verbal statement made by the other person produced an immediate knowledge to the tenth person causing him the direct realization that he is the tenth. In the same way the śruti statement, though it is only verbal, can produce immediate knowledge leading to the realisation that the soul is identical with Brahman.

Even this explanation, Vedānta Deśika contends, does not prove that verbal testimony causes immediate knowledge. In the statement—'thou art the tenth person'—there are two aspects : (*a*) 'thou', and (*b*) the person being the tenth. The 'thou' aspect which refers to the self is already known to the individual because it is self-evident and on that account the knowledge of that aspect is immediate. The other aspect in the statement that he is the tenth person is conveyed to him by means of a verbal statement, and this knowledge therefore is mediate (*parokṣa*). As the 'thou' aspect is so obvious and is of immediate nature, the latter mediate knowledge is easily mistaken to be of immediate nature. If it is contended that *śabda* could generate immediate knowledge, then the distinction drawn between *pratyakṣa* and *parokṣa* would cease to exist. The correct position is that knowledge which arises through direct perception is alone immediate (*aparokṣa*), whereas the knowledge that arises on the basis of inference and *śabda* is always mediate (*parokṣa*) in character.[44]

---

of the identity of Brahman as generated by the scriptural texts and the knowledge which constitutes the very *svarūpa* of Brahman. These are discussed in detail in the *Śatadūṣaṇi* and rejected by Vedānta Deśika as untenable. See SD, Vāda 43. See also AV, pp. 144-45.

[44]TMK II-46.

For still another reason verbal testimony cannot generate immediate knowledge of the object denoted by it. When we hear a verbal statement we get only perceptual knowledge of the sound (*śabda-viṣayaka-pratyakṣa*) but not of what is denoted by the statement. The knowledge of the fire which arises on the basis of the perception of smoke in the hill is *parokṣa*. Only smoke is perceived, whereas fire is inferred. Hence the knowledge of the fire is mediate. In the same way, the knowledge of 'thou' aspect which is self-evident and already known is immediate, whereas the characteristic feature of his being the tenth is only known mediately by the verbal statement conveyed to him. This illustration thus shows that it is not possible to prove that verbal testimony causes immediate knowledge.

After refuting the theory that *vākyārtha-jñāna* is the means to *mokṣa*, Vedānta Deśika proceeds to point out that the acceptance of such a theory would lead to several difficulties. In the first instance, the teaching of the Upaniṣad by a teacher to a pupil is not tenable, because, according to the metaphysical position held by the Advaitin, there is no second, real individual other than Brahman.[45] If it be accepted that the pupil exists as a real individual and is different from the teacher, then the teaching of identity of souls is absurd. If the teacher has realised the identity, then he would be teaching to a non-existent individual.

Even if some distinction between the teacher and taught is plausible, the knowledge which arises from the teaching of the scriptural text 'That Thou Art' cannot remove the cosmic illusion. If everything other than Brahman is illusory, even the scriptural text which teaches the identity of Brahman and *jiva* is illusory. If this text as well as the knowledge arising out of it is illusory, how could that remove the cosmic illusion? The criticism is based on the assumption that what is illusory can only be sublated by what is real.

To this objection the Advaitin may reply that it is not necessary that the cognition which sublates the illusory experience should be real. For example, a person mistakes a rope for snake. Another person nearby tells him that it is not a snake. If the individual having the illusion believes that the statement of the

[45]TMK II-47.

other person is false, it cannot remove his illusion. In the same way, once it is realised that the knowledge arising from the teaching of the scriptural text is illusory in character, it can no longer remove the cosmic illusion.

The Advaitin adopts a different argument in support of his theory. The scriptural texts teaching the identity of Brahman and *jiva* are not absolutely unreal like the sky-flower. Prior to the onset of the knowledge of Brahman, it is viewed as something real.[46] As long as knowledge of Brahman has not arisen, these texts are capable of generating knowledge of Reality. Further, what is illusory can cause effects which are of real nature.[47] There are numerous examples of what is real being revealed by what is not real. The shell-silver which is illusory causes joy. The objects experienced in dream cause pleasure of real character. One's reflection in the mirror causes the knowledge of one's face.

The Viśiṣṭādvaitin does not accept this argument. In all these instances cited by the Advaitin, it is not the illusory object but the knowledge of those objects that cause the real effects. Knowledge in this system is real. Even if the object be illusory, its cognition is real. The content of the knowledge does not determine the nature of the cognition because the latter is real by virtue of its intrinsic character.[48]

Another difficulty is pointed out in respect of the position held by the Advaitin. The knowledge which arises from the teaching of the scriptural text 'That Thou Art' is supposed to remove the cosmic illusion. It is asked whether or not this knowlege which is different from Brahman persists after the removal of the cosmic illusion. If it persists, then, it being different from Brahman, there would be no total release. If another knowledge is sought for its removal, it would lead to an infinite regress. To overcome this problem, the Advaitin maintains that this *nivartaka jñāna*, vanishes by itself just as the last bit of flame of the jungle fire gets itself extinguished.

[46]See SB I-1-4 and II-1-14.

[47]This is known as *asatyāt-satya-siddhi-vāda* advanced by the author of *Brahma-siddhi*.

[48]TMK II-49. Detailed criticism of this theory may be found in *Śatadūṣaṇī*, see Vāda, 30. Also AV, pp. 20-24.

In reply to this Vedānta Deśika says that it would not be correct to say that the knowledge which removes the entire cosmic illusion becomes removed of its own accord. Even in the case of the jungle fire, the last flame is not self-extinguished. On the contrary, it gets extinguished through the help of the wind. In fact, the jungle fire which is real has a real cause; with the cessation of the cause its effect too ceases to exist. In the case of the *vākyārtha-jñāna*, it is *mithyā* or illusory in character, and what is illusory is to be sublated by another knowledge negating it (*bādhaka-jñāna*). If what is illusory could cease to exist on its own accord, then the cosmic illusion too should have been removed of its own accord. But this is not so. Hence one *nivartaka-jñāna* needs another one for its removal and in this way it would lead to an infinite regress. If the *nivartaka-jñāna* does not get removed, then *mokṣa* also would not become possible.[49]

Further, what is the content of the *nivartaka-jñāna*? Is pure Brahman its content or Brahman associated with *māyā* or the universe itself which is other than Brahman or the *mithyātva* of the universe? None of these alternatives is tenable. If pure Brahman is the content, it becomes knowable (*vedya*) insofar as it becomes the content of knowledge. This position is not acceptable to the Advaitin. Nor is Brahman conditioned by *māyā* its content. In that case, the *jñāna* has for its content an illusory entity, because the conditioned Brahman for Advaitin is not ultimately real, and it is therefore absurd to say that *mokṣa* is attained through means which is illusory in character. The same objection also holds good for the third alternative. The fourth alternative is equally untenable. Is *mithyātva* of universe real or unreal? The former leads to the position of accepting two realities. In the latter case, if *mithyātva* of the universe itself is *mithyā*, it leads, like two negatives implying a positive, to the logical conclusion that the universe is *satya*. If it is devoid of content, then it ceases to be knowledge.[50]

What is the *āśraya* of the *nivartaka-jñāna* which brings about the *mokṣa* of the individual? Either it has to be the *jiva* or the Brahman. If it be the former, *jiva* being illusory (*mithyā*), it also stands sublated with the cessation of all that is illusory other than Brahman (*sarva-mithyātva-jñāna*). This would give

[49]TMK II-50. [50]TMK II-51.

rise to a situation in which no individual would ever strive for one's own destruction. It may be contended that *jiva* is not totally illusory, as the critic supposes. *Jiva* in the Advaita system is nothing other than Brahman as conditioned by *antaḥkaraṇa*. Even if the adjunct in the form of *antaḥkarṇa* is removed, the universal consciousness remains unaffected. *Jiva* is not, therefore, totally annihilated. This explanation does not improve the position, because the empirical *jiva* or the ego in the name of *antaḥkaraṇa* which actually is the aspirant for *mokṣa* stands annihilated in the state of *mokṣa*. How could a *jiva* which ceases to exist in the state of *mokṣa* ever strive for it.[51]

To avoid this difficulty Brahman may be regarded as the *locus* of *nivartaka-jñāna*. But then would this *āśrayatva* or the quality of being the locus for *jñāna* be real or unreal? If real, then Brahman having such a quality becomes *saviśeṣa* which is not acceptable to the Advaitin. If, on the contrary, the *āśrayatva* is unreal, the assumption of such a view cannot be fully justified.[52]

Further, what is it that is achieved by the *vākyārtha-jñāna* which is supposed to remove cosmic illusion? Obviously, it is the *mokṣa* for the *jiva*. What is the nature of this *mokṣa*? If it means the very *svarūpa* of Brahman (i.e. realisation of the true nature of Brahman), then it would follow that *mukti* has already existed, for *Brahma-svarūpa* is always in existence and there is nothing new that is achieved by *mokṣa*. If *mukti* is different from Brahman, then it becomes *mithyā*, because every thing other than Brahman is *mithyā*. In that case all that is *mithyā* gets annhilated by *tattva-jñāna* and even *mokṣa* stands cancelled. In other words, the possibility of achieving *mokṣa* by means of *jñāna* is inconceivable, if the ontological position of Advaita is accepted. Thus, the theory that *vākyārtha-jñāna* is the means to *mokṣa* is untenable.[53]

As explained earlier, knowledge derived from the study of the scriptural text should develop itself into the form of meditation which alone can serve as means to *mokṣa*.

IV. THE PLACE OF KARMA IN THE SPIRITUAL DISCIPLINE

What is the role of karma[54] in the spiritual discipline? Accord-

[51]TMK II-53. [52]TMK II-53. [53]TMK II-52.

[54]The word *karma* is used here in the sense of the observance of religious duties as laid down by scripture in accordance with one's *varṇa* and *āśrama*.

ing to the Viśiṣṭādvaitin, *karma* is an important subsidiary to *bhakti-yoga* or *upāsanā* which is the direct means to *mokṣa*. As opposed to this theory, there are two important schools of thought which lay greater emphasis on *karma*. According to one school, ascribed to Bhāskara, both *jñāna* (understood in the sense of *upāsanā*) and *karma* (in the sense of performance of rituals) constitute the means to *mokṣa*. This is known as *jñāna-karma-samuccaya-vāda*. Yādavaprakāśa also supports this view except with the modification that though both *karma* and *jñāna* play important parts, the former removes the obstruction in the way of attaining *mokṣa*, whereas the latter actually leads to *mokṣa*. The other school of thought expounded by Mīmāṁsakas maintains that *karma* or the performance of the rituals alone as enjoined in the Vedas is the means to *mokṣa*, whereas *jñāna* is only subsidiary to *karma*. The Advaitin whose theory we have already examined maintains that knowledge being the sole means of *mokṣa*, *karma* or religious acts are not required as direct aids to it. The religious acts are useful for securing mental purity and thereby *jñāna*, but once *jñāna* arises *karma* may be dispensed with.

Vedānta Deśika rejects these views. According to the Viśiṣṭādvaitin, both *jñāna* (*upāsanā*) and *karma* have an important place in the spiritual discipline, but the latter is subsidiary to the former which is the principal means to *mokṣa*. *Karma* is understood in the Viśiṣṭādvaita system as the performance of the various religious duties laid down in the Vedas according to one's *varṇa* and *āśrama* (*varṇāśrama-dharma*). It is an important means to *bhakti-yoga* insofar as it helps to remove the sins of the past, develop the inner purity of mind and thereby promote *bhakti*. This view is strongly supported by the *Vedānta-sūtra* which is based on the scriptural text which states that by means of the study of Vedas, rituals, charity, austerity and fasting, Brahman is known.[55] Just as certain ethical virtues such as *śama* (control of mind) and *dama* (control of senses) help the development of *bhakti*, in the same way *varṇāśrama-dharma* too serves *bhakti* by way of removing the sins of the past and purifying the mind which is essential for

[55]Br IV-4-22. *tametam vedānuvacanena brāhmaṇā vividiṣanti yajñena dānena tapasā anāśakena*. See VS III-4-26. *sarvāpekṣā ca yajñādiśruteraśvavat*. See also BG XVIII-5.

the practice of *bhakti-yoga.*[56] The statements[57] which emphasise both *karma* and *jñāna* as necessary to achieve *mokṣa* are to be understood in the sense that mere *upāsanā* by itself is not sufficient to achieve *mokṣa*. As *karma* is a subsidiary means to it, both are necessary. But this is not to be taken to mean, as Bhāskara believes, that *upasanā* and *karma* as combined together constitute the means to *mokṣa*. As explained earlier, *upāsanā* or *bhakti-yoga* is the direct means to *mokṣa* whereas *karma* is the subsidiary means to it.

According to the Mīmāṁsakas, *karma* or the preformance of rituals enjoined in the Vedas is the means to *mokṣa*. Knowledge of the Self or Brahman derived from the study of the Upaniṣadic portion of the Vedas serves only as an auxiliary means to *karma* insofar as it serves as a purificatory act (*saṁskāra*) to the individual who is engaged in the performance of rituals. The Mīmāṁsakas who emphasise the supremacy of the moral law of *dharma* and the performance of the Vedic rituals for this purpose, attach greater importance and authority to the ritualistic portion of the Vedas known as *pūrvakāṇḍa*. The Upaniṣads, according to them, only teach the nature of the individual self who is the performer of rituals. As the Mīmāṁsakas do not accept the existence of God (*Paramātmā*), Brahman mentioned in the Upaniṣad is, in their opinion, the individual self who has achieved a higher status through the performance of rituals. The knowledge of the self gained by the study of Upaniṣads thus serves as a purificatory act for the *jiva*.

Vedānta Deśika criticises this theory. *Jñāna* as the *upāsanā* of Brahman which is enjoined as the means to *mokṣa* and which is so different in nature from *karma* cannot serve as a purificatory act for the *jiva* engaged in the performance of rituals. Besides what stands as a means for a specific goal cannot be the means to achieve something else.[58] Further, *upāsanā*, unlike *karma*, cannot give the result with one-time observance. It has to be pursued continuously almost till the end of one's life. The eightfold discipline described in the *yoga* system and the need for a steadfast mind, steady posture, proper place and time, etc. as

[56]TMK II-33.
[57]*hatam jñānam kriyāhīnam, hatā ca ajñāninām kriyā.*
[58]TMK II-34.

explained in the *Vedānta-sūtras* constitute the *aṅga* or subsidiary means to *jñāna* in the form of *upāsanā*.

If *jñāna* cannot be the subsidiary means to *karma*, is it possible that *karma* or rituals subserve *jñāna*? This is a question raised by the Mīmāṁsakas. According to them, the rituals prescribed in the earlier portion of the Vedas (*pūrvakāṇḍa*) cannot become subsidiary to *jñāna*. The basis for this objection is that in the *mokṣadharma* (a section of the *Mahābhārata*), it is repeatedly stated that only those who have unshakable faith in and devotion to *Paramātman* will be able to achieve *mokṣa*.[59] The rituals prescribed in the Vedas refer to the worship of other deities such as Indra, Sūrya and Agni. The objectives of *Brahmavidyā* and the performance of rituals are different and the two are also opposed to each other. *Karma* cannot therefore subserve *jñāna* in the form of steadfast devotion to *Paramātman*.

Vedānta Deśika sets aside this objection. According to the Vedāntin, the terms Indra, Agni and Prajāpati referred to in the ritualistic texts denote ultimately the *Paramātman* who is the indweller of all the other deities as their inner controller. This is the interpretation adopted in the *Pratardana-Vidyā* of Vedānta.[60] Accordingly, in the case of a *mumukṣu* who is engaged in *Brahmaupāsanā*, Agni does not refer to the deity Agni but *Paramātman* who is the *antaryāmi* or indweller of Agni. The worship of Agni involved in a ritual amounts to the worship of *Paramātman*. The observance of the *varṇāśrama-dharma* by the *upāsaka* of Brahman is fully justified and *karma* therefore can become the auxiliary to *jñāna*.

It is contended by some that *varṇāśrama dharma* is to be renounced by one who is a *upāsaka* of Brahman. Accordingly, the per-

[59]See SS II-35, p. 91. *pratibuddhastu mokṣabhāk. . . pratibuddhāḥ na sevante.*

[60]This is one of the *vidyās* taught in the Upaniṣads and is referred to in the *Kauṣītakī Upaniṣad*. It bears that name because it was taught to Pratardana by Indra. Pratardana prays to Indra to confer on him a boon which is considered to be the highest good of man. The latter directs the former to meditate on Indra, who describes himself as *prāṇa* and *prajñātmā*. The question raised here is whether the meditation on Indra as *prāṇa* means the individual self (the *jīva* of Indra) or the Supreme Being (*Paramātmā*). Rāmānuja, on the strength of a later statement in the same passage describing *prāṇa* as supreme consciousness and immortal, interprets that the meditation on Indra here means the meditation on Brahman as the indwelling spirit of Indra. See RB I-1-29.

formance of *karma* does not necessarily subserve *Brahma-vidya*. This view is rejected on the strength of the teachings contained in the *Bhagavad-gītā*. According to the *Gītā*, *tyāga* or renouncement is of three kinds: *sāttvika*, *rājasa* and *tāmasa*.[61] Of these, what is approved by the Lord is *sāttvika tyāga* which means the performance of the prescribed religious duties without any desire for the results and shedding the notion that the individual is the doer. The *Gītā* also emphasises that under no circumstances the prescribed religious duties should be given up. It says: *karma* such as sacrifice, charity, austerity should not be given up but should be performed.[62] Commenting on this verse, Rāmānuja points out that the religious duties such as *yajña*, charity, austerity, etc., which are laid down as mandatory by Vedas should never be given up by an aspirant for *mokṣa* and that these have to be observed right up to the end of one's life (*āprayāṇād-aharahaḥ kāryameva*). One who gives up the performance of such rituals is doing so out of ignorance (*moha*).[63]

In the case of one who is in *samādhi* or trance, the performance of *karma* might have been suspended during the state of *samādhi*. This does not really amount to the renouncement of *karma*, since the *yogi* is deeply absorbed in the realisation of the goal (*aṅgi*) in the form of *Brahmānubhava* and *karma* as *aṅga* has become part of *aṅgi*, the goal. The goal being important the temporary rejection of its *aṅga* is permissible. That is, temporary suspension of religious duties while one is in *samādhi* is acceptable.

A question is raised based on a superficial meaning of an Upaniṣadic statement which uses the expression '*atyāśrami*' or one who has transgressed *varṇāśrama-dharma*, whether it would be necessary to observe *karma* as *aṅga* to *Brahma-vidyā*. The expression *atyāśrami*, according to Vedānta Deśika, means those who belong to the *uttamāśrama* or the best stage of life.[64] This refers to the *saṁnyāsin* or the one who has renounced all worldly objects. Even the *saṁnyāsins*, according to the Viśiṣṭādvaitin, have to observe the religious duties enjoined by the Vedas.[65] Therefore, it is not apporpriate to conclude that rituals are not required for *upāsaka*.

[61]BG XVIII-6.

[62]*Ibid.*, XVIII-5. *yajña-dāna-tapaḥ-karma na tyājyam kāryameva tat.*

[63]BG XVIII-5. *mohāt tasya parityāgaḥ.*

[64]SS II-36, p. 91.

[65]RB III-4-19. See also Ch V-10-1.

V. KARMA AND UPĀSANĀ

In connection with the consideration of *karma* as auxiliary to *bhakti-yoga*, we have to bear in mind the types of *karma* which subserve *Brahmopāsanā*. There are three types of *karma—nitya, naimittika* and *kāmya*. The *nitya karmas* are the prescribed religious duties which are mandatory and these have to be performed unconditionally and the failure to do so will result in sin. *Naimittika karmas* are such prescribed rituals as have to be observed necessarily but only on certain occasions or for certain specific purposes such as expiation of sins. The *kāmya-karmas* are those which have to be performed only when one desires to attain some specific results such as heaven or wealth. The first two are obligatory duties, whereas the third are purely optional. Only *nitya karmas* and certain *naimittikas* are regarded as auxiliary for *Brahmopāsanā* and not the third.

In this connection a few objections are raised by the critics of Viśiṣṭadvaita. First of all, the distinction between *nitya* and *kāmya* is not well determined and as such it cannot be emphasised that only *nitya karmas* are subsidiary means to *upāsanā*. Secondly, *nitya karmas* are also mandatory for persons of different stages of life (*āśramas*). How could these which are auxiliary to *āśrama* also subserve *upāsanā*? Thirdly, even *bhakti-yoga* whose goal is *mokṣa* could be a *kāmya karma* insofar as the persons practising it have a desire for *mokṣa*. All these issues are discussed by Vedānta Deśika and clarified.

Regarding the first issue, the critic is of the view that even a *nitya karma* would be in a sense *kāmya*, because no one would attempt to perform it without some motivation. The motivation could be two-fold : either for the purpose of achieving some good result or for the purpose of avoiding sin which may arise as a result of its nonobservance.

This is not a correct view, argues Vedānta Deśika. If one performs *nitya karma* with the purpose of avoiding sins that may arise due to its nonperformance, it would not become a *kāmya karma*. A *karma* becomes *kāmya* if only it is done with the motive of achieving some specific result in the form of greater happiness, wealth or heaven. The desire on the part of a person to avoid what is considered to be undesirable (*aniṣṭa*) is a natural one and is common to all. If one performs the *karma* with such a desire to avoid the undesirable consequence, such a *karma* should not be regarded as *kāmya*. If it is done purely for achieving some specific result, it becomes a *kāmya karma*.

The distinction between *nitya* and *kāmya karma* is also well defined by the sacred texts (*śāstra*). Injunctions are of two types: one is in the form of command (*ājñā*) and the other is in the form of general suggestions laid down for observance if so desired (*anujñā*). *Nitya karmas* come under the first category. These have to be performed without fail. The *kāmyas* fall under the second category. These are optional. If one so desires, one may perform them.

Similarly the distinction between *nitya* and *naimittika* is clear, though the avoidance of sin is common to both. The word *naimittika* means that which is to be observed due to the special circumstances(*nimittāt āgataḥ naimittikaḥ*). Accordingly, *naimittika karma* is that which is performed as and when a need arises to atone a sin. In the case of *nitya karma*, it is to be performed without fail in order to avoid the sin that will arise as a result of its nonperformance.

Naimittika karma is of two kinds: *karma* in the form of *prāyaścitta*, expiation of sin and *karma* to be done on certain specified occasions or time, such as the *śrāddha* ceremony on a new moon day. The former could also be regarded as a *kāmya* since it is optional.[66] That is, the *karma* may be done if one desires to atone the sin committed. Non-performance of it does not result in sin, unlike the *nitya karma*. The latter type of *naimittika karma* is equivalent to a *nitya karma*, since its nonperformance results in sin.[67]

Karmas are also classified into *pravṛtta* and *nivṛtta*. According to Manu, who draws this distinction, *pravṛtta karma* are those which are performed for the attainment of some desired results either in this world or the higher realms.[68] The *nivṛtta karma* is that which is performed without any desire for results (*niṣkāma*) but purely for the purpose of *mokṣa*.[68a] In this context a question is raised whether the *karmas* which are observed as auxiliaries

[66]TMK II-40. *pāpaśāntyartham ekaṁ tat syāt kāmyena tulyam.*
[67]*Ibid. akaraṇataḥ doṣakṛt nityatulyam.*
[68]SS II-41, p. 93. *Iha vā amutra vā kāmyaṁ pravṛttam.*
[68a] *niṣkāmasya jñānapūrvam tu nivṛttam.*

to *upāsanā* for the purpose of *mokṣa* could be strictly considered *niṣkāma* since these are done with a desire (*kāmanā*) for *mokṣa*. It cannot be said that the *mumukṣu* performs them purely for the pleasure of *Īśvara* and not for achieving any desired results such as *svarga* or heaven, because it is impossible to perform any *karma* solely for the pleasure of *Īśvara* without at the same time having some selfish interest like *mokṣa*. The aspirant for *mokṣa* is aware of the fact that by earning the grace of *Īśvara*, he will also get his *mokṣa* and to this extent some selfish element is involved in it.

In reply, Vedānta Deśika points out that there is no room for the above objection if we understand correctly the implication of the words, *pravṛtta* and *nivṛtta*. The *nivṛtta karmas* are those which are helpful to overcome the fear of being caught up in bondage, and as such one is drawn away from *saṁsāra*. The *pravṛtta karmas* are those whose observance will lead one towards bondage and cause further bondage. In other words, what takes one away from further bondage is *nivṛtta karma* and what leads one towards further bondage is *pravṛtta karma*. *Mokṣa* is the supreme goal of life, and if one desires to achieve it, it does not become a *kāmanā*, that is, something to be achieved for selfish purposes. *Mokṣa-kāmanā* is not *kamanā* as understood in the ordinary sense of the term. It is a desire directed towards the removal of bondage and is to be sought for as the *summum bonum* of life. What is to be rejected by the *mumukṣu* is the desire for other results, because it drags one into bondage.[69]

VI. REMOVAL OF PUṆYA AND PĀPA BY UPĀSANĀ

Mukti is possible when the individual soul becomes totally free from the shackles of *karma*[70] in the form of both *puṇya* and *pāpa*. The meditation on Brahman is enjoined as the means to achieve it. The question arises whether the *upāsanā* on Brahman is efficacious enough to remove all the sins and also the merit (*puṇya*) accumulated by the *jiva* from time immemorial. This doubt

[69]TMK II-41.

[70]The word *karma* here refers to the merit (*puṇya*) and sin (*pāpa*) acquired as a result of the good or bad deeds respectively performed by an individual in the past lives.

arises because *karma* seems to be never ending, and, unless it is overcome by performing suitable expiatory rituals (*prayaścitta*), it will not cease to exert its influence on the individual. It is almost impossible in one's life time to get rid of the entire *karma* by expiatory rituals. Further, *prāyaścitta* is prescribed only for sins committed but not for removing the *puṇya*. The śruti says that by *dharma*(meaning Vedic rituals)only sins are overcome.[71] But it does not speak of the removal of *puṇya*. How can it be claimed that all *karmas* in the form of both *puṇya* and *pāpa* are overcome by *Brahmopāsanā*?

The above objections are not valid, argues Vedānta Deśika. Men of wisdom who have deep Vedic knowledge have declared that *Brahma-vidyā* or the meditation on Brahman itself constitutes the *prāyaścitta* for all sins committed by the individual.[72] The main objective of *Brahma-vidyā* is to remove all obstacles that stand in the way of Brahman-realisation. In view of this it is possible that the same *Brahma-vidyā* which is prescribed for Brahman-realisation could also serve the purpose of *prayaścitta* for sins. Insofar as it is capable of removing all obstacles including *karma* in the form of *puṇya* and *pāpa*, *Brahma-vidyā* is regarded as *prayścitta* for sins. The *Gitā* also states that self-knowledge in the form of fire (*jñānāgni*) burns all the *karmas*.[73]

The Upaniṣadic text says that *Brahma-vidyā* takes away all sins (*pāpmānaḥ*).[74] The word *pāpmānaḥ* (sins) expressed in plural is intended to mean both sin as well as merit (*puṇya*). Though the word *puṇya* is not explicitly mentioned in the śruti, it becomes included in the word *pāpma*, because for an aspirant to *mokṣa* even *puṇya* has the same effect as *pāpa* insofar as it stands in the way of attainment of *mokṣa*.[75] Even *dharma* becomes *adharma* from the standpoint of an aspirant for *mokṣa*. *Dharma* is that which is a means to achieve a desired end. In the case of one who is aiming at *mokṣa*, what serves to achieve that goal is *dharma* and what comes in its way is *adharma*. Since *puṇya* is an obstacle for *mokṣa*, it has also to be got rid of. The very Upaniṣad speaks of all merit arising from *dharma*, *artha* and *kāma* – the three goals of

[71]Tait *dharmeṇa pāpam apanudati.*
[72]TMK *tādṛg vidyaiva tanniskṛtiḥ.*
[73]BG IV-37. *jñānāgniḥ sarvakarmāṇi bhasmasāt kurute tathā.*
[74]Ch V-24-3. *sarve pāpmānaḥ pradūyante.*
[75]TMK II-55.

life—as *pāpa*. It also mentions clearly that both *sukṛta* (merit) and *duṣkṛta* (demerit) are to be cast off. After mentioning specifically both *sukṛta* and *duṣkṛta*, the text says in one sweeping statement *sarve pāpmānaḥ*.[76] Therefore, *Brahma-vidyā* destroys not only all sins but all *puṇya* too accumulated by the individual.

It is claimed on the authority of the Upaniṣadic texts that a *Brahma-jñāni* or the one who has Brahman-realisation is untouched by sin. Thus, the *Chāndogya Upaniṣad* says: 'Just as water does not cling to a lotus leaf, so the evil deeds do not touch the Brahman-knower.'[77] In the same way the *Vedānta-sūtra* states that Brahman-knower is also untouched by *puṇya*. What are the implications of these statements? Do they mean that all kinds of sin, both of the past and those done after the commencement of *upāsanā* (*uttarāgha*) do not affect the *Brahma-jñāni* ? If this be so, the Upaniṣadic text[78] which states that unless one is free from all sins one will not be able to achieve *mokṣa*, becomes meaningless. That is, if *puṇya* and *pāpa* do not affect the *Brahma-jñāni*, why should he have to get rid of them totally for attaining *mokṣa*.

Vedānta Deśika clarifies this doubt by presenting the correct position based on the interpretation offered by Rāmānuja. *Pāpa* is of two kinds: one which is committed intentionally and the other done unintentionally. The former needs to be overcome by suitable expiatory rituals. Only the latter does not affect the *Brahma-jñāni* because his *upāsanā* of Brahman is capable of counteracting it. The *Kaṭha Upaniṣad* therefore refers to the need of overcoming such sins as committed intentionally.[79]

In the same way it is to be understood that only *puṇya* or merit acquired by a *Brahma-jñāni* unintentionally will not bear any result for him. This is the significance of his not being affected by *puṇya*. A *jñāni*, for example, might do pious acts unintentionally such as some service to the community or the creation of a flower garden for worship. Such acts, though not done for any selfish purpose, may bear fruits, but the fruits of such good deeds do not touch the *jñāni* in the same way as the sins committed unintentionally do not affect him.[80]

[76]Ch VIII-4-1. *na sukṛtaṁ na duṣkṛtaṁ sarve pāpmāno'to nivartante.*

[77]Ch IV-14-3. *pāpam karma na śliṣyate.* See also VS IV-1-14.

[78]Ka 2-24. *nāvirato duścaritāt.*

[79]TMK II-56. [80]TMK II-57.

It is stated in the Upaniṣads that at the time the Brahman-knower casts off his mortal remains, his merit goes to his friends and his sins go to his enemies.[81] Is such a transfer of one's *puṇya* and *pāpa* possible? *Karma* which is the cause of bondage is of two kinds : one which is accumulated prior to the commencement of *Brahmopāsanā,* and the second which arises after the *upāsanā* is started. The first one is of two types : that which has already begun to give result and that which is yet to ripen and give its effect. The former is to be endured by experiencing it till the end of one's life. The latter is eradicated by *upāsanā.* The *karma* which is acquired after the commencement of *upāsanā* is of two kinds. The first is that which is caused by the deeds done intentionally and the second is that which arises as a result of acts done unintentionally. We have already pointed out that the latter does not affect the *upāsaka*. The former is to be experienced either in this life or in another life. If this is the case, where is the scope for any *karma* in the form of *puṇya* and *pāpa* to be transferred to someone else at the time the *upāsaka* casts off his physical body?[82]

Vedānta Deśika explains the meaning and significance of the transfer of *puṇya* and *pāpa* and also the eradication of the same by *Brahmopāsanā*. According to Viśiṣṭādvaita, *puṇya* and *pāpa* are respectively the *anugraha* (favourable disposition or pleasure) and *nigraha* (unfavourable disposition or displeasure) of *Īśvara.* When a meritorious deed is performed, *Īśvara* becomes pleased; when an evil deed is done, He becomes displeased. *Puṇya* and *pāpa* of an individual consist in causing pleasure or displeasure respectively to *Īśvara.* In view of this, the statement that *puṇya* and *pāpa* do not affect the *Brahma-jñāni* and that these are obliterated implies that the *saṅkalpa* of God in the form of His grace or displeasure on the individual doing *upāsanā* does not operate.[83] As regards the transfer of *puṇya* and *pāpa* to friends and foes, there is no such transfer of *puṇya* or *pāpa* from one to the other. All that it means is that *Īśvara* showers grace or shows displeasure towards the friends and foes of the *Brahma-jñāni* taking into consideration the kinds of good services done or offences

[81]*tasya putrā dāyam upayānti*; *suhṛdaḥ sādhukṛtyām dviṣantaḥ pāpakṛtyām* (quoted by Rāmānuja in his commentary on VS-IV-1-17).

[82]See SS II-58, p. 103.

[83]TMK II-58. *karmāśleṣa praṇāśau tadupadhibhagavan nigrahādeḥ nivṛttiḥ.*

committed by them towards the knower of Brahman (*Brahmavit*). At the time the Brahman-knower sheds his physical body, all the *puṇya* and *pāpa* he has acquired and which have taken the form of pleasure or displeasure of *Īśvara* cease to bear result due to the influence of *bhakti-yoga*. Nevertheless, God, at the time the *Brahma-jñāni* is on his way to *mokṣa*, dispenses *puṇya* and *pāpa* separately corresponding to his *puṇya* and *pāpa* to his friends and foes in the form of showing special favours or displeasures to them.[84] This is what is known as *puṇya-pāpa-saṅkramaṇa* or the transfer of sin and merit to others.

An objection may be raised against this theory of transfer of one's *karma* to another. There is a settled order insofar as one who performs that *karma* should reap its fruits. If someone else were to get its fruits, it would upset the law of *karma*. God, who is the dispenser of the fruits, would be transgressing His limits. Therefore, transfer of *karma* to another individual is untenable.

The above position is not correct, because God dispenses good or bad results to the friend and foes of *Brahma-jñānī* in accordance with the good and bad deeds done to the *jñāni* by these persons. As already explained, there is no transfer of the good or bad *karma* of the Brahman-knower to his friends and foes. The latter are awarded the results to the extent they have done good and bad to the *Brahma-jñānī*. Thus each one's *karma* bears its fruit. The law of *karma* is not ignored. Nor does *Īśvara* transgress His own limits.[85]

The Path to Mokṣa

What happens to the *jiva* of *Brahma-jñāni* when it leaves the physical body at death? The Upaniṣads give a vivid description of the spiritual path through which the *jivas* march towards the final state of *mokṣa*. These details are not discussed in *Tattva-muktā-kalāpa* but they may be found in Rāmānuja's commentary on the relevant *Vedānta-sūtras*.[86] The path through which the *jiva* of an individual who has done *Brahmopāsanā* is technically known as *arcirādi mārga*—the path of the Gods. There seem to be apparent conflicts between the different Upaniṣadic texts[87]

[84]TMK II-58. *tat-tulyau eva (nigrahānugrahau) viduṣi prayati tac-chatru-mitreṣu devaḥ dhatte.* [85]TMK II-59. [86]VS IV-3-2 and IV-3-3.

[87]See Ch IV-15-5 and VIII-6-5; Br. VIII-2-15 and VII-10-1; also *Kauṣītaki Upaniṣad* I-21.

as there is some variation in the description of the presiding deities who receive the *jiva* on the way to *mokṣa*. But Rāmānuja reconciles these conflicts and points out while commenting on the relevant *Vedānta-sūtra* that the *arcirādi mārga* is one only.[88] Based on Rāmānuja's views, Vedānta Deśika presents the correct position in regard to the *arcirādi mārga*, with a view to clearing up any confusion. The *arcirādi* path comprises the following: *jyotis* or flame, *ahas* or the day, *śukla-pakṣa* or the bright fortnight of lunar month, *uttarāyaṇa* or the bright half of the year when the sun travels northward, *saṁvatsara* or the year, *vāyu* or air, *mārtaṇḍa* or the sun, *tārakeśa* or the moon and *vidyut* or the lightning accompanied by Varuṇa, Indra and Prajāpati.[89] These deities are commanded by God to be guides to the *jivas* proceeding to *mokṣa*. The presiding deity of vidyut is known as *amānava* or *mānasa*. Flame, day, etc. does not refer to the physical entities but rather to the presiding deities. They are known as *ātivāhikas*, those who serve as guides on the way.[90]

VII. THE NATURE OF MUKTI

According to the Viśiṣṭādvaita Vedānta, *mokṣa* is not merely freedom from bondage but it is also a positive state of existence for the *jiva* in a supra-mundane realm (*parama-pada*) without losing its individuality. It is described by Vedānta Deśika as *paripūrṇa-brahmānubhava*, the full and perfect enjoyment of the bliss of Brahman. Prior to the state of release, *jiva's* knowledge was restricted in scope being subjected to *karma*. In the state of *mokṣa*, *jiva* becomes totally free from the shackles of *karma* and as such its *jñāna* manifests itself in its fullness. *Jiva* becomes omniscient and is thus capable of comprehending Brahman in all its splendour. As the concluding *Vedānta-sūtra* points out, when once this state is reached by *jiva* there is never a return to the state of bondage (*na ca punarāvartate*).

On the strength of the scriptural texts, it is admitted that *jiva* attains a status in *mokṣa* almost equal to Brahman. Thus, the śruti says that the *jiva* in the state of *mukti* enjoys supreme equality with *paramātman*(*parama-sāmya*).[91] The real implication of

[88]RB IV-3-1, p. 851. *arcirādireka eva mārgaḥ sarvatra pratipādyate.*

[89]TMK II-60. [90]RB IV-3-4.

[91]Mund 3-1-3. *nirañjanaḥ paramam sāmyam upaiti.*

parama-sāmya or equality with Brahman needs to be understood. According to Advaita Vedānta, the individual self becomes identical with the Absolute. The Advaitin takes his stand on the scriptural text *brahma veda brahmaiva bhavati.*[92] The text which is understood literally is interpreted to mean that the knower of Brahman becomes Brahman, which implies the identity of the individual self and the Brahman. The Viśiṣṭādvaitin points out that this text does not so much refer to identity (*tādātmya*) as to equality (*sādharmya*). The justification for adopting this view is that Brahman itself becoming Brahman cannot constitute the goal as it has already been accomplished. Nor is it possible for one different from Brahman to become Brahman itself as it would result in an *apasiddhānta*. Two different entities cannot be identical. It would be therefore logical to hold that the individual self attains the status of Brahman (*sādharmya*) rather than that it becomes one with Brahman. This interpretation is also in consonance with other Upaniṣadic texts declaring in unambiguous terms the equality (*sāmya*) of the self with Brahman.[93]

If *jivatmā* in the state of *mukti* enjoys equal status with *paramātmā*, the question arises whether the former has also the power to create and dissolve the universe? If this is not admitted, how could we conceive that *jiva* is absolutely free in *mukti*, as the śruti declares (*sa svarāṭ bhavati*).[94] The reply to this objection is that *jiva* is not equal to *Īśvara* in every respect. As *Vedānta-sūtra*[95] points out, it does not have the function of creation and dissolution of the universe, since this is unique to Brahman only, as established by the scriptural texts. The equality between the two is only in respect of the enjoyment of bliss (*bhogamātra-sāmya*).[96] The Upaniṣadic text clearly points out that the *jiva* also enjoys the *vibhūtis* of Brahman. Thus, the text says: *so'śnute sarvān kāmān saha.*[97] The word *saha* indicates that Brahman together with his *vibhūtis* is experienced by the individual self. The freedom of the *jiva* is not however restricted. He is permitted by *Paramātman* to act freely in all other respects.[98]

[92] *Ibid.*, 3-2-9. [93] Mund 3-1-3. [94] Ch 7-25-2.
[95] VS IV-4-17. *jagadvyāpāravarjaṁ prakaraṇād asannihitatvācca.*
[96] VS IV-4-21. [97] Tait 1-2. [98] TMK II-63.

Even though *jīva* is equal to *Īśvara* except in respect of the function of creation of universe, *jīva* is dependent on *Paramātman*. A question may be raised whether such a subordination to *Īśvara* does not cause suffering to *jīva*, because in our ordinary experience dependence on others is a source of suffering. How then can *jīva* enjoy bliss in the state of *mokṣa*?

This criticism, according to Vedānta Deśika, is based on an improper understanding of the *dāsatva* or subordination of *jīva* to *Īśvara*. It is bondage in the form of *puṇya* and *pāpa* that causes suffering of the individual self but not the mere *dāsatva*. *Dāsatva* or dependence is the very *svarūpa* or nature of *jīva*. What constitutes an essential characteristic of *jīva* will not cause any suffering to *jīva*. The real cause of suffering to *jīva* is *karma*, and since that is totally rooted out in the state of *mokṣa* there is no scope for any suffering.[99]

Another question may be raised in this connection. If *jīva* is totally dependent on *Paramātman* who is *svatantra* or absolutely free will there be a possibility of the latter sending back the former to bondage. This is ruled out, says Rāmānuja in his commentary on the concluding *Vedānta-sūtra*. *Paramātman* is full of love and compassion for the individual soul (*atyartha-priyaḥ*).[100] He will never let the *jīva* return to the state of bondage once the latter has attained *mokṣa*. The scriptural as well as smṛti texts reaffirm the truth that there is no return under any circumstances to bondage.[101]

We have observed earlier that *jīva* becomes omniscient in the state of *mokṣa*, as is evident from the scriptural text.[102] It may be noted that the omniscience is not something that is newly produced in the *jīva*. The *jīva* by its very nature is omniscient, but its omniscience was not manifest in the state of bondage owing to *karma* with which it was overlaid. With the removal of *karma*, the true nature of self becomes manifested. This is comparable to the lustre of a gem which is hidden by dirt and which is made manifest by merely removing the dirt. Similarly, the self becomes almost equal to Brahman in every respect except in the

[99]TMK II-64. [100]BG VII-17.
[101]Ch 8-15-1. *na ca punarāvartate*. VS IV-4-22; also BG VIII-15-16.
[102]Ch VII-26.2. *sarvam ha paśyaḥ paśyati*.

matter of the creation, sustenance and dissolution of the universe which belong exclusively to *Paramātman*.

Does the *jiva* have a body and sense organs even in the state of *mokṣa* in order to enjoy the bliss? Such a question arises because the *Chandogya Upaniṣad* states that *jiva* in *mokṣa* is capable of eating, playing, moving from place to place, etc.[103] If *jiva* be associated with a body, would it not cause bondage, because association of the *jiva* with the body is considered bondage. The same Upaniṣad declares in another context that there is no release for an individual as long as it is associated with body.[104]

It is admitted that the individual soul in the state of *mokṣa* could assume a body out of its free will (*saṅkalpa*) for the purpose of enjoying bliss or for movemet. Such a body assumed by the *jiva* is not a *karmic* body and as such no bondage is caused to it. The *jiva* could also remain without a body if it so desires. The body which the *jiva* sheds for attaining release is the one caused by *karma* while the body assumed by it in its state of *mukti* is of its own creation and totally free from *karma*. Thus there is no conflict between the two śruti texts, one speaking of a bodily form and the other requiring the physical body to be cast off.

VIII. CRITICISM OF OTHER THEORIES OF MUKTI

The concept of *mokṣa* as advocated by Viśiṣṭādvaita could be appreciated better if we consider the other theories of *mokṣa* advanced by other schools of thought. There are several theories and these are all summed up in one verse[105] by Vedānta Deśika. These are:

(1) *Mukti* is a state of identity of soul and Brahman (*Brahmaṇaikyam*). This is the view of the Advaitin for whom *jiva* is really non-different from Brahman.

(2) *Mukti* is total cessation of all *vāsanās* and thereby *vijñāna* alone persisting devoid of *vāsanās* (*vāsanoccheda mātram*).

[103]Ch. 8-12-3. *sa tatra paryeti jakṣan, krīḍan, ramamāṇaḥ.*
[104]Ch. 8-12-1. *na ha vai saśarirasya sataḥ priyāpriyayor apahatirasti.*
[105]TMK II-75.

This is the view of the Vijñānavādins for whom *jīva* is a series of momentary mental states.

(3) *Mukti* is total destruction or cessation of all *vijñāna* series, a view held by one section of Mādhyamika Buddhist.

(4) *Mokṣa* is a state of void (*śūnyādvaitam*), a theory advanced by the Mādhyamikas.

(5) *Mukti* is the continuous upward movement of the soul (in the higher region), a view held by the Jainas.

(6) *Mukti* is the existence of the self similar to a dead stone free from all experience. This is the view of the Vaiśeṣikas.

(7) *Mukti* is the manifestation of the soul with its natural characteristics, viz. eternal knowledge and eternal bliss, a view held by one school of thought in Nyāya system.

(8) *Mukti* is the experience of the happiness of one's own self by the mind (*svātma-saukhyānubhavam*). This is the view held by the Bhāṭṭa school of Mīmāṁsā.

(9) *Mukti* is perfect freedom of the individual soul. This seems to be the view of one school of ancient Śaiva sect.

(10) *Mukti* is the state in which soul becomes equal to Śiva (*paśupati-samatā*), a view held by Pāśupata religion.

All these views, which are considered as purely speculative in character and formulated according to one's fancies, are summarily rejected on the ground that they are opposed to what is established on the basis of scriptural texts. In a lighter vein, Vedānta Deśika says: 'Let śrutis come to their help in understanding the correct nature of *mukti*.'[106] However, it may be observed that most of these theories advocate a negative concept of *mokṣa* rather than a positive one to be achieved by an aspirant for *mokṣa*. If individuality of *jīva* in *mokṣa* is not accepted, it cannot be a real *puruṣārtha* or *summum bonum* of spiritual life worth striving for.

Vedānta Deśika takes up for detailed examination the theories of Vaiśeṣika and Sāṅkhya. According to Vaiśeṣika, *mokṣa* is the cessation of all the qualities of the soul.[107] Knowledge, pleasure,

[106] *Ibid. muktau jalpatām vaḥ śrutiḥ upakṛtaye kalpatām.*

[107] *aśeṣa-viśeṣa-guṇocchedaḥ.*

pain, desire and aversion are the special characteristics or attributes of the soul. These are not permanent attributes, unlike knowledge of *ātman* in the Viśiṣṭādvaita system. Whatever is *anitya* or non-permanent cannot persist in the state of *mokṣa* which is an eternal state. Therefore, *mokṣa* consists in the cessation of pain and all cognitional activity of *jīva*. In order to prove this theory, the Vaiśeṣikas adopt the following syllogistic argument : '*Jīva* is at some stage devoid of all characteristics (*aśeṣa-viśeṣa-guṇa-śūnya*), because such characteristics possessed by *jīva* are non-permanent; just as the pot in the first moment of its production is.'[108]

This argument is refuted on the ground that it is in direct conflict with the śruti text which clearly says that *jīva* in the state of *mokṣa* sees everything.[109] Further, when Vedānta speaks of *mukti* as a state of bliss (*ānandasvarūpa*), it is inappropriate to advocate a negative concept of *mukti*, equating it with the nature of a stone. No one would ever aspire for such a state !

The syllogistic argument also suffers from logical fallacies. The *sādhya*, viz. *aśeṣa-viśeṣa-guṇa-śūnya* does not exist in the illustration. That is, the pot which is cited as illustration is not totally free from all qualities at the first moment of its production. According to the Naiyāyika, an object at the first moment of its production is supposed to be devoid of all qualities. This is not accepted by the Viśiṣṭādvaitin. What is cited as illustration should be acceptable to both the disputants. The *hetu* or probans is also not established. That is, it cannot be proved that *jīva* prossesses non-permanent characteristics. For the Viśiṣṭādvaitin, *jñāna* which is an attribute of *jīva* is eternal and the qualities such as desire, aversion, pain, pleasure are its modifications. The probans therefore suffers from the fallacy of *asiddha*.

According to the Sāṅkhya system, *mokṣa* which is known as *kaivalya* consists in the existence of the individual self or *puruṣa* in its true form, absolutely unassociated with matter (*prakṛti*). *Puruṣa* and *prakṛti* are the only two ultimate reals in the system. Of these, *puruṣa* is of the nature of pure consciousness, eternally free and unchanging (*kūṭastha*) ; *buddhi* or intellect is material

[108]SS II-69, p. 109. *jīvāḥ kadācit aśeṣa-viśeṣa-guṇa-śūnyaḥ anityāviśeṣaguṇa-vattvāt, utpatti-kṣaṇe ghaṭavat.*

[109]Ch 7-2-2.

in character but is always subject to constant modification. When *puruṣa* becomes reflected in *buddhi*, it falsely assumes the doership (*kartṛatva*) as if it belongs to it, and similarly the intellect assumes intelligence which is rightly the property of the self. This conjunction of intelligent *puruṣa* with the non-intelligent *buddhi* is the root cause of bondage. Release or freedom from bondage consists in their disjunction—the ultimate realization of *puruṣa* and *prakṛti* as separate through discriminatory knowledge. The final psychosis (*antya-vijñāna-vṛttiḥ*) which causes the realisation that self is distinct from matter puts an end to bondage and leaves the individual self in its pure and free state. This is *kaivalya*. In a sense, *puruṣa* is always free by virtue of its intrinsic nature, but in *mokṣa* it realises this truth by breaking away its undesirable association with matter. It is more a negative state of riddance from evil than the realisation of positive bliss.

Vedānta Deśika refutes this theory. The criticism is mainly based on the untenability of the reflection of *puruṣa* in the intellect. Reflection is normally possible only when the media in which reflection takes place has a colour base (*rūpa*). When *buddhi* is devoid of any colour, how could *puruṣa* be reflected in it? Similarly, *puruṣa* is also devoid of any form. How could *puruṣa* reflect itself in the intellect.[110]

Further, *puruṣa* in this system is untouched by any afflictions or imperfections (*nirlepa*). How could such a *puruṣa* become bound? How could the *puruṣa* who is absolutely pure and free from all activity become deluded with bondage? If it be said that because of some *upādhi* or conditioning factor bondage takes place, then *puruṣa* will have to remain deluded for all time since such an *upādhi* would be present always. In such a position, how would the self ever realise that it is separate from matter? The self never had any form of bondage on an earlier occasion; nor will it have it later. What then is *mokṣa* for the self?[111]

Other difficulties arise in the Sāṅkhya theory of *mokṣa*. In this system, *prakṛti* is one and *vibhu* or all-pervasive. It is common to all *puruṣas* or individual selves. All selves are *vibhu*. The experience of pleasure and pain by individual selves takes place due to their association with *prakṛti*. As the association with

[110]TMK II-71. [111]*Ibid*.

prakṛti is common to all *jivas*, the experience of pleasure and pain should be common to all.[112] It may be possible to say that *buddhi* or intellect is different for each individual, and therefore there is difference in the experience of pleasure and pain. But this explanation does not hold good because even the intellect in this system is only the product of *prakṛti*. If *buddhi* were the property of the soul, it would be possible to account for the differences in experience. This is not so. Thus, the theory of *mokṣa* as formulated by Sāṅkhya on the basis of their ontological position is unsound.

IX. CRITICISM OF THE THEORY OF JĪVAN-MUKTI

We have already considered the untenability of the theory of *mukti* in Advaita. We shall consider here whether it is possible to achieve *mukti*, while one is still associated with the physical body? Such a possibility is accepted by Advaita system. According to the Advaitin, *mokṣa* is *Brahma-sākṣātkāra*, the realisation of the identity of the individual self with the Absolute. By repeated meditation on the oneness of the *jiva* and Brahman, as enunciated in the scriptural text *tattvamasi*, it is considered possible for one to realise this identity. He thus becomes *mukta* even while he is embodied since the ignorance about Brahman or *avidyā* which is the cause of bondage is removed by Brahman-realisation. Though *avidyā* is removed, the traces of it still persist, and, as a result of it, even after the realisation of Brahman the body persists. Such a state of *mukti* is technically called *jivan-mukti*.

The concept of *jivan-mukti* is a self-contradiction, says Vedānta Deśika. *Mukti*, in the correct sense of the term, is that state of the individual self in which it is totally dissociated from the vital breath, sense organs and physical body.[113] An individual soul connected with *prāṇa*, *indriyas* and physical body is its embodied state (*jivana*). The two states—disembodied and embodied—are mutually opposed to each other. One who is embodied cannot therefore be *mukta* or disembodied. Then, how do we understand the statements found in the religious literature

[112] See VS II-3-32.

[113] TMK II-73. *muktiḥ prāṇākṣadehādibhir upādhibhir atyanta-viśleṣa-rūpā.*

which speak of *jīvan-mukti.*[114] Vedānta Deśika points out that the expression of *jīvan-mukti* in such statements is to be understood in a secondary sense meaning that this is a state similar to *mukti* (*tatsamāvasthā*).

The Advaitin justifies the theory of *jīvan-mukti* on the basis of the possibility of traces of *avidyā* persisting even after the removal of *avidyā* by means of Brahman-realisation (*badhitānuvṛtti*). Because of the traces of *avidyā* persisting, the individual continues with the body, even though he has realised Brahman. This is explained on the analogy of the vision of the double moon. An individual that perceives the moon as double due to the defect in the eye which is caused when the eyeball is pressed. Though he knows that there is one moon and not two, he continues to see the moon as two because of the persistence of the defect in the eye. However, it does not cause him any delusion, since he already has a correct knowledge about the moon.

The explanation offered to support the theory does not hold good. In the case of the vision of double moon, the optical defect is real; and as long as this condition persists the appearance of moon as double will continue in spite of his awareness that there is only a single moon. However, since he is convinced that the moon is single, the sense of fear or wonder does not exist. Such an explanation does not hold good in respect of the removal of *avidyā*. According to the ontological position of Advaita, everything else other than Brahman is illusory. When Brahman-realisation takes place, there should be a total cessation of *avidyā*, and there is absolutely no room for the continuance of its traces.

Even granting that the trace of *avidyā* continues, how is its removal effected? The Advaitin's answer is that it gets removed on its own as in the case of the last flame, the final wave of the sound and the final *saṁskāra* (*carama-saṁskāra*). This explanation does not stand to reason, argues Vedānta Deśika. What removes a thing cannot itself be the thing removed. In other words, the destroyer and the destroyed connot be identical since the two are incompatible. The pot, for instance, is destroyed never by itself. The analogies of the flame, etc. cited by the

[114] *Ibid.* SS II-73, p. 113. *jīvanmuktā bhavanti.*

Advaitin do not hold good here. According to Vedānta Deśika, in all these instances their destruction is effected by the will of God with the help of the particular spatial and temporal factors.[115] Thus, the possibility of the traces of *avidyā* persisting even after Brahman-realisation being ruled out, the doctrine of *jivan-mukti* becomes untenable.

From the foregoing critical evaluation of the different theories of *sādhana* and *mukti*, Vedānta Deśika comes to the conclusion that if *mokṣa* is the *summum bonum* or the supreme goal of life, it is to be conceived as the final liberation of the soul from the cycle of births and deaths, leading to a positive state of existence for the individual self in a supramundane realm enjoying fully the eternal bliss of Brahman. The true means or *sādhana* to achieve such a state is *bhakti* or constant and continuous meditation on Brahman along with the requisite ethical and religious discipline.

[115]SD Vāda 31; also SS II-74, p. 114.

CHAPTER TEN

Prakṛti and Its Evolutes

Prakṛti or the primordial cosmic matter is one of the six metaphysical entities (*tattvas*) admitted in the Viśiṣṭādvaita system. Unlike *Īśvara* and *jiva*, it is non-sentient (*jaḍa*) in character. It is eternal (*nitya*) but subject always to modification. It has three qualities, *sattva*, *rajas* and *tamas*, and is the field of action (*karma*) for the *jivas*.[1] Though it is real and eternal, it is not absolutely independent as in the Sāṅkhya system but is controlled by *Īśvara* and is dependent on Him for its very existence. It is regarded as *parārtha* or intended for others which implies that the sole purpose of its evolution into the physical universe of space and matter is to provide the necessary ground and opportunity for the individual souls to function and strive for release from bondage.

I. NATURE AND ORDER OF EVOLUTION

As in the Sāṅkhya system, Viśiṣṭādvaita also accepts the evolution of *prakṛti* into twenty-three *tattvas—mahat*, *ahaṁkāra*, *manas*, five *jñānendriyas* and five *karmendriyas*, five *tanmātras* and five *bhūtas*. Except the five *bhūtas* (gross elements), these are supersensuous in character and cannot be known through perception. The Sāṅkhyas attempt to prove their existence on the basis of inference. According to Vedānta Deśika, it is not possible to prove their existence by means of inference. The validity of inference depends upon the soundness of the probans (*hetu*) adopted and the establishment of logical concomitance (*vyāpti*) between the probans and probandum, as in the case of fire and smoke on the basis of observed facts. Such a thing is not possible in respect of entities which are beyond the scope of our per-

[1]See *Rahasyatrayasāra*, Ch. V (quoted from *Paramasaṁhitā*). *acetanā parārthā ca nityā satatavikriyā; triguṇā karmiṇāṁ kṣetraṁ prakṛteḥ rūpam ucyate.*

ceptual experience. The only *pramāṇa* by means of which these could be established is the āgamas or the revealed scripture including smṛti and itihāsa whose validity is accepted as unquestionable.[2]

Prakṛti which evolves itself into *mahat* and other *tattvas* is characterised by three *guṇas*, viz. *sattva*, *rajas* and *tamas*. In the Sāṅkhya system, the three *guṇas* are the components of *prakṛti*. That is, *prakṛti* is constituted of these three *guṇas*. Vedānta Deśika does not accept this position. If *guṇas* are components, they would be like three substances and the total number of *tattvas* would then be twenty-seven instead of twenty-five. The *guṇas* are therefore to be admitted as the essential characteristics of *prakṛti*. Though they are distinct from *prakṛti*, they are inseparably related to them. *Sattva* represents, as in the Sāṅkhya system, whatever is fine or light; *rajas* whatever is active and *tamas* whatever is heavy. These qualities are not present in equal proportion. There is variation in the sense that one or the other is predominant. Because of this variation, evolution takes place.

The first evolute of *prakṛti* is known as *mahat*. As an evolute of *prakṛti*, *mahat* also is characterised by the three *guṇas*. From *mahat*, *ahaṁkāra* evolves. This is also characterised by the three *guṇas* and accordingly it is of three kinds: *sāttvika*, *rājasa* and *tāmasa*. From the *sāttvika ahaṁkāra* in which the *sattva* element is predominant, the eleven sense organs including *manas* are evolved. From the *tāmasa ahaṁkāra*, the five *tanmātras* or the subtle elements evolve. *Rājasa ahaṁkāra* serves as an accessory for both the *sāttvika* and *tāmasa ahaṁkāra* in their evolution.

The order of evolution as explained by the Viśiṣṭādvaitin slightly differs from that of the Sāṅkhya system. According to Sāṅkhya, all the five *tanmātras* evolve together out of the *tāmasa ahaṁkāra*. According to Viśiṣṭādvaita, which takes its stand on the scriptural testimony, only *śabda-tanmātra* or the sound essence comes out of *tāmasa ahaṁkāra*. From the *śabda-tanmātra* arises *ākāśa* or the gross space; from *ākāśa* comes *sparśa-tanmātra*, the touch essence; *sparśa-tanmātra* causes *vāyu* or air; from *vāyu* comes *rūpa-tanmātra* or colour essence; from this comes *tejas* or fire; *tejas* produces *rasa-tanmātra* or taste essence; *rasa-tanmātra* causes *jala* or water; from *jala* comes *gandha-tanmātra* or odour essence

[2]TMK I-11.

and from this evolves *pṛthivī*—the gross element of earth. The order of evolution is as follows:

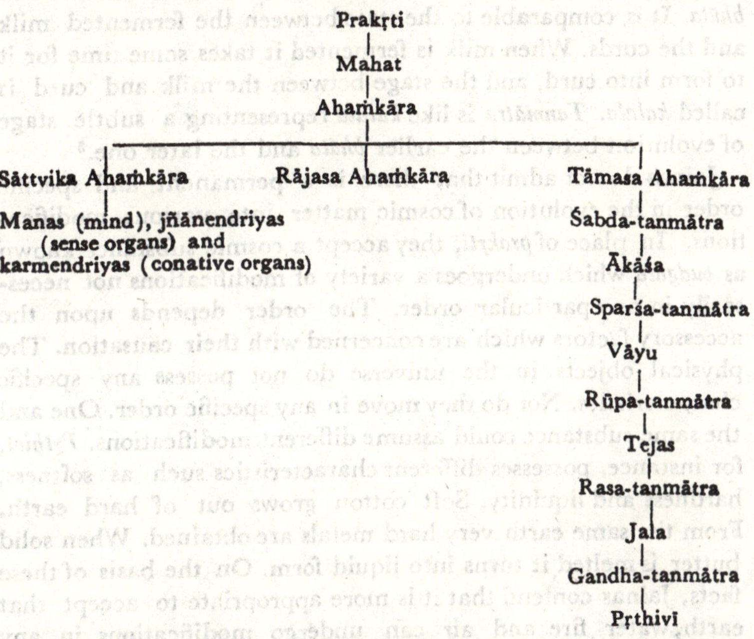

The main justification for holding the above order of evolution is that the scriptural texts speak of such an order. Thus the *Taittirīya Upaniṣad* says: 'From *ākāśa* comes *vāyu*, from *vāyu agni*, from *agni ap* and from *ap pṛthivī*.'[3] But this statement does not explicitly mention that the *tanmātras* cause the corresponding gross elements. However, the *Subāla Upaniṣad*,[4] while describing the order of dissolution (*laya*) of the five elements, indicates the merging of each of the elements in the corresponding *tanmātras*. It is therefore taken that each *bhūta* or gross element is caused by its corresponding subtle element. That is, *pṛthivī* or earth is caused by the *gandha-tanmātra* or the subtle element of odour; *jala* or water by the *rasa-tanmātra* or the subtle water element, etc. The difference between *tanmātra* and *bhūta* is one of degree. The former constitutes the fine or subtle element (*sūkṣma*),

[3]Tait II *ākāśād vāyuḥ; vāyor agniḥ; agner āpaḥ; adbhyaḥ pṛthivī.*

[4]Sub II. *ākāśam indriyeṣu, indriyāṇi tanmātreṣu; tanmātrāṇi bhūtādau līyante. Bhūta* is interpreted as *ahaṁkāra-tattva*. See the commentary of Sudarśana Sūri, p. 602 and p. 624. See also SS I-12, pp. 15-16.

whereas the latter stands for the gross form of the element (*sthūla*). What is a subtle state as *tanmātra* becomes manifest as *bhūta*. It is comparable to the state between the fermented milk and the curds. When milk is fermented it takes some time for it to form into curd, and the stage between the milk and curd is called *kalala*. *Tanmātra* is like *kalala* representing a subtle stage of evolution between the earlier *bhūta* and the later one.[5]

Jainas do not admit that there is a permanent and specific order in the evolution of cosmic matter into various modifications. In place of *prakṛti*, they accept a cosmic substance known as *pudgala* which undergoes a variety of modifications not necessarily in any particular order. The order depends upon the accessory factors which are concerned with their causation. The physical objects in the universe do not possess any specific characteristics. Nor do they move in any specific order. One and the same substance could assume different modifications. *Pṛthivi*, for instance, possesses different characteristics such as softness, hardness and liquidity. Soft cotton grows out of hard earth. From the same earth very hard metals are obtained. When solid butter is melted it turns into liquid form. On the basis of these facts, Jainas contend that it is more appropriate to accept that earth, water fire and air can undergo modifications in any order.

If it is the view of the Jainas that only one primary substance undergoes different modification, it is acceptable to the Viśiṣṭādvaitin. But what he cannot agree with is that there is no specific order in the evolution for the obvious reason that such a view goes against the teaching of the scripture. The scriptural texts declare in categorical terms that both evolution and dissolution of the universe take place in an order. It is not therefore proper to deny the authoritativeness of the scriptural teachings by merely resorting to logic.[6]

As against this it is argued that the very Vedas offer conflicting views regarding the classification as well as the order of evolution. Thus the Atharvaṇa śruti points out that of the twenty-four *tattvas*, eight are of the nature of *prakṛti* and the rest are *vikṛtis*.[7] Here *prakṛti* means what serves as the cause of

[5]TMK I-12. *tanmātra-bhūta-bhedaḥ kalala-dadhi-nayāt tattvavidbhiḥ kalpitaḥ.*
[6]TMK I-14.
[7]SS I-15, p. 17. *adhīyate hi kecidātharvaṇikāḥ:aṣṭau prakṛtayaḥ ṣoḍaśa vikārā iti.*

another *tattva* and *vikṛti* means that which is not the cause of another *tattva.* According to Sāṅkhya, eleven *indriyas* and five *bhūtas* constitute the *vikṛtis* and the rest are *prakṛtis.*[8] For the Viśiṣṭādvaitin, only the eleven *indriyas* and *pṛthivi* are *vikṛtis* and the rest are *prakṛtis*. Even with regard to the order of evolution there are conflicting statements. The *Subāla Upaniṣad* while describing the order of dissolution speaks of the merger of *ākāśa* in *indriyas* and of *indriyas* in *tanmātras.*[9] In another place, it is said that *agni* comes from *ap* (water), whereas the accepted view is that *ap* comes from *agni*. How then do we decide the matter on the basis of scripture ?

In reply Vedānta Deśika points out that the classification and enumeration of *tattvas* into *prakṛti* and *vikṛti* is not of much relevance as long as the total number of *tattvas* and the order of their evolution remain undisputed. Some attempts have been made to reconcile such apparent conflicts found between what is described in some of the *purāṇas* and in the Sāṅkhya system but philosophically such explanations are not of much significance.[10]

Theory of Pañcikaraṇa

The evolution of *prakṛti* into the five gross elements through various stages in a particular order as outlined above is called *samaṣṭi-sṛṣṭi* or creation of the aggregate universe. This may be regarded as the primary evolution or evolution of *prakṛti* up to the stage of five gross elements. After this stage is reached, the creation of the physical universe with all its diversity starts. This is known as *vyaṣṭi-sṛṣṭi* or creation of the universe of space and matter with all its diversity. This may be regarded as the secondary evolution or the formation of the physical universe. It is done by the admixture of different parts of the five elements in certain proportion. This is technically called *pañcikaraṇa* or quintuplication of the five elements.

This is done as follows : first the aggregate of each of the five elements—*ākāśa*, *vāyu*, *agni*, *jala* and *pṛthivi*—is divided into equal parts; then each half is subdivided into four parts; in the next stage, taking this one-eighth portion of each of the five elements, it is mixed with the half part of each of the *bhūtas*. This means

[8]See *Sāṅkhyakārikā*, verse 3.

[9]Sub II. [10]TMK I-15. *cintā-sāphalya-māndyāt* ... udāsi.

that each element such as *ākāśa* comprises half of that element and one-eighth portion of other four elements. The illustration given below explains the position :

Ākāśa	
Ākāśa	Vāyu
	Agni
	Jala
	Pṛthivi

Vāyu	
Vāyu	Ākāśa
	Agni
	Jala
	Pṛthivi

Agni	
Agni	Ākāśa
	Vāyu
	Jala
	Pṛthivi

Jala	
Jala	Ākāśa
	Vāyu
	Agni
	Pṛthivi

Pṛthivi	
Pṛthiv i	Ākāśa
	Vāyu
	Agni
	Jala

The rest of the creation of the physical universe with all its diversity is made out of the *pañca-bhūtas* or the five elements thus mixed up.

The *Chāndogya Upaniṣad* speaks of the admixture of three elements only (*ap, tejas* and *pṛthivi*).[11] This is known as *trivṛtkaraṇa.* Vedānta Deśika explains that this should not be taken as contradicting the *pañcikaraṇa* theory which has been supported by several other Upaniṣadic texts. The *Chāndogya* śruti refers to the admixture of *bhūtas* at the first stage of evolution (*vyaṣṭi-sṛṣṭi*) and not at the second stage (*samaṣṭi-sṛṣṭi*).

The *pañcikaraṇa* theory is justified by the fact that all objects in the universe including the human body are constituted of all the five elements. All these elements are not, however, present in them in the same proportion. While one or the other element is predominant, others exist in a negligible proportion. In the physical body the element of *pṛthivi* is predominant and it is therefore classified as *pārthiva.* In *jala,* the element of water is predominant, while *pṛthivi* and other elements are negligible. In the same way, *tejas, vāyu* and *ākāśa* are to be understood. Rāmā-

[11]Ch VI-3-3. *hantāham imo tisro-devatāḥ... tāsāṁ trivṛtam trivṛtam ekaikam karavāṇīti.*

nuja accounts for some cases of illusion such as the mirage on the basis of quintuplication theory.

Criticism of Sāṅkhya and Naiyāyika Theories of Evolution

Before we proceed to consider the nature of the other evolutes, we should take note of one important point regarding the evolution of *prakṛti* into the physical universe. According to the Sāṅkhya, *prakṛti* evolves itself into the universe through the various stages as already outlined without the aid of *Īśvara* as its controller. This means that *prakṛti* is the direct material cause of the universe. According to the theory of causality accepted by the Sāṅkhyas, an effect exists in a potential form in its cause and the causation is the manifestation of what is unmanifest. The Vedāntins have rejected this theory of evolution as philosophically unsound. Evolution of *prakṛti* on its own account is untenable because a non-intelligent entity cannot evolve itself in such a perfect order except with the control or guidance of an intelligent agent. To meet this criticism, the Sāṅkhyas argue that the presence of *puruṣa*, the eternal individual self, should be sufficient to start the evolution of *prakṛti* into *mahat*. Such an explanation is also considered unsatisfactory. *Puruṣa* in the Sāṅkhya system is present eternally and it is difficult to account for the origin of the evolutionary process at any particular point of time on that basis. The author of the *Vedānta-sūtras* has advanced elaborate arguments to disprove the theory that *prakṛti* is the cause of the universe.[12] On the strength of the Upaniṣadic texts, the Viśiṣṭādvaitin maintains the view that Brahman as the inner controller of *prakṛti* and its evolutes causes evolution from one stage to another.[13]

The Naiyāyikas who uphold the atomic theory do not admit *prakṛti* as an independent and eternally real entity apart from the five gross elements. According to them, the *paramāṇus* or the

[12]VS II-2-1 and 9.

[13]TMK I-16. *sa paraḥ hetutattvaiḥ śarīrī (san) niśśeṣam kāryatattvam janayati.* See also RB II-3-14, p. 569. The *Chāndogya Upaniṣad* (VI-2-3) says: 'The *tejas* thought, may I be many.' 'The *ap* thought, may I be many.' What is non-sentient (*acetana*) cannot have the function of thinking (*Īkṣaṇa*). Therefore these texts signify, according to Rāmānujā, that Brahman as embodied in *tejas*, *ap*, etc. as its inner controller, wills to become many. *Īkṣaṇam tattatśarīrakasya parasyaiva brahmaṇa upapadyate.*

atoms which are the eternal, partless, infinitesimal and supra-sensible reals are the material cause of the physical universe. The five gross elements—earth, water, fire, air and *ākāśa*—are only derived from such atoms. Without going into the details of this theory, we may just note here how the process of origination of physical objects takes place. When two atoms (as, for example, of earth) come together, they form a binary compound known as *dvyaṇuka*. Like the primary atoms, it is infinitely small in size and is therefore super-sensuous. Three such binaries suitably adjusted produce a triad known as *tryaṇuka*, which is identified with the dust particle we notice in the sunbeam and is regarded as the visible entity. Its magnitude is finite and all other finite objects are made out of such triads.

This theory has come up for severe criticism at the hands of the Vedāntin. Based on the *Vedānta-sūtra* both Śaṁkara and Rāmānuja have rejected the theory as untenable. The main point of criticism, as stated by Vedānta Deśika, is directed towards the impossibility of atomic combination. When two *paramāṇus* come together, do they combine as a whole or only in parts? If they combine as whole then there is complete interpenetration (one submerging in the other) and as such the *dvyaṇuka* formed out of it is not of bigger magnitude. How then could such *dvyaṇukas* produce the things bigger than themselves? If, on the contrary, atoms combine in parts, then the atom must be regarded as possessing parts. For the Naiyāyikas atoms are partless. In the case of two physical objects, we can speak of their coming together only in respect of part only. But such a possibility is ruled out in respect of atoms which do not possess any spatial property. If the combination of the two atoms cannot be explained satisfactorily, it is not possible to regard the atoms as the material cause of the physical universe.[14]

II. NATURE OF THE SENSE ORGANS

After explaining the order of evolution of *prakṛti*, Vedānta Deśika takes up for consideration the nature of the other evolutes since there is some difference of opinion in this regard bet-

[14]TMK I-18. For other criticisms against this theory, see RB II-2-10 and 11.

ween the Viśiṣṭādvaitin and the Nyāya-Vaiśeṣika. We have already noticed that the eleven sense organs including the mind (*manas*) are the products of *sāttvika ahṁkāra*. The Vaiśeṣikas hold the view that the five cognitive sense organs are caused successively by the five gross elements (*pañcabhūtas*) and as such they are physical in character (*bhautika*) rather than psychical.

The following argument is put forward in support of it: 'The visual organ (*cakṣus*) is the product of the element of light (*taijasam*), because it cognises only colour (*rūpa*) and not any other qualities of the elements such as taste, as, for example, the flame of a lamp (*dīpavat*).' By adopting the same kind of argument, it is contended that the tactile organ is made up of air, the gustatory organ of water, the olfactory organ of earth and the auditory organ of ether.

Vedānta Deśika questions the validity of the argument. The Vaiśeṣikas assume that the sense organ is an important and specific instrument (*karaṇa*) for the perception of colour. This is not correct. It constitutes one of the accessories for the apprehension of the quality. In the act of perception many accessories are involved such as the subject, object, light, sense organs, sense contact and absence of obstruction, and it is therefore difficult to single out the visual organ as the most important *karaṇa* or instrument for perception of colour. Merely on the basis of the fact that the visual organ cognises only colour, it is wrong to suppose that this sense faculty is constituted of the same element, viz. *tejas*, because the visual organ is not by itself responsible for the perception of colour. The lamp which is cited as an example is only an accessory cause and not the direct means for the perception of colour. It is therefore not correct to assume that the sense organs are made up of the same stuff as their corresponding physical elements, ignoring the scriptural testimony which asserts that these are the products of *ahaṁkāra tattva*.

Regarding the number of *indriyas*, there is a difference of opinion between the Naiyāyika and the Vedāntin. While the latter maintains that *indriyas* are eleven including *manas*, the former only accepts six *indriyas*, the five cognitive organs and mind, and do not consider the conative organs as *indriyas*. This is not a correct stand, argues Vedānta Deśika. Whatever is the basis on which the cognitive organs are admitted, the same principle holds good for the conative organs. If the cognitive organs are treated as *indriyas* because of the reason that these serve as *karaṇa* or means of knowledge, the same reason holds good for the conative organs since these too serve as *karaṇa* or means of physical movements. If it be possible to account for physical movements without the acceptance of *karmendriyas* on the basis of the respective physical organ, this should hold good even in the case of the *jñānendriyas*. Then it would follow that the concerned physical counterpart of the sense organ, as for instance, the mere eye balls in the case of vision causes the apprehension of colour. But we often find that the mere physical aspect of the organ such as presence of eye balls do not cause the vision and it is therefore necessary to postulate some subtle organ of the centre of sight as the real sense organ. The same explanation holds good even for the conative organs. An individual may have legs but he may not have the movement. As in the case of the cognitive organs, even for conative organs there are subtle organs which really cause the movements of their physical components. Realising this truth, the Vedic seers have stated that *indriyas* are eleven.

Manas or mind, as already pointed out, is an internal sense organ. In the Sāṅkhya system the internal organ known as *antaḥkaraṇa* is described as three-fold, viz. *manas* or mind, *buddhi* or intellect and *ahaṁkāra* or ego.[15] Each one has a different function and as such they are regarded as three different faculties or parts of the psychic apparatus. The Yoga system admits an additional faculty known as *citta*. Both these theories are not correct, says Vedānta Deśika, because scriptural texts relating to the evolution of *indriyas* do not speak of such distinct entities other than *manas*. If there are some references in the scripture to both *manas* and *citta*, these are not intended to imply that they are distinct faculties. The postulation of such a theory is unwarranted. *Buddhi*, *ahaṁkāra* and *citta* are different states or functions of the mind. The śurti text[16] itself acknowledges this fact and says that *kāma* (desire), *saṅkalpa* (will), *vicikitsā* (doubt) *śraddhā* (faith), etc. are only mental modifications. There is only one internal sense organ, viz. *manas* and the same has different

[15]See SS I-37. *antaḥkaraṇaṁ trividham*.

[16]Br III-5-3. *kāmas-saṅkalpaḥ . . . sarvaṁ mana eva*.

functions or modifications in the form of *buddhi*, ego and *citta*.[17]

One other important point in regard to the sense organs which is emphasised in the Viśiṣṭādvaita system is that the *indriyas* are not merely the external physical organs but the subtle sense faculties which are monadic in character (*aṇu*).[18] The basis for such a theory is that the Upaniṣads speak of the exit of the *indriyas* from the body along with the *jiva* after the death of a person. If *indriyas* are all-pervasive (*vibhu*), as some believe, their exit from the body along with *jiva* is inconceivable. What is *vibhu* cannot have movement. For the same reason they cannot be of the size of the body (*madhyama-parimāṇa*). If they were of the size of the body, they should be destroyed along with the physical body.

That *manas* is atomic is also proved by the fact that, even though all the five *indriyas* have connection with their corresponding external objects, the latter are not comprehended simultaneously but, on the other hand, knowledge of the respective objects takes place only in succession. This is due to the fact that mind being atomic in character is not connected with all the *indriyas* at the same time. If, on the contrary, mind were all pervasive or if it occupied the span of the body, then the cognition by all the five sense organs should arise at one moment. This is not so. Mind is therefore *aṇu* in character.

If *indriyas* are atomic, how do they cognise objects which are far from them? The *indriyas* operate through their *vṛttis*.[19] *Vṛtti* is the outflow of the energy of the sense organ which is generated by the respective element, as for example, light (*tejas*), in the case of visual organ and *ākāśa* for the auditory organ.[20] It moves out almost with the speed of light and grasps its objects. Thus the *indriyas* comprehend the objects, lying near and also at a distance through their *vṛttis*. They are capable of grasping a vast area and as such their potential power is extensive. It is in this

[17]TMK I-37. *manasaḥ vṛtti-vaicitrya-yogāt.* See also RB II-4-5. *adhyavasāyābhimāna-cintā-vṛtti-bhedāt mana eva buddhy-ahaṁkāra-citta śabdair vyapadiśyate.*

[18]The term *aṇu* is used in the sense of *sūkṣmatva* or subtle in character and not in the sense of smallest dimension.

[19]TMK I-39.

[20]*Ibid. vṛttiḥ āpyāyanārthaiḥ bhūtaiḥ jātaḥ prasarpaḥ.* This theory differs from that of the Sāṅkhyas. According to the latter *vṛtti* transforms itself in the form of the object, whereas for the Viśiṣṭādvaitin *vṛtti* only comes into direct contact with the object. What reveals the object is the *jñāna* or knowledge through the sense organs.

sense that the Upaniṣadic text describes *indriyas* as *ananta* which means that they are infinite in their scope but not *vibhu* or all-pervasive.[21]

How does the auditory organ (*śrotrendriya*) grasp the sound which emanates at a distance? Two explanations are offered in this regard. According to one view, which is held by the Sāṅkhyas, the auditory organ grasps sound through its *vṛtti* which is the space extending outside the ear. Though the organ of hearing is inside the ears, the space outside it, which is all-pervasive, connects the sound with the auditory organ. In whatever direction the sound emanates, the *vṛtti* flows in that direction, and this enables the auditory organ to grasp the sound.

The second view which is favoured by Vedānta Deśika offers a better explanation. The sound arising at a distance reaches one's ears in the form of sound waves, and as it comes in contact with the ear the auditory organ grasps it. When the sound is first produced, it takes a few seconds for it to travel, and as it traverses from a distance it becomes gradually weaker and weaker. If the auditory organ reached the area through its *vṛtti*, it should then be able to hear the sound with its full intensity. But this is not so. The sound heard at a distance is of less intensity than at the spot where it was produced. This is due to the fact that, as the sound travels from a distance in the form of sound waves, its intensity becomes gradually diminished. He therefore concludes that the auditory organ grasps the sound when it reaches the ears.[22]

III. THEORY OF SPACE (ĀKĀŚA)

Ākāśa is the first of the five gross elements caused by the *śabda tanmātra*, which is an evolute of *tāmasa ahaṁkāra*. As a product of the *ahaṁkāra tattva*, it is not eternal (*nitya*), nor is it infinite (*vibhu*). The Vaiśeṣikas on the contrary hold the view that *ākāśa* is *nitya* and *vibhu*. They adopt the following inference in support of the theory : '*Ākāśa* is *nitya* because it is partless.' This view is rejected on the ground that the syllogistic argument suffers from the logical fallacy. Because an entity is partless (*niravaya dravya*), it does not necessarily follow that it should be *nitya*. The *paramāṇu*

[21] TMK I-39. See also RB II-4-6. [22] SS I-41, p. 49.

for the Viśiṣṭādvaitin is partless but is *anitya*. What is partless can also be *anitya*. Further, śruti declares that *ākāsa* is produced. Thus the Upaniṣad says: *ākāśa* is caused.[23] What is well established by śruti cannot be contradicted by inference. The former is of greater validity than the latter. The śruti also points out that *vāyu* or air is caused by *ākāśā* (*ākāśāt vāyuḥ*). *Vāyu* is a corporeal substance and its cause also should be of the same character. This goes against the Vaiśeṣika theory.

Ākāśa as a separate element is not accepted by the Buddhists and Cārvākas. For them it is the mere absence of obstruction (*āvaraṇābhāva*). It does not have any specific characteristic because it is non-existent (*tuccha*).

This theory is not correct, contends Vedānta Deśika. *Ākāśa* manifests itself as a positive entity and it does exist. It is not the mere non-existence of obstruction. Non-existence (*abhāva*) presupposes the knowledge of its counter-correlate and knowledge of its location. That is, when we speak of non-existence, the question arises of what and where. Non-existence being a relative term, it becomes meaningless if it is not related to its counter-correlate and a particular location. In the case of *ākāśa* we do not have either the knowledge of its counter-correlate or its location. If *ākāśa* is regarded as *āvaraṇābhāva*, as long as *avaraṇa* which is the counter-correlate of *abhāva* exists, the *āvaraṇābhāva* cannot exist at the same time. *Ākāśa* cannot therefore be mere *āvaraṇābhāva.*

Ākāśa, according to the Viśiṣṭādvaitin, is perceived by the visual organ. That it is perceptible is evident from the fact that we see the blue sky. The open space is *ākāśa*, and we perceive the open space when we notice the birds moving in the sky or when we look inside a well.

It is argued that the sky is devoid of colour and touch, and as such it cannot be perceived by the visual and tactile organs. The sense organs of smell, hearing and taste are not capable of grasping a substance. The mind too which is an internal organ cannot congnise the external object directly. Therefore, *ākāśa* cannot be the object of perception.

This view is not valid. The experience of sky is so obvious to perception that it cannot be denied. It is not necessary that an object should possess colour in order to be cognised by means of

[23]Tait II. *ākāśaḥ sambhūtaḥ*. See RB II-3-2. *asti tu ākāśasya utpattiḥ.*

perception. Saṁkhyā or number, for instance, is devoid of colour, but nevertheless it is admitted to be the object of perception. If we accept the *pañcikaraṇa* theory which we have already explained, subtle particles of *pṛthivi* element are also present in *ākāśa*. Even though the sky by virtue of its true character is colourless, it looks blue because of the presence of material elements in it. This is explained by the analogy of a piece of white cloth which is soiled with dirt. The dirt is not the true colour of the cloth, but still it enables us to perceive the cloth. Even though the whiteness of the cloth is not visible, the cloth becomes visible along with the soiled colour.

The Vaiśeṣikas attempt to prove the existence of *ākāśa* by means of inference in an indirect way. *Śabda* or sound for Vaiśeṣika is a *guṇa* or quality. What is a *guṇa* should necessarily inhere in a substance. Of the nine substances admitted in this system, the eight substances such as *pṛthivi*, etc. cannot be its substrate. Only the ninth *dravya* which is *ākāśa* should be the substrate or *ādhāra* for *śabda*. Such a kind of inference is known as *pariśeṣānumāna* (deduction by a process of elimination).

The argument, according to Vedānta Deśika, does not hold good as it suffers from logical fallacies. If a *guṇa* should necessarily inhere in a substance, then the Vaiśeṣikas, who reckon twenty-four *guṇas*, should postulate the existence of twenty-four substances, one for each of the *guṇas*. Thus the very basis of the argument adopted by them is wrong. *Śabda* actually is a *guṇa* or attribute of *ākāśa*, one of the five gross elements, and there is no need to adopt an inference to prove the existence of *ākāśa* which, as already explained, is obvious to perceptual experience.

The Vaiśeṣikas use another argument to prove the existence of *ākāśa*. Thus the *Vaiśesika-śūtra* says : 'The act of entering and coming out (of a room) is the proof of *ākāśa*.'[24] The implication of it is that unless there be an open space, neither is it possible to enter into the room nor come out of it and such an open space is *ākāśa*.

This is not a sound view. *Ākāśa* being all-pervasive, it exists inside the room even without the act of one going in or coming out of the room. It cannot be said that because of the obstruction in the form of a wall on the four sides, exit or entry is not possible. In that case, the cause of exit or entry of a person to

[24]*niṣkramaṇam praveśanam iti ākāśa-liṅgam.*

the room is not so much due to the presence of *ākāśa* but the absence of obstruction. The argument adopted by the Vaiśeṣika is thus defective and inference cannot therefore prove conclusively the existence of *ākāśa*. Perception is the *pramāṇa* in support of it.

Besides *ākāśa* as an ethereal substance, the Vaiśeṣikas admit *dik* as a separate substance. *Dik*[25] is one, all-pervasive and eternal substance. Though it is one, it is regarded as different on account of *upādhi*, such as the movement of the sun in the sky. Thus the direction associated with the rising sun is regarded as east; when the same is associated with the setting sun, it is called west. On the basis of the *Meru* (a mythological mountain), north and south are determined.

Vedānta Deśika questions the soundness of postulating *dik* as a separate substance other than *ākāśa* or ether. If on the basis of sun's position in the sky the positional relations such as east and west could be explained, there is no need to postulate a separate substance as *dik* other than the *upādhi* for the purpose. The sky itself with the help of such *upādhis* can account for the different directional relations. Even for the purpose of explaining the spatial relations such as proximity and distance, *dik* alone cannot do it; *upādhi* is needed for the purpose. *Ākāśa* with the help of *upādhis* could also account for spatial relations. It is not therefore necessary to postulate *dik* as a separate category. Further, among the ontological categories mentioned by the sacred texts, *dik* is not included unlike *kāla* or time.[26]

IV. NATURE OF OTHER ELEMENTS

The Elements of Vāyu

Vāyu or air is the next important physical element in the cosmic evolution. There are a few disputed points with regard to *vāyu* and these are discussed by Vedānta Deśika. According to the Vaiśeṣikas, *vāyu* is not directly perceived. What we comprehend is the quality of touch (*sparśa*). *Vāyu* is inferred from the fact that *sparśa* is a *guṇa* which must inhere in a substrate

[25]*Dik* is normally understood as direction such as East, West, North, South, etc. For the Nyāya-Vaiśeṣikas it means the *space*, as distinct from *ākāśa* or ether. For the Viśiṣṭādvaitin *ākāśa* itself is space.

[26]TMK I-50.

and that substrate is *vāyu*. *Vāyu* is also a colourless entity, and it cannot therefore be the object of visual perception. The assumption is only that which has a *rūpa* or colour can be grasped by the visual organ.

Vedânta Deśika questions the soundness of these arguments. When we see a lamp with the flame, we make the judgment 'lamp burns', and this experience is admitted as perceptual. The experience in the form 'wind blows' is similar to it, and it should also be accepted as perceptual. It cannot be said that in this case we only grasp the quality of touch but not the *vāyu* which is its substrate, and that the latter is only inferred on the basis of the fact that a quality must necessarily inhere in a substance. If that were the case, the apprehension of a jar by a blind person through touch would have to be treated as an inferential knowledge. This is not acceptable even to the Vaiśeṣikas. It is admitted that the same object can be seen as well as touched. The fact that an object is not seen by eyes but experienced by other sense organs should not rule out the possibility of its being perceptual.

Vâyu may be colourless (*rūpa-śūnya*) and as such it may not be seen by the eyes. Nevertheless it can be an object of perception insofar as it is grasped through the tactile organ. When both the visual as well as tactile organ can apprehend a substance (*dravya*), it is inappropriate to say that the tactile organ grasps only the quality of touch and not the substance (*vāyu*). If *vāyu* is not admitted as an object of perception on the ground that it is devoid of colour, then fire too should be regarded as imperceptible because it does not possess the quality of taste. Fire, though it is devoid of odour and taste, is cognised both by the visual and tactile organs. In the same way, *vāyu* is also known through tactile perception. There is no need to resort to inference to prove its existence.[27]

It may be asked if *vāyu* is cognised by touch, then its characteristics such as number and dimension should also be known by means of touch. This is acceptable to the Viśiṣṭādvaitin. When there is a big storm, we do experience that it is one and also that it is heavy. It is no doubt true that only a few qualities of air are experienced. But it is not necessary that all the qualities

[27]TMK I-51.

of the entity should be known when its cognition takes place. The Vaiśeṣikas have to accept this position because in the case of individual self all its characteristics are not known along with self-knowledge.[28]

While considering the nature of *vāyu*, the question is raised whether *prāṇavāyu*, the vital breath, is an independent *tattva* or whether it is only a modification of the gross element of *vāyu*. On the strength of the scriptural text, Vedānta Deśika rules out that *prāṇa* is not mere *vāyu*.[29] The Upaniṣadic text says : 'From this arises *prāṇa*, *manaś*, all *indriyas*, ether, *vāyu*, etc.[30] As *prāṇa* and *vāyu* are mentioned separately in the same text, the two are not identical. Nor is it a function (*kriyā*) of *vāyu*, because it is mentioned along with *dravyas*.[31] That which is a *dravya* cannot be a function or quality. It is not even an independent *tattva* like *tejas*, because in the enumeration of the twenty-four *tattvas*, *prāṇa* does not figure.[32] It is therefore concluded that *vāyu* itself assumes different modifications and *prāṇa-vāyu* is one such modified form of *vāyu*, in the same way as water in the cloud becomes solid hail-stones (*ghana jalakara*). The same *prāṇa-vāyu* assumes ten different functions in our body and is called by different names such as *prāṇa*, *apāna*, *samāna*, *vyāna*, *udāna*, etc.[33]

The word *prāṇa* is synonymous with the word *indriya* (sense organ). Besides, *prāṇa* is found very useful to *jīva*. In view of this, some believe that *prāṇa* is a special sense organ (*indriya-viśeṣaḥ*). This is not a correct view. Even though the word *prāṇa* is applicable to both *indriya* and *prāṇa-vāyu*, it is not an *indriya*. The primary import of the word *prāṇa* is not *indriya*. It is only in a secondary sense that *prāṇa* is understood as *indriya*. Further, *prāṇa* cannot be regarded as *indriya* merely on the ground that it is serviceable to *jīva*. In that case even the physical body which is more serviceable to *jīva* would have to be accepted as *indriya*. *Indriyas* are the evolutes of *sāttvika ahaṁkāra*. *Prāṇa* is not such an evolute, and it is not therefore an *indriya*.[34]

[28]TMK I-52. [29]TMK I-53. *na prāṇo 'vāyumātram*.

[30]Mund 2-1-3. *etasmāj-jāyate (prāṇo) manaḥ sarvendriyāṇi ca; khaṁ vāyurjyotirāpaḥ pṛthivī....*

[31] See VS II-4-8. *na vāyukriye pṛthag upadeśāt.*

[32]See RB II-4-9. *nāyam bhūtaviśeṣaḥ.*

[33]TMK I-53.

[34]TMK I-54. See also RB II-2-16.

The Element of Agni

Agni or fire is the next evolute in the order of five gross elements caused by the corresponding *tanmātras*. There is no difference of opinion with regard to the nature of this *tattva* between the Viśiṣṭādvaitin and other schools except on two minor points. One issue is whether the *agni* in the human body, which is described as *vaiśvānarāgni* (the digestive fire or energy), is the same as *jīva*. The second point is whether the light (*prabhā*) radiated by the flame (*dīpa*) of the lamp is a quality of the *dīpa*.

With regard to the first point, Vedānta Deśika says that the *vaiśvānarāgni* is material (*jaḍa*) in nature and as such it cannot be the *jīva*. However, as in the case of *vāyu*, it is very useful to *jīva* since it is believed to help in the digestion of food with the assistance of *prāṇa* and *apāna vāyu*.[35]

As regards the second point, he clarifies that *prabhā* is a quality (*dharma*) of the *dīpa* and the two are distinct. The justification for holding this view is that light manifests itself as a quality of flame. We also notice the brightness of the light when it is closer to the flame, and when the same is farther it becomes dimmer.[36] According to the Naiyāyikas, the two are not distinct. The light itself radiates in the form of minute particles and on this basis the brightness or dimness of the light is accounted for. As the particles spread further and further, the light becomes dimmer. If the particles are closer to the lamp, the light is brighter.

Vedānta Deśika does not agree with this view. *Prabhā* is the *dharma* or quality of *dīpa*. This is similar to the lustre of the diamond. In the case of the diamond, its lustre does not spread out in the form of minute particles. If that were so, it would be subject to destruction. The lustre is the *dharma* of the diamond. In the same way, it is appropriate to regard the *prabhā* as a *dharma* of the *dīpa*. *Dīpa* or flame is a substance (*dravya*) constituted of the element of fire (*agni*)—and *Prabhā* or light is its *dharma*.[37]

One another minor point which is considered in this connection is whether or not gold as a metal is constituted of *tejas*.

[35]TMK I-55. See also BG XV-14.

[36]TMK I-56. *ekā prabhā dharmaḥ bhāti.*

[37]TMK I-56.

According to Vaiśeṣika, it is a *dravya* consisting of the element of *tejas*. The Viśiṣṭādvaitin does not agree with this view. Gold is hard and has weight. Its colour is like that of earth. It therefore contains predominantly the earth element (*pārthiva*).

The Element of Pṛthivī

After *agni* comes *ap* or water, but there are no disputed points to discuss regarding water. Next in order comes *pṛthivī* or earth. With regard to *pṛthivī*, Vedānta Deśika takes up for discussion only one issue relating to *tamas* or darkness. Vaiśeṣikas believe that *tamas* is not a substance because it is a negative concept (*abhāva-rūpa*) meaning the non-existence of light. The Viśiṣṭādvaitin does not agree with this view because *tamas* is a material substance (*pārthiva-dravya*)—a substance constituted of *pṛthivī* element. He advances two arguments in support of his view. First, *tamas* possesses a dark blue colour which is the special characteristic of earth. Secondly, it has movement and is subject to changes such as becoming thicker or thinner. It is not merely a quality in the form of dark blueness, as some believe. Because what is a quality cannot subsist by itself but must inhere in a substance Besides, as a quality it cannot have the changes in the form of becoming thicker or thinner. *Tamas* is therefore a *dravya* or a substance.[38]

A few objections may be raised against this theory. *Tamas* cannot be moved from one place to another like a jar, and it cannot therefore be an independent substance. Against this it is replied that *tamas*, though not an independent substance, is a *dravya* dependent on something, like the shadow whose movement is controlled by the objects to which it belongs (*chāyāvat-pāratantryam*).

The second objection is that if *tamas* is constituted of *pṛthivī* it should have some hardness in it and be capable of being felt by touch. In reply it is said that it is not necessary that *tamas* in order to be material should have hardness in it. The lustre of an emerald stone possesses the green colour but it is not open to touch. In the same way, *tamas* which is obvious to perception cannot be denied even though it is devoid of touch.

The third argument is that physical objects need light in order

[38]TMK I-60.

to be seen. If *tamas* were a substance, we should have needed the help of light for its cognition. But *tamas* is seen without light and therefore it cannot be a substance. This objection is set aside on the ground that physical objects can be seen even without light. Thus, for instance, a person who has applied a special ointment (*añjana*) to the eyes can see objects even in darkness. An owl can see clearly anything in darkness without the aid of light. In the same way, darkness can be perceived without the aid of light and it is a material substance.[39]

Vedānta Deśika further points out that *tamas* is not of the nature of pure negation (*abhāva*). Darkness is always perceived in a positive form as of dark colour. Though there is absence of light wherever darkness is present, it is not a mere non-existence of light. It is more than that because we perceive it as dark colour. The dark colour seen in darkness is not an illusion. If that were so, then at some later stage somebody should get an experience in the form that it is not dark colour as in the case of illusion of snake in a rope. Even if it is assumed that dark colour is an illusion, then darkness should also have appeared as of some other colour. The fact that only dark blue colour is noticed by all where darkness exists cannot be a case of illusion.

The theory of the Viśiṣṭādvaitin is also supported by the scripture. The śruti text states that in the state of dissolution there was neither darkness nor light.[40] *Bhāva* (existence) and *abhāva* (non-existence) are contradictory. Both cannot be either asserted together or denied. Light and darkness are mutually opposed and it is not possible to say that either both exist or both do not exist. But the sacred texts speak of non-existence of both at the same time during the state of dissolution. The implication of this is that *tamas* and *jyotis* referred to in the text are two contrary substances and not contradictories. In other words, *tamas* should be regarded as a positive entity and not mere non-existence of light, and it can therefore coexist with light. The same śruti text further says that both *tejas* and *tamas* are *śarira* for *Īśvara*.[41]

[39] *Ibid.*

[40] SS I-62, p. 64. *nāsīt tamo jyotirabhūn na cānyat.*

[41] Br V-7-17-18. *yasya tejaḥ śarīram; yasya tamaḥ śarīram.*

V. THE THEORY OF TIME (KĀLA)

Kāla is one of the six *dravyas* admitted in the Viśiṣṭādvaita system. It is an independent and real substance, enjoying the same status as *prakṛti*. It is not part of *prakṛti*, as is the case with the Sāṅkhyas. It exists along with *prakṛti*. It has neither a beginning nor an end. This means that it is *nitya*, like *jīva* and *prakṛti*. But it is not outside the ultimate Reality but is coexistent with Brahman. It is infinite in nature (*vibhu*). Like *prakṛti* it is *jaḍa* (non-sentient), and as a primary substance it also undergoes modifications in the form of moments, minutes, hours, days, months, years, etc. In fact, what we regard as time in terms of hours, days, weeks, etc. are modifications or different states of the one infinite *kāla* (*akhaṇḍa-kāla*). The above theory is developed by the Viśiṣṭādvaitin on the strength of scriptural texts, as will be evident from the criticisms offered against the views of other schools of thought and particularly those of Nyāya-Vaiśeṣika.

According to some, it should be possible to account for the variations of time on the basis of other factors such as the movement of the sun in the sky, and it is not therefore necessary to postulate time as a separate entity. Vedānta Deśika does not agree with this view. As pointed out by the smṛti text,[42] even after dissolution of the entire universe (including the sun, sky, etc.) *kāla* exists and it is not subject to either destruction or origination. Like *prakṛti* and *jīva*, *kāla* is also eternal and an entity different from Brahman.[43] *Kāla* is not the same as *Īśvara*, though it is stated in the *Gītā* and *Viṣṇupurāṇa* that Bhagavān is *kāla*.[44] Such statements are to be understood to imply that *Paramātman* is the inner controller (*antaryāmi*) of *kāla*. This signifies that *Īśvara* and *kāla* are distinct but inherently related like the body to the soul. In view of this in the *Gītā* Lord Kṛṣṇa says: 'I am *kāla*.' Besides, *kāla* is mentioned separately along with other sentient and non-sentient entities in the universe.

According to some, *kāla tattva* is *anitya*, and like *mahat* and other evolutes of *prakṛti* it is subject to origin and destruction. This view is not accepted by the Viśiṣṭādvaitin. Anyone who

[42]VP I-2-26. *anādirbhagavān kālo nāntosya dvija vidyate.*
[43]TMK I-65. *prakṛti-puruṣavad brahmaṇaḥ anyat rūpam iti munibhiḥ nirdiṣṭaḥ.*
[44]BG XI-32. *kālo'smi.* VP 1-2-26. *anādirbhagavān kālaḥ.*

says *kāla* is *anitya* will have to admit that *kāla* did not exist before it was produced, and similarly it ceases to exist after it is destroyed. If time were produced, it would imply that it was non-existent prior to the production. Similarly, if time were destroyed, it should be non-existent after destruction. The very concept 'prior to the origin of *kāla*' involves the notion of time. Unless the time factor is admitted, it is not possible to speak of anything prior to the origin of time. If this be admitted, then the statement that time did not exist prior to its origin would amount to self-contradiction. The same kind of self-contradiction arises with regard to the expression 'after *kāla* is destroyed'. The concept 'after' also implies the notion of time.

There are a few stray statements in the purāṇas describing that *kāla* was brought into existence by *Īśvara*. Vedānta Deśika explains that such statements are to be understood in the sense that the physical objects with which *kāla* is associated are produced. If such an interpretation were not accepted, the same self-contradiction referred to above would arise even with regard to *Īśvara*. If it is said that *kāla* is produced by *Īśvara*, it would presuppose the notion of time prior to its production. If existence of time prior to its production is admitted, it cannot be said that it was produced. *Kāla* therefore exists eternally (*nitya*).

Time is directly perceived as a quality of all perceived objects.[45] The Vaiśeṣikas maintain the view that time is only inferable. This view is rejected by the Viśiṣṭādvaitin. When an object is perceived, it is also known as characterised by a quality. The quality that characterises an object also reveals that particular object is different from another one. Thus, for instance, in the case of a blue jar, the blue colour of the jar distinguishes it from a brown jar. In the same way, when we make the statement that an object is done in a moment, the time element associated with that object reveals that it is different from another object which has taken a day to be done. The judgment 'pot is here' shows that pot is conditioned by a specific space. Similarly, the statement 'pot exists now' reveals that pot is qualified by a particular time factor. In all such cognitions of objects characterised by time factors, time is also perceived along with the object seen.[46]

[45]TMK I-68. *kālaḥ adhyakṣāvaseyaḥ*. [46]*Ibid.*

It may be argued that all our experiences relate to the present and as such in the cognition of objects by perception there is no notion of time as before and after. Thus, there is no direct perception of time. In reply to this it is stated that when an object is seen in the form 'I see this', it becomes known as belonging to the present time. Just as the object is known by means of perception, the present time in which it exists also becomes perceptible.[47]

It is contended that the time factor involved when we say later and earlier differentiating an younger brother from an elder brother is not directly perceived but is only inferred. Time cannot therefore be perceptible. Against this argument, Vedānta Deśika explains that *paratva* (later) and *aparatva* (earlier) are the mere association of the notion of time with the persons concerned. The person who is connected with longer span of time is called the older brother (*para*); the person connected with shorter span of time is regarded as the younger (*apara*). This may be a case of inference for others. But the parents of the younger and older children do have direct experience of the time factor associated with them.

Though time is one and infinite, it is regarded as conditioned and divisible into many units in the form of minute, hour, day, week, month, year, etc. only due to the conditioning objects such as the movement of the sun. This is similar to the one and the same substance appearing as many and different in respect of the various states it passes through (*avasthā-bheda*). This is explained on the analogy of *ākāśa* which, though one and all-pervasive, is regarded as many because of the conditioning objects. Similarly, on account of *upādhi*, *kāla*, though it is one and infinite, is regarded as many.

There is another view ascribed to Yādavaprakāśa, according to which *kāla* is beginningless and endless but continuously transforms itself through moments by which the divisions of time as hours, days and nights can be spanned, through which again the transformation of all changeable objects can be measured.[48] In this view, the conditions are relative from the point of view of each person, who collects the passing time units and forms his own conception of minutes, hours and days from his own point of calculation, according to his own needs.

[47]TMK I-68. [48]See SS I-69, p. 69.

If *kāla* itself undergoes modifications into many time units, is there any need for the acceptance of limiting conditions to account for the different time units? Vedānta Deśika answers this question in the affirmative. Even though *kāla* is considered to undergo transformation into moments, etc. the modification cannot take place in an orderly manner without a cause. The limiting adjuncts (*upādhi*) are necessary for the modification of one infinite time into parts.

Kāla, though it is conceived in terms of moments, hours, etc. is eternal in itself. Eternal means that it has neither a beginning nor an end. It is thus co-existent with God. It is the material cause with reference to its own modifications and is the efficient cause with reference to everything else.[49] The all-pervasiveness of God does not affect *kāla* being all-pervasive because the two are coexistent.

VI. THE DOCTRINE OF NITYA-VIBHŪTI

We have seen how *prakṛti* or the cosmic matter characterised by the three *guṇas* is the basic source of all the things in the universe, both mental and physical. Besides the cosmic matter, Viśiṣṭādvaita Vedānta admits the existence of transcendental matter which is known as *nitya-vibhūti*. It is also named as *śuddha-sattva* implying that it is a spiritual substance characterised only by unalloyed *sattva*, unlike the physical matter which has all the three *guṇas*, *sattva*, *rajas* and *tamas*. In view of this, Vedānta Deśika defines *śuddha-sattva* as that which possesses *sattva* only as different from the substance characterised with the three guṇas.[50] It is also described as that which possesses the quality of *sattva* being at the same time self-luminous in character.[51]

According to the above definitions, the *śuddha-sattva* has two important features. First, it is *ajaḍa* or non-material in the same way as *Īśvara*, *jīva* and *jñāna* are. *Ajaḍa* implies that it is spiritual in character and like *jñāna* it is self-luminous (*svayam-prakāśa*). The second important feature is that *śuddha-sattva* is *acetana* like

[49]SS I-69, p. 70. *nitya-vyāpinaḥ kālasya sarvakāryahetutvam.*
[50]See NS p. 235. *triguṇa-dravya-vyatiriktatve saty sattvavattvam.*
[51]*Ibid. svayaṁprakāśatve saty sattvavattvam.*

dharma-bhūta-jñāna. That is, unlike self it cannot know but manifests itself always for others (*parāk* or *parasmā eva bhāsamāna*). In this respect it is different from *Īśvara* and *jiva* which are self-revealed (*pratyak*).

The main justification for admitting such an entity is that several śruti as well as smṛti texts speak of the existence of an eternal abode (*sthāna-viśeṣa*) which is constituted of *śuddha-sattva*. Thus śruti says : 'The enlightened seers always see the supreme abode of Viṣṇu.'[52] The *Mahābhārata* describes it as celestial abode which is ageless, immeasurable, incomprehensible, primordial and knowable through scriptures.[53] According to Viśiṣṭādvaita, there are eternally released souls, besides the souls which have become free from bondage. *Mukti* in this system is a positive state of existence for the individual souls enjoying the supreme bliss in a supra-mundane place. Religious literature speaks of the existence of eternal abode for *Īśvara*. As we have observed in an earlier chapter, *Īśvara* has a bodily form which is eternal (*nitya*) and not made of *karmic* material stuff but of spiritual substance. The *jivas* also in the state of *mukti* can assume bodies out of free will for purpose of divine service. Such bodies are not the products of *karma* but are made out of the *śuddha-sattva*. According to the Āgamas, the idols which are consecrated in the places of worship are permeated with *śuddha-sattva*, as otherwise they would not be spiritual and worthy of worship. If all these facts are taken into consideration, the acceptance of *nitya-vibhūti* as a separate spiritual substance is justified.

A question may be raised whether the existence of an eternal transcedental matter does not go against Upaniṣadic teaching which emphasises that in the state of dissolution there was nothing other than the Absolute Being. Vedānta Deśika replies that the *nitya-vibhūti* falls outside the purview of the universe to be created. As śruti speaks of the eternal existence of the *nitya-sūris* or the eternally free souls in a supra-mundane existence, the *nitya-vibhūti* is not covered by the scriptural text referring to the creation of the universe.[54] If this interpretation were not

[52] *Yajurveda* VI-5. *tad viṣṇoḥ paramaṁ padaṁ sadā paśyanti sūrayaḥ*. See also Tait II-1. *yo veda nihitam guhāyāṁ parame vyoman. ādityavarṇaṁ tamasaḥ parastāt.*

[53] The *Mahābhārata*. *divyaṁ sthānam ajaram ca aprameyam durvijñeyam ca āgamair gamyam-ādyam*. See also VP I-6-38.

[54] TMK III-61. *sṛṣṭeḥ prāg ekameva iti nigama-vacopi srakṣyamāna-vyapekṣam.*

accepted, then even *māyā*, which is the *upādhi* for Brahman, would become dissolved in the state of dissolution, and consequently there would be no scope for the creation of the universe.

According to some Viśiṣṭādvaitins *śuddha-sattva* is *jaḍa* or material in character. The reason for holding this view is that, in the *Rahasyāgama*,[55] *nitya-vibhūti* is described as of the nature of *jñāna* like that of *Īśvara*, and in view of this, they argue that all the six essential attributes of God should be admitted in respect of it. But such a view does not sound good and hence they maintain that it is to be regarded as *jaḍa*. As regards the description of *nitya-vibhūti* as *jñāna* they contend that it is to be taken in a secondary sense. Vedānta Deśika does not agree with this explanation. It is stated by the sacred texts that *Īśvara* is of the essence of *jñāna*. The *vigraha* or the bodily form of such a Being cannot be made of anything else other than pure *sāttvika* element. Therefore, it is appropriate to accept that *śuddha-sattva* is of the nature of knowledge implying that it is purely spiritual in character.

If as a spiritual entity it is self-luminous, the question arises for whom it manifests itself? The released souls, who are omniscient, can apprehend it even if it be devoid of self-luminosity. The embodied souls do not cognise it in any way as it is transcendental. What is the purpose of its being self-luminous? In reply to this objection, Vedānta Deśika explains that it is not necessary that what is self-luminous by its very nature should be the object of cognition. *Īśvara* is self-luminous but He is not perceived by us as such. In the same way, *suddha-sattva* is also self-luminous, whether or not it is cognised by us. The important point to be noted is that it is necessary to accept the spiritual character of the transcendental substance since the body of *Īśvara* is made out of it. It cannot be a material stuff which is subject to change or mutation.

One other objection is raised against this theory. If the released souls assume body made out of pure *sattva*, it would imply that, as in the case of the material stuff, the *śuddha-sattva* too would be subject to modification or mutation. How then do we claim that it is *nitya* in character?

[55]*Rahasyāgama* is *ekāyana-śākhā*, a branch of the Vedas, and is not extant.

In reply to this objection, Vedānta Deśika points out that the kind of modification to which *śuddha-sattva* is subjected is different in nature from what obtains in the material world. In the latter case, the changes which are constant are due to the variation in the *guṇas* and they are not of permanent nature; whereas in the *nitya-vibhūti* the modification or mutation being spiritual or non-material in character is permanent. Though the terms or concepts used to describe the entities in *nitya-vibhūti* are similar to what is current in the empirical world, there is a wide difference between the two. To make this distinction clear, the spiritual transcendental matter is described as *nitya-vibhūti* or matter without mutability, whereas the cosmic universe is designated as *līlāvibhūti* or matter subject to constant mutation. However, both are the property of *Īśvara* as he is the ground (*ādhāra*) and the inner controller (*niyantā*) for them.

CHAPTER ELEVEN

Fundamental Attributes

We shall consider in this chapter ten fundamental attributes mentioned by Vedānta Deśika under the category of *adravya* as well as the *guṇas* and other *padārthas* (categories) enumerated by Nyāya-Vaiśeṣika system. Though these attributes are generally accepted by the other schools of thought, there is some variation with regard to the description of their nature. We shall give a brief account of each of the attributes as discussed in *Tattva-muktā-kalāpa*, with a view to bringing out their philosophical and logical significance.

I. VIŚIṢṬĀDVAITA THEORY OF ATTRIBUTES

Attributes of Cosmic Matter

Sattva, *rajas* and *tamas* are the three fundamental attributes of *prakṛti* or the cosmic matter. According to the Sāṅkhya system, these are not the qualities but the very components of *prakṛti*. As against this view, the Viśiṣṭādvaitin maintains that *prakṛti* is characterised by these essential qualities (*pradhāna-bhūta-guṇāḥ*). As we have already observed in the chapter on *prakṛti*, the justification for holding such a view is that both the scriptural texts and the *Bhagavad-gītā* describe *sattva*, *rajas* and *tamas* as *guṇas*.[1] If these were regarded as substances, as the Sāṅkhyas believe, then *prakṛti* would be three-fold instead of one entity, and the total number of *tattvas* would be more than twenty-four.

The *guṇas* characterise *prakṛti* which is constantly undergoing modification both in its causal and effect state. In the causal state of *prakṛti* *guṇas* remain in equilibrium even though they are active. In the state of evolution, variation takes place in the *guṇas* by way of one of them being dominant while others

[1]BG XIV-5. *sattvam rajastama iti guṇāḥ prakṛti-sambhavāḥ*. See also RB. *prakṛteḥ svarūpānubandhinaḥ svabhāvaviśeṣāḥ*.

being subdued. In fact, evolution is the disturbed state of the *guṇas*, while dissolution is the state of their equilibrium. Thus, the *guṇas* are present in all the evolutes of the *prakṛti* including the gross physical objects of the universe. *Sattva* stands for whatever is fine or light (*prakāśa*) and causes happiness (*sukha*). *Rajas* represents whatever is active and is the cause of suffering (*duḥkha*). *Tamas* is whatever is heavy and is responsible for ignorance (*moha*). All these facts have been established on the basis of scriptural authority.[2]

Attributes of the Five Elements

Śabda (Sound). The five attributes of the gross elements are *śabda* (sound), *sparśa* (touch), *rūpa* (colour), *rasa* (taste) and *gandha* (odour). Each one of these is cognised by the corresponding sense organ. Though *śabda* is an essential characteristic of *ākāśa* (space), it is also found in all the other elements. Thus, *vāyu* (air) possesses the quality of *śabda* besides *sparśa*; *agni* (fire) has the quality of *śabda* in addition to *sparśa* and *rūpa*; *jala* (water) contains the qualities of *śabda* in addition to *sparśa*, *rūpa* and taste; and *pṛthivi* (earth) possesses all the qualities including *śabda*. The presence of colour in *ākāśa* as noticed in the blue sky is due to the presence of some element of earth in it. Similarly, *vāyu* has odour because of its association with *pṛthivī*. According to the *Pañcīkaraṇa* theory explained in the previous chapter, each element possesses some aspect of the other elements. However, the specific attribute of each element is determined in the process of the evolution itself and it is not produced as a result of its association with other elements.[3]

According to the Naiyāyikas, *śabda* is an exclusive attribute of *ākāśa* only and it is not found in the other four elements. They adopt the following inferential argument in support of their view: *śabda* is not a *guṇa* of any of the other four elements such as *pṛthivi*, because it is only heard through the ears. The assumption of this argument is that *śabda* as a *guṇa* cannot be separated from its substrate which is *ākāśa*. If it were the quality of *pṛthivi*, the auditory organ cannot grasp it. Since there is *ākāśa* inside the auditory organ, it is possible to grasp the sound. *Śabda* is therefore the exclusive attribute (*guṇa*) of *ākāśa*).

[2]SS V-16, p. 271. *te ca . . . śāstra-siddham.* See also BG XIV-6-8.
[3]TMK V-18.

Vedānta Deśika refutes this argument. The inference is fallacious because by the process of elimination (*pariśeṣānumāna*), it cannot be conclusively proved that *śabda* is a *guṇa* of *ākāśa* only. Besides, such a view is in direct conflict with the scriptural texts which point out that other elements besides *ākāśa* possess *śabda*. Thus, *vāyu* is extolled as *śabda*.[4] Even in our ordinary experience, we speak of sound of water, sound of drum, etc. *Śabda* is therefore found in all the five elements.

The Vaibhāṣika school of Buddhists hold the view that *rūpa*, *rasa*, *gandha* and *sparśa* are the only four real entities (*padārthas*) which are technically named as *dhātus*, and that *śabda* which is audible by the organ of hearing is a *dharma* of all these four and not different from them. This view is criticised by Vedānta Deśika. Why is *śabda* non-different from the *dhātus*? Is it because the difference between *śabda* and the *dhātus* is not known or is it due to the fact that the difference is negated by another stronger *pramāṇa*? The former alternative is not tenable because we do have a clear awareness of the distinction between *śabda* as a quality (*ādheya*) and its inherence in a substance (*ādhāra*). Nor is the second alternative correct because there is no *pramāṇa* which contradicts the difference between the two. *Śabda* is therefore a separate attribute.[5]

The Bhāṭṭa school of Mīmāṁsakas hold the view that *śabda* is a *dravya* (substance). The Viśiṣṭādvaitin rejects this on the ground that *śabda* as an attribute is dependent on its substrate, and as such cannot be an independent entity. The śruti and smṛti texts also describe *śabda* as an *avasthā-viśeṣa*—a modification that takes place in the air (*vāyu*). In the order of evolution described by the śruti texts, only the five elements (*pañcabhūtas*) are enumerated and not *śabda* as an independent evolute. *Śabda* is mentioned along with other four qualities.[6]

The Mīmāṁsakas adopt an inferential argument to prove that *śabda* is a *dravya*. '*Śabda* is a *dravya* because it is cognised directly through the contact with sense organs, like any physical object' Vedānta Deśika rejects the argument because the probans (*hetu*) in this syllogism is fallacious. According to the epistemological position of the Viśiṣṭādvaitin, the sense organs cannot

[4]Tait. *namaste vāyo tvameva pratyakṣam brahmāsi.*
[5]TMK V-21.
[6]Tait. *śabda-sparśa-rūpa-rasa-gandhā me śudhyantām....*

have any direct contact (*saṁyoga*) with the qualities of objects. The contact with the qualities takes place only indirectly through the object to which they belong. It may be possible to say that *śabda* is apprehended directly if only it could be established that *śabda* is a *dravya.* The inference advanced by the Mīmāṁsaka cannot prove it, because the *hetu* adopted stands unproved. It is also not correct to say that the ears are of the nature of *ākāśa*, and as such there is direct contact between the auditory organ and *śabda.* The auditory organ, according to the Viśiṣṭādvaitin, is not *ākāśa.* On the contrary, it is one of the eleven sense organs, according to the accepted theory of evolution of cosmic matter.[7]

The Digambara sect of the Jainas upholds the theory that the primal cause of the universe known as *pudgala*, a subtle matter similar to the *paramāṇus* of Nyāya-Vaiśeṣika, evolves itself into the form of *dhvani* (sound) which takes the form of letters (*varṇa*). Such a theory is not proved either by perception or any other *pramāṇa*, says Vedānta Deśika. No other school of thought subscribes to the view that the term *śabda* as commonly used is applicable to the kind of *śabda* conceived by the Jainas. What is audible to the ears is known as *śabda*. It is an attribute of *ākāśa* which is an evolute of cosmic matter.[8]

While discussing the nature of *śabda*, Vedānta Deśika examines the issue whether or not the letters (*varṇa*) are eternal. According to one school of Mīmāṁsā (Kumārila), *śabda* is of two types: one in the form of letters (*varṇa*) and the other in the form of sound (*dhvani*). The latter is a quality of air and not a substance (*dravya*), whereas the former is a substance and also eternal (*nitya*).[9] The fact that a letter is pronounced in the same uniform way by all and the recognition (*pratyabhijñā*) that arises in the form that it is the same letter prove the permanent character of letters. If there is variation in the pronunciation of a letter with hard or soft sound, this is due to the imposition of the hardness or softness inherent in the air, which causes the manifestation of the letters. A person riding on a horse is described as running fast. Actually it is the horse which is running, but the activity of the horse is superimposed on the person riding it. In the same way the loudness or softness of the sound which are the qualities of air are superimposed on the letters.

[7]TMK V-22. [8]TMK V-23. [9]SS V-22, p. 274.

Vedânta Deśika rejects this theory on the ground that it is clearly established by the śruti and smṛti texts that *varṇas* are subject to destruction.[10] According to the theory of evolution and dissolution, based on the scriptural statements, *śabda-tanmātra* or the subtle sound becomes merged in the *ahaṁkara.*[11] Thus, what is subject to dissolution cannot be eternal. Further, *śabda* in the form of *dhvani* which is grasped by the auditory organ is regarded by the Mīmāṁsaka as the modification (*avasthā-viśeṣa*) of *vāyu*. In the same way, even the fifty-two alphabets which are *varṇas* should also be regarded as modifications of air because these too are grasped by the auditory organ. What is an *avasthā* or modification cannot be a *dravya*. The softness or hardness of the sound belongs to *varṇa* or letter. It is therefore difficult to establish that *śabda* in the form of *varṇa* is *dravya*.

The Mīmāṁsakas consider the *varṇas* as eternal in order to uphold the eternity of the Vedas. According to Vedânta Deśika, even if *varṇas* are non-eternal it would not follow that Vedas are non-eternal. Varṇas by themselves do not constitute the Vedas. On the other hand, *varṇas* existing in a particular sequence (*ānupūrvi*) constitute Vedas. In other words, the letters are not eternal. The letters themselves do not constitute the Vedas. The combination of letters forms words, and these words appearing in a particular sequence constitute the Vedas. This sequence of words in respect of Vedas do not change. At the beginning of the creation, Vedas are taught by *Īśvara* in the same order. In this sense Vedas are regarded as *nitya.*[12]

Sparśa (Touch). This is an essential attribute of air (*vāyu*) which is cognised by means of the tactile organ. It is also present in the other three elements, light water and earth. The Vaiśeṣikas speak of a separate quality of touch which is neither hot nor cold (*anuṣṇāśita*). Such a quality is supposed to exist in earth and air. That is, *pṛthivī* and *vāyu* are neither hot nor cold; these are therefore characterised as non-hot-cold. This is not mere absence of hotness and coldness; if that were so, even *ākāśa* in which these two qualities are absent should have been experienced by touch. It is therefore a separate quality.

[10]TMK V-24. *naigamaiḥ asya nāśaḥ nigaditaḥ.*

[11]Sub II. *tanmātrāṇi bhūtādau vilīyante.* The term *bhūtādi* here is interpreted as *ahaṁkāra* which is the cause of the *tanmātras.*

[12]TMK V-26. *nityaika-rūpa-krama-niyama-vaśān nityabhāvaḥ śrutīnām.*

Vedānta Deśika does not accept this view. Coldness is the quality of water and hotness, that of fire. If these qualities are found in the elements of earth and air, it is due to the association of the elements of water and fire. If *pṛthivi* and *vāyu* are felt as cold, it is due to the presence of water element in them. In the same way, due to the presence of the element of fire, water and earth are considered hot.[13]

Rūpa (Colour). *Rūpa* or colour is an attribute of the elements of fire, water and earth only. *Ākāśa* and air are devoid of colour. In the *Mantra Śāstra*, each element is described as having a specific colour. Thus, earth is described as of yellow colour, water as white, fire as red, air as grey and sky as blue. This gives the impression that each element is of a specific colour. This is not correct, according to Vedānta Deśika. The mention of specific colour for each element is intended for purposes of meditation.[14] The admission of specific colour for each element would go against our perceptual experience and śruti texts. It is an accepted fact that both sky and air are colourless. Earth is not found to possess yellow colour. The śruti text states that it is of dark colour (*kṛṣṇa*).[15] This does not rule out the presence of other colours in earth. *Pṛthivi* possesses certain special qualities, unlike other elements. Touch and odour, which are the two other attributes of earth, undergo change as a result of heating. The elements of water and fire assume different colour as a result of their association with earth. The change of colour in earth is therefore due to the heating. Water, when it is heated, does not undergo any change in colour. It however undergoes change of colour only as a result of its association with earth. Fire can cause change of colour in respect of earth only but not water.

The Vaiśeṣikas admit variegated colour (*citra-rūpa*) as a separate quality. According to them, the parts (*avayavas*) are distinct from the whole (*avayavi*). The different colours found in the parts, as for instance the different colours of the threads, cause variegated colour in the whole, a piece of cloth woven out of the multi-coloured threads. The multi-colour found in the

[13]TMK V-27.

[14]TMK V-29. *dhyānārtham mantra-varṇeṣviva kathitam idam.*

[15]SS V-29, p. 277. *yat kṛṣṇaṁ tadannasya.*

whole is a separate quality as distinct from the different colours of the parts.

This theory is unsound. It may be asked whether the variegated colour exists in each part or whether it exists only in the whole. The former is not acceptable even to the Vaiśeṣikas, because each part has a specific colour of its own. It would then follow that the variegated colour only belongs to the whole (*avayavī*) since it is different from parts. But the Viśiṣṭādvaitin does not admit that the whole exists as distinct from the parts. Cause and effect in this system are not two distinct entities, but are different states of the same one substance. The same colours which exist in the different parts become manifest in the whole as well.

Rasa and Gandha (Taste and Odour). These are the two attributes of water and earth elements respectively. Even though *rasa* is present in earth, *gandha* is its exclusive quality. As there are no controversial points with regard to these two *guṇas*, there is nothing further to add to what has been accepted by Nyāya-Vaiśeṣika and other schools of thought.

Śakti as an Attribute of Causal Substance

Śakti or potency is one of the ten *adravyas* accepted in the system. It is that property of a causal substance by virtue of which it produces the effect.[16] It is a special quality (*dharma-viśeṣaḥ*) inherent in the causal substance which brings out the necessary effect. The special power inherent in the Supreme Being is also regarded as *śakti*, as it is the cause of all magnificent creations. This divine power is not the very nature (*svarūpa*) of *Īśvara*; nor is it illusory (*kalpita*). It is other than the *svarūpa of Īśvara* and is real in character.[17]

The Naiyāyikas do not admit *śakti* as a separate category. According to them, *śakti* is the absence of obstruction for the production of an effect. The example given to illustrate this point is the fire, which has natural power to burn, is prevented from doing so due to the influence of certain special gem (*maṇi*) or the efficacy of certain *mantras*. The absence of such obstructive elements could as well be regarded as the *śakti* or power of the fire. In other words, the absence of obstructive elements

[16]TMK V-98. *hetoḥ kāryopayuktam yadiha bhavati tat śaktiśabdābhilapyam.* ı.
[17]*Ibid.*

such as *maṇi* and *mantra* is the *śakti* of the fire, because while they are present fire does not burn and in their absence it functions. If, on the contrary, a separate power as inherent in the fire is to be admitted, how then that *śakti* which is destroyed by the *maṇi* and *mantra* is again produced in the fire? We do not see any new cause for its reappearance. If it is argued that *śakti* is not destroyed but only its operation is arrested, it would be more appropriate to say that fire itself did not function rather than admitting *śakti* as a separate quality.

All these arguments are untenable, contends Vedânta Deśika. That the Divine Being possesses variegated power (*śakti*) is well established by śruti texts.[18] In the case of the physical causal entities, our experience reveals that they possess certain inherent power as, for example, the burning capacity in fire and the attractive power in magnet. When something is well established by scripture as well as experience, the arguments based on logic do not hold good.

Saṁyoga as Relation

This is the tenth *adravya* admitted in the system. As in the Naiyâyika system, it is a form of relation that holds good between two physical objects as between two jugs or the floor and the jug. It is considered to be an important relation, because the very creation of universe is possible only as a result of *saṁyoga* between *prakṛti* and *puruṣa*. All the various modifications in the universe right from Brahmâ to the blade of grass are to be accounted for by the different types of *saṁyoga* between a soul and its body. Knowledge arises only as a result of *saṁyoga* between *buddhi* and external objects. Seeds sprout as a result of their *saṁyoga* with water and earth. Hence *saṁyoga* is accepted as a separate fundamental attribute under *adravyas*.

There are different views on the nature of *saṁyoga* relation as advanced by other schools of thought. These are critically examined by Vedānta Deśika. The Buddhists do not accept *saṁyoga* as a separate quality. The mere absence of space between two objects (*antarālābhāva*) is considered as *saṁyoga*. In other words, when two objects are not conjoined, there is space left between them. This is known as *antarāla*. When the two objects are brought close to each other, then the *antarāla* or

[18] Svet VI-8. *parāsya śaktiḥ vividhaiva śrūyate*....

the space in between them disappears. The absence of it is itself *saṁyoga* and there is no need to postulate a separate category as *saṁyoga*.

This is not a correct theory. It is an admitted fact that when a cloth is made out of the threads the former as an effected state is caused by the conjunction of the threads. It cannot be said that the cloth is not a separate product but the very threads, because the operation of other causal factors such as loom, weaving, etc. would become futile. Nor can it be said that everything being momentary, the later state of cloth is different from the threads and as such the causal operation is not futile. The Viśiṣṭādvaitin does not accept the doctrine of momentariness. As a matter of fact, even *antarālābhāva* is a positive entity, since *abhāva* as will be explained later is *bhāvāntara* for the Viśiṣṭādvaitin. It cannot therefore constitute *saṁyoga*[19] For the Viśiṣṭādvaitin *saṁyoga* or conjunction is a separate category.

In connection with *saṁyoga*, an important question is raised. *Saṁyoga* normally takes place between two physical objects. Could there be *saṁyoga* between partless entities (*niravaya vastu*)? According to the Jainas, all objects in the universe including the *paramaṇus* are constituted of parts (*sāvayava*), as otherwise it is impossible to have *saṁyoga* of one object with another. Two partless entities such as *paramāṇu* and *ākāśa* cannot have *saṁyoga*. If a *saṁyoga* between them is admitted, either the *paramāṇu* will have to be of the size of *ākāśa* or *ākāśa* of that of *paramāṇu*. That which is small cannot conjoin with that which is large. Therefore, all entities will have to be composed of parts (*sāvayava*) for the purpose of conjunction. This is the view of the Jainas.[20]

Against this theory, Vedānta Deśika points out that *saṁyoga* can take place even between two partless entities (*niravayava dravya*). It is evident from perception that between two *sāvayava* objects *saṁyoga* takes place in respect of a part only. That is, when two physical objects are conjoined, only a side or part of it comes into contact with a part of another object. On the basis of the same principle, we have to admit *saṁyoga* of two partless entities in respect of a part only as caused by some kind of limiting factor (*upādhi*)[21]

[19]See p. 378. [20]See SS V-53, p. 287.

[21]TMK V-53. *aupādhikī aṁśakliptiḥ*. See also SS, pp. 287-88.

Vedānta Deśika further points out that *saṁyoga* is possible even in respect of two *vibhu dravyas*, the entities which are all-pervasive. Two *vibhu dravyas* exist together all the time (*nirantara*). If there be any space left between them, they cannot be *vibhu*. When they exist together all the time, they have *saṁyoga*. The Vaiśeṣikas contend that *saṁyoga* is only brought about by some kind of action (*kriyā*) in either of the entities; and since such a *kriyā* is absent in the case of *vibhu* entities, *saṁyoga* relation is not possible between them. This objection is not valid. How do we account for the rise of knowledge in God? In the case of God, it is believed that His knowledge is *nitya* (eternal) and it functions without the aid of sense organs. On the basis of the same logic, it is possible to conceive that without *kriyā* or action, the two eternal *vibhu* entities are conjoined eternally. That two *vibhu dravyas* such as *kāla* (time) and *Īśvara* are conjoined is proved on the basis of scriptural evidence. Such a *saṁyoga* between *Īśvara* and *kāla* is eternal.[22]

II. NYĀYA-VAIŚEṢIKA THEORY OF ATTRIBUTES

We have so far considered the ten fundamental attributes which are grouped under *adravyas*. We shall now examine the other attributes which are classified as *guṇas* by the Nyāya-Vaiśeṣikas. The Vaiśeṣikas have enumerated twenty-four such *guṇas*. Six of these *guṇas*—*śabda, sparśa, rūpa, rasa, gandha* and *saṁyoga*—are included under *adravyas* of Viśiṣṭādvaita system. With the exception of *buddhi* or knowledge which is a *dravya*, the remaining *guṇas* mentioned below are not accepted by Vedānta Deśika as separate attributes (*atirikta-guṇa*). He therefore examines each one of them critically in order to bring out their true character. These may be grouped together for the purpose of our examination under the following headings :

(1) MATERIAL ATTRIBUTES: *sneha* (lubricity), *gurutva* (heaviness), *saṅkhyā* (number), *parimāṇa* (dimension), *pṛthaktva* (separateness), *vibhāga* (disjunction), *paratva* and *aparatva* (priority and posteriority).

(2) MENTAL ATTRIBUTES: *sukha* (pleasure), *duḥkha* (pain), *icchā*

[22]TMK V-54.

(desire), *dveṣa* (aversion), *yatna* (effort), *saṁskara* (latent impression).

(3) Ethical attributes: *dharma* (merit), *adharma* (demerit) and *adṛṣṭa* (unseen potency).

Material Attributes

Sneha (Lubricity). According to the Vaiśeṣikas, lubricity (*sneha*) is a separate quality of liquid such as water. This is evident to perception by the fact that water has the capacity of converting the earth particles into a lump of clay. Lubricity is not the same as liquidity (*dravatva*) or the very quality of water itself (*jalatva*). The melted gold is liquid but it lacks lubricity as it cannot convert the earth particles into a lump of clay. The lustre of diamond is described in Sanskrit literature as *snigdha* meaning that it is shining like a lubricant (oil), but it does not possess the quality of liquidity.

Vedānta Deśika points out that lubricity is not a separate quality of water. Water itself has the capacity to convert the earth particles into a lump of clay, and it is not necessary to postulate a separate quality for this purpose.[23] The magnet, for instance, has the capacity to attract iron but we do not postulate the presence of a separate quality in magnet to account for it other than the special characteristic of the object itself. In the same way water has the special capacity to solidify earth particles. Further, *snehatva* is not unique to water alone, as Vaiśeṣikas believe. It is also found in a few earthly elements.

Liquidity (*dravatva*) is also not a separate quality. Water has the capacity to flow downward. What causes the flow is the heaviness and smoothness of water. According to some Naiyāyikas, the initial flow is caused by the liquidity, a quality present in water. Vedānta Deśika does not question this. Whether or not liquidity is a separate quality is not relevant. What is important is that we should admit that water has natural liquidity (*sāṁsiddhika dravatva*).[24] As compared to this, the *ghee* (melted butter) possesses liquidity but this is caused by heat. The same is the case with melted gold. In the case of oil, liquidity is caused by the presence of water element in it.

[23]TMK V-33.

[24]TMK V-35. *toye svabhāvāt dravatvam dṛṣṭaṁ.*

Gurutva (Heaviness). *Gurutva* is that quality by virtue of which things fall to the ground. The basis for accepting it as a quality by the Vaiśeṣika is that objects have a tendency to fall. Water and all material objects are examples of heaviness.

The acceptance of *gurutva* as a separate quality is considered superfluous in order to account for the fall of the objects. Fall is a downward motion which is common to water and material objects. Even fire and air have motion, the former moving upward and the latter in oblique direction, but the Vaiśeṣikas account for such motions on the basis of *adṛṣṭa* or unseen potency. Vedānta Deśika urges that the same explanation could as well be offered for the downward movement of objects. If *gurutva* is to be accepted in order to account for the difference in the weight of two objects, this could as well be explained on the basis of the difference in the quantity of the two objects. If the quantity of one object is more than the other, the former is naturally weightier than the latter. On the same basis the variation in the speed of the downward motion can be explained.[25]

According to some Vaiśeṣikas, weight is cognised by the tactile organ. This is not correct. We do not apprehend the weight of an object by touching either its surface or bottom. Weight is only inferred on the basis of weighing an object. When we lift an object, we begin to feel its weight, and on the basis of it we infer that it has weight but not by mere touch.

According to the Sāṅkhyas, *gurutva* or heaviness in the material objects is caused by the *tamoguṇa*.. This is also not a sound theory. If *tamas* is the cause of *gurutva*, then the Sāṅkhyas should admit that *sattva-guṇa* is the cause of lightness in fire. In the Sāṅkhya system, *sattva* stands for lightness (*sattvam laghu*), and *tamas* for heaviness. But no one admits including the Sāṅkhyas that fire is of light weight. If *gurutva* as a quality is to be accepted in order to account for the fall of the objects, then this can be explained on the basis of the *tamoguna* itself which is the very constituent of the physical object.[26] Thus there is no need to postulate *gurutva* as a separate quality.

Saṅkhyā (Number). According to the Vaiśeṣikas, *saṅkhyā* (number) is a separate quality belonging to things which generates the apprehension and the empirical usage as one, two,

[25]TMK V-36. [26]TMK V-38.

three, etc.[27] The number 'one' or the notion of oneness is eternal in respect of eternal objects such as *paramāṇu* (atom). It is non-eternal in respect of a diad and triad as these are caused by the combination of *paramāṇus*. As regards the numbers two, three, etc. the knowledge of these arises only after the person gets the cognition separately of each single entity. That is, if a person has to get the knowledge of two, he has first to apprehend separately that this is one and that is also one; on the basis of this apprehension, there arises the quality of twoness (*dvitva*), and this leads to the knowledge of two. The knowledge of two is thus dependent on the cognition of oneness of each of the two entities by an individual. This is technically known as *apekṣā-buddhi* or dependence on the cognition of the particular subject. From this it follows that *dvitva* or being two does not belong to the objects, but, on the contrary, it arises as a result of the cognition of each of the entity as one by a particular individual. On the basis of the knowledge of *dvitva*, the judgment that it is two arises. This is the explanation offered by the Vaiśeṣika.

Vedānta Deśika rejects this theory as unsound. It is not necessary to postulate *dvitva* as a separate quality to be generated by the *apekṣā buddhi* and on that basis to account for the empirical usage that it is two. The very *apekṣā-buddhi*, that is, the cognition of the two objects, each of them separately as one, could as well lead to the knowledge that they are two. That is, the *dvitva* knowledge itself causes the *dvitva vyavahāra*, and there is no need to postulate *dvitva* as a separate quality for this purpose. Further, *dvitva* as a numerical quality does not exist. The judgments that we make as two or three arise as a result of the cognition of two or three objects.[28]

Does oneness (*ekatva*) as a numerical quality exist? And if so, what is its nature? In Sanskrit the term *eka* has different meanings.[29] It means *kevala* that is, 'one only'. The term used in this sense denies the existence of other things. But oneness as a numerical term has a positive implication, and does not negate the existence of others, and it is not therefore to be equated with the term *kevala*. By *eka* is also meant what is the most important (*mukhya*). This also cannot be the correct meaning of oneness as

[27]TMK V-39. [28]TMK V-40.
[29]SS V-41. p. 282. *mukhya anya kevaleṣu ekam.*

a numerical term, because it is applicable in respect of unimportant things as well. *Eka* is also used to mean *anya* or other. But *ekatva* as numerical concept is applicable to all objects, and it cannot therefore be equated with *anya*. It is also not correct to use the word *ekatva* in respect of a collective whole (*saṅghāta-ikyam*), because the collective whole is a group of objects of the same nature, and the numerical number 'one' is not applicable to it except in a secondary sense being one collective whole. It may be said that *avayavi* as one is different from the *avayava*, but such a theory is not acceptable to the Viśiṣṭādvaitin. Vedânta Deśika therefore comes to the conclusion that *ekatva* as a number is to be accepted, but in its primary sense it is applicable to the individual *paramāṇu* which is partless and not forming a group or whole (*asaṅghātarūpa*). In the same way it is also applicable to *Paramātman*. Whether the number one is *nitya* or *anitya* depends upon the object to which it belongs. In the case of *Paramātman*, it is *nitya* and in the case of *paramāṇu* it is *anitya* according to Viśiṣṭādvaita.[30] When the word *eka* is applied to other material objects as well as the qualities (*adravya*), it is to be understood only in a secondary sense (*aupacārika*).[31]

Parimāṇa (Dimension). Dimension is that quality of things by virtue of which one is able to apprehend them as big or small, long or short. It is of four kinds: *anu* or the smallest like the atom, *mahat* the extremely big like *ākāśa*, *dirgha* the long and *hrasva*, the short. Dimension is eternal in eternal substances and transient in non-eternal ones.

According to some, *parimāṇa* is not a separate quality but it is the spatial limitation, that is, space conditioned by different objects (*deśa-vyāptiprabhedaḥ*).[32] Thus, *ākāśa* which is all-pervasive becomes conditioned by a jug or a house; the conjunction of the object with the space causes the difference in respect of the size of the area as small or big depending upon the size of the adjuncts. The jug occupies less space than the house, and the former is, therefore, regarded as small and the latter as big in dimension.

[30] *Paramāṇu* is understood in the Viśiṣṭādvaita system as the smallest particle which is regarded as *tryaṇuka* or the triad identified with the dust particle observed in the sunbeam passing through a narrow hole. Such a *paramāṇu* is *anitya*.

[31] TMK V-41. [32] TMK V-45.

This is not a correct view, because the objects themselves which condition the space have a dimension of their own. Besides, if largeness or smallness of the objects is determined on the basis of the largeness or smallness of the area they occupy, it would lead to a vicious circle. If it is asked why pot takes less space and the house more space, the answer will be that pot is small and the house is large. If we ask why pot is small and house is large, the reply will be that pot occupies less space whereas house takes more space. In other words, the variation in the area is due to the variation in the dimension of the objects and the variation in the dimension of the objects is due to the variation in the space they occupy. Thus, it involves a vicious circle. In order to overcome this difficulty, it is necessary to admit that objects themselves possess dimension of their own. This is the position in the case of individual objects. With regard to the collective objects such as a heap of grains, the area or space occupied by the grains (*deśa-sambandha*) is the dimension of the heap of grains (*dhānya-rāśi*).[33] As regards *paramāṇu*, which is the smallest indivisible particle, it has a dimension of its own.

Does Brahman have any dimension? According to one view, which is based on the Upaniṣadic text[34] describing Brahman as not of gross matter (*asthūla*), not monadic (*anaṇu*) not long, not short, etc. Brahman has no dimension. This is not a correct view, according to Vedānta Deśika. The Upaniṣad declares that Brahman is bigger than the *pṛthivī*, bigger than the *ākāśa* and bigger than all the universe.[35] It is evident from this that Brahman possesses *vibhuparimāṇatva*, which is known as *parama-mahattva*, implying the all-pervasive character of Brahman. The text, which speaks of Brahman as *asthūla*, *anaṇu* etc. only negates the empirical dimension that is applicable to material objects. Even if the text is understood in the sense of negation of all dimension, it would only imply that Brahman exists as *vibhu*, which is its natural form (*svābhāvika parimāṇa*), because, according to Viśiṣṭādvaitin, *abhāva* means *bhāvāntara* or existence in some other form.

[33]Such an explanation is necessary because according to the Naiyāyikas, the *dhānya-rāśi* is not, unlike the pot, the *avayavī* (whole) as different from *avayava* (part).

[34]Br III-8-8. [35]Ch III-14-3.

The question is raised whether it would be possible to account for *parama-mahat-parimāṇa* in the Viśiṣṭādvaita system which does not accept the distinction between *avayava* and *avayavi* (part and whole) as conceived by the Naiyāyikas. According to the Nyāya system, the conglomeration of several *paramāṇus* or atoms constitute the large dimension (*mahat-parimāṇa*). This is *avayavi* or whole of parts. If *avayavi* is denied, what remains are only the individual *paramāṇus* which cannot be regarded as of large dimension. In the same way, even *madhyama-parimāṇa* or the larger dimension is also not possible. If *mahat-parimāṇa* is not possible, the theory that God is of *parama-mahat-parimāṇa* also does not hold good.

In reply to this objection, Vedānta Deśika asserts that the concept of *mahat-parimāṇa* is accepted by the Viśiṣṭādvaitin. Whether it is different from what the Naiyāyikas say or whether it is the same as *parimāṇa* in general may be disputed. But, as long as *mahat-parimāṇa* is accepted, the admission of *parama-mahat-parimāṇa* also stands justified. *Parama-mahattva*, as already explained is the natural form of *Īśvara*.

In the same way *aṇutva* or atomic dimension is the natural form of *jiva*. As in the case of physical objects, *aṇutva* is not caused by any extraneous factor. It is the very nature or *svarūpa* of *jiva*. In the case of all other material objects, dimension is the characteristic of the very objects. This is proved by the fact that objects are seen as possessing dimension.

Pṛthaktva (Separateness). According to Nyāya-Vaiśeṣika, *pṛthaktva* or separateness is that quality in the objects by virtue of which one object is regarded as different from the other.[36] Vedānta Deśika points out that *pṛthaktva* is the same as *bheda* or difference, and as such the postulation of it as a separate *guṇa* is superfluous. There are three terms—*pṛthak*, *bheda* and *itarat*—and all of them have the same meaning, viz. different. If the concept of *bhinna* is different from the concept of *pṛthaktva*, the Naiyāyikas should accept *itarattva* also as a separate concept. If it be argued that *bhinna* and *itarattva* are different only in words and not in their meaning, the same argument holds good in respect of *bhinna* and *pṛthaktva*. In fact, *pṛthaktva* and *bheda* have the same meaning. When we say blueness is *pṛthak* from yellowness, the blueness

[36]NS, p. 262. *pṛthaktvam pṛthag-vyavahāra-kāraṇaṁ r. pṛthag-guṇa iti kāṇādādayaḥ.*

itself which is the essential characteristic of blue object constitutes the difference from the yellow object.

It may be argued that *bheda* is a negative term because it presupposes the knowledge of the counter-correlate, whereas *pṛthaktva* is a positive term and as such the two are not the same. This is untenable because *pṛthaktva* also presupposes the knowledge of the counter-correlate. The judgment that this is separate from the other (*pṛthak*) cannot arise unless the counter correlate is known. The two terms are therefore synonymous. *Pṛthaktva* is not therefore a separate *guṇa* but the same as *bheda*.

Paratva and Aparatva. According to Nyāya-Vaiśeṣika, these are two separate qualities which cause in us the apprehension of long time and short time, remote and near. Vedānta Deśika points out that it is not possible to prove them as separate qualities on the basis of the change in the duration of time which is connected with the movement of the sun.[37] We say that a particular individual is older and another younger. The concept of older and younger implies only difference in time. Similarly, the concept of remote and near implies spatial difference. The variation in time or in space is actually determined by the movement of the sun (*sūrya-calana*). Apart from the temporal and spatial variation dependent upon the movement of the sun, we do not perceive any separate qualities as belonging to the material objects.[38]

Vibhāga or Disjunction. Vibhāga or disjunction is considered by the Naiyāyikas as a separate quality. When two things are conjoined, the movement of one of the two or both causes disjunction. The Viśiṣṭādvaitin does not accept disjunction as a separate quality. The removal or destruction of conjunction itself (*saṁyoga-nāśa*) is disjunction. When two objects are conjoined and what is thus conjoined is separated as a result of the movement of either of the objects, we regard such a state as *vibhāga*.[39] *Saṁyoga-nāśa* is not caused by disjunction in which case disjunction as a separate quality will have to be admitted. On the other hand, the *kriyā* or the movement of the objects itself is the cause of *saṁyoga-nāśa*, and there is no need to postulate a separate quality as *vibhāga* for the purpose.

[37]TMK V-58. [38]*Ibid.* [39]SS V-56, p. 289.

Mental Attributes

Among the twenty-four *guṇas* enumerated by the Nyāya-Vaiśeṣikas, *buddhi* (knowledge) and five other qualities which may be broadly treated as mental are included. These are: *icchā* (desire), *dveṣa* (aversion), *sukha* (pleasure), *duḥkha* (pain) and *prayatna* (effort). All these including *buddhi* are the qualities of the individual self. According to the Viśiṣṭādvaitin, knowledge is not a *guṇa* in the sense the Nyāyā-Vaiśeṣika understands, but it is a substance (*dravya*) inseparably related to the individual self. This is discussed in the chapter on Theory of Knowledge. As regards the other five qualities, Vedānta Deśika maintains the view that these are not the qualities of the self but are only different states (*avasthās*) of the *dharmabhūtajñāna* or knowledge as understood in this system.[40] Thus, when knowledge arises in the form of a desire towards some object, it assumes the name of *icchā*; similarly, knowledge in the form of aversion towards a particular thing is *dveṣa*. It does not follow that *jñāna* and *icchā* are the same. The fact that both are basically of the nature of knowledge does not lead to the conclusion that these are synonymous. Thus, for example, recognition (*pratyabhijñā*) and determinate perception (*savikalpaka pratyakṣa*) are perceptual in character, but they are not synonymous. If such an explanation is not accepted, then other mental qualities such as jealousy, hatred, fear, compassion, courage, etc. would have to be accepted as distinct qualities of the soul. If these be regarded as different mental states, then on the same principle even *icchā*, *dveṣa*, *sukha*, *duḥkha*, etc. should be accepted as the states of knowledge.[41]

Icchā itself assumes two different names as *rāga* and *dveṣa* depending upon the difference in its content. When there is a desire to have something, it is known as *rāga*; when the desire is not to have something, it becomes *dveṣa*.[42] *Rāga* and *dveṣa* are not therefore two separate states of knowledge. When *rāga* or desire is intensive, it is known as *kāma* or passion. Similarly, an intensive aversion becomes *krodha* or anger. In the same way, the different states of knowledge assume different names depending upon the nature of their content. If each state of knowledge is to be regarded as a separate quality of the soul, as Naiyāyikas do, there would be any number of *guṇas* of the soul.

[40]TMK V-68. *icchā-dveṣa-prayatnaḥ sukham itaradapi jñānato nātiriktāḥ.*

[41]*Ibid.* [42]TMK V-70.

Icchā (desire) and *prayatna* (effort) are two distinct states of knowledge. According to some, desire itself results in action and it is not necessary to regard the latter as a separate state. Vedānta Deśika does not agree with this view. A person may develop a desire, but it does not necessarily lead to action. Thus, for example, a person may desire to have natural cool breeze during hot weather, but he cannot make any effort in this direction. During a dark night one may desire moonlight, but no effort in this direction is possible. Desire therefore is of general nature, while effort is of specific nature. The two are different states of knowledge and cannot be the same.

Sukha (pleasure) and *duḥkha* (pain) are also two different states of *jñāna*. *Sukha* is not merely the absence of *duḥkha* (*duḥkhābhāva*). If that were so, then absence of *sukha* should be *duḥkha*. This is not so. They are therefore two distinct states. Knowledge arising in an agreeable form is pleasure (*anukūlatva-jñāna*), and knowledge in a disagreeable form is pain (*pratikūlatva-jñāna*). If both pleasure and pain are absent, then it is a state of indifference (*audāsinya*). Thus, these are different states of experience.[43] What causes the different states in the form of pleasure or pain is the *karma* of the individual. The external objects as such are not the causes of happiness or suffering for an individual. If that were so, the same object should cause pleasure to all uniformly. An object which is a source of delight to one may be a source of suffering to another. The attitude of an individual towards the objects is therefore responsible for the different types of experience in the form of pleasure or pain. What is responsible for such attitudes of a person is his own past *karma*. When an individual becomes totally free from the influence of *karma*, then his knowledge manifests itself in its fullest form. Such a state of knowledge not influenced by *karma* is considered the supreme happiness (*ānanda*) which is really the absolute *sukha*.[44] The same is regarded as *Brahmānanda*. As compared to it, the *sukha* of our ordinary experience and even the happiness attained in the state of *kaivalya* is a drop in the ocean.

Some hold the view that there is nothing like happiness in this world. Vedānta Deśika does not agree with it. As there is

[43]TMK V-74. [44]*Ibid.*

more suffering than happiness in life, one may take such a view. But such statements totally denying *sukha* are to be understood in a secondary sense. If happiness is altogether denied, the term *sukha* becomes meaningless (*vyutpattihinam*). If wise men describe the life in this world as *duḥkha* (suffering), it is intended to emphasise the fact that happiness is either mixed with suffering or that it may eventually lead to some kind of suffering.[45]

Saṁskāra is that which causes the recollection at a later period of what was previously experienced without the aid of the external sense organs.[46] It assists the mind in recollecting the experience of the past as and when a suitable stimulus is provided by seeing an object similar to what was experienced earlier. The previous experience alone cannot cause the recollection because an experience of the past has ceased to exist any more. Nor does the mere apprehension of a similar object (*sadṛśa-vastu-darśana*) is the cause of the memory, because an object which was not previously seen does not cause the memory. Therefore, only the *saṁskāra* generated by previous experience is the cause of memory.[47]

What is the *saṁskāra* which is regarded as different from the previous experience as well as the apprehension of a similar object? Vedānta Deśika points out that *saṁskāra* is a state of knowledge (*avasthāviśeṣa*). Knowledge in this system is a permanent, separate entity (*dravya*) and is subject to modifications. When knowledge is in contact with the external objects through the sense organs, it flows out and reveals the object. The previous experience of an object is thus a modification of knowledge. The *saṁskāra* generated by the previous modification of knowledge is responsible for its recollection when a similar object again presents itself to knowledge. Thus, *saṁskāra* is a state of *jñāna* and inheres in it. Such an explanation of *saṁskāra* is plausible in this system because of the acceptance of *dharmabhūtajñāna* as a *dravya* capable of undergoing modifications. The Naiyāyikas believe that *saṁskāra* is a quality of the *ātman* and as such inheres in it. There are difficulties in accepting such a theory. A *saṁskāra* inhering in the soul can-

[45]SS 296. *duḥkhottaratvāt duḥkhatvam abhidhiyate.*

[46]TMK V-101. *bāhyākṣāder avṛttau ciraviditamapi smaryate yena so'yaṁ saṁskāraḥ.*

[47]NS, p. 258. *anubhavajā smṛtihetuḥ vāsanā.*

not cause modification in knowledge. *Ātman* is *nirvikāra.* It is therefore appropriate to accept modifications in *dharmabhūta-jñāna* for which *ātman* is the *ādhāra*. The changes that take place apply to *jñāna* but not to *ātman.* In so far as *ātman* is the *ādhāra* for *jñāna*, the changes taking place in the latter are regarded as if they belong to the *ātman.*[48]

According to Nyāya-Vaiśeṣika, *saṁskāra* is of three kinds: *bhāvanā* or mental impressionability by which the soul is able to recollect things already experienced; *vega* or velocity which keeps a thing in motion; *sthitasthāpaka* or elasticity by virtue of which a thing reverts to its orignal state when it is disturbed, as for example, a folded skin of deer. We have already considered that *bhāvanā* as *saṁskāra* is not a separate quality of *ātman* but a quality of knowledge generated by previous experience. Vedānta Deśika rejects the other two types of *saṁskāra* as separate qualities.

Vega or velocity is a special feature of motion (*karmātiśaya*). When we say that a person goes fast, all that is implied is that the person moves fast. Apart from the action (*karma*) in the form of movement, we do not see any separate quality as *vega.* Even the Naiyāyikas determine the variation in the movements as fast, slow, etc. on the basis of the variation found in *karma* (action). Fastness of motion itself is velocity.[49]

The Naiyāyikas adopt an argument to prove velocity as a separate quality. The first motion of an arrow in the bow is caused by the contact of the hand with the arrow; after the arrow is released from the bow, the contact of the hand ceases. How does the next motion of the arrow take place? The answer of the Naiyāyikas is that a quality known as *vega* or velocity is created in the arrow, and this causes further motion in the arrow.

The above argument is fallacious. It is possible to account for the second motion of the arrow on the basis of the very action (*karma*) which caused the first motion. Just as *śabda* or sound causes another *śabda,* the previous motion can cause the succeeding one. It cannot be said that a *karma* can be caused only by a *guṇa* and not by another *karma.* Even *karma,* according to the Viśiṣṭādvaitin, is a *guṇa,* since it inheres in a substance,

[48]SS IV-103, p. 308. [49]TMK V-104.

and it is therefore appropriate to say that one motion causes another motion. Velocity is thus the fast motion itself and not a separate quality.

Regarding *sthitasthāpaka* or elasticity as a separate quality, Vedānta Deśika asks: where does this quality inhere? The Naiyāyikas reply that it exists in the special structure of the objects possessing this quality (*avayava-sanniveśa*). For instance, the folded deer skin is stretched flat, but when it is loosened it goes back to its original position. The quality of elasticity which is responsible for this exists in the special structure of the deer skin. If this is the case, then it would be more appropriate to accept the special structure of the concerned object as the cause of this peculiar movement rather than accepting a separate quality to account for this behaviour. It is not necessary to assume elasticity as a separate quality in order to explain the slow or fast movement of the objects to their original position. Such variation in the speed can also be due to the very nature of those objects.[50]

The Vaiśeṣikas maintain that elasticity is a peculiar quality of material objects. This is also not a sound view, because such elasticity as a peculiar behaviour of the objects could as well be found in water and fire. When water is thrown up, it has natural tendency to move downward. Similarly, when fire is blown, it comes back to its normal position as soon as the act of blowing stops. It is, therefore, concluded that *sthitasthāpaka* as a separate quality is untenable. It is the property of the very objects which have elasticity.

Ethical Attributes

The concepts of *dharma* and *adharma* as well as *adṛṣṭa* are accepted by most of the Indian schools of thought and constitute an important part of the moral teaching and spiritual discipline. However, there is a diversity of views with regard to their nature, particularly the theory of *adṛṣṭa*. Vedānta Deśika critically examines these views and explains the theory as developed in the Viśiṣṭādvaita system.

According to the Nyāya-Vaiśeṣika, *dharma* and *adharma* are two separate specific qualities (*viśeṣa-guṇa*) that belong to the self. *Dharma* is the quality, the presence of which enables the

[50]TMK V-105.

soul to enjoy happiness or to attain salvation. *Adharma* is the opposite quality, the presence of which in the soul causes suffering to the person. Accordingly, *dharma* and *adharma* do not stand for right or wrong deeds; they signify rather the merit (*puṇya*) and demerit (*pāpa*) resulting respectively from the performance of the right deeds and the indulgence in the wrong deeds.

The Mīmāṁsā and Vedānta systems do not accept the above theory. *Dharma* and *adharma* refer to the good and bad deeds to be determined on the authority of the revealed scripture. In other words, *dharma* stands for the deeds prescribed and *adharma* for the deeds prohibited by the Vedas. According to the Mīmāṁsakas, *dharma* refers to the rituals (*kriyā*) prescribed by the sacred texts for achieving certain good results.[51] *Adṛṣṭa* is accepted by them as different from *dharma* and *adharma*. It is a special potency generated by the performance of the prescribed rituals and which confers the desired result at a later period. The rituals in the form of sacrifices, etc. are not permanent. The desired result comes at a much later period. As there is no direct causal relation between the *kriyā* and the result in the form of *svarga* to be achieved, a medium is considered necessary to confer the desired result at a later period. This unseen potency caused by the performance of deed is known as *adṛṣṭa*. The same is technically called *apūrva* by the Mīmāṁsakas.

The concept of *adṛṣṭa* is also accepted by other schools of thought but their views differ from that of the Mīmāṁsakas. For the Naiyāyikas, *adṛṣṭa* is a quality of the individual self. It is generated in the soul by the performance of religious duties. Sāṅkhya and Yoga system regard it as a modification of the *antaḥkaraṇa*, the internal organ (the same known as *citta* in Yoga). The Buddhists believe that *adṛṣṭa* is the *vāsanā* or latent impression of the mind. One school of Jainas maintains that it is a type of *vibhu-dravya*. Some other Jainas regard this as *pudgala*, the cosmic entity which is the cause of the universe.

Vedānta Deśika rejects the above views as mere speculations (*kalpanā*). According to the Viśiṣṭādvaita Vedānta, *adṛṣṭa* is *Īśvara-buddhi-viśeṣa*, that is, the mental disposition of God as

[51]TMK V-76. *tattatphalakaraṇatayā śāstrasiddham kriyādi dharmaḥ adharmaśca*. See also SS, p. 296.

influenced by the performance of the deeds by an individual.[52] Unlike the common belief held by a few other schools of thought, *adṛṣṭa* is not a separate entity in the form of *apūrva*, or a quality generated in the self or mind, but a modification (*pariṇati*) that takes place in *Īśvara-buddhi*. In other words, the performance of the good deeds as prescribed by the sacred texts results in causing pleasure or a favourable disposition in *Īśvara* towards the individual. This is known as *anugraha* or showering of the grace by God. This itself is *puṇya* or merit of the individual. Similarly, if an individual indulges in bad deeds which are prohibited by the sacred texts, then it causes displeasure or unfavourable disposition in *Īśvara* towards the individual. This is known as *nigraha* or award of punishment. The same is the *pāpa* or sin of an individual. Both *anugraha* and *nigraha* are the *saṅkalpa* or mental dispositions of *Īśvara*. Acquisition of *puṇya* by an individual means becoming an object of God's grace and acquisition of *pāpa* means becoming the object of His wrath. *Adṛṣṭa* which is caused by the performance of deeds, operates only through the *will* of God. It is neither an unseen potency nor a quality of the soul.

What is the proof of such a theory of *adṛṣṭa*? According to Vedānta Deśika, the proof rests only on the strength of the sacred texts. Neither can it be known by means of perception nor is it proved by means of inference. Naiyāyikas attempt to establish their theory on the basis of inference. The argument adopted by them is that if *adṛṣṭa* in the form of *dharma* and *adharma* is not accepted, the good deeds performed by pious individuals in the universe becomes meaningless. Vedānta Deśika does not agree with this explanation. The argument of Naiyāyikas may hold good in so far as *adṛṣṭa* is understood in a general sense. The details regarding the variation in the merit or demerit of an individual, the different types of deeds to be performed for the purpose, the manner in which these have to be observed and the means to be adopted to acquire *puṇya*, etc. cannot be established by means of logical arguments. For such matters one has to resort to the Vedic texts. If this be the position, then one should as well have recourse to the scripture for accepting *adṛṣṭa*. In such transcendental matters as *svarga*,

[52]SS V-76, p. 296. *tattatkarmācaraṇapariṇata Īśvarabuddhiviśeṣa eva adṛṣṭam iti tattvavidām sampradāyaḥ.*

mokṣa, etc. and the means to be adopted for achieving them, the revealed scripture alone is the guide and not logic.

Mīmāṁsakas also attempt to prove their theory of *apūrva* on the basis of logical arguments. These, when subjected to critical analysis, fall to the ground. One of the arguments to which we have already referred earlier is based on the assumption that as there is a long interval between the time of the performance of a *yāga* or sacrifice and the time the result is to be achieved, an unseen power (*śakti*) as generated by the sacrifice is to be admitted which actually gives the result at the appropriate time. Against this theory the question is asked as to where such a potency exists. As a *dharma* or quality generated by the *yāga* it should subsist somewhere. Either it should inhere in the *yāga* itself or in the *svarga* which is its result. Neither the *yāga* nor the *svarga* exists soon after the *yāga* is completed. The only possible explanation, which may not be acceptable to the Mīmāṁsakas, is that the pleasure or displeasure caused to the concerned deities to whom sacrifices are offered constitutes the potency or *śakti* that gives the desired result.[53] This explanation has the support of the scriptural evidence. *Yāga* is defined as worship to the higher deities (*yaja devapūjāyām*). The śruti itself says that the specific deity awards the result.[54] When good deeds are performed for specific results, the concerned divine beings for whom sacrifices are offered become supremely pleased with it and through their *grace* the results accrue to the individuals concerned at the appropriate time.

An objection is raised by the Mīmāṁsakas against the above explanation. The divine beings (*devatās*) are not eternal, unlike *Īśvara*. At the time of dissolution of the universe they cease to exist, and when new evolution starts taking place new divine beings also come into existence. The same deities who were worshipped in the earlier epoch (*kalpa*) will not be present after the new evolution takes place. How could the new *devatās* who were not worshipped earlier be expected to award the fruits?

This objection is met on the basis of the ontological position taken by the Viśiṣṭādvaitin. According to Viśiṣṭādvaita, the Supreme Being who is the indweller (*antaryāmi*) in all divine

[53]TMK V-81. *devatā-prīti-koṭau tattatphalāpteḥ dvāraṁ śrutibhiḥ avadhṛtau.*
[54]*sa evainaṁ bhūtiṁ gamayati.*

beings is the giver of the fruit. Although the individual deities are worshipped, the one who really confers the results eventually is *Īśvara*. In view of this, He is described as *sarva-karma-samārādhya*. Indra and Agni may come and go, but the *paramātman*, who is their *antaryāmi* is eternal. It is *paramātman* who is pleased with the good deeds performed by the individuals and He alone, through the *media* of the concerned divine beings, awards the fruits.[55] Śrutis and smṛtis are His commands. The scrupulous obedience of the divine command causes pleasure to *Īśvara*; disobedience of His command causes displeasure to Him. *Adṛṣṭa* is nothing other than the pleasure or displeasure (*anugraha* and *nigraha*) of *Īśvara*. This is to be accepted on the strength of scriptural texts. If scripture were not accepted as an authority, even the performance of *yāgas* which is laid down in it would have to be given up.

III. OTHER CATEGORIES

Nyāya Theory of Karma

We have so far examined the various attributes known as *guṇas* enumerated by the Nyāya-Vaiśeṣika, and pointed out that with the exception of a few they do not constitute distinct qualities (*atirikta-guṇa*). Along with the consideration of the *guṇas*, Vedānta Deśika also takes up for critical examination the other categories such as *karma* (action), *sāmānya* (generality), *viśeṣa* (individuality), *abhāva* (non-existence) and *samavāya* (inherence). All these are regarded by the Nyāya-Vaiśeṣika as separate categories (*padārthas*).

Karma or action refers to movement. According to the Nyāya-Vaiśeṣika, there are five kinds of movement: (1) upward movement (*utkṣepaṇa*); (2) downward movement (*apakṣepaṇa*); (3) contraction (*ākuñcana*); (4) expansion (*prasaraṇa*); and (5) movement in general such as going forward or backward (*gamana*). All kinds of movement (*karma*) belong to the *dravya* (substance) and cause the things to move. Their relation to *dravya* is similar to that of *guṇas*. *Karma* is not perceptible but it is proved by means of inference.

[55]TMK V-84. *sa ekaḥ sarvārādhyāntarātmā na hi galitapadaḥ nāpi suptaḥ ṭadāpi.*

There is a view, according to which *karma* is what is brought about by the association or conjunction of an object with another spatial entity. According to another view, *karma* is not mere conjunction of one object with another spatial entity. Thus, for instance, the fishes found in a continuously flowing river are found stable and the fact that they are associated with the moving water does not cause a movement in them. To take another example, the flowing river is in conjunction with the *ākāśa* or sky over it but the latter is not regarded as having movement. The mere conjunction of an object with a moving entity is not *karma*. It is something more than that.[56]

According to Vedānta Deśika, *karma* is that which causes in us the awareness that the object is moving.[57] In other words, it is movement (*calana*). While he agrees with the Naiyāyika with regard to the general nature of *karma*, he questions the soundness of classification of *karma* into five kinds. There is no justifiable criterion on the basis of which such a classification could be maintained. If, on the basis of four directions (east, west, south and north) and movement in general (*gamana*), *karma* is divided into five types, then there should have been ten types of *karma*, because of ten directions. If it be some other determining factor on the basis of which classification is made, there would be indefinite number of *karmas* in so far as the determining factor is not specific. It may be said that the specific effort of an individual which leads to action is the determining factor. Even this will not hold good, because it is found that one single effort may lead to several actions and sometime several efforts may lead to one single action.[58]

Vedānta Deśika also rejects the view that *karma* is not perceptible but it is to be inferred. The following syllogistic argument is adopted by the Naiyāyikas in support of their view: '*Karma* is not capable of being known through perception because it is *karma*, as for example the movement of the sun which is not an object of perception.' This syllogism is fallacious. If *karma* is never an object of perception, logical concomitance (*vyāpti*) on which the soundness of the syllogism rests is not possible. The invariable concomitance between two

[56]SS V-107, p. 309. *deśāntaraprāptiḥ adhikam karma.*

[57]NS, p. 264. *calanapratyayaviṣayaḥ karma.*

[58]TMK V-110

entities is possible only when these are perceived. If all *karmas* are outside the purview of sense perception, how is it possible to prove that the *hetu* is correlated with the *sādhya*? The illustration cited is also defective. The movement of the sun is capable of being known through perception. But if we do not have a direct vision of it, it is only due to the distance. If *karma* is not perceptible, then it stands unproved (*apramāṇa*) Insofar as it is not established by the *pramāṇas*. The Naiyāyikas might say that it is valid because it is inferred on the basis of the fact that an object has moved from one place to another (*deśāntara-sambandha*). What causes such a movement is *karma*. In the opinion of Vedānta Deśika, such an explanation is unnecessary to prove *karma*. Whatever is the cause of the *karma* as conceived by the Naiyāyika, the same may be accepted to explain the movement of an object from one place to another. The assumption of an additional factor as *karma* besides the movement of the object from one place to another is superfluous. Further, *saṁyoga* or conjunction involves two objects, and if *karma*, is accepted as a separate quality it should be present in both the relata. But in the case of the *saṁyoga* of the bird with the hill, movement belongs only to the bird but not to the hill. If Nyāya explanation is accepted, then movement should also apply to the hill. But this is opposed to our experience. It should therefore be admitted that movement of the object itself is *karma* which is perceptible.[59]

Nyāya Theory of Sāmānya

This is admitted as an independent category (*pādārtha*) by the Vaiśeṣikas. It refers to the feature or property common to two or more things. Thus, when we see several cows we get the notion that they are all the same. The cognition of sameness in respect of objects which are different from each other does not arise without some reason. As the cows are also seen as different they cannot be regarded as non-distinct (*aikya*). It cannot be said that it is purely a mental construction (*jñānākāra*), because knowledge which is internal cannot assume the form of what exists externally. The generality found among the cows exists externally. Nor can it be said that the awareness of sameness is superimposed since what does not exist anywhere cannot be

[59]TMK V-108.

superimposed. Therefore, we have to admit that there is some characteristic common to all (*anugata-dharma*). This is what is known as *sāmānya*, according to Vaiśeṣikas. The same is also called *jāti* or generic character. *Gotva* or cowness is the general feature which is common to all the cows. Cowness (*gotva*) is therefore the *sāmānya* of cows. According to the Vaiśeṣikas, it is a separate category and exists in all the three *padārthas*: *dravya*, *guṇa* and *karma*. Though it is existent in all the three, it has an independent reality. It is one, eternal and subsists in many. There are gradations of *sāmānya*. *Sattā* or Being is the highest universal (*parajāti*), for it is found to characterise the largest number of entities; and the others, known as *apara jāti* or lower universals, follow it in a descending order, like *dravyatva*, *pṛthivitva* and *ghaṭatva*, each characterising less and less numerous things.

The theory of *sāmānya* has been subjected to severe criticism by the Buddhists who deny it altogether. Where does *sāmānya* or *jāti* exist? Does it exist in between the two objects such as pots? This cannot be so, because it is against our experience. If it does not exist in between the two objects, then the two pots cannot be regarded as the same. Again, does potness (*ghaṭatva*) which is *sāmānya* exist in the entire pot or only in a part of it? If it be the first alternative, potness being in the entire pot would not be found in other pots. If it be the latter alternative, then *jāti* would become an entity with parts (*sāṁśa-padārtha*). In other words, partial existence presupposes possession of parts. What is single, eternal and ubiquitous cannot have parts. If *sāmānya* exists in its entirety in one individual, it cannot exist in other individuals having exhausted itself in one. Further, if the object (*dharmi*) in which it subsists is destroyed, *sāmānya* which is its *dharma* also ceases to exist. *Sāmānya* has no movement and it cannot therefore move out into another individual object.[60]

These dialectical arguments are refuted by the Vaiśeṣikas as untenable on the ground that what is well established by experience is to be accepted.[61] By way of direct reply, the Vaiśeṣikas urge that *sāmānya* being single and ubiquitous cannot be thought of as existing either in parts or as a whole. It exists in

[60]TMK V-114.

[61]See SS V-114, p. 312. *pratyakṣaviruddhatvāt adūṣaṇam.*

the relation of inherence with its substratum; the same universal exists in each of the individuals in a similar way without changing its feature. Only such an existence of an unchanged and single thing can account for the cognition of similarity in the object of the same class.

The Buddhists have another theory by means of which they disprove the existence of *sāmānya*. According to this theory, known as *apoha-vāda,* the nature of cognition is negative in character. When a cow is perceived, it is not directly seen as cow but as something different from all the things that are different from it (*gavetarāpoha*). The *sāmānya* of cow is nothing but the difference from animals other than cow such as horse. What differentiates a cow from horse is its *sāmānya.* In other words, the sameness as cow is the negation of all non-cows, and this is represented in consciousness as the sameness as cow.

This is not a correct theory, because negation of non-cows is a negative perception, whereas the sameness perceived as cow is a positive perception. *Gotva* or cowness is not a negative concept implying its difference from others but rather it is a positive concept only implying the true characteristic of a cow. If *gotva* is not accepted as a positive concept as Buddhists claim, it would lead to a vicious circle.[62] That is, if a cow is to be known as that which is not a non-cow, we should first have to know what a cow is; to know this non-cow, we will have to know what a cow is. Thus the cognition of cow depends upon the knowledge of non-cow which again depends upon the former.

Viśiṣṭādvaita Concept of Jāti

After having in general outlined the Vaiśeṣika theory of *sāmānya* and defended it against the criticisms of Buddhists, Vedānta Deśika proceeds to present the Viśiṣṭādvaita theory of *jāti*. The term *jāti* is used in place of *sāmānya* mentioned by the Nyāya-Vaiśeṣika. Though the Viśiṣṭādvaitin accepts the concept of *jāti*, he does not regard it as an independent category or as one and ubiquitious. According to this system, *jāti* is the *asādhāraṇa-dharma,* the unique characteristic of the object. It is the specific structure of the object (*saṁsthāna-viśeṣa*) as, for ex-

[62]TMK V-115.

ample, the dewlap, in the case of the cow. Apart from this, there is no separate entity as *jāti*, as the Nyâya-Vaiśeṣikas believe.[63]

The Vaiśeṣikas accept *sāmānya* as a separate category in order to account for the notion or the awareness of similarity which we get when we see the different objects of the same class. That which causes such a notion of similarity is the *sāmānya* or generality that exists in those objects. Vedānta Deśika points out that the postulation of *sāmanya* as a category other than the special structure of the objects is superfluous, because the latter itself can account for the notion of similarity. Thus, for instance, *bhūtatva* or being an element is a common feature of all the *pañcabhūtas* (five gross elements); this is the generality or *sāmānya* of the *bhūtas*. Even, according to the Vaiśeṣikas, it is a specific characteristic (*viśeṣaguṇa*) and not a separate category, It is known as *upādhi* or a qualifying character. If such an *upādhi* could cause the notion of similarity among the *bhūtas*, the same explanation should hold good in respect of other physical objects. Thus, for instance, *gotva* or cowness is the *sāmānya* or *jāti* of the cow-class and *gotva*, as already explained, is not a separate quality but the special physical feature of the cows in the form of dewlap. If the judgment that all cows are the same could take place on the basis of the special structure found in the cows, it is not necessary to postulate an additional category as *sāmānya* for the purpose.

For the Vaiśeṣikas, the physical objects which are known as *avayavi* (the whole) are the conglomeration of parts (*avayavas*); apart from the structural composition of the parts, there is no other characteristic as *sāmānya*. It is therefore appropriate to accept the similarity that exists in respect of the special physical structure of the objects as the basis for the notion of similarity among the different objects of the same class. As there is a perfect similarity of all *avayavas* of individual objects (*atyantasādṛśya*), it is possible to get the notion that all of them are the same.

The admission of *jāti* as a separate *dharma* other than the structure of the object leads to certain difficulties. According to the Vaiśeṣikas, the physical structure of the object (*ākṛti*) is the revealer (*abhivyañjaka*) of *jāti*. *Ākṛti* itself is a common character found in all kinds of material objects and as such it would

[63]TMK V-116. *tasmāt saṅghātavargeṣu avayavaracanābhedato anyat na siddhyet.* See also RB I-1-1, p. 54. *saṁsthānam eva jātiḥ.*

constitute a *jāti*. Then the question arises whether there is something which would reveal this *jāti* in the form of *ākṛti*. If the reply is in the affirmative, it would lead to the fallacy of infinite regress. To overcome this difficulty, if it be said that *ākṛti* does not require another *ākṛti* to reveal itself but, on the contrary, it reveals itself as well as the *jāti*, then why accept *jāti* as a separate *dharma* in order to account for similarity (*sādṛśya*)? It may be argued that the physical structure of the object (*ākṛti*) being different from each other cannot constitute a common character of all objects as a *jāti* but nevertheless it can serve the purpose of revealing the *jāti*. If that be the case, it would follow that the special structure of the object (which is the very *ākṛti*) gives rise to the notion of similarity, and as such there would no need to admit *sāmānya* as a separate *dharma*.[64]

By way of further clarification Vedānta Deśika states that some of the characteristics in the objects manifest themselves as similar to others. On the basis of such similarity observed in the objects of the same class, one recollects the similarity in respect of other objects of the same class as and when seen, and thereby gets the awareness that they are all the same. The recollection of the common characteristic found in all is responsible for the awareness that all are the same. It is therefore obvious that the cause of the *anugata-vyavahāra* or the notion of generality is not a separate entity such as *sāmānya* or *jāti* but the very structure of the objects which is common to all.[65]

An objection may be raised against this conclusion. Is *sādṛśya* or similarity, which is responsible for the notion of generality, a separate quality or property recurrent in all the objects of the same class? If it is so, then that itself is the *jāti* as conceived by the Naiyāyikas. If, on the contrary, it is said that *sādṛśya* is not a separate property common to all the objects, then it cannot form the basis for getting the notion of generality. In reply to this objection, Vedānta Deśika says that *sādṛśya* is not accepted by the Viśiṣṭādvaitin as a separate quality recurrent in all the objects of the same class. It is no doubt a separate characteristic feature of the object in the form of the special structure (as for example, the dewlap of the cow) but subsisting in each

[64]SS V-117, p. 313.

[65]TMK V-118. *anyonyataikasmṛtiviṣayatayā tattadekāvamarśaḥ*.

individual object.[66] However, the concept of similarity (*sādṛśya*) is relational in character, because the moment we say it is similar the question arises : similar to what? It is only when two objects of the same class are cognised together, we make the judgment that they are similar. In the same way, all such other objects of the same class which have similarity come to our mind. What is an *anugata-dharma* is a *buddhi-viśeṣa*. That is, it is a notion or a mental picture and not a separate characteristic known as *jāti* as recurrent in all objects. Further, *anugata-vyavahāra* or the notion of generality need not arise necessarily on the basis of *jāti* only. Take, for instance, the non-existence (*abhāva*) of heat in objects other than fire. We have noticed that only fire possesses the quality of heat. The notion of non-existence of heat in all objects other than fire (as *anugata-dharma* or common feature) arises automatically even without the apprehension of *jāti*.

Another important objection is raised against the Viśiṣṭādvaita theory of *jāti*. If the physical feature (*ākṛti*) in the form of some special structure of the object (*avasthā-sanniveśa*) is *jāti*, how do we account for *jāti* in respect of quality such as odour and *ātman* which do not possess any physical structure (*niravayava*)? In reply to this Vedāntā Deśika points out that only in respect of material objects, which possess physical features, the *saṁsthāna* or the special physical structure constitutes the *jāti* or the basis for the notion of generality. In the case of entities such as odour which is a *guṇa*, the very *guṇa* itself serves the purpose of *jāti* for the notion of generality.[67] Similarly, in the case of *ātman*, the distinguishing characteristic of *ātman* (*ātmatva*) constitutes the *jāti* for it. Even the Naiyāyikas who raise the above objection have to adopt such an explanation. According to them, the physical feature (*ākṛti*) is the revealer of *jāti* in respect cf material objects. *Guṇas* do not have physical form. Nevertheless, *gandhavattva* which is *jāti* inheres in *gandha* and not in any other quality. In the same way, the Viśiṣṭādvaitin also mainatins that the very nature of the entity, whether it be a substance or attribute, should be the determining factor for the notion of similarity.

[66]TMK V-119. *ekaikasthaṁ tu tais tair nirupadhiniyatais sapratidvandvikaṁ syāt.* See also SS, p. 314.

[67]SS V-121, p.315. *guṇādiṣu tattad asādhāraṇalakṣaṇameva tattadvyavahāraniyāmakam.*

The Concept of Viśeṣa

According to the Vaiśeṣikas, *viśeṣa* or individuality is a special and separate quality that subsists in eternal objects and on the basis of which one object is distinguished from the other. It is the differentia of ultimate objects which are otherwise alike. Thus, two atoms of earth or two souls . their intrinsic form resemble each other in every respect, and, if they are still regarded as two, we should admit a distinctive feature in each. That feature is its *viśeṣa*. The ultimate objects which are supposed to possess *viśeṣa* are atoms, souls, time, space (*dik*), ether (*ākāśa*) and mind (*manas*).

Vedānta Deśika criticises this theory. The individuality or *viśeṣa* is not a separate quality subsisting in objects. The very objects serve the purpose of distinguishing one from the other, and it is not therefore necessary to postulate a separate concept. It should be possible to distinguish the objects on the basis of temporal as well as spatial factors or with reference to the distinguishing characteristics they possess. Even the Vaiśeṣikas admit this. Thus, in our ordinary experience when we see an object, we describe it as possessing a specific generic character as existing in a particular place and time and of having specific qualities. When another object as different from it is seen by us, it is described as not possessing any of these qualities. Thus, objects perceived by us are characterised by time, space, generic character and qualities.[68] What is, thus, characterised is the *viśeṣa* of the object. *Viśeṣa* of an object is therefore to be determined by temporal, spatial factors and the characteristics it possesses.

In the case of eternal entities such as the eternally free souls (*nitya-muktas*) which are all alike, their individuality is explained on the basis of the special characteristics they possess on the authority of the sacred texts.[69] As regards the released souls (*muktātmā*), it is possible to distinguish between them on the basis of the functions they perform in the released state. This is also determined on the authority of the sacred texts. Their individuality could also be established on the basis of the types of *karma* they were associated with prior to release. It may be asked

[68]TMK V-123. See also SS, p. 316. *loke hi deśakālādiviśeṣādvastūnām viśeṣo dṛśyate.* [69]*Ibid.*

as to how we know this. The answer is that the *yagis* or those with supernormal perception could apprehend such distinctions. Thus, some special characteristics exist in all entities including the ultimate substance, and by means of this their individuality is established. It is not necessary to psotulate *viśeṣa* as a separate quality.

The Vaiśeṣikas have felt the need to admit the *viśeṣa* as a separate quality in order to account for the distinction between the *paramāṇus* and the *muktātmans*, in the same way as between an elephant and a horse. This is unnecessary, contends Vedānta Deśika, because the Vedāntins do not accept the existence of *paramāṇus* and that of the released souls as totally devoid of consciousness.

Vedānta Deśika further points out that the postulation of *viśeṣa* as a separate quality serves no useful purpose either to the ordinary human beings or the *yogis*. It is not useful to us because it is not at all perceptible being a supersensuous entity. The *yogis* could have a vision of them, but it is not of any use to them since they are not interested in the empirical world. The *yogis* who are omniscient could apprehend all objects as they are. What is not proved by perception could be established by inference, but this is not of any relevance since *viśeṣa* as a quality serves no useful purpose. The Āgamas also do not support the theory since there are no scriptural texts referring to it.[70]

The Concept of Abhāva

Some of the later followers of Nyāya-Vaiśeṣika system have admitted *abhāva* as an independent category. The Vedāntins and the Prābhākaras do not accept it as a separate category. According to the Viśiṣṭādvaita Vedānta, *abhāva* is a positive concept and is a different state of existence (*bhāvāntara*). Non-existence of an object means that it exists in some other state, or it exists in a different place or time. When we say that the pot does not exist here at present, a statement implying *abhāva* of the pot, it only means that the pot exists elsewhere at some other time or it exists in the state of a lump of clay (*piṇḍatva*). *Abhāva* is, thus, a determining factor which characterises an object with reference to time, space and condition.[71]

[70]TMK V-125.

[71]TMK V-129. *daśā-deśa-kālādi-bhedaḥ yaḥ svabhāvam niyamayati, saḥ abhāvaḥ.*

If the above explanation is accepted, would it not imply that in the judgment 'blue jar' blueness is negation of yellow colour? Vedânta Deśika replies that it is not so. Blueness is not the absence of yellowness, because in the cognition of a blue jar, blueness is perceived as a positive characteristic of the jar, whereas when we cognise non-existence of jar, we do not cognise any other object except the absence of jar. The two judgments—'blue jar' and 'jar does not exist'—have different implications. The former refers to the special quality of the jar, whereas the latter refers to the absence of the jar.

The Naiyâyikas have recognised four types of *abhāva*: taking the case of a jar, there is first the antecedent non-existence or prior negation (*prāgabhāva*), and there is only the clay or the two halves (*kapāla*) of it. This type of *abhāva* is considered beginningless but comes to an end when the object in question is produced. When again the jar is destroyed leaving only the potsherd behind, there is subsequent non-existence or posterior negation (*pradhvaṁsābhāva*). It has a beginning but is endless, since the identical jar will never again come into existence. These two negations characterise the clay and the potsherd respectively. The third type is known as absolute or total negation (*atyantābhāva*) as in the example of the bare ground with no jar on it. The last type is mutual negation (*anyonyābhāva*) which is only another word for difference (*bheda*) between two objects each having its own identity as, for example, the statement that jar is not cloth. While Vedânta Deśika agrees in general with these details, he points out consistent with the general theory of *abhāva* as positive concept, that *prāgabhāva* is a series of states in the form of lump of clay that exists from eternity prior to the production of pot. Similarly, the posterior non-existence is an endless series of states of potsherd that follow soon after destruction of the pot. The *svarūpa* of a substance in this system is *nitya* (eternal); therefore *prāgabhāva* of an object is *anādi* and its *pradhvaṁsābhāva* is *ananta*. If, on the contrary, it is maintained that the prior non-existence and posterior non-existence are two distinct categories, we have to admit an endless series of *abhāvas* both prior to the production and after destruction of the pot, and it would lead to an infinite regress. It is therefore more appropriate to accept a theory which is in conformity with experience and which is acceptable to all.

An objection may be raised against the Viśiṣṭādvaita view of *abhāva*. The modifications in the form of origin and destruction take place only in a substance in succession. That is, a pot is brought into existence (origin); it exists and it is then destroyed. In this way origin and destruction take place in a sequence. This amounts to saying that one state (*avasthā*) of a substance assumes another state (*avasthā*) and so on *ad infinitum*. If one *avasthā* becomes another *avasthā*, the concept of origin and destruction does not find a satisfactory explanation. If *abhāva*, on the contrary, is accepted as a negative concept, such a difficulty does not arise.

This objection is untenable, contends Vedānta Deśika. *Avasthās* or modifications in the form of origin and destruction are mutually opposed. When a substance passes from one state to another, it is considered to have been produced. When it is subjected to destruction, the *avasthā* that it assumes at that stage is regarded as destroyed. The *avasthās* belong to the substance and whatever names are given to the modified substances, the same do hold good for those *avasthās*. The changes in the *avasthās* account for the origin and destruction not only in themselves but also in the substances in which they inhere. There are six types of modifications taking place in a substance: (1) being or existence (*asti*); (2) origin (*jāyate*); (3) growth (*vardhate*); (4) transformation (*pariṇamate*); (5) decay (*apakṣiyate*); and (6) destruction (*naśyati*). All these are modifications which account for the different states of a substance and cause the notion of origin, destruction, etc. of the substance. Vedānta Deśika therefore comes to the conclusion that there is no justification to regard *abhāva* as a separate negative concept. It is only a positive state (*bhāvāntara*).

Samavāya (Inherence). This is another important category admitted by the Nyāya-Vaiśeṣika as an independent *padārtha*. It refers to the internal relation that exists between two inseparable entities (*ayutasiddha*) as between a substance and an attribute. We have already examined this theory separately in the earlier chapter.[72] According to Vedānta Deśika, the postulation of *samavāya* as a separate relation between two inseparable entities is superfluous. It is also logically untenable as it leads to the fallacy of infinite regress.

[72]See Section 'Nyāya-Vaiśeṣika Theory of Samavāya' in Chapter I.

It may be observed from the foregoing discussion that the Nyāya classification of the metaphysical categories or *padārthas* and the enumeration of the nine *dravyas* and twenty-four *guṇas* is done in an arbitary way without sufficient logical justification. With a view to overcoming the apparent defects, Vedānta Deśika has classified the metaphysical categories under the broad concepts of *dravya* and *adravya*. The two concepts as defined by him are comprehensive and exclusive in character. Under the *dravyas* are included the six entities—*Īśvara*, *jiva*, *buddhi* (knowledge), *prakṛti* (cosmic matter), *kālā* and *nityavibhūti* (the transcendental matter)—all of which are real and eternal (*nitya*) in character. Under the *adravyas*, the ten fundamental or basic attributes are included. All the other objects and the attributes in the universe come under these sixteen categories.

It may be asked whether it would be justifiable to claim that *padārthas* are only this much and no more. If there are more than what is enumerated, then the claim becomes false; if there are no more *padārthas*, then the claim is meaningless.

This is not a relevant question, contends Vedānta Deśika. The implication of the above claim is that whatever entity could be established on the basis of valid *pramāṇas*, that falls under the broad categories enumerated by the Viśiṣṭādvaitin. Such an explanation should be acceptable even to the critic. It is only after the nature of the metaphysical entities or the fundamental attributes is determined on the basis of the *pramāṇas*, it is possible to ask the question whether or not there could be anything else which is not covered. In other words, the question whether or not there is any more entity or attribute arises only after we have established what the ultimate categories are. Thus, on the basis of an impartial and careful philosophic enquiry conducted in conformity with the valid *pramāṇas*—perception, inference and revealed scripture—Vedānta Deśika formulates the *dravyas* and *adravyas*. As we mentioned earlier, it is for the first time in the history of Viśiṣṭādvaita system that such a critical study of this important doctrine has been carried out in the *Tattva-muktākalāpa*. Herein lies the greatness and importance of this philosophic classic and its contribution to the study of Vedānta.

CHAPTER TWELVE

General Estimate and Conclusion

In the preceding chapters we have discussed in detail the fundamental doctrines of Viśiṣṭādvaita Vedānta relating to *jñāna*, *jīva*, *Īśvara*, *prakṛti*, *kāla* and *nityavibhūti*, the six metaphysical entities accepted in the system. We have also discussed comprehensively the fundamental metaphysical concepts and the categories. The theory of knowledge forms the basis on which the metaphysics of Viśiṣṭādvaita is founded. The three realities—*Īśvara* *jīva* and *prakṛti*—as an organic unity constitute the Metaphysical Absolute or Brahman described in the Upaniṣads. The doctrine of substance and attribute, as explained in the first chapter, provides the justification for upholding the unity or oneness of Reality while at the same time maintaining the difference or plurality.

How far are these doctrines sound? Are they philosophically and logically tenable? While examining critically the corresponding doctrines of rival schools of thought, Vedānta Deśika has anticipated all possible criticisms against the theories of Viśiṣṭādvaita and answered them fully. These have been mentioned in the respective chapters. We need not reiterate them here. We shall take up in this chapter a general and overall evaluation of Viśiṣṭādvaita as a sound system of philosophy.

There are two important issues which require critical examination in order to establish the soundness of Viśiṣṭādvaita as a system of philosophy. Viśiṣṭādvaita accepts the personal God of Religion as the Ultimate Reality, and regards it as identical with the Absolute of Metaphysics. In other words, it rejects the concept of the undifferentiated transcendental Absolute or *nirviśeṣa* Brahman and upholds that the Supreme Being as a personality or *saviśeṣa* Brahman is the only Ultimate Reality. Is it philosophically justifiable to regard the *saviśeṣa entity* as the Ultimate Reality? Secondly, if Reality is *saviśeṣa* Brahman, that is, Brahman which includes in itself *cit* and *acit* and also the numerous other attributes, would it be justified to consider such a complex entity as one in the strict sense of the term?

I

The first issue, insofar as it is confined to Vedânta, is raised on the assumption that the Upaniṣads on the basis of which the Vedânta system is developed refer to two realities—a higher Brahman as undifferentiated Being and a lower Brahman endowed with qualities as the creator of the universe. The former is regarded as the Absolute of Metaphysics, whereas the latter is the God of Religion. Râmânuja rejects the former as inconceivable and accepts the latter by adopting a theistic interpretation of the Upaniṣads. Śaṁkara, on the contrary, adopts a non-theistic interpretation of the Upaniṣads, and accepts the undifferentiated Absolute as the Ultimate Reality. However, realising the need for religion, he also admitted God which for him is the *saguṇa* Brahman or the Brahman as conditioned by *mâyâ*. We shall examine how far these claims are justifiable.

Do the Upaniṣads really speak of two Brahmans? Prima facie, the answer is in the affirmative. In reply to a question whether there are two Brahmans as *para* and *apara*, Saṁkara in his commentary on *Vedânta-sûtra* says on the strength of the *Praśna Upaniṣad* that Brahman is conceived in two ways.[1] *Para*. or higher Brahman is that which is described by the Upaniṣad as free from all the limiting conditions caused by the influence of *avidyâ*. The *apara* or lower Brahman is that which is qualified by limiting conditions and which is intended for purposes of *upâsanâ*. Thus the Upaniṣad which is quoted in support of the higher Brahman says: 'It is neither gross nor minute, neither short nor long, neither redness nor moisture, neither shadow nor darkness, neither air nor space, unattached without odour, without eyes or ears, without vocal organ or mind, non-luminous, without vital breath or mouth, without measure and without interior or exterior.'[2] The lower Brahman with positive attributes, on the other hand, is described as: 'He, whose body is spirit, whose form is light, whose thoughts are true, whose

[1]Śaṁkara Bhâṣya on VS IV-3-14. *kiṁ dve brahmaṇī param aparaṁ ca iti? bâḍham dve; 'etadvai satyakâma paraṁ ca aparaṁ ca brahma yadoṁkâraḥ' ityâdi darśanât*. See *Praśna: Upaniṣad* 5-2.

[2]Br III-8-8 (according to SB).

nature is like *ākāśa*, from whom all works, all desires, all odours and all tastes proceed, encompassing this whole world.'[3] There are Upaniṣadic texts which speak of Brahman as devoid of qualities, while there are also texts which declare Brahman as endowed with attributes. In some passages, the Reality is presented as acosmic or all-exclusive (*niṣprapañca*). In some others again, it is stated to be cosmic or all-comprehensive in its nature (*saprapañca*).

Some Advaitins take the view that the Upaniṣads do not refer to two Brahmans, but they only describe Brahman as having two aspects : the one devoid of attributes (*nirviśeṣa*) and the other endowed with qualities (*saviśeṣa*). Brahman, it is argued, is one only without a second and that the same Brahman has been described in two ways from two different points of view. The one is called the empirical point of view (*vyāvahārika*) and the other transcendental (*pāramārthika*). The first is upheld by those who regard the world as real and therefore describe Brahman as its omnipotent and omnipresent creator, sustainer and destroyer. Such a Brahman is *saguṇa* or *saviśeṣa*, endowed with attributes. But, according to the second view, the world of names and forms is finally unreal, and only Brahman exists. This Brahman is unconditioned and devoid of all attributes.

The question whether the Upaniṣads refer to two Brahmans —*para* (higher) and *apara* (lower)—or whether they describe only two aspects of Brahman is not so important. Even the Viśiṣṭādvaitin is prepared to accept two aspects of Brahman as *nirākāra* or *sākāra* though in a different sense.[4] The relevant issue for a student of philosophy is what is the nature of the ultimate Reality, according to the Vedānta? Is the Ultimate Brahman *nirviśeṣa* or *saviśeṣa*? The answers to this crucial ontological issue as provided by Śaṁkara and Rāmānuja are too well known. They hold a diametrically opposite view. According to some modern scholars, the Upaniṣads present conflicting views on the nature of Ultimate Reality, and it may not therefore be possible to come to a decisive conclusion on the basis of it. However, according to Śaṁkara, the purport of the Upaniṣads is non-dualism and that Brahman alone without a second

[3]Ch III-14-2.

[4]See '*Jitanta-Stotra. na te rūpam na cākāraḥ nāyudhāni na cāspadam/ tathāpi puruṣākāraḥ bhaktānām tvaṁ prakāśase//*

(*ekameva advitiyam*) is the ultimate Reality. The implication of this is that Brahman is undifferentiated. This view is upheld primarily on the strength of the Upaniṣadic texts.

Rāmānuja does not accept this view. According to him, the Upaniṣads speak of only one Brahman which is *saviśeṣa* or *saguṇa*. He examines critically all the Upaniṣadic texts quoted by Śaṁkara in support of the *nirviśeṣa* Brahman, and comes to the conclusion that the true import of these texts, taken in their relevant contexts and also with reference to other śruti texts, is only a Brahman as endowed with attributes. We need not go into a discussion of the interpretation of the relevant Upaniṣadic texts as this will require an independent study of the Upaniṣads and falls outside the scope of this book. We may only consider the logical soundness of the underlying principles and arguments adopted for the interpretation of the relevant Upaniṣadic texts to determine the nature of the ultimate Reality. This will help us to assess the relative merits of the conclusions drawn by Śaṁkara and Rāmānuja regarding the ultimate Reality.

In matters which are supersensuous, the revealed scripture is the most authoritative *pramāṇa*. This is the fundamental postulate accepted by all the Vedāntins. Thus, the *Vedānta-sūtra* asserts that *śāstra* or sacred texts is the only source of authority for ascertaining the philosophic truth (*śāstrayonitvāt*). Inference or logic cannot conclusively establish the nature of ultimate Reality, because it is possible for one to advance arguments on the basis of logic to disprove what is asserted by means of inference.[5] Logic has its own limitation. While it can be adopted to support what is taught by scripture, it cannot be the sole means of knowing the Reality.

Besides revealed scripture, we have to depend on two other sources for understanding the nature of Reality. Vedānta as a system of philosophy (*darśana*) is founded on the Upaniṣads, the *Vedānta-sūtras* and the *Bhagavad-gita*—the triple foundation known as *prasthānatraya*. Of these the Upaniṣads constitute the primary source, and naturally enjoy greater authority. The other two texts are equally important as these are accepted as the authoritative sources of Vedānta. The *Vedānta-sūtras* compiled by Bādarāyaṇa are not merely intended to present the

[5]See VS II-1-11. *tarkāpratiṣthānādapi.*

teachings of the Upaniṣads in a systematic manner but also to provide guidance for interpreting the Upaniṣadic texts. They are, in fact, according to tradition, meant to reconcile the apparent conflicts found in the Upaniṣads and present a coherent view of Reality.[6] Further, in the case of other systems or *darśanas* such as Nyāya, Vaiśeṣika, Yoga and Pūrva-Mīmāṁsā, the respective *sūtras* are taken as the basic source for the concerned system. In the same way, the *Vedānta-sūtras* should also be taken to constitute the basic source for the Vedānta system.

As regards the *Bhagavad-gītā*, though it does not enjoy the same status as revealed scripture, it is accepted as an important authoritative source-book for Vedānta, because it aims to elucidate the teachings contained in the Upaniṣads. It is therefore regarded as an *upabṛṁhaṇa* or that which lucidly explains the abstract truths contained in the Vedas.[7]

In determining the nature of ultimate Reality, we should therefore take into consideration the teachings contained in all the three *prasthānas*—Upaniṣads, *Vedānta-sūtras* and *Gītā*. An objective study of all the three texts taken together would inevitably lead to the conclusion that Brahman is *saviśeṣa*. Even if each one of these treatises is taken individually, the conclusion cannot be different.

The *Vedānta-sūtras* do not generally support the theory of *nirviśeṣa* Brahman. That the *sūtras* are not in consonance with the doctrine of Reality advocated by the Advaitin is amply demonstrated with convincing arguments by Vedānta Deśika in his *Śatadūṣaṇi*.[8] To give a few instances: the very first aphorism, 'Then therefore the desire to know Brahmaṇ' is in direct conflict with the concept of undifferentiated Reality. *Jijñāsā* or desire to know arises when an object is known in respect of general features and when its specific features are yet to be understood. If Brahman is *nirviśeṣa* and the same is also not the object of knowledge, *jijñāsā* becomes untenable. The second *sūtra* points

[6]The *sūtras* string together the teachings of the Upaniṣads and present them in a systematic way. See *Śaṁkara-bhāṣya* I-1-2. *vedānta-vākya-kusuma-grathanārthatvāt sūtrāṇāṁ; vedānta-vākyāni hi sūtrair udāhṛtya vicāryante*. *Vedānta-sūtras* are also regarded as *Naya-sūtras* meaning that these serve as logical arguments supporting the teachings of the Upaniṣads.

[7]See RB II-2-1, p. 442. *upabṛṁhaṇam ca śrutipratipannārthaviśadīkaraṇam*.

[8]*Śatadūṣaṇī* Vāda 66 *paramate sūtra-svārasya-bhaṅga-vādaḥ*. See also RB I-1-2.

out that Brahman is that from which the origin, etc. of the universe proceeds. This aphorism is intended to define the nature of Brahman which is the object of philosophic enquiry. According to this *sūtra* which is based on the *Taittirīya Upaniṣad* text, Brahman is the cause of universe. The functions of creation, sustenance and dissolution of universe are applicable only to a *saviśeṣa* Brahman or personal God. In the same way, Vedānta Deśika points out that the subsequent topics dealt with in the *Vedānta-sūtras* do not favour the *nirviśeṣa* Brahman.[9]

The two aphorisms in the *ubhayaliṅgādhikaraṇa*[10] which are claimed by the Advaitin as teaching explicitly the undifferentiated character of Brahman bring out, according to the interpretation offered by Rāmānuja, the two-fold characteristics of Brahman, viz. that it is free from all imperfections and also the abode of numerous auspicious qualities as declared by the Upaniṣads.[11]

The *Bhagavad-gītā* also does not favour the doctrine of *nirviśeṣa* Brahman. The substance of the *Gītā*, as is beautifully summed up in one verse by Yāmuna, is that the *para* Brahman is Nārāyaṇa who is to be attained by means of meditation (*bhakti*) developed by the observance of *karma* and *jñāna yoga*.[12] The teachings of the *Gītā* right from the beginning to the end refer to a personal God as distinct from *jīva* (*kṣetrajña*) and matter (*kṣetra*). Those few verses in the *Gītā* which are claimed to lend support to the theory of *nirviśeṣa* Brahman bear a different meaning, according to the interpretation offered by Rāmānuja.

Do the Upaniṣads advocate the doctrine of *nirviśeṣa* Brahman? We have already observed that the Upaniṣads contain conflicting statements regarding the nature of ultimate Reality, and it may be somewhat difficult to arrive at a decisive conclusion solely on the basis of the Upaniṣads without the help of *Vedānta-sūtras* and the *Gītā*. If the Upaniṣadic texts are interpreted in the

[9] *Ibid.*

[10] VS III-2-11. *na sthānato' pi parasya ubhayaliṅgam.* VS III-2-14. *arūpavadeva hi tatpradhānatvāt.*

[11] RB III-2-11, p. 653. *sarvatra śrutismṛtiṣu, paraṁ brahma ubhayaliṅgam ubhaya-lakṣaṇam abhidhīyate; nirastanikhiladoṣatva-kalyāṇa-guṇākaratva-lakṣaṇopetam.*

[12] See the opening verse of *Gītārtha-saṅgraha. svadharmajñānavairāgyasādhyabhaktyaikagocaraḥ; nārāyaṇaḥ paraṁ brahma gītāśāstre samīritaḥ.*

light of the *Vedānta-sūtras* and the *Gītā*, one is led to the conclusion that ultimate Reality is *saviśeṣa* in character.

It may be argued that the *Vedānta-sūtras* and the *Gītā* are only derivative sources for Vedānta system, and they are not as important as the Upaniṣad which is the primary source. The *sūtras* and the verses of the *Gītā* have therefore to be interpreted in consonance with the Upaniṣads.

If the Upaniṣads are to be depended on primarily to determine the nature of ultimate Reality, then one should accept them in their entirety. It would be wrong to select a few statements as the most authoritative and reject the rest as of lesser validity. Even if we confine our discussion to the ten or thirteen principal Upaniṣads accepted by both Śaṁkara and Rāmānuja, the majority of the texts found in them do not lend support to the theory of *nirviśeṣa* Brahman.

We may examine another important argument adopted in defence of the Advaitin's theory of Reality. It is contended by the Advaitin that the main purport of the Upaniṣads is non-dualism. This is determined on the basis of the interpretation of the principal Upaniṣadic texts with the help of the six-fold criterion governing authenticity of interpretation. The *Sadvidyā* of *Chāndogya Upaniṣad*, which contains the most crucial statements such as 'This was Being alone in the beginning, one only without a second' and 'That thou art', points out that Brahman alone as devoid of all differentiation is the ultimate Reality and that idealistic monism or Advaita is the purport of the Upaniṣads. When once it is established that non-dualism is the purport of the Upaniṣads, the other texts as well as the *Vedānta-sūtras* will have to be interpreted in consonance with the main doctrine. According to the Advaitin, the Upaniṣads speak of two *vidyās*: two types of philosophic knowledge or 'grades' of teaching known as *parā* and *aparā*.[13] The *parā vidyā*, which refers to the transcendental Reality or the absolute truth, is intended for those who have reached a higher stage of philosophic wisdom and who have the direct intuition of Reality, and for such persons Brahman is *nirviśeṣa*. On the other hand, the *aparā vidyā* or lower knowledge which deals with *saguṇa* Brahman is meant for those who are at the empirical level and who have not attained the highest philosophic wisdom. For such persons, the

[13]Mund I-1-4.

teachings of the Upaniṣads, the *Vedānta-sūtras* and the *Gītā* referring to *saviśeṣa* Brahman are intended. Thus, all the Upaniṣadic texts as well as the teachings of the *Vedānta-sūtras* and the *Gītā* are valid.

The above argument is based on certain important postulates. In the first place, it is maintained that the main purport of the Upaniṣads is idealistic monism, and that Reality is therefore pure undifferentiated Being. Secondly, it is believed that there are two levels of philosophic knowledge—higher and lower. Thirdly, it is assumed that there are two truths, transcendental (*pāramārthika satya*) and empirical (*vyāvahārika satya*). According to the critics of Advaita, all these are questionable postulates.

Without entering into the controversies on the interpretation of the concerned scriptural statements, we may make some general observations on these points. According to the Viśiṣṭādvaitin, it is not possible to assert that non-dualism is the sole purport of the Upaniṣads, because the Upaniṣads also speak of the real difference between ontological entities such as *jīva*, *Īśvara* and cosmic matter.[14] In his opinion, the crucial statement in the *Sadvidyā* of *Chāndogya Upaniṣad* does not prove the absolute identity of the individual self and Brahman as understood by the Advaitin. As will be shown presently, the words *sadeva*, *ekameva* and *advitīyam* in the Upaniṣadic text do not mean that Reality is devoid of all differentiation. Rāmānuja has discussed this issue in great detail both in the *Vedārtha-saṁgraha*[15] and *Śrī-bhāṣya*,[16] and established that the very *Sadvidyā*, which the Advaita Vedāntin holds in favour of his doctrine, supports the theory of *saviśesa* Brahman as conceived by the Viśiṣṭādvaitin by adopting the same six-fold principle of interpretation.

The mention of two *vidyās* as *parā* and *aparā* in the Upaniṣad does not imply two kinds of philosophic knowledge as interpreted by Śaṁkara. According to Rāmānuja, the subject matter of both the kinds of knowledge is *saviśeṣa* Brahman itself. The difference lies in it that the *aparā vidyā* refers to the knowledge obtained by the study of the scriptural texts, while *parā vidyā* refers

[14]See p. 270.

[15]*Vedārthasaṁgraha*, pp. 31-36.

[16]RB I-1-1, p. 89 and II-1-15, p. 483. See also *Śrutaprākāśikā* I-1-1. *asyāḥ sadvidyāyāḥ saviśeṣa-vastunyeva ṣaḍvidha-tātparyaliṅgam vidyate.*

to the intuitive knowledge of Brahman which arises as a result of continuous meditation on Brahman. The former is the verbal knowledge (*parokṣa jñāna*) derived from the study of the scripture which leads to *upāsanā* or meditation on Brahman. The latter is regarded as a kind of intuitive knowledge (*aparokṣarūpa jñāna*). The admission of two stages of teaching in order to accord validity to a large number of scriptural statements referring to *saviśeṣa* Brahman is unwarranted.

The postulation of two kinds of truth as *pāramārthika* (transcendental) and *vyāvahārika* (empirical) is also rejected by the Viśiṣṭādvaitin. It may be a necessity for the Absolutists or the schools of thought upholding idealistic monism to postulate the doctrine of two truths in order to account for the phenomenal universe. The Buddhists too make a distinction between *paramārtha satya* or absolute truth and *samvṛti satya* or truth as conventionally believed in common parlance.[17] This theory is criticised by Kumārila.[18] He points out that *samvṛti* (which is similar to *avidyā* of Advaita) is not strictly speaking real (*satya*), and it is therefore absurd to draw a distinction between the two grades of reality. If *samvṛti* is actually real, it ceases to be *samvṛti*; if it be unreal, how can it be categorised as *satya* or real ? The *satyatva* cannot be a common feature of what is real and what is unreal, as the two are diametrically opposed to each other in their nature. To escape this objection if it be said that there are no two real objects to which *satyatva* is applicable but *samvṛti* is just a postualation in order to account for the practical activities, then it would amount to a non-entity (*nirvastu*). This criticism equally applies to the doctrine of two grades of reality admitted by Advaita. The Advaitin adopts the concept of *sad-asad-vilakṣaṇa* (different from *sat* and *asat*); and on that basis he considers that what is empirically real is not non-existent like the sky-flower. He also advances the theory of sublation (*bādhyatva*) to account for the distinction between the absolute reality and empirical reality. But as we have discussed in an earlier chapter, all these theories when subjected to logical scrutiny are untenable. Either a thing is

[17]*dve satye samupāśritya buddhānām dharmadeśanā|*
loke samvṛtisatyam ca satyam ca paramārthataḥ||

[18]See *Ślokavārtika*, p. 216. *saṁvṛteḥ na tu satyatvaṁ satya-bhedaḥ kuto nvayam satyaṁ cet saṁvṛtiḥ keyaṁ mṛṣā cet satyatā katham.*

absolutely real or absolutely unreal, and there cannot be a third alternative. It is not possible to justify two grades of reality.[19]

There are no doubt apparent conflicts in the Upaniṣadic statements such as the texts describing Brahman as *nirguṇa* and those referring to Brahman as *saguṇa*. There are also texts which emphasise the identity of *jiva* and Brahman and the negation of the universe in respect of Brahman. As we have explained in the earlier chapters such apparent conflicts can be resolved by adopting proper interpretation on the basis of the principles laid down by the Mīmāṁsakas. Thus, in the case of the *saguṇa* and *nirguṇa* śrutis, the conflict is overcome by adopting the rule of the exception or what is known as *utsargāpavāda-nyāya*. Negation only refers to the qualities other than what are affirmed. In the same way, the texts referring to the identity of *jiva* and Brahman have to be understood as oneness in the sense of a substance as qualified by attribute on the basis of the principle of *sāmānādhikaranyaṁ*.

We may leave aside scriptural testimony and consider whether it would be possible to prove by means of any other *pramāṇa* that the ultimate Reality is *nirviśeṣa*. Rāmanuja has discussed this matter thoroughly in the Mahāsiddhānta section of *Śri-bhāṣya*, and shown that it is not possible to prove the existence of a *nirviśeṣa* entity on the basis of any of the accepted *pramāṇas*, either perception or inference or verbal testimony.[20] Epistemologically, it is inconceivable because all knowledge reveals an object as qualified.[21] Metaphysically, it is untenable because an absolutely transcendental entity beyond all thought and speech and having no bearing or relation to the universe is a mere abstraction and amounts to a non-entity or *avastu* like a non-existent object. We therefore come to the conclusion that the ultimate Reality or Brahman is *saviśeṣa*.

II

Brahman as *saviśeṣa* includes in itself the two reals, *cit* and *acit*. In other words, *cit*, the sentient souls, and *acit*, the non-sentient matter, subsist in Brahman all the time (*sarvadā*), both in the state of dissolution and even after creation. Would it be then

[19]See SS III-48, p. 151. *paraspara-virodhe hi na prakārāntara-sthitiḥ.*
[20]RB I-1-1, pp. 48-50. [21]See p. 75.

philosophically sound to regard such a complex entity as absolutely one without a second? This question is raised with reference to the crucial *Chāndogya Upaniṣadic* text which forms the pivot of Advaita Vedānta. The text reads as follows: *Sadeva saumya idamagra āsit ekameva advitiyam.*[22] The literal meaning of this text is : 'In the beginning, my dear, this was Being alone; one only, without a second.' The fuller meaning of this text, according to Śaṁkara's interpretation, is that the universe of name and form (*idam*) was only Being (*sadeva*) prior to creation (*agre*); there is no second to it (*ekameva*) and there is no other object than Being (*advitiyam*). The term *sadeva* or Being only implies absence of difference from any other entity of different kind (*vijātiya-bheda*); the term *ekameva* signifies difference from another entity of same kind (*sajātiya-bheda*); the term *advitiya* refers to the absence of internal difference in the form of characteristic (*svagata-bheda*). *Sat* or Brahman is devoid of all three kinds of differences. In other words, nothing else other than Being exists. Taking into consideration the two phrases 'one only' and 'without a second' in the light of the above interpretation, there seems to be no scope for the admission of *saviśeṣa* Brahman as the ultimate Reality.

Prima facie, this view seems to be unquestionable, because the word 'one' which is a numerical term (*saṅkhyāvācaka*) denotes generally the substantive aspect of the entity without any reference to the attributes it may possess. Thus, when we say 'one pot', we mean pot as a substance is one, and we do not take into consideration its several qualities. But, in the case of this particular Upaniṣadic text, the term *eka* needs to be understood with reference to the context in which the statement appears and also with reference to the statement that follows immediately. The context here refers to the origin or creation of the manifested universe of name and form; the statement which follows immediately is : 'The Being willed: "Let me become many", "Let me multiply"' (*tadaikṣāta bahusyām prajāyeya*).[23] The word 'one' is to be interpreted with reference to the word 'many' mentioned in the subsequent statement. The word *bahu* here means *bahutvāvasthā*; and *eka* which is its counter-correlate should naturally mean *ekatvāvasthā*. What is the *ekatvāvasthā* and *bahutvāvasthā* of Brahman and

[22]Ch VI-2-1. [23]Ch VI-2-3.

how are we justified in assuming such states in respect of Brahman? In the context of 'one' becoming 'many', the two *avasthās* refer to the unmanifested and manifested states respectively of *cit* and *acit*, which subsist always in Brahman. In the state of dissolution *cit* and *acit* exist in Brahman in an unmanifested form without differentiation through name and form. This is regarded as the *ekatvāvasthā* and that is the meaning of the term *ekameva* (*nāma-rūpa-vibhāgābhāva*).[24] That is, the *sat* or Brahman existed prior to creation with *cit* and *acit* in their subtle state without differentiation through names and forms. The *bahutvāvasthā* signifies that the same *sat* or Brahman becomes many with *cit* and *acit* as differentiated with name and form.

This interpretation is justified for more than one reason. According to the doctrine of causality advocated by the Viśiṣṭādvaitin, an effect cannot be caused from what does not exist. The very passage in question, which propounds a real causal relation between Brahman and the universe, denies the possibility of an effect originating from what does not exist, when it raises the question: 'How can Being originate from Non-Being?' The implication of this is that the universe before creation was not non-existent but was one with Being. This is what is meant by the statement that *idam* (this universe) *sadeva āsit* (was Being only) signifying that it existed in an unmanifested form without differentiation through names and forms.[25] Causation means the modification of the same substance from one state to another. Further, the statement that *sat* alone existed in the state of dissolution is meaningful if *sat* or Being was in a different form from what it is after creation. For the Advaitin *sat* is undifferentiated both in the state of dissolution and even after creation. To say that it was *sat* only in the beginning does not carry any special significance. That *cit* and *acit* existed in Brahman in the state of dissolution in an unmanifest form is also supported by the *Bṛhadāraṇyaka Upaniṣad*. Thus it says: 'This was in the beginning unmanifest and the same evolved with name and form.'[26] In the words of Rāmānuja, Brahman is at all times differentiated by the sentient and non-sentient

[24]See RB II-3-18.

[25]See *Vedārtha-saṁgraha*, p. 31; Also *Śrutaprakāśikā* I-1-1.

[26]Br 3-4-7. *taddhedaṁ tarhi avyākṛtam āsīt tan nāmarūpābhyām eva vyākriyata.*

beings which constitute its body, and it can be said to be one only without a second prior to creation. At that time, differentiation in terms of names and forms did not exist. What makes the difference between plurality and unity is the presence or absence of differentiation through names and forms.[27]

Further, it is not possible to conceive the existence of the mere *svarūpa* of Brahman as totally devoid of any other element in the state of dissolution. Even the Advaitin has to admit the presence of *māyā* or *avidya* in Brahman in the state of dissolution; otherwise, creation of the universe in the sense of the illusory appearance of Brahman as manifold universe becomes inexplicable. The schools of Bhâskara and Yâdava also admit the presence of a real *upādhi* or conditioning element in the form of *avidyā* (for Bhâskara) and the three-fold *śakti* or energy (for Yâdava). Nevertheless, all the schools regard Brahman as one only (*ekameva*) in the state prior to creation. It should not therefore be philosophically unsound to maintain that Brahman as associated with *cit* and *acit* in their unmanifest form is one in the state of dissolution. This view has the merit of being supported fully by scripture.

Unity or oneness does not necessarily imply absence of internal differentiation (*svagata-bheda*). When we say 'one pot' the term 'one' refers to a single substance. But it does not exclude the characteristics it possesses. It means that the pot as characterised by potness is one. It is also wrong to assume that the admission of internal difference in the form of attributes affects the unitary character of the substance.[28] Any number of qualities may be attributed to a substance. But insofar as the qualities, which also inhere in the same substance, are not mutually opposed to each other, they do not disintegrate the substance (*viśeṣya*). If the qualities are opposed to each other and they cannot inhere in the same substance, then they cannot denote one entity. Thus, for example, in the judgment 'Devadatta is *śyāma* (of fair complexion) and *yuvā* (youthful)', the

[27]RB II-3-18, p. 574.

[28]This assumption of the Advaitin is based on the Buddhist argument that *dharmas* disintegrate the *svarūpa* or *dharmī* of the entity *upayan apayan dharmaḥ vikaroti hy dharmiṇam*. Kumārila has criticised this view. The mere association of an entity with a *dharma* should not affect the integrity of the entity *vikriyāmātravācitvāt na hy ucchedaḥ asya tāvatā*. Thus, for example, *ākāśa* has the association with *vāyu* but the former is not affected in any way.

two qualities can inhere in one person and as such the two, even though bearing different connotations, are attributed to one individual. The attribution of these two qualities to one person does not in any way affect his integrity as one individual. Take the statement : 'The cow with broken horn, the cow without horn.' Here the qualities are opposed to each other and each quality denotes a different entity.[29] A substance as characterised by qualities is one. The admission of internal difference does not therefore affect the unitary character of substance.

Even on philosophical ground, it is not possible to uphold the view that Brahman is absolutely one devoid of all differentiation. Absolute oneness implies the denial of reality of the universe and the existence of infinite number of souls. Such a theory can only be justified if it is established with valid proof that the universe is illusory (*mithyā*) and the multiplicity of souls is not ultimately real. The Advaitin attempts to prove the phenomenal character of the universe and souls by adopting the doctrine of *māyā* or *avidyā*. But as we have discussed in the chapter on Brahman and universe, the doctrine of *māyā* is logically untenable. The Upaniṣadic texts also do not support the doctrine. The words *māyā* and *avidyā* used in a few scriptural texts do not refer to the concept in the sense in which it is conceived by the Advaitin. In the absence of any valid proof in support of it, it just remains a questionable postulate. The universe consisting of the sentient and non-sentient beings cannot therefore be illusory. The souls are real and eternal as evidenced by the scriptural texts. So also the cosmic matter. If they are real and eternal, they have to remain in some form or the other even after dissolution of the entire universe. In view of these facts, the Viśiṣṭādvaitin maintains that *cit* and *acit* subsist in Brahman prior to creation in an unmanifest form. Brahman and universe of *cit* and *acit* are inseparable being organically related like the body to the soul and they exist all the time, both prior to creation and after evolution. The ultimate Reality or Brahman is therefore *saviśeṣa*.

If Brahman as ultimate Reality includes in it both *cit* and *acit*, it would amount to the admission of three reals—Brahman, *cit* and *acit*. The three are not only absolutely real but they are

[29] See Section 'Import of Samānādhikarana Vākya' in Chapter III.

also absolutely different from each other. How then is it possible to assert at the same time that the Reality is one except in a secondary sense as an aggregate whole? To overcome this difficulty, if all the three entities are regarded as one 'existentially', then it is difficult to maintain a distinction between them. Logically, difference (*bheda*) and non-difference or unity (*abheda*) are mutually opposed. If the three reals are absolutely different, we cannot speak of unity; on the contrary, if they are non-different, difference between them cannot be maintained. It is possible to overcome this difficulty by predicating both non-difference and difference between Brahman and universe as the Bhedābhedavādin does. But Rāmānuja rejects this concept as self-contradiction The concept of *apṛthaksiddhi* or inseparability is adopted by Rāmānuja to account for unity while at the same time acknowledging difference. But such a concept is objected to on the ground that what is considered inseparable cannot be two but one.

These objections are based on certain misunderstanding of the Viśiṣṭādvaita concept of Reality. It is true that Rāmānuja admits three real entities—*cit, acit* and *Īśvara*. But it must be noted that all the three are not *ultimately real* as the critics suppose. Of the three, only one is ultimately real, that is Brahman or God, while the other two are real but dependent on *Īśvara* for their existence. Vedānta Deśika describes Brahman as *para tattva* and the other two reals as *apara tattva*. The former is absolutely independent Reality and is the ground (*ādhāra*) and controller (*niyantā*) of everything other than itself that exists in the universe. The latter are dependent for their very existence and are also controlled by the former.[30] What is dependent on something else does not become less real, as Advaitin assumes. Each entity enjoys absolute reality even though it may be dependent for its existence on another. The lack of independence does not render the entity unreal or less real. Here we need to understand the metaphysical category of substance and attribute. As explained in an earlier chapter, the substance and attribute are distinct by virtue of their intrinsic character. The attribute does not have an independent existence except as related to the substance. Similarly, the substance, though not dependent on the attribute for its existence,

[30]Vedānta Deśika's *Tattvapadavī* (opening verse).

needs the latter for the purpose of determining its nature. The attribute though dependent for its existence on the substance is real, as is warranted by experience. The substance and attribute, though distinct, are inseparable. As substance and attribute the two are distinct, but as a substance characterised by the attribute it is one. The same logical explanation holds good between Brahman and the universe of *cit* and *acit*. The *cit* and *acit* are the *modes* or the inseparable attributes of Brahman; Brahman as ground of all beings in the universe and the inner controller is the primary substance. The relation between the two is that of body to soul. Brahman as organically related to *cit* and *acit* is the one ultimate Reality as an *organic unity*.

The concept of *apṛthaksiddhi* is criticised on the assumption that what is inseparable cannot admit distinction. We have explained at great length in an earlier chapter that this is not the correct view. *Apṛthaksiddhi* is not a mere postulate either to unite what are considered to be separate or to separate what is one. It is a term used to describe the nature of two relata which are by their very nature inherently related like the substance and attribute as well as the soul and body. It holds good only where two entities are by their very nature found to be inherently related. This may be contrasted with the two separable physical objects where the relation is one of *saṁyoga* or conjunction—an external relation. There are two types of entities in the universe—one which is separable and the other inseparable. In the case of the former, there is absolute difference between the two and they are always apprehended as distinct; that is, the type of difference that exists between such separable entities does not allow for non-difference or unity. In the case of the inseparable entities, such as substance and attribute, though they are distinct by virtue of their intrinsic character, they are apprehended as inherently related in the form of one substance characterised by the attribute. Here the kind of difference that exists between the two inseparable entities allows for non-difference or unity as a characterised entity. Logically, the concept of unity and difference in respect of a *viśiṣṭa* entity is justifiable. This is the case with Brahman, *cit* and *acit*. The three are distinct, but Brahman as organically related to *cit* and *acit* is one as a *viśiṣṭa* entity. It is therefore perfectly justifiable both on logical and philosophic ground to uphold that ultimate Reality as *saviśeṣa* Brahman is one.

The above conclusion should not be taken to mean that the Viśiṣṭādvaitin upholds *bhedābheda*. That is, the *cit* and *acit* are both different as well as non-different from Brahman. This is the theory of Bhāskara and Yādava. Such a theory is rejected by Rāmānuja, because it involves self-contradiction. The Viśiṣṭādvaitin does not affirm difference as well as non-difference in respect of the same one Reality. The *cit, acit* and *Īśvara* are absolutely different by virtue of their intrinsic character. To this extent plurality or difference is true and real. The unity or non-difference admitted by the Viśiṣṭādvaitin is not in the sense of the three entities being absolutely identical (*svarūpaikya* or *tādātmya*). If that were the case, his theory of Reality would be open to the criticism levelled against the Bhedābhedavādin. The unity or oneness is accepted in the sense of the three reals being one as an organic unity (*viśiṣṭaikya*). As Vedānta Deśika has explained, Brahman is the one ultimate Reality as organically related to the *cit* and *acit* (*aśeṣa-cid-acit-prakāraṁ brahmaikameva tattvam*).[31] Thus the unity with difference is maintained without involving any self-contradiction.

The acceptance of Brahman as *saviśeṣa* is the only way to find a satisfactory solution to fundamental metaphysical and religious problems. The major problem of metaphysics is to explain how the 'one' becomes the 'many' and how the one Reality is related to this manifold universe. The problem of religion is to account for the relation of the universe to God and satisfy the religious needs of individual souls. An absolute transcendental Reality does hardly offer any solution to these problems except by treating ethical and religious matters as phenomenal in character by taking recourse to the doctrine of *avidyā*. This doctrine which is the pivot of idealistic monism becomes highly vulnerable to criticism. The only other way to resolve these problems is to admit Reality as both transcendent and immanent and accept the *pariṇāmavāda* or the *viśiṣṭa-Brahman* as the material cause of the universe.

If we look at the development of Vedānta from an historical standpoint, we see that *Brahmapariṇāmavāda* has been in vogue

[31] *Nyāya-siddhāñjana*, p. 1.

[32] See p. 311.

from the earliest times, as is evident from references made to it by Śaṁkara· and other Vedāntins. The earliest exponent of this theory is Bhartṛprapañca who flourished long before Śaṁkara. He advocated the *Brahmapariṇāmavāda* or that Barhman itself evolves into the universe of matter and sentient souls and the *bhedābhedavāda* or the theory that universe and souls are both different as well as non-different from Brahman on the analogy of the sea and the waves. The Mādhyamika Buddhists who developed the *śūnyavāda* rejected the theory of a permanent eternal Reality. They also denied independent reality to the external world and introduced the concept of *saṁvṛti* to account for the phenomenal character of the universe. The school of Vedānta represented by Śaṁkara attempted to restore the reality of Brahman by the refutation of the doctrine of *śūnyavāda*. In place of *saṁvṛti*, the concept of *avidyā* was postulated and on the basis of it the *vivartavāda* or the theory that the universe is an illusory appearance of Brahman was introduced. The Bhāskara school of Vedānta found the *māyāvāda* of Śaṁkara unsatisfactory and rejected it totally. They accepted the reality of the universe and also of the individual souls, as distinct from Brahman and conceived that there is difference as well as non-difference between the two. In order to explain the causal relationship between Brahman and the universe, they adopted the older *pariṇāmavāda* of Bhartṛprapañca with a modification that Brahman as associated with the *upādhi* known as *avidyā* is the material cause of the universe. Brahman which is one becomes many as individual souls because of the limiting adjunct, viz. *avidyā*, like the one all-pervasive space becoming conditioned by a pot or other objects. *Avidyā* for Bhāskara is real unlike in Advaita. The school of Vedānta, represented by Yādavaprakāśa, found Bhāskara's theory philosophically unsound, because the defects found in the *jīvas* would apply to Brahman as the two being essentially non-different. In order to preserve the unchanging character of Brahman, Yādava introduced the concept of three-fold *śakti*—*cit-śakti*, *acit-śakti* and *Īśvara-śakti*—and attributed to *śakti* the actual transformation. The three-fold *śakti* evolved itself into *Īśvara*, *cit* and *acit*. Even this doctrine was found defective by Rāmānuja. If *śakti* were non-different from Brahman, the defects of the soul would apply to Brahman. To overcome this difficulty, if *śakti* be considered different from Brahman, then causality would apply to *śakti* only and Brahman cannot be regarded as the material cause.

Thus each of the theories advanced by the Bhedābhedavādins and Māyāvādin to explain the causality of the universe suffers from serious difficulties. Philosophically, they are unsound. If one were to accept the reality of the material universe and the individual souls and at the same time explain the causal relationship between them and Brahman, without affecting the unchanging character of the latter, one has to admit necessarily that Brahman as organically related to *cit* and *acit* is the ultimate Reality. Idealistic monism (*Advaita*), in the sense of absolute identity devoid of any internal or external differentiation, cannot therefore be justified by having recourse to the *vivartavāda*. If everything other than Brahman is illusory, no sound philosophic theory or religion can be propounded. A system, which is developed on the basis of valid *pramāṇas* in conformity with experience as well as logic and which at the same time maintains the validity of all scriptural statements by way of reconciliation of apparent conflicts, is philosophically sounder than the one developed on the basis of questionable postulates.

Glossary

abhāva: non-existence.
abheda: non-difference.
abheda-jñāna: knowledge of the identity of *jīva* and Brahman.
abhimāna: attachment.
ābhimukhya: juxtaposition.
abhivyañjaka: that which causes the manifestation.
abhivyakti: manifestation.
abhyāsa: repetition.
ācārya: preceptor.
acetana: non-sentient.
acit: non-sentient matter; primordial cosmic matter.
ādhāra: sustainer; supporter.
adharma: deeds prohibited by the sacred texts: evil resulting from the performance of prohibited deeds.
ādheya: the sustained; the supported.
adhiṣṭhāna: substratum; objective basis for illusion.
adhyakṣa: sense-perception.
adhyāsa: superimposition.
adravya: non-substance; an attribute which cannot be the basis for another quality.
adṛṣṭa: unseen potency caused by the performance of deeds.
advaita: non-dualism; system of philosophy associated with Śaṁkara.
advitīya: one without a second; absence of second similar to Brahman.
āgama: revealed scripture.
āgantuka-dharma: accidental quality.
agni: fire.
agnihotra: offering oblations to the sacred fire.
ahamartha: the entity denoted by the notion of 'I'; the individual self.
ahaṁkāra: egotism; an evolute of cosmic matter.
ahas: the day.
aikya: identity.
aiśvarya: lordship.
aitihya: tradition.
ajaḍa: sentient; revelation for itself.
ājñā: command.
ajñāna: ignorance; absence of knowledge.
ākāra: image; impression of an object.
ākāra-samarpaṇa: transference of the image of an object.
ākāśa: ether; space.
akhaṇḍārtha: impartite and non-relational sense.

akhyāti: theory of error; the non-apprehension of the difference between two cognitions.

ākṛti: physical structure of an object.

alaukika: non-empirical.

amala: pure; free from imperfections.

amānava: the presiding deity of the lightning who guides the soul to ***mokṣa***.

amṛta: immortal.

aṁśa: a part; an integral part of a complex whole; an essential and inseparable attribute of a substance.

aṁśin: the complex whole having parts; Brahman as organically related to *cit* and *acit*.

anādi: beginningless; that which has no origin.

anaikāntika: a logical fallacy involving an inconclusive reason leading to more than one conclusion.

ānanda: bliss.

ānandamaya: blissful.

ānanda-svarūpa: the substance constituted of bliss.

anantam: infinite; that which is not conditioned by time, space or another entity.

ananya: non-distinct.

anavasthā: infinite regress.

anekānta: manifold in nature; the doctrine of relative pluralism.

anirvacanīya: indeterminable.

anirvacanīya-khyāti: the theory of error according to which the object seen in error is inexplicable.

anṛta: unreal; *karma* that causes contraction of knowledge; sin.

antaḥkaraṇa: internal sense organ; mind.

antaryāmin: the indwelling self; the immanent supreme self.

antarāla: space in between two objects.

antarātmā: inner controller of all beings in the universe.

aṇu: monad or atomic.

anubhava: experience.

anubhūti: knowledge; transcendental consciousness.

anudhyāna: repeated contemplation.

anugraha: God's grace.

anukūla: agreeable feeling.

anumāna: inference.

anumiti: knowledge derived by means of inference.

anupalabdhi: non-apprehension; a *pramāṇa* for proving the non-existence of an object.

anupapatti: logical untenability.

nupūrvi: recitation in a particular order.

anuvāda: restatement.

anuvyavasāya: mental perception.

anvaya-vyāpti: concomitance based on positive agreement between *hetu* and *sādhya*.

anyathākhyāti: theory of error caused by an apprehension of an object other than what it is.
anyonyābhāva: mutual non-existence.
anyonyāśraya: a logical fallacy; an argument involving a vicious circle.
apaccheda-nyāya: the name of the principle formulated by the Mīmāṁsakas to determine which one is an earlier event and which one is a later event in connection with the expiatory rites; the principle of the later sublating the earlier.
apakṣepaṇa: downward movement.
apara: lower.
aparokṣa: immediate; direct.
apasiddhānta: a conclusion opposed to one's own tenet.
apauruṣeya: not ascribed to human author.
apṛthakpratīti: that which cannot be cognised separately.
apṛthaksiddha: inseparability; integrally related as substance and attribute, body and soul.
apṛthaksthiti: that which cannot exist independently.
apūrva: an unseen agency that rewards and punishes merit and demerit.
arcā: incarnation of God by entering into the idols chosen by devotees.
arcāmūrti: idols worshipped in the temples.
arcirādimārga: the path of the divine beings leading to *mokṣa*.
artha: meaning; object denoted by words.
artha-prakāśa: manifestation of object.
arthāpatti: presumption; a means of knowledge.
arthavāda: glorificatory statement.
asādhāraṇa-dharma: an essential attribute inseparably related to an entity.
asat: non-real; the non-existent; the cosmic matter in unmanifest form.
asatkāryavāda: the theory of causality advocating that the effect does not exist in the cause.
asatkhyāti-vāda: the theory of Mādhyamika Buddhist asserting that in error what does not exist appears as existent.
āśrama: stages of life such as bachelor, householder, ascetic and forest dweller
āśraya: locus; basis.
astitva: existence.
ātivāhikas: the deities commanded by God to serve as guides to the soul on its march to *mokṣa*.
ātmajñāna: knowledge of the self.
ātmakhyāti: theory of knowledge advocating that the external objects are the projection of *vijñāna* or the knowledge.
ātman: the self; the individual self.
ātmānubhava: experience of the self.
ātmāśraya: a logical fallacy; *ignoratio elenchi*.
atyantābhāva: absolute non-existence.
audāsīnya: indifference.
avacchedavāda: theory that *jīva* is the appearance of Brahman as conditioned by *avidyā*.
avācya: indescribable by words.

avāptasamastakāma: one whose desires are all fully achieved without obstruction; God.

āvaraṇa: concealment (by *avidyā*).

avasthā: an accidental modification of a substance.

avatāra: incarnation of God.

avayava: the part of a whole.

avayavī: the whole consisting of parts.

avedya: unknowable; not being an object of knowledge.

avidyā: ignorance; the cosmic principle which is the cause of world-illusion.

avyākṛta: unmanifest; devoid of manifestation with name and form.

avyakta: unmanifest.

ayutasiddha: that which exists as inseparable entity.

bādha: sublation.

bādhaka: that which sublates.

bādhita: sublated; contradicted.

bādhitānuvṛtti: persistence of the trace of *avidyā* even after it is sublated.

bādhya: that which is sublated.

bala: strength.

bhakti: devotion to God; meditation.

bhakti-yoga: unceasing loving meditation on God as means to *mokṣa*.

bhautika: constituted of the elements.

bhāvanā: mental impression.

bhāvāntara: existence in some other form.

bhāvarūpa: that which is positive in character (as, for example, *ajñāna* for Advaitin).

bheda: difference.

bhedābheda: difference-cum-nondifference; identity in difference.

bheda-vāsanā: the latent impression causing the cognition of difference.

bhinna: different.

bhoktā: one who experiences; the individual self which experiences pleasure and pain.

bhrama: error; wrong knowledge.

bhrānti: illusion.

bhūtas: five gross elements such as earth, water, fire, air and ether.

bhūyodarśana: repeated observation.

bimbapratibimbavāda: the theory that the *jīva* is a reflection of Brahman in the internal organ.

boddhā: knower; the individual self which is cogniser.

Brahman: the Absolute of philosophy; the ultimate Reality; the personal God.

Brahmānanda: the supreme happiness derived from the experience of blissful Brahman.

Brahmānubhava: experience of Brahman.

Brahma-sākṣātkāra: realisation of Brahman.

Brahmavidyā: spiritual knowledge of Brahman.

Brahmopāsana: meditation on Brahman.

buddhi: intellect; mind; internal organ.
buddhi-yoga: supreme devotion; *para-bhakti*.

caitanya: consciousness.
cakraka: a logical fallacy involving circular reasoning.
cakṣus: eyes; visual organ.
carama-saṁskāra: the final residual impression of experience.
ceṣṭā: activity.
cetana: sentient; that which possesses consciousness.
cid-acid-viśiṣṭa-brahma: Brahman as organically related to sentient beings and non-sentient matter.
cintana: contemplation; meditation.
cit: sentient being; the individual self; consciousness.

dama: self-restraint.
darśana: realisation of the self; specific type of contemplation characterised by vividness; a system of philosophy.
dāna: charity.
dāsya: serviceability.
dayā: compassion.
dehātmabhrama: the illusion of the self in the body.
deśa: place; space.
dharma: attribute.
dharmabhūtajñāna: knowledge as an essential attribute of the self.
dharmī: substratum; the substantive aspect of an entity.
dharmijñāna: knowledge which constitutes the essence of the self.
dhī: knowledge.
dhruvānusmṛti: steadfast contemplation.
dhyāna: contemplation; meditation.
dik: direction as east, west, etc.; space (according to Naiyāyikas).
dīpa: light (of the lamp).
doṣa: defect.
dravatva: liquidity.
dravya: substance; that which serves as the substratum for modification.
dṛḍhatara: well-established.
dṛg: seer; subject; self.
dṛṣṭānta: illustration.
dṛśyatva: cognisability; objectivity.
duḥkha: suffering; sorrow.
duṣkṛta: evil deed.
dveṣa: hatred.
dvitva: the notion of being two.
dvyaṇuka: dyad, combination of two atoms.

ekajīvavāda: the theory that there is only one individual self (*jīva*).
ekatva: oneness, the notion of number one.

gamana: movement.

gandha: odour.
gaurava: prolixity of assumption.
guṇa: quality; attribute.
guṇin: that which possesses the *guṇa*.
guru: the teacher; preceptor.
gurutva: heaviness.

hetu: reason, probans in the syllogistic argument.
hetvābhāsa: fallacy relating to *hetu*.
heyaguṇa: imperfect qualities or attributes.
hita: means to achieve the supreme goal of life.
hrasva: short.

icchā: desire.
indriyas: sense organs (cognitive and conative).
Īśvara: God; the supreme self as the inner controller of all beings.

jaḍa: inert; matter.
jala: water.
jāti: generic character: the distinguishing characteristic of an object.
jijñāsā: desire to know.
jīva: individual self; empirical self.
jīvanmukti: release of an individual while he is still embodied.
jīvātman: the individual self as distinct from *paramātman*, the supreme self.
jñāna: knowledge; consciousness.
jñānāśraya: that which is the locus of knowledge; the subject of knowledge.
jñāna-svarūpa: knowledge constituting the essence of the self.
jñāna-yoga: the spiritual discipline as means to self-realisation.
jñānendriyas: the cognitive organs.
jñātā: the knowing subject; the knower.
jñātṛtva: cognisership; the state of being the knower.
jvālābhedānumāna: the inference which proves that the flames of a lamp are distinct, succeeding one another.
jyotis: light.

kaivalya: self-realisation; the existence of the self in its true form as totally liberated from bondage.
kalāpa: an ornament.
karaṇa: that which serves as an accessory.
karma: action; rituals; past deeds and their results in the form of merit and sin.
karmakāṇḍa: parts of the Vedas dealing with rituals.
karma-vaśya: one who is conditioned by the influence of past *karma*.
kartā: agent of action; the doer.
kartṛtva: responsibility for action.
kathā: philosophic debate.
kāla: time.

kālātyayāpadeśa: a logical fallacy in which the probans asserts something, the opposite of which is ascertained to be true by other evidence.

kāma: desire.

kāmya-karma: religious observances prompted by desire for results.

kāraṇa: cause.

kāraṇa-śruti: the scriptural text which speaks of the causality of the universe.

kārya: effect.

kevala-vyatireki: kind of inference established only on the basis of agreement in absence between probandum and probans.

kevalānvayi: kind of inference based only on agreement in presence between the *hetu* and *sādhya*.

kṛti: effort

kriyā: activity; the performance of rituals.

krodha: anger.

kṣaṇa: absolute instant; the conglomeration of causal factors which have not been operative in producing an effect (according to Visiṣṭādvaitin).

kṣaṇika: momentary.

kṣaṇikavāda: the doctrine which upholds that everything is momentary.

kṣetra: the body as the field where one reaps the fruits of past deeds.

kṣetrajña: the knower of the body, the individual self.

lakṣaṇa: definition.

lakṣaṇa-vākya: a sentence or statement purporting to offer definition.

lakṣaṇā: secondary import.

laukika: empirical.

līlā: sport.

līlā-vibhūti: the cosmic universe as the property of the Supreme Being.

lipi: letters; script.

mahat: the great; the evolute of the primordial matter (*prakṛti*).

mahāvākya: the supreme upaniṣadic texts emphasising the identity of *jīva* and Brahman (according to Advaitin).

manana: logical reflection.

manas: mind.

maṇi: special gem; precious stone.

mantra: incantation.

māyā: cosmic principle which gives rise to world-illusion; the phenomenal character of the universe; that which is an instrument of wonderful creation; the primordial matter (*prakṛti*).

māyāvāda: the doctrine of Advaitin which advocates that everything except Brahman is illusory.

meru: name of a mythological mountain.

mithyā: illusory.

mithyātva: illusoriness.

moha: delusion.

mokṣa: liberation of the soul from bondage; union with the Absolute; attainment of the status of Brahman.

mukhyārtha: primary meaning.

mukhya-vṛtti: primary import.

mukta: one who is liberated from bondage; released soul.

mukti: state of final liberation from bondage.

mumukṣu: an aspirant for *mokṣa*; one who is desirous of release from bondage.

nāimittika: rituals prescribed for specific occasions or specific purposes.

nāma-rūpa: name and form.

nāyaka: the Lord of the universe; God.

naya-sūtra: aphorism expressed in the form of logical argument.

nididhyāsana: contemplation; steadfast meditation.

nigraha: unfavourable disposition of God.

nigrahasthāna: points of defeat raised during philosophic debate.

niranvaya: total (destruction).

niravadya: free from all defects.

niravayava: incapable of physical division; partless.

nirdharmaka: devoid of *dharmas* or attributes.

nirguṇa: devoid of qualities;

nirguṇa-brahma-vāda: the doctrine which upholds that Brahman is undifferentiated Being.

nirguṇa-śruti: scriptural texts describing Brahman as devoid of attributes.

nirukta: one of the six Vedāṅgas; a treatise containing glossarial explanation of Vedic terms.

nirupādhika: unconditioned; natural form.

nirūpita-svarūpa-viśeṣaṇa: secondary attributes; qualities which become known after the *svarūpa* of the objects is known.

nirvikalpaka: indeterminate.

nirvikāra: immutable.

nirviṣaya: knowledge devoid of content.

nirviśeṣa: undifferentiated; devoid of all characteristics.

niṣkāma: free from any desire for results.

niṣkarṣaka śabda: words having fixed denotation

niṣprapañca: acosmic; Brahman as unrelated to universe.

nitya: eternal.

nitya-karma: religious duties laid down as mandatory.

nitya-mukta: soul that is eternally free from bondage.

nitya-saṁsārī: soul eternally caught up in bondage.

nitya-vigraha: eternal spiritual body of God.

nivartaka-jñāna: knowledge which removes the ignorance about Reality.

nivṛtta-karma: *karma*, performed without any desire for results; *karma* which takes one away from bondage and leads to *mokṣa*.

nivṛtti: cessation; removal.

niyāmya: that which is controlled.

niyantā: controller of all beings; God.

niyoga: Vedic injunction; unseen result generated by observance of Vedic injunction.

padārtha: category (logical and metaphysical); denotation of words.
pakṣa: the subject of syllogism.
pañcīkaraṇa: quintuplication of the five elements.
pāpa: sin accrued as a result of performance of evil deeds; unfavourable disposition of God.
parāk: that which manifests for the self as, for example, *jñāna*.
paramāṇu: atom.
parama-pada: supreme abode of Brahman.
pāramārthika: transcendental; absolutely real.
parama-sāmya: attainment of equal status with Brahman by the *jīvas* in *mokṣa*.
paramātman: supreme self; God.
parārtha: what is intended for the use of others.
parārthānumāna: a syllogistic argument adopted to convince another about an established truth.
parasmā-eva-bhāsamāna: that which manifests always to others such as knowledge in Viśiṣṭādvaita.
parataḥ-prāmāṇya: validity derived from extraneous factors.
paricchinna: limited; conditioned by time, space or object.
parimāṇa: dimension.
pariṇāma: change; transformation; modification.
pariśeṣānumāna: inference by a process of elimination.
parokṣa: mediate.
prabhā: light.
pradhāna-pratitantra: a major doctrine which is unique to a system and not accepted by others.
pradhvaṁsa: destruction.
prakāra: mode; attribute; *jīva* as a mode of Brahman.
prakārin: a substance which has modes; Brahman.
prakāśa: illumination; manifestation; knowledge.
prakāśya: what is revealed by knowledge; object.
prakṛti: primordial matter.
pralaya: dissolution of the universe.
pramāṇas: means of valid knowledge; evidence.
prameyas: objects of valid knowledge; ontological doctrines.
prapatti: absolute self-surrender to God.
pratibandi: a type of counter-argument.
pratibimba: reflection.
pratitarka: counter-argument.
pratīti: awareness; cognition.
pratyabhijñā: knowledge by recognition.
pravṛtti: activity; initiation into action.
pravṛtta-karma: *karma* or deeds which are performed for results and thereby leading to further bondage.
prāgabhāva: prior non-existence.

prākaṭya: manifestation.

prāmāṇya: validity (of knowledge).

prāṇa: breath.

prāṇa-vāyu: vital breath; a modification of *vāyu* (air).

prāyaścitta: expiatory rites.

prīti: love.

pṛthak: separate; different.

pṛthivī: element of earth.

pudgala: the name given to the cosmic matter which undergoes modifications according to Jainas.

puṇya: merit accrued as a result of performance of good deeds; favourable disposition of God.

puruṣārtha: ends of human endeavour.

puruṣottama: the supreme self; personal God.

pūrvapakṣa: prima facie view.

rāga: desire.

rajas: one of the cosmic attributes; that quality which causes suffering.

rasa: flavour; taste.

rūpa: colour; form of an object.

śabda: sound; verbal testimony.

śābdabodha: comprehension of the meaning of words.

sādhana: discipline; means for spiritual realisation; means to *mokṣa*.

sādharmya: equality.

sādhya: what is sought to be proved; probandum.

sadasad-vilakṣaṇa: different from the real and the unreal; illusory.

sadvidyā: meditation on Brahman as the *sat* without a second as described in the *Chāndogya Upaniṣad*.

saguṇa-brahman: Brahman endowed with attributes.

saguṇa-śruti: scriptural statements describing Brahman as qualified by attributes.

sahopalambha: invariable association.

śākhā-vibhāga: division of Vedas into different branches.

śakti: potency; energy; import of a word.

śakti-jñāna: knowledge of the import of the words.

sāmagrī: accessories.

samānādhikaraṇa-vākya: a sentence or judgement where terms are found in apposition.

sāmānādhikaraṇya: syntactic equation of terms denoting the same one entity but connoting different attributes.

sāmānya: generality; a feature common to two or more things; generic chararter (*jāti*), according to Viśiṣṭādvaitin.

samavāya: inherence; internal relation.

sambandha: relationship.

saṁjñā-pada: a word denoting a specific individual only.

saṁśaya: doubt.

saṁskāra: residual impression of experience; purification caused by rituals (according to Mīmāṁsaka).
saṁsthāna: structure; exclusive characteristic of an object; the generic character.
saṁvit: knowledge.
saṁvṛti: the categorising function of mind; that which causes phenomenal appearance.
saṁyoga: conjunction; external relation.
saṅkalpa: will.
saṅkhyā: number.
saṅkoca: contraction.
sānvaya-vināśa: partial destruction.
saptabhaṅgi: seven-fold description of the nature of reality as enunciated by Jainas.
sara: strand.
śarīra: body; that which is necessarily supported by the self, controlled by it and subserves its purpose.
śarīra-śarīri-sambandha: the organic relation of the body to the soul and of the cosmic universe of *cit* and *acit* to *Iśvara*, according to Rāmānuja.
śarīrin: the owner of the *śarīra*.
sarveśvara: Supreme Being; God.
śāstra: sacred texts.
satkāryavāda: the theory of causality which believes that the effect exists in the cause in a potential form (according to the Sāṅkhyas); the view that an effect is a modified state of the causal substance (according to Viśiṣṭādvaita).
satkhyāti: the theory which upholds that all knowledge is of the real.
sattā: existence.
sattva: one of the three qualities of *prakṛti*.
satyam: truth; reality.
savikalpaka: determinate; differentiated.
saviśeṣa: that which is characterised; Brahman as qualified by attributes.
saviśeṣādvaita: non-dualism of the organic unity.
sayūthya: of the same flock; followers of same school of thought.
śeṣa: one who exists for the purpose of the *śeṣin*; individual self as *śeṣa* of God.
śeṣin: one who utilises the *śeṣa* for his purpose.
siddhānta: final view; established conclusion; final truth of an argument.
siddha-sādhana: proving of what has already been accepted by the opponent.
sphoṭa: word essence.
śrīpati: consort of Goddess Śrī or Lakṣmī; Nārāyaṇa.
śrotra: ears.
śruti: revealed scripture; the Vedas including the Upaniṣads.
śuddha-sattva: spiritual substance characterised by unalloyed *sattva*; transcendental spiritual matter.
sukha: happiness.
sukṛta: merit earned by performance of good deeds.
śūnya: void.

śūnyavāda: nihilism; the doctrine advocated by the Mādhyamika Buddhist that nullity is the ultimate nature of Reality.

suṣupti: deep, dreamless sleep.

svabhāva: the nature of an object; characteristics of an object.

svalakṣaṇa : a term used by the Buddhist referring to the bare unrelated particular presented in the initial stage of perception.

svaparanirvāhaka: that which is capable of explaining itself as well as another thing.

svarūpa: essential nature; being.

svarūpa-nirūpaka-dharma: attribute which determines or defines the essential nature of an object.

svasmai-bhāsamāna: that which reveals itself.

svataḥ-siddha: self-established.

svataḥ-prāmāṇya: self-validity.

svayaṁ-prakāśa: self-luminous; that which does not require to be manifested by anything else.

tādātmya: absolute identity.

tamas: one of the three qualities of *prakṛti*; darkness; primordial matter.

tanmātra: subtle elements.

tapas: austerity.

tarka: logic; counter-argument.

tattva: real entity which exists: metaphysical category.

tattva-jijñāsā: enquiry into the nature of Reality.

tattva-sākśātkāra: realisation of Reality; intuition of Brahman.

tirodhāna: concealment; obscuration.

tṛvitkaraṇa: triplication or admixture of three elements of water, fire and earth.

tryaṇuka: triad, combination of three atoms.

tuccha: non-existent.

tyāga: renouncement.

ubhayaliṅgādhikaraṇa: a topic in the *Vedānta-sutra* dealing with the two-fold nature of Brahman as perfect and free from imperfections.

upabṛṁhaṇa: that which elucidates the meaning of the scriptural texts; smṛtis and purāṇas.

upādāna-kāraṇa: material cause.

upadeśa: imparting the philosophic knowledge.

upādhi: adjunct; a limiting condition.

upahita-Brahma: Brahman as conditioned by *māyā*.

upajīvaka: that which depends on another.

upajīvya: that which offers subsistence.

upapatti: explanation; logical tenability.

upakrama: commencement; opening statement of a passage.

upasaṁhāra: conclusion; concluding statement.

upāsanā: contemplation; steadfast meditation.

upāya: means.

ūrdhvagamana: upward march of the soul (according to Jaina).
utkṣepaṇa: upward movement; one of the five types of motion accepted by Vaiśeṣika.
utsarga: general rule.
uttarāgha: sins committed after the commencement of *upāsanā* for *mokṣa*.

vācaka: that which denotes (an object).
vācya: what is denoted by a word.
vāda: philosophical discussion aimed at the ascertainment of truth.
vaibhavokti: exaggerated statement.
vaiśvānarāgni: the digestive fire or energy.
vākyārtha: meaning of a sentence.
vākyārtha-jñāna: knowledge generated by the study of the upaniṣadic texts.
varṇa: letters.
varṇāśramadharma: the religious duties as prescribed by the sacred texts according one's birth and stages of life.
veda: revealed scripture.
vedana: knowledge; loving meditation.
vega: velocity.
vibhāga: disjunction.
vibhavāvatāra: incarnation of God in different human or other forms for the worship of the devotees.
vibhu: all-pervasive.
vibhūti: property of God.
vigraha: bodily form of a deity.
vijñāna: knowledge.
vijñātā: knower; subject of knowledge.
vikāra: modification; change.
vikṛti: an evolute of *prakṛti* which does not serve as a cause of another evolute.
vikṣepa: projection of the illusion of universe.
vināśa: destruction.
viparyaya: wrong knowledge.
virodha: opposition; obstruction; contradiction.
viṣaya: object; content (of knowledge).
viṣayi: subject; knowledge (as related to object).
viśeṣa: individuality; one of the seven categories accepted by Nyāya-Vaiśeṣika.
viśeṣaṇa: qualification; attribute; mode.
viśeṣya: that which is the basis for qualities or attributies; substance.
viśiṣṭa: that which is qualified with attributes; a characterised entity; a complex whole.
viśiṣṭādvaita: the system expounded by Rāmānuja; the non-dualism or oneness in the sence of an organic unity; the theory that ultimate Reality or Brahman is one as organically related to *cit* and *acit*.
viśiṣṭaikya: unity in the form of an organic whole including several attributes.

vitaṇḍā: argument adopted solely for the purpose of defeating an opponent.
vivartavāda: the theory that the universe is an illusory appearance of Brahman.
vṛtti: the outflow of the energy of sense organs or mind.
vṛttijñāna: knowledge of the psychosis.
vyabhicāra: a logical fallacy; the presence of the probans without the probandum.
vyakti: individual entity.
vyaṣṭi-sṛṣṭi: creation of the universe of space and matter with all its diversity.
vyavahāra: empirical usage.
vyāvahārika satya: phenomenal or relative reality.
vyāvarta: changing.
vyūha: one of the five divine manifestations.
vyutpatti: derivation; etymology; origin.

yāga: religious sacrifice.
yajña: religious worship; religious sacrifice.
yathārtha-khyāti: the theory that all knowledge is of the real.
yatna: effort.
yogyānupalabdhi: competent non-cognition; the *pramāṇa* by means of which non-existence is apprehended.

Bibliography

SANSKRIT WORKS

ĀLAVANDAR, *Āgamaprāmāṇyam*, Rāmānuja Research Society, Madras.

———, *Siddhitraya*, ed. R. Ramanujachari, Annamalai University Philosophy Series.

RĀMĀNUJA, *Śrī-Bhāṣyam* (2 vols.), ed. Uttamur T. Viraraghavacharya, Madras, 1968.

———, *Gītā-Bhāṣya with Tātparya-Candrika*, ed. P. B. Annangaracharya, Conjeevaram

———, *Vedārtha-Saṁgraha*, ed. S.S. Raghavachar.

———, *Vedāntadīpa*, ed. Uttamur T. Viraraghavacharya, Madras.

———, *Vedantasāra*, Adyar Library, Madras, 1953.

RANGARĀMĀNUJA, *Upaniṣad-Bhāṣya* (vols. 1-4), ed. Uttamur T. Viraraghavacharya, Ubhaya Vedānta Granthamala Series.

———, *Bṛhadāraṇyakopaniṣad-Bhāṣya*, ed. Uttamur T. Viraraghavacharya, Sri Venkatesvara Oriental Institute, Tirupati.

ŚAṀKARA, *Brahma-Sūtra-Bhāṣyam*, ed. Narayan Ram Acharya, Nirnayasagara Press, Bombay.

ŚRĪNIVĀSA, *Yatīndramatadīpikā*, ed. Swami Adidevananda.

SRINIVASACHAR, L., *Darśanodayam*.

SUDARŚANA ŚŪRI, *Śrutaprakāśikā* (2 vols), ed. Uttamur T. Viraraghavacharya, Madras.

VEDĀNTA DEŚIKA, *Adhikaraṇasārāvalī*, ed. P.B. Annangaracharya.

———, *Nyāya-Pariśuddhi*, ed.———.

———, *Nyāya-Siddāñjana*, ed.———.

———, *Rahasya-Trayasāram*, ed.———.

———, *Śatadūṣaṇī*, ed.———.

———, *Tattvaṭīkā*, ed.———.

———, *Tattva-muktā-kalāpa with Sarvārthasiddhi*, ed.———.

———, *Tattva-muktā-kalāpa and Sarvārthasiddhi with the Commentaries Ānandadāyinī and the Bhāvaprakāśa* (vols. 1-3), Oriental Research Institute, Mysore.

———, *Tattva-muktā-kalāpa and Sarvārthasiddhi with the Commentaries Gūḍhārthavivṛti, Guḍhārthaprakāśa and Alabhyalābhaḥ*, pub. Uttamur T. Viraraghavacharya.

ENGLISH WORKS

ANANTHARANGACHAR, N. S., *The Philosophy of Sādhanā in Viśiṣṭādvaita.*

CARMAN, J. B., *The Theology of Rāmānuja.*

BHARADWAJ, K.D., *The Philosophy of Rāmānuja.*

BHATTA, S.R., *Studies in Rāmānuja Vedānta.*

DASGUPTA S.N., *A History of Indian Philosophy* (5 vols).

DEUSSEN, P., *The System of the Vedânta.*

HIRIYANNA, M., *Outlines of Indian Philosophy.*

LOTT, ERIC. J., *God and the Universe in the Vedantic Theology of Râmânuja.*

MAHADEVAN, T.M.P., *The Philosophy of Advaita.*

MAX MULLER, *Six Systems of Indian Philosophy.*

NAGARAJASARMA, R.N., *Reign of Realism.*

RADHAKRISHNAN, S., *Indian Philosophy* (2 vols).

———, *The Brahma Sūtra.*

———, *The Principal Upaniṣads,*

RAGHAVACHAR, S.S., *Introduction to the Vedārtha-Saṅgraha.*

———, *Śrī Rāmānuja on the Upaniṣads.*

———, *Viśiṣṭādvaita* (Madras University Lectures).

RAJAGOPALA AYYANGAR, M.R., *Śrīmad Rahasyatrayasāra* (Translation with Introduction).

RAMANUJACHARĪ, V.K., *The Three Tattvas.*

RANGACHARYA, M., *The Vedānta-Sūtras with the Śrī-Bhāṣya of Rāmānuja* (vols. i-iii), Education Publishing Co., Madras.

SINGH, SATYAVRATA, *Vedānta Deśika: His Life, Works and Philosophy.*

SRINIVASACHARI, P.N., *The Philosophy of Viśiṣṭādvaita.*

———, *Ramanuja's Idea of The Jinite Self.*

SRINIVASACHARI, S.M., *Advaita and Viśiṣṭādvaita.*

THIBAUT, G., *Vedānta Sūtras with Rāmānuja's Commentary* (SBE Series), vol. xlviii.

VARADACHARI, K.C., *Rāmānuja's Theory of Knowledge.*

VARRDACHAR, K.S. *Tattva-muktā-kalāpa* (with commentary in Kannada language), pub. Parakal Mutt, Mysore.

VIDYARTHI, B.P., *Rāmānuja's Philosophy and Religion.*

———, *Knowledge, Self and God in Rāmānuja.*

INDEX

Abbreviations: A=Advaita; Bh=Bhāskara; R=Rāmānuja; S=Śaṁkara; V=Viśiṣṭādvaita; Y=Yādava; N.V.=Nyāya-Vaiśeṣika; M=Mīmāṁsaka; V.D.=Vedānta Déśika; accg. to=according to; re.=regarding